CONTENTS AT A GLANCE

Introduction
1 Data Storage Alternatives
2 Database Design
3 Security
4 Off to See the Wizard
5 The DataSet Family of Objects
6 Database Connections
7 XML Databases
8 Bound Controls
9 Data Safety
10 A Single-User Example
11 Multi-User Programming
12 Query by Example
13 Discovering Database Structure
A SQL
B The Visual Basic .NET Development Environment
Index

Visual Basic® .NET Database Programming

Rod Stephens

201 W. 103rd Street
Indianapolis, Indiana 46290

Visual Basic® .NET Database Programming

Trademarks

All terms mentioned in this book that are known to be trademarks or service marks have been appropriately capitalized. Que Publishing cannot attest to the accuracy of this information. Use of a term in this book should not be regarded as affecting the validity of any trademark or service mark.

Warning and Disclaimer

Every effort has been made to make this book as complete and as accurate as possible, but no warranty or fitness is implied. The information provided is on an "as is" basis. The author and the publisher shall have neither liability nor responsibility to any person or entity with respect to any loss or damages arising from the information contained in this book.

Executive Editor
Candy Hall

Acquisitions Editor
Jenny Watson

Development Editor
Sean Dixon

Technical Editor
Karl Hilsmann

Managing Editor
Thomas Hayes

Project Editors
Natalie Harris
Karen Shields
Christina Smith

Copy Editor
Linda Seifert

Indexer
Kevin Broccoli

Proofreader
Abby Van Huss

Team Coordinator
Cindy Teeters

Media Developer
Michael Hunter

Interior Designer
Anne Jones

Cover Designers
Alan Clements
Anne Jones

Page Layout
Cheryl Lynch
Michelle Mitchell

TABLE OF CONTENTS

Introduction   1

Intended Audience   2

How This Book Is Organized   2

How To Use This Book   5

Necessary Equipment   6

Example Databases   7

Online Samples, Updates, and
Changes   8

1   Data Storage Alternatives   9

Compiled In Data   9

Registry   11
   CSV Files   14
   Fixed-Length Records   15
   INI Files   17
   XML   21

Relational Databases   23
   Relationships   24
   Ordering Data   26
   Indexes   26
   Stored Procedures   27
   Security   27

Specific Relational Database Engines   27
   Microsoft Access   27
   SQL Server   29
   MSDE   30
   Oracle   30
   Others   30

More Exotic Databases   31

Summary   32

2   Database Design   35

Application Design Approaches   35

Requirements   36

Entities   36

Refining the Design   38

Master-Detail Relationships   40

Normalization   41
   First Normal Form   41
   Beyond 1NF   41
   Second Normal Form   42
   Beyond 2NF   45
   Third Normal Form   46
   Beyond 3NF   47
   Denormalization   47
   A Reformatted Database Diagram   47

Keys   48

Indexes   49
   Good and Bad Indexes   49
   Composite Indexes   50
   Duplicates In Indexes   51

Constraints   51
   Range Tables   52
   Cascading Updates and Deletes   53

Design Tools   54

Designing Databases With Microsoft
Access   55
   Using the Database Wizard   55
   Building a Database By Hand   57

Building a Database with SQL   61

Summary   66

3   Security   67

Degrees of Security   67
   No Security   67
   Database Passwords   68
   User Passwords   68
   Physical Security   71

Controlling Privileges **72**
GRANT **73**
DENY **75**
REVOKE **76**

Controlling Access with Views **76**

SQL Server Security Procedures **77**
SQL Server Access **78**
Database Access **79**
Changing Login Information **80**
Defining Roles **80**
Creating Roles **81**
Obtaining Information **82**
Stored Procedure Summary **84**

Summary **85**

4 Off to See the Wizard 87

Data Link Properties **87**

The Data Form Wizard **90**
Customizing Data Forms **95**
Customizing Grid Forms **95**
Customizing Single Record
Forms **97**

Query Builder **97**

Data Adapter Configuration Wizard **99**

Using The Data Adapter **101**

Summary **104**

5 The DataSet Family of Objects 105

DataSet **105**
Clear **106**
HasChanges **106**
AcceptChanges and
RejectChanges **106**
HasErrors **107**
GetChanges **107**
Merge **110**
Clone and Copy **110**
GetXml, WriteXml, and
ReadXml **111**

GetXmlSchema, WriteXmlSchema, and
ReadXmlSchema **113**

DataTable **113**
TableName **114**
Columns **114**
Rows **114**
CaseSensitive and Select **114**
ImportRow **115**
LoadDataRow **115**
NewRow **116**
PrimaryKey **116**
ChildRelations and
ParentRelations **117**
Constraints **117**
HasErrors, AcceptChanges,
RejectChanges, Clear, and
GetChanges **121**
GetErrors **122**
Clone and Copy **124**
DataTable Events **124**

DataRow **126**
Item **126**
ItemArray **127**
Error Methods **127**
RowState **128**
AcceptChanges and
RejectChanges **128**
BeginEdit, CancelEdit, and
EndEdit **128**
Delete **129**
GetChildRows, GetParentRow,
GetParentRows, and
SetParentRow **129**
SetUnspecified **133**

DataColumn **133**
AllowDBNull, MaxLength, ReadOnly,
Unique, and DefaultValue **133**
DataType **134**
AutoIncrement, AutoIncrementSeed,
and AutoIncrementStep **134**
ColumnMapping **136**
ColumnName **137**
Expression **137**
Ordinal **138**

DataRelation **138**
    Constructor **140**
    ChildColumns and
    ParentColumns **140**
    ChildTable and ParentTable **141**
    ChildKeyConstraint and
    ParentKeyConstraint **141**
    RelationName **141**

DataView **141**
    RowFilter and RowStateFilter **142**
    AllowNew, AllowEdit, and
    AllowDelete **143**

DataView **143**
    Count and Item **144**
    AddNew and Delete **144**
    Sort and Find **144**

DataRowView **145**
    Item **145**
    Row **145**
    RowVersion **145**
    Delete **146**

Summary **146**

6 Database Connections 147

Data Connection Methods **147**

Program-Generated Data **147**

XML Data **149**

SQL Server **150**
    SqlConnection **151**
    SqlCommand **157**
    SqlParameter **169**
    SqlDataAdapter **170**
    SqlCommandBuilder **174**
    Example Program Use
    DataAdapter **175**
    SqlDataReader **177**
    SqlTransaction **179**

OLE DB **182**

Example Program RunScript **183**

Summary **191**

7 XML Databases 193

What Is XML? **193**
    Single-Table **194**
    Multi-Table **195**
    Deep Multi-Table **195**
    Other Formats **196**

Editing XML Files **197**

Schemas **200**

Loading XML Data in Visual Basic **201**

Saving XML Data From Visual
Basic **204**

Overwriting Files **207**

Summary **207**

8 Bound Controls 209

Basic Binding **209**
    Connecting to the Database **210**
    Defining a DataSet **211**
    Displaying Data **214**
    Displaying Pictures **215**
    Navigating Through the DataSet **216**
    Adding and Deleting Records **218**
    The Contacts Program **218**

Record Selection with Bound
Controls **224**

Selecting a Calculated Field **225**

A TreeView Display **228**

DataViews **233**

Binding Controls with Code **236**

DataGrid **238**

Summary **239**

9 Data Safety 241

EasyDraw **241**

Storing Data **242**

Drawing Existing Objects **243**

Drawing New Objects **244**

DataSafe **248**

Menu Commands **249**

MRU List **254**

Data Validation **258**

Summary **261**

10 A Single-User Example 263

A One-Form Design **263**
Database Design **264**
Loading Data **265**
Displaying Data **271**
Adding Records **273**
Deleting Records **275**
Canceling Changes **276**
Saving Changes **276**

A Tabbed Design **280**
Global Control **281**
The Customer List Form **282**
The Customer Detail Form **285**

Summary **288**

11 Multi-User Programming 289

Program OrderEntryMultiUser **289**

Database Redesign **290**

Reservations **292**

Source Code **294**

Modifications **298**
Query-By-Example **298**
Real-Time Customer Lists **298**

Picking Customers **299**
Displaying Reservations **299**

Summary **300**

12 Query By Example 301

Features **302**

Programming the RecordList Form **303**
AddField **306**
InitializeForm **307**

RecordList Form Internals **308**
The FieldInfo Class **308**
Initializing the Form **309**
Selecting Records **312**
Displaying Results **315**
Raising the RecordSelected
Event **317**
ListView Output **317**
Sorting Records **318**
DisplayResults **321**
Raising the RecordSelected
Event **322**

Summary **323**

13 Discovering Database Structure 325

Learning About Servers **325**
sp_server_info **325**
sp_helpserver **326**
sp_who **327**

Learning About Databases **327**
sp_databases **327**
sp_helpdb **328**
sp_helpfile **329**
sp_spaceused **329**
sp_help **329**

Learning About Tables **329**
sp_tables **330**
sp_depends **331**

Learning About Relationships **331**
sp_pkeys **331**
sp_fkeys **331**

sp_helpconstraint   332
sp_helpindex   332

Learning About Fields   332
Filling a DataTable   333
Filling a SqlDataReader   335
Using GetSchemaTable   336
sp_columns   338
sp_column_privileges   338

Meta-Learning   338
sp_stored_procedures   338
sp_helptext   339
sp_datatype_info   340

Program ExploreServer   341

Program ExploreRelations   345

Summary   349

A SQL   351

DROP DATABASE   354

ALTER DATABASE   355

CREATE TABLE   355
Data Types   356
IDENTITY   359
Column Constraints   359
Table Constraints   362

ALTER TABLE   363

DROP TABLE   365

CREATE INDEX   365
FILLFACTOR   366
PAD_INDEX   367
DROP_EXISTING   367

DROP INDEX   368

CREATE VIEW   368

DROP VIEW   369

SELECT   370
SELECT   370
INTO   371
FROM   371
WHERE   372
GROUP BY   373
HAVING   374
ORDER BY   374
UNION   375

INSERT   376

UPDATE   377

DELETE   378

Aggregate Functions   379

Joins   380
INNER JOIN   381
LEFT JOIN   381
RIGHT JOIN   382
FULL JOIN   382

Summary   383

B The Visual Basic .NET Development Environment   385

Getting Started   385

Creating a New Solution   387

Toolbars   387

Toolbox Tabs   389

Properties   391

Finding Lost Windows   392

Summary   393

Index   395

ABOUT THE AUTHOR

Rod Stephens began life as a mathematician but, in the 1980s at MIT, discovered the joys of computer algorithms and has been programming professionally ever since. During his tenure at GTE Laboratories, he used relational databases to build several large award-winning applications that are still in use today. More recently he has worked on projects ranging from tax software for the state of Minnesota to a training system for professional football teams.

Rod has written 12 programming books that have been translated into several languages, and more than 150 magazine articles covering Visual Basic, Visual Basic for Applications, Delphi, and Java. His popular VB Helper Web site (www.vb-helper.com) receives more than a million hits per month. VB Helper includes information on Rod's books, essays, tutorials, and more than a thousand example programs for Visual Basic programmers.

TELL US WHAT YOU THINK!

As the reader of this book, *you* are our most important critic and commentator. We value your opinion and want to know what we're doing right, what we could do better, what areas you'd like to see us publish in, and any other words of wisdom you're willing to pass our way.

As an executive editor for Que Publishing, I welcome your comments. You can fax, e-mail, or write me directly to let me know what you did or didn't like about this book—as well as what we can do to make our books stronger.

Please note that I cannot help you with technical problems related to the topic of this book, and that due to the high volume of mail I receive, I might not be able to reply to every message.

When you write, please be sure to include this book's title and author's name as well as your name and phone or fax number. I will carefully review your comments and share them with the author and editors who worked on the book.

Fax: 317-581-4770

E-mail: feedback@quepublishing.com

Mail: Candy Hall
           Executive Editor
           Que Publishing
           201 West 103rd Street
           Indianapolis, IN 46290 USA

INTRODUCTION

Simply put, a database is a piece of software that lets a program store and retrieve data. Usually programmers think of the database as also including the actual data stored on a hard disk or some other media. Sometimes developers think of the database as only including the data. That makes some sense when you speak of backing up the database because you only back up the data, not the data access software. But because the data isn't useful without the data access routines, it makes the most sense to think of the two pieces together as shown in Figure I.1.

All programs work with data to some extent, and business systems often work with large amounts of data. It is common for a large business system to work with thousands or even millions of customer records, product listings, and inventory items.

With this in mind, it is easy to understand why most Visual Basic developers use databases. Although you can write programs that manipulate data without databases, those approaches can be a lot more work. Standardized database products can provide more features such as sorting, searching, and reporting without adding a huge amount of extra work for the developer. If you are writing an application that tracks payments made by a few million customers, you undoubtedly have enough to do without worrying about low-level data storage details.

Visual Basic .NET Database Programming explains how you can use databases in your Visual Basic.NET applications. It talks briefly about several different ways a program can manage data but focuses heavily on the most common type of database in use today: a relational database. Using a relational database and Visual Basic .NET, you can build programs that store, modify, find, and display data quickly and easily.

Figure I.1
A database includes stored data and data access software.

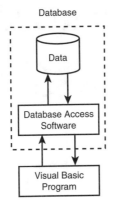

Database

Data

Database Access Software

Visual Basic Program

INTENDED AUDIENCE

Visual Basic .NET Database Programming is for Visual Basic developers who want to manipulate large amounts of data in their programs. It is for those who want to be able to store and manipulate data in a consistent manner, search for specific pieces of data, and fetch different groups of records arranged in various ways.

This book provides a detailed introduction to database programming with Visual Basic .NET. It does not assume you have any previous experience with databases.

This book does assume you have at least some familiarity with some version of Visual Basic. If you have never used Visual Basic before, you might want to start with a more general Visual Basic book. After you know a little about Visual Basic, you can read this book without becoming bogged down in syntactic details.

If you have used a previous version of Visual Basic, ASP, or VBScript, you will be able to follow the examples in this book easily. While Visual Basic .NET and previous versions of Visual Basic have many differences, they are similar enough that you should have few problems understanding the code. Some of the details may be new to you, but the major database concepts will be clear. Appendix B, "The VB .NET Development Environment," contains a quick primer to help you get used to some of the new development environment features.

HOW THIS BOOK IS ORGANIZED

Visual Basic .NET Database Programming provides a broad introduction to database programming in Visual Basic. Chapters in the beginning of the book explain tasks that lie outside of your actual program, such as designing and building a database. The next few chapters explain how to use Visual Basic's automated database tools to provide database support in simple ways. Later chapters explain how to interact directly with databases to provide sophisticated data processing capabilities.

Chapter 1, "Data Storage Alternatives," explains in greater detail what databases are and how programs can use them. It describes several different kinds of data storage techniques you can use when you don't really need the full power of a relational database. It also briefly describes a few less common types of databases in addition to the relational databases that are the book's focus.

Chapter 2, "Database Design," explains how to design a relational database. It tells you how to design, normalize, and construct a database. It explains master-detail relationships, keys, indexes, constraints, and other database construction concepts that you need to understand to build an efficient database.

Chapter 3, "Security," explains security, focusing on the security implemented by SQL Server and MSDE databases. It tells how to grant and deny privilege to connect to a server or a particular database. It tells how to use account IDs and roles to control the access each user gets to the database. For example, it shows how to give a user permission to create tables in a database, or how to allow a user to view but not modify data in a particular table.

Chapter 4, "Off to See the Wizard," describes the most useful database-related wizards that come with Visual Basic .NET. The simpler wizards can help you build SQL queries, initialize database connections, and configure data adapters. The more complicated Data Form Wizard can automatically build a complete database access form for your application. Although the results often require some customization, this wizard can save you a lot of time when starting a new application.

Chapter 5, "The DataSet Family of Objects," describes the DataSet class and classes that work closely with it. It explains how a DataSet object contains DataTable objects. A DataTable object in turn contains DataColumn objects that describe the columns of data and DataRow objects that hold the data. This chapter shows how a program can use DataRelation objects to define relationships between different DataTable objects and how a program can use a DataView object to manipulate a subset of a DataSet's values.

Chapter 6, "Database Connections," explains different ways an application can connect to a database. It shows how a program can initialize its data objects internally, load them using XML data, and connect to SQL Server or OLE DB databases. Once an application has connected to a database, it can manipulate the database. The RunScript program described in this chapter shows how a program can manipulate a database's structure and data quickly and flexibly with remarkably little code.

Chapter 7, "XML Databases," explains one of the newest technologies in data storage: XML (Extensible Markup Language). It explains how a program can load, manipulate, and save XML data. Although relational databases provide far more features for sorting, searching, updating, and grouping data, XML files provide a simple text-based alternative to relational databases that is sometimes useful.

Chapter 8, "Bound Controls," explains how bound controls automatically let a user view, modify, and delete data. These controls cannot perform extremely complex database operations but they can let you build simple database programs in remarkably little time. This chapter also explains how a program can use DataViews to bind a control to a subset of the data and how to use CurrencyManager objects to manage the position of the bound controls in the data.

Chapter 9, "Data Safety," shows how a program can implement data safety features to ensure that no changes are lost without the user's permission. Using a simple drawing program as an example, this chapter shows how a program can implement standard File menu items including New, Open, Save, Save As. It also shows how a program can build a most recently used file (MRU) list.

Chapter 10, "A Single-User Example," uses a simple order entry program to demonstrate several important single-user application techniques. It starts with a big form containing many controls. It refines the initial design to create an MDI interface that can tell when the user modifies a customer's data so it can ensure that the changes are saved safely.

Chapter 11, "Multi-User Programming," continues to improve upon the example built in Chapter 10 to demonstrate techniques useful in multi-user applications. The program developed in Chapter 10 has two serious drawbacks. First, it loads all of its data at once so it cannot handle extremely large databases. Second, this program does not protect users from each other. One user's changes can overwrite another's or they can make the program crash. The example presented in this chapter addresses these issues to make the program more efficient and safe for multiple users.

Chapter 12, "Query By Example," describes a specific technique for selecting records from a database. A query-by-example form lets even inexperienced users perform complex database queries without worrying about all the details. You can add the form described in this chapter to your programs so users can select records using a variety of criteria quickly and easily. In many applications, this is the only record selection method the users will need.

Chapter 13, "Discovering Database Structure," explains how an application can learn about a database's structure. It shows how a program can use Visual Basic's database objects and SQL Server stored procedures to learn about the databases on a server, the tables in a database, and the columns in a table. It shows how to use stored procedures to identify the columns that form a table's primary key and how to determine which fields refer to a column as a foreign key.

Appendix A, "SQL," summarizes some of the more important features of Structured Query Language (SQL). SQL plays an important t role in many database applications and many of the examples described in this book use SQL to perform tasks such as adding, modifying, and deleting database records, and modifying the database structure itself. This chapter summarizes the most useful commands provided by SQL.

Appendix B, "The VB .NET Development Environment," provides a quick introduction to the tools you will use to make Visual Basic .NET applications. It explains the features you can use to customize the environment, possibly making your environment look different from the pictures in this book.

How To Use This Book

The chapters in *Visual Basic .NET Database Programming* are arranged roughly in order of increasing complexity so you can certainly read the chapters in order. Depending on your previous experience and what you want to accomplish, however, you may be able to skip around a bit.

If you have some experience with databases, you may only need to skim Chapters 1 through 3. If you will be writing programs to access a database that someone else will build and manage, you can skim these chapters to get to those later chapters that show how to use a database in a Visual Basic application.

If you want to build a quick-and-dirty application to let other programmers modify the data, or if you only need to provide simple data display, you may be able to get by using the wizards and bound controls described in Chapters 4 and 8. These methods let you get a database application up and running very quickly, though they may allow you less flexibility and can be hard to extend.

If you know your program needs more sophisticated access to the data, you may want to skim those chapters and focus on Chapters 5 and 6, and Chapters 9 through 13. Those chapters explain how to manipulate data in more sophisticated ways programmatically.

Chapter 11 talks about multi-user programming issues. If you plan to build only single-user applications, you can skip it. Some of the techniques this program uses to build its MDI interface make it more efficient, however. Read this chapter to learn how to apply those techniques to single-user systems, as well.

Chapter 12 describes a specific technique for letting the user select records quickly and easily. Read this chapter to learn about the techniques the example uses. Often you can adapt this example to use in your own applications, so you should at least skim this chapter so you know what it does in case you will need it later.

Chapter 13 explains ways a program can learn about a database's structure. If your database is well documented, you may never need to find out what databases are available on a server or to learn the definition of a certain stored procedure. In that case, skim this chapter or skip it completely.

Appendix A describes the most useful SQL commands. If you are unfamiliar with SQL, you should at least skim this appendix and then refer to it later as you encounter specific SQL statements in the examples throughout the rest of the book.

Appendix B provides a quick primer on the Visual Basic .NET development environment. If you have not used Visual Basic .NET before, you should read this material. If you have been using Visual Basic .NET for a while, you can safely skip this appendix.

Table I.1 shows which chapters cover each of the major topics discussed in this book.

TABLE I.1   CHAPTER SUMMARY

Topic	Chapters
Database Basics	1
Database Design and Structure	2–3, 13
Quick-and-Dirty Applications	4, 8
Accessing Data Programmatically	5–6
XML Databases	7
Specific Techniques	9–12
SQL	Appendix A
Visual Basic .NET Primer	Appendix B

NECESSARY EQUIPMENT

The code in this book is written in Visual Basic .NET so you will need a copy of Visual Basic .NET to use the code. Don't even try to run the examples using a previous version of Visual Basic. There are many differences between Visual Basic 6 and Visual Basic .NET, and database programming is one of the areas that changed drastically. If you want to build database applications in an earlier version of Visual Basic, you should probably get an older book.

To run the examples you will also need a computer capable of running Visual Basic .NET. That means a relatively new computer with a reasonably large amount of disk space and memory. Your exact hardware requirements depend on the specific combination of Visual Studio components you install. Table I.2 summarizes Microsoft's current recommended hardware configuration for a typical installation. For their latest recommendations, check Microsoft's Web site at http://msdn.microsoft.com/vstudio/prodinfo/sysreq.asp.

TABLE I.2   RECOMMENDED HARDWARE CONFIGURATION

Item	Recommended	
CPU	450 MHz Pentium II or faster	
Operating System	Windows NT 4.0 or later	
Memory:	Windows NT 4.0 Workstation	64MB
	Windows NT 4.0 Server	160MB
	Windows 2000 Professional	96MB
	Windows 2000 Server	192MB
	Windows XP Pro	160MB
Disk Space:	Standard Edition	2.5GB

Item	Recommended	
	Professional Edition	3.5GB
	Enterprise Edition	3.5GB
Media	CD-ROM or DVD drive	

TABLE I.2   CONTINUED

The system used to build the examples in this book is a 1GHz Pentium III with 128MB of memory and a 20GB hard drive running Windows 2000 Professional. That system was adequate but some additional memory would probably have given me a quicker response. Those examples were built using the non-optimized beta versions of Visual Basic .NET, and the production version should be faster. However, given my experiences I would use the values in table I.2 as minimum requirements for a development computer, particularly for CPU speed and memory.

EXAMPLE DATABASES

Many of the examples in this book use Microsoft Data Engine (MSDE). MSDE is a restricted subset of SQL Server with some size limitations. Because MSDE is a subset of SQL Server, it provides a relatively easy migration path if you need to upgrade your database. You can initially build your application using MSDE and then switch to SQL Server if you need a bigger database.

The MSDE examples described in this book were built on the MSDE server named NETSDK on the computer Bender. You will need to modify the connect strings and Windows NT user names used in the examples to work on your server. For example, the following connect string lets a program connect to the Customers database on the server Bender\NETSDK.

```
Dim connect_string As String = _
    "user id=sa;password=;Data Source=Bender\NETSDK;Database=Customers"
```

If you build an MSDE server named VBDB on the computer FastBox, you would need to change the connect string to this:

```
Dim connect_string As String = _
    "user id=sa;password=;Data Source=FastBox\VBDB;Database=Customers"
```

You can get more information on MSDE, including instructions for obtaining and installing it, on Microsoft's Web site http://msdn.microsoft.com/vstudio/msde.

After you create your MSDE server, you can build databases on it using database design tools or programs of your own. Chapter 2, "Database Design," describes scripts you can use to build databases. The code for Chapter 2, available on this book's Web site, contains sample scripts for creating and populating test databases. You can use the RunScript program explained in Chapter 6, "Database Connections," to execute those scripts to build databases on your server.

ONLINE SAMPLES, UPDATES, AND CHANGES

At this book's Web site (www.vb-helper.com/vbdb.htm) you can:

- Download the examples in the book
- Download other database programming examples
- View updates and corrections for this book
- Read other readers' comments and suggestions

The main VB Helper Web site (www.vb-helper.com) also includes more than a thousand tips, tricks, and example programs, mostly from previous versions of Visual Basic.

If you have corrections, comments, or suggestions you would like to make, please e-mail them to RodStephens@vb-helper.com.

Data Storage Alternatives

There are many ways a program can store and retrieve data. It can store values in the system registry, in comma-separated value (CSV) files, INI files, XML files, object databases, and relational databases.

When most developers think of databases, they think of relational databases such as Access, SQL Server, Oracle, and Informix. The other techniques mentioned in the previous paragraph are useful under some circumstances, however, and so I describe each of them in this chapter. Before you start using a relational database, you should be certain you need one. There's no point in using a database system when a simpler solution will work. In cases where you don't need the full power and flexibility of a relational database, other methods are often faster, easier, and less expensive.

This chapter describes some of the different methods you can use to store data. It discusses the advantages and disadvantages of each, and gives some tips for picking the best solution under different circumstances.

Compiled In Data

The simplest way to load data into an application is to put the data right into a program's source code. This method is extremely simple so it is easy to implement and debug. The program loads the data quickly and the data cannot get lost.

If a program needs a simple piece of data that will never change, compiling the data into the code is a perfectly acceptable technique. Example program CompiledIn1, shown in Figure 1.1, uses the following code to load its State ComboBox. The Form's Load event handler declares and initializes the array states to hold the names of the 50 U.S. states, plus D.C. Then it calls the ComboBox's Items.AddRange method to add the values to the ComboBox:

```
' Load cboStates.
Private Sub Form1_Load(ByVal sender As System.Object, _
  ByVal e As System.EventArgs) Handles MyBase.Load
    Dim states() As String = { _
        "AK", "AL", "AR", "AZ", "CA", "CO", "CT", "DC", "DE", "FL", _
        "GA", "HI", "IA", "ID", "IL", "IN", "KS", "KT", "LA", "MA", _
        "MD", "ME", "MI", "MN", "MO", "MS", "MT", "NC", "ND", "NE", _
        "NH", "NJ", "NM", "NV", "NY", "OH", "OK", "OR", "PA", "RI", _
        "SC", "SD", "TN", "TX", "UT", "VA", "VT", "WA", "WI", "WV", _
        "WY"}
```

```
        cboState.Items.Clear()
        cboState.AddRange(states)
    End Sub
```

Figure 1.1
This program loads a
ComboBox with state
values.

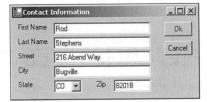

Alternatively, you can select the ComboBox in the development environment, click the ellipsis to the right, and enter the list of states at design time. In that case, Visual Basic places the list of states in the section labeled "Windows Form Designer Generated Code" at the beginning of the form's module. The following code fragment shows the resulting code. The line continuation characters were added to make the code fit on the page. In the actual code, the states are all listed on one very long line:

```
'
'cboState
'
Me.cboState.DropDownWidth = 48
Me.cboState.Items.AddRange(New Object() { _
 "AK", "AL", "AR", "AZ", "CA", "CO", "CT", "DC", "DE", "FL", _
 "GA", "HI", "IA", "ID", "IL", "IN", "KS", "KT", "LA", "MA", _
 "MD", "ME", "MI", "MN", "MO", "MS", "MT", "NC", "ND", "NE", _
 "NH", "NJ", "NM", "NV", "NY", "OH", "OK", "OR", "PA", "RI", _
 "SC", "SD", "TN", "TX", "UT", "VA", "VT", "WA", "WI", "WV", _
 "WY"})
Me.cboState.Location = New System.Drawing.Point(72, 104)
Me.cboState.Name = "cboState"
Me.cboState.Size = New System.Drawing.Size(48, 21)
Me.cboState.TabIndex = 4
```

The drawback to both of these methods is that you cannot modify the data without recompiling the program. This is probably not an issue in this example because it is unlikely that the United States will add or remove a state in the near future.

If your application was a point-of-sales system covering the western United States, however, this could be a problem. If your sales area expanded to include a new state or part of Canada or Mexico, you would need to recompile the application and redistribute it to all users.

These techniques also do not allow the user to modify the data. That's not a problem for state lists and other data that the user will never modify, but it makes these methods unsuitable for storing values such as user preferences, customer data, and order information.

In cases like these, where the data may change, compiled in data is not a good solution.

REGISTRY

Visual Basic's SaveSetting and GetSetting routines let a program save and restore values in the system Registry. GetSetting has this syntax:

```
value = GetSetting(AppName, Section, Key, Default)
```

Here *AppName* is the name of the application. GetSetting uses this parameter to keep the values stored by this application separate from those used by other programs.

The *Section* parameter allows the program to categorize the values stored for the program. For example, the program might use separate sections for user configuration settings, user log in information, internationalization data, and so forth.

The *Key* parameter tells GetSetting the name of the value that it should fetch from the Registry. GetSetting returns *Default* if the value is not in the part of the Registry used by the indicated *AppName*, *Section*, and *Key*.

The SaveSetting routine's syntax is similar.

```
SaveSetting(AppName, Section, Key, Setting)
```

The *AppName*, *Section*, and *Key* parameters are the same as those used by GetSetting. The *Setting* parameter gives the value SaveSetting should store in the Registry.

The GetAllSettings function takes as parameters the application's name and a section name, and returns a list of the setting names and values in that section. The DeleteSetting routine deletes a value or section from the Registry.

Example program Registry, shown in Figure 1.2, uses the following code to save and restore a small note. When the program starts, the Form's Load event handler uses GetSetting to load the saved value. When the program ends, the Form's Closing event handler uses SaveSetting to save the current note value:

```
' Load the saved note value.
Private Sub Form1_Load(ByVal sender As Object, _
  ByVal e As System.EventArgs) Handles MyBase.Load
    txtNote.Text = GetSetting("Registry", "Settings", "Value", _
      "Enter a note to save here")
    txtNote.Select(0, 0)
End Sub

' Save the current value.
Private Sub Form1_Closing(ByVal sender As Object, _
  ByVal e As System.ComponentModel.CancelEventArgs) Handles MyBase.Closing
    SaveSetting("Registry", "Settings", "Value", txtNote.Text)
End Sub
```

Figure 1.2
Program Registry
saves and restores a
small message in the
system Registry.

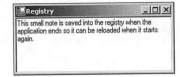

Using the Registry, an application can save and restore a limited number of simple values. You can even use the Registry to save more complex values such as arrays. Example program MRU uses the code shown in Listing 1.1 to save and restore a most recently used file list (MRU). The Form `Load` event handler calls subroutine `LoadMruList`. That routine uses `GetSetting` to retrieve the values `FileName0`, `FileName1`, `FileName2`, and `FileName3` from the MRU List section of the MRU program's Registry area. It removes the path information from each MRU filename and displays the result in the program's File menu.

In a real application, the program would update the MRU list as the user opens and saves files. When the program exits, the Form's `Unload` event handler calls subroutine `SaveMruList` to save the current MRU filenames. That routine loops through the MRU list, saving each of the MRU values back into the Registry.

LISTING 1.1   SAVING AND RESTORING AN MRU

```
' The MRU file names.
Private m_MruFileNames(4) As String

' Load the saved MRU list entries.
Private Sub Form1_Load(ByVal sender As Object, _
  ByVal e As System.EventArgs) Handles MyBase.Load
    ' Load saved MRU values.
    LoadMruList()
End Sub

' Load the saved MRU file list.
Private Sub LoadMruList()
    Dim i As Integer

    ' Get the file names.
    For i = 0 To 3
        ' Get the name.
        m_MruFileNames(i) = GetSetting("MRU", "MRU List", _
            "FileName" & Format$(i), "")

        ' Display the title.
        Select Case i
            Case 0
                mnuFileMRU1.Text = FileTitle(m_MruFileNames(i))
            Case 1
                mnuFileMRU2.Text = FileTitle(m_MruFileNames(i))
            Case 2
                mnuFileMRU3.Text = FileTitle(m_MruFileNames(i))
            Case 3
                mnuFileMRU4.Text = FileTitle(m_MruFileNames(i))
        End Select
```

LISTING 1.1   CONTINUED

```
    Next i
End Sub

' Return the file's title without the path.
Private Function FileTitle(ByVal file_name As String) As String
    Dim pos As Integer

    pos = InStrRev(file_name, "\")
    FileTitle = Mid$(file_name, pos + 1)
End Function

' Save the current MRU list.
Private Sub Form1_Closing(ByVal sender As Object, _
  ByVal e As System.ComponentModel.CancelEventArgs) _
  Handles MyBase.Closing
    SaveMruList()
End Sub

' Save the currrent MRU file list.
Private Sub SaveMruList()
    Dim i As Integer

    For i = 0 To 3
        SaveSetting("MRU", "MRU List", "FileName" & Format$(i), _
          m_MruFileNames(i))
    Next I
End Sub
```

Chapter 9, "Data Safety," has more to say about MRU lists and provides more realistic examples.

Although you can store simple values like MRU lists in the Registry, this is not an ideal place to store large amounts of data. If you need to save a large array of data, you would probably be better off using a file or a database.

The Registry resides on a particular computer. This can be an advantage or a disadvantage depending on what you want to accomplish. Because each computer has its own Registry, it is easy to save user configurations in the Registry. You can store values using SaveSettings without worrying about which user is using the program.

On the other hand, that means these values stay with the computer rather than the user. If you normally work on one computer but you sometimes use another, any settings saved in the Registry will not follow you. Sometimes this can be confusing because the application doesn't look the same on all computers. This is particularly likely in a networked environment where users expect to be able to use the same application on several computers.

If you want to make settings follow the users, you should use some other data storage technique. For example, you can store settings identified by the users' names in a file, database, or other location shared across the network. When the user logs on, the program looks up the user's name and retrieves the settings for that user.

CSV FILES

Comma-separated value (CSV) files are text files that contain values separated by commas. Similar file formats that separate values with other delimiters such as semicolons or tabs are also useful, particularly if the data values may contain commas. Often a CSV file begins with one record that lists the names of the fields the file contains, as shown in the following example:

```
FirstName,LastName,Street,City,State,Zip
Rod,Stephens,1234 Programmer Way,Bugville,CO,80333
Snortimer,Canid,827 E Cat Chaser's Ct,Hoot,AZ,98765
Cobe,Cat,POB 12763,Reno,NV,90219
```

Visual Basic provides tools that make loading delimited files like this easy. Example program CSV uses the code shown in Listing 1.2 to load a list of customers from a CSV file. The `LoadCustomers` subroutine calls the `GetFileContents` function to grab the CSV file's contents all at once. It uses Visual Basic's `Split` function to move the file's lines into an array of strings. `LoadCustomers` loops through the array of lines and uses `Split` again to break each line into fields. It adds the fields to an output string and, when it is finished processing all the lines, it displays the result.

LISTING 1.2 LOADING A CUSTOMER LIST

```vb
' Load the customer list.
Private Sub Form1_Load(ByVal sender As Object, _
  ByVal e As System.EventArgs) Handles MyBase.Load
    LoadCustomers()
End Sub

' Load the customer list from Customers.csv.
Private Sub LoadCustomers()
    Const DELIMITER = ","
    Dim result As String
    Dim file_contents As String
    Dim records() As String
    Dim field_names() As String
    Dim fields() As String
    Dim record_num As Integer
    Dim field_num As Integer

    ' Grab the file contents.
    file_contents = GetFileContents(Application.StartupPath & "\Customers.csv")

    ' Break the file into lines.
    records = Split(file_contents, vbCrLf)

    ' Break the first record into field names.
    field_names = Split(records(0), DELIMITER)

    ' Process the remaining records.
    For record_num = 1 To records.GetUpperBound(0)
        ' Watch for empty entries that may
        ' appear at the end of the file.
        records(record_num) = records(record_num).Trim
```

LISTING 1.2   CONTINUED

```
        If records(record_num).Length > 0 Then
            ' Break the record into fields.
            fields = Split(records(record_num), DELIMITER)

            ' Add the record to the output.
            result = result & vbCrLf
            For field_num = 0 To fields.GetUpperBound(0)
                result = result & _
                    field_names(field_num) & ": " & _
                    fields(field_num) & vbCrLf
            Next field_num
        End If
    Next record_num

    ' Display the result.
    txtCustomers.Text = result.Substring(vbCrLf.Length)
    txtCustomers.Select(0, 0)
End Sub

' Return the file's contents in a string.
Public Function GetFileContents(ByVal file_name As String) As String
    Dim stream_reader As New StreamReader(file_name)
    Dim text As String = stream_reader.ReadToEnd()

    stream_reader.Close()
    Return text
End Function
```

Note

If the file used delimiters other than a comma, you would need to change the definition of the constant DELIMITER, but you could leave the rest of the code unchanged.

FIXED-LENGTH RECORDS

In a file containing fixed-length records, each data field has the same length in every record. In the following example, the records have 10-character FirstName, 10-character LastName, 30-character EmailAddress, and 30-character Picture fields. The total size of each record is 80 characters. Depending on the exact file format, records may be separated by carriage returns, some other character, or they may be run together back to back:

```
FirstName LastName  EmailAddress                 Picture
Rod       Stephens  RodStephens@vb-helper.com    www.vb-helper.com/rod.jpg
Snortimer Canid     Snortimer@vb-helper.com      www.vb-helper.com/dog.jpg
Cobe      Cat       Cobe@vb-helper.com           www.vb-helper.com/cats.jpg
```

Example program FixedLength uses the code shown in Listing 1.3 to read this data. Subroutine LoadCustomers loads the file's contents into a string and uses Split to break it into lines as before. If the records in the file were all run together on a single line, the program would need to count characters to see where one record ended and the next began.

Next `LoadCustomers` pulls the field names out of the first line of text. The `field_lengths` array tells it how long each field is and from that the subroutine can calculate where each field begins. The program uses a similar technique to separate and display the fields in the file's remaining records.

LISTING 1.3   READING AND DISPLAYING FIXED-LENGTH DATA

```
' Load the customer list.
Private Sub Form1_Load(ByVal sender As Object, _
  ByVal e As System.EventArgs) Handles MyBase.Load
    LoadCustomers()
End Sub

' Load the customer list from Customers.fix.
Private Sub LoadCustomers()
    Dim result As String
    Dim file_contents As String
    Dim records() As String
    Dim record As String
    Dim field_names() As String
    Dim record_num As Integer
    Dim field_num As Integer
    Dim field_start As Integer
    Dim field_lengths() As Integer = {10, 10, 30, 30}

    ' Grab the file contents.
    file_contents = GetFileContents(Application.StartupPath & "\Customers.fix")

    ' Break the file into lines.
    records = Split(file_contents, vbCrLf)

    ' Get the field names.
    ReDim field_names(field_lengths.GetUpperBound(0))
    field_start = 0
    For field_num = 0 To field_names.GetUpperBound(0)
        record = records(0)
        field_names(field_num) = _
            record.Substring(field_start, field_lengths(field_num)).Trim
        field_start += field_lengths(field_num)
    Next field_num

    ' Process the remaining records.
    For record_num = 1 To records.GetUpperBound(0)
        ' Watch for empty entries that may
        ' appear at the end of the file.
        record = records(record_num)
        If record.Length > 0 Then
            ' Add the fields to the output.
            result = result & vbCrLf
            field_start = 0
            For field_num = 0 To field_names.GetUpperBound(0)
                result = result & _
                    field_names(field_num) & ": " & _
                    record.Substring(field_start, _
                    field_lengths(field_num)).Trim & _
                    vbCrLf
```

LISTING 1.3   CONTINUED

```
                    field_start += field_lengths(field_num)
            Next field_num
        End If
    Next record_num

    ' Display the result.
    txtCustomers.Text = result.Substring(vbCrLf.Length)
    txtCustomers.Select(0, 0)
End Sub

' Return the file's contents in a string.
Public Function GetFileContents(ByVal file_name As String) As String
    Dim stream_reader As New StreamReader(file_name)
    Dim text As String = stream_reader.ReadToEnd()

    stream_reader.Close()
    Return text
End Function
```

Note that the LoadCustomers subroutine must know how long each field is. If the field lengths change, you will need to update the field_lengths array's initialization code.

INI FILES

Before the Registry was invented, Windows operating systems stored values in INI (initialization) files. Microsoft introduced the Registry, told developers to use it instead of INI files, and has been gradually reducing support for INI files ever since.

An *INI file* is a text file that contains values grouped into sections. Each section begins with the section's name in brackets. Within a section, items consist of a name followed by an equals sign followed by a value. Comments begin with a semicolon and go to the end of the line. The following example shows a small INI file containing configuration parameters for a mapping application:

```
[Position]
; The main form's position.
MainLeft=100
MainTop=300
MainWidth=800
MainHeight=600

; The map form's position.
MapLeft=400
MapTop=400
MapWidth=500
MapHeight=500

[Colors]
; Colors used to draw the map.
StreetColor=000060      ; Streets
HighwayColor=60FFFF      ; Highways
TrackColor=000000       ; Railroad tracks
WaterColor=0000FF       ; Rivers and lakes
```

Because INI files are outdated, you should try to avoid them in your applications. XML files provide much more flexibility and power, and Visual Basic supports them directly.

If you need to load data from an INI file, you may want to convert it into an XML file. Example program INI2XML, shown in Figure 1.3, uses the code shown in Listing 1.4 to convert INI files into XML files.

Figure 1.3
Program INI2XML converts INI files into XML files.

Most of the work is performed by subroutine IniToXml. That routine uses the Split function to break the INI file into lines. It makes the XML file's top-level tag <AllValues>. It then loops through the INI file's lines.

For each line, the routine removes the line's comment if one is present. It then uses Trim to remove any spaces from the ends of the result.

If the line is still non-blank, IniToXml examines its first character. If the first character is an open bracket, the line marks the beginning of a new section. In that case, the program checks its section_name variable to see if a previous section is open. If a section is open, IniToXml adds that section's closing tag to the XML result. For example, if the routine is reading the Colors section, it adds the tag </Colors> to the output. After ending the previous section, the subroutine saves the new section's name and adds the new section's opening tag to the XML result.

If the trimmed line does not begin with a bracket, it contains an item name, equals sign, and an item value. The subroutine locates the equals sign and uses the text on either side to build a tag containing the value. For instance, if the line contains the text BackColor=&HFFFFFF, then the subroutine generates the output <BackColor>&HFFFFFF</BackColor>.

After it has processed the INI file's last line, the subroutine closes the final section and the XML document itself.

LISTING 1.4   PROGRAM INI2XML USES THIS CODE TO CONVERT INI FILES INTO XML FILES

```vb
' Open an INI file.
Private Sub mnuFileOpen_Click(ByVal sender As System.Object, _
    ByVal e As System.EventArgs) Handles mnuFileOpen.Click
    Dim file_name As String
    Dim xml_contents As String

    ' Let the user select the INI file.
    If dlgOpenINI.ShowDialog() = DialogResult.Cancel Then Exit Sub

    ' Load the INI file.
    file_name = dlgOpenINI.FileName

    ' Load the file and convert it into XML.
    xml_contents = IniToXml(GetFileContents(file_name))

    ' Save the results.
    file_name = file_name.Substring(0, file_name.Length - 3) & "xml"
    SetFileContents(file_name, xml_contents)

    ' Display the results.
    txtXml.Text = xml_contents
    txtXml.Select(0, 0)
End Sub

' Convert the INI file into an XML file.
Private Function IniToXml(ByVal ini_contents As String) As String
    Dim xml_contents As String
    Dim lines() As String
    Dim line_num As Integer
    Dim section_name As String
    Dim new_line As String
    Dim pos As Integer
    Dim item_name As String
    Dim item_value As String

    ' Break the INI file into lines.
    lines = Split(ini_contents, vbCrLf)

    ' Create the XML output.
    xml_contents = "<AllValues>" & vbCrLf
    For line_num = 0 To lines.GetUpperBound(0)
        ' Remove comments and trim the line.
        new_line = lines(line_num).Trim()
        pos = new_line.IndexOf(";")
        If pos >= 0 Then
            new_line = new_line.Substring(0, pos)
        End If
        new_line = new_line.Trim()

        ' See if this line begins a new section.
        If new_line.Length > 0 Then
            If new_line.Substring(0, 1) = "[" Then
                ' This begins a new section.
                ' Close the previous section.
                If section_name <> "" Then
```

LISTING 1.4 CONTINUED

```
                            xml_contents &= "  </" & section_name & ">" & vbCrLf
                End If

                ' Save the new section name.
                section_name = new_line.Substring(1, new_line.Length - 2)

                ' Start the new XML section.
                xml_contents &= "  <" & section_name & ">" & vbCrLf
            Else
                ' This is a value. Find the =.
                pos = new_line.IndexOf("=")
                item_name = new_line.Substring(0, pos)
                item_value = new_line.Substring(pos + 1)
                xml_contents = xml_contents & _
                    "    <" & item_name & ">" & _
                    item_value & _
                    "</" & item_name & ">" & vbCrLf
            End If
        End If
    Next line_num

    ' Close the last section.
    If section_name <> "" Then
        xml_contents &= "  </" & section_name & ">" & vbCrLf
    End If

    ' End the XML document.
    xml_contents &= "</AllValues>" & vbCrLf

    ' Return the results.
    Return xml_contents
End Function

' Return the file's contents in a string.
Public Function GetFileContents(ByVal file_name As String) As String
    Dim stream_reader As New StreamReader(file_name)
    Dim text As String = stream_reader.ReadToEnd()

    stream_reader.Close()
    Return text
End Function

' Write a file from a string.
Public Sub SetFileContents(ByVal file_name As String, _
  ByVal file_contents As String)
    Dim stream_writer As New StreamWriter(file_name)

    stream_writer.Write(file_contents)
    stream_writer.Close()
End Sub
```

The following text shows the XML file produced by program INI2XML for the previous INI file:

```
<AllValues>
  <Position>
    <MainLeft>100</MainLeft>
    <MainTop>300</MainTop>
    <MainWidth>800</MainWidth>
    <MainHeight>600</MainHeight>
    <MapLeft>400</MapLeft>
    <MapTop>400</MapTop>
    <MapWidth>500</MapWidth>
    <MapHeight>500</MapHeight>
  </Position>
  <Colors>
    <StreetColor>000060</StreetColor>
    <HighwayColor>60FFFF</HighwayColor>
    <TrackColor>000000</TrackColor>
    <WaterColor>0000FF</WaterColor>
  </Colors>
</AllValues>
```

Some INI file formats contain other characters than those handled by program INI2XML. Some use ## to indicate comments instead of a semicolon. The INI standard also allows escape sequences to insert special characters into the file. For example, the sequence \t represents the tab character. This simple version of INI2XML doesn't handle these cases, so you will need to modify it if you encounter such an INI file.

XML

The latest thing in text-based data storage is *Extensible Markup Language* (XML). XML stores data using tags similar to those used in HTML. HTML uses tags such as <H1>...</H1> and <B>...</B> to define the style of a piece of text. The <H1> tag indicates the enclosed text should be in heading style number 1 and the <B> tag indicates the text should be bold.

Whereas HTML uses tags to define the appearance of text, XML uses tags to define data content. One important difference between HTML and XML tags is that HTML tags are defined by the HTML standard but you can define the XML tags.

For example, the XML document shown in the previous section (the one produced by program INI2XML) stores configuration information in two sections: Position and Colors. Within those sections other tags hold specific configuration values.

All XML files must have a single root tag that includes all other elements. In the XML document I just noted, all the document's elements are included in an AllValues tag.

XML is just as easy to read as CSV files, files containing fixed-length records, and INI files. Furthermore, Visual Basic .NET provides much better support for XML files than for files of the other types. Using the XmlDocument class, an application can load an XML file, modify it, and save any changes. XmlDocument and other related classes let you search for specific items in the document, iterate over a collection of document elements, and even perform some simple sorting operations.

Example program XML uses the code shown in Listing 1.5 to load position information from an XML file. Subroutine `LoadConfiguration` opens the file `Settings.xml`. It uses the `XmlNodeValue` function to retrieve the values of the XML file's `MainLeft`, `MainTop`, `MainWidth`, and `MainHeight` elements, and it uses those values to position the program's form.

Function `XmlNodeValue` uses an XPath expression to identify the node it should select. In general, the XPath language is complex but the examples used here all have a form similar to `//MainLeft`. The `//` characters indicate that the selection can include any ancestors in the XML document hierarchy. `MainLeft` means the document element should be named MainLeft. That means the XPath expression `//MainLeft` would match any element named MainLeft.

The `XmlNodeValue` function calls the `XmlDocument` object's `SelectSingleNode` method, passing it the XPath expression it received as a parameter. If `SelectSingleNode` fails to find a matching node, `XmlNodeValue` returns a default value. If `SelectSingleNode` does find a matching node, `XmlNodeValue` returns the text contained within the node. That text is whatever lies between the node's start and end tags.

LISTING 1.5 LOADING POSITION INFORMATION FROM AN XML FILE

```
Imports System.Xml

... Code deleted ...

' Load configuration information from Settings.xml.
Private Sub LoadConfiguration()
    Dim xml_document As New XmlDocument()

    ' Open the XML document.
    xml_document.Load(Application.StartupPath & "\Settings.xml")

    ' Position the form.
    Me.StartPosition = FormStartPosition.Manual
    Me.SetBounds( _
        XmlNodeValue(xml_document, "//MainLeft", Me.Location.X), _
        XmlNodeValue(xml_document, "//MainTop", Me.Location.Y), _
        XmlNodeValue(xml_document, "//MainWidth", Me.Size.Width), _
        XmlNodeValue(xml_document, "//MainHeight", Me.Size.Height))
End Sub

' Return the value of a node.
Private Function XmlNodeValue(ByVal xml_document As XmlDocument, _
  ByVal xpath As String, Optional ByVal default_value As String = "") As String
    Dim xml_node As XmlNode

    xml_node = xml_document.SelectSingleNode(xpath)
    If xml_node Is Nothing Then
        ' The node doesn't exist. Return the default.
        Return default_value
    Else
        ' Return the node's value.
        Return xml_node.InnerText
    End If
End Function
```

XML, XPath, and other related technologies are extremely flexible and there's no room to do them justice here. For more information, see a book on XML, such as my book *Visual Basic.NET and XML* (2002, Stephens and Hochgurtel, John Wiley & Sons).

RELATIONAL DATABASES

A relational database provides three main levels of data storage: *field*, *record*, and *table*. A *field* stores a single piece of data such as a last name or a salary.

A *record* stores a record of related fields. For example, a record might store fields giving a particular employee's name, address, phone number, job title, and salary.

A *table* holds a collection of records that all contain the same kinds of fields. For instance, a table named Employees would hold records containing data for all the company's employees. Each record would contain the same fields (FirstName, LastName, Street, and so forth), though the fields would have different values in different records.

A physical analogy to this structure is a filing room. The room (database) holds a collection of filing cabinets (tables). Each filing cabinet holds folders (records) that contain pieces of data (fields).

This analogy is imperfect for several reasons. Perhaps most importantly, every record in a table must contain exactly the same fields, though with different values in each record. The folders in a filing cabinet can hold just about anything.

Figure 1.4 shows a more correct view of a relational database.

Figure 1.4
A relational database contains tables that hold records that hold fields.

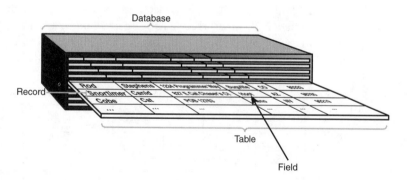

You can think of a table as a large grid similar to a spreadsheet or a text file containing fixed-length records. Because tables have this grid-like structure, the records and fields in a table are often called rows and columns (see Table 1.1).

TABLE 1.1   AN EXAMPLE TABLE

FirstName	LastName	EmailAddress	Picture
Rod	Stephens	RodStephens@ vb-helper.com	www.vb-helper.com/rod.jpg
Snortimer	Canid	Snortimer@ vb-helper.com	www.vb-helper.com/dog.jpg
Cobe	Cat	Cobe@ vb-helper.com	www.vb-helper.com/cats.jpg
...	...	...	...

RELATIONSHIPS

If a relational database were nothing more than a collection of grid-like tables, it would provide little advantage over simple text files containing fixed-length records. The word "relational" hints at the real power of these databases. A relational database provides an assortment of tools for creating and analyzing relationships among different pieces of data.

For example, suppose you have a test score database with two tables named Students and Scores. The Students table contains fields that identify the students: FirstName, LastName, Period, and StudentId. The Scores table contains fields that identify a particular student's score on a specific test: StudentId, TestNumber, and Score.

In this example, the two tables' StudentId fields link the tables as shown in Figure 1.5. If a record in the Students table has the same StudentId field value as a record in the Scores table, the corresponding student received that score on a test. For example, the values in Figure 1.5 show that Cindy Smith received a score of 98 on Test Number 1 and a score of 95 on Test Number 2. Other records in the Scores table, but not shown in Figure 1.5, would hold Cindy's scores for other tests.

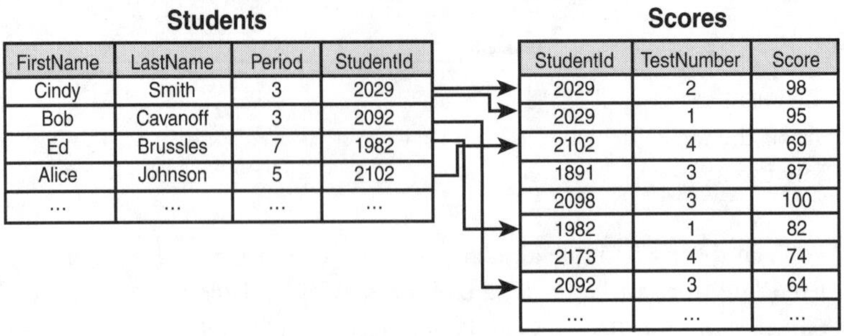

Figure 1.5
Matching fields in tables define the tables' relationships.

Students

FirstName	LastName	Period	StudentId
Cindy	Smith	3	2029
Bob	Cavanoff	3	2092
Ed	Brussles	7	1982
Alice	Johnson	5	2102
...	...	...	...

Scores

StudentId	TestNumber	Score
2029	2	98
2029	1	95
2102	4	69
1891	3	87
2098	3	100
1982	1	82
2173	4	74
2092	3	64
...	...	...

To find a pupil's scores manually, you would look up his record in the Students table and find his StudentId. Then you would find all the records in the Scores table that have a matching StudentId field.

You could easily write a program to perform this operation, but a relational database can do this for you using Structured Query Language (SQL, often pronounced "sequel"). SQL is an intuitive industry-standard language for working with relational databases. It includes statements for building tables, creating records, modifying values, deleting records, and relating tables to each other.

By executing the following SQL statement, a program can make the database return a list of scores for student 2029:

```
SELECT TestNumber, Score FROM Scores WHERE StudentId = 2029
```

This statement tells the database to return the values of the TestNumber and Score fields in the Scores table where the corresponding StudentId value is 2029.

The result of this query in a tabular format looks like this (assuming there are only two Scores records for Cindy Smith):

TestNumber	Score
2	98
1	95

This query still isn't very convenient because it requires you to supply the StudentId. To find the scores for Cindy Smith, you would need to look through the Students table until you found her record and then look up her StudentId. The following SQL statement selects Cindy's scores using her name:

```
SELECT TestNumber, Score
FROM Students, Scores
WHERE FirstName='Cindy'
  AND LastName='Smith'
  AND Students.StudentId = Scores.StudentId
```

This statement's SELECT clause tells the database to select the TestNumber and Score fields. The FROM clause tells the database that the fields come from the Students and Scores tables. In this case, the SELECT clause does not select any fields from Students, but that table must be listed here because it is used in the WHERE clause.

The WHERE clause tells the database which records to select and how to join them. The first part of the WHERE clause indicates that the records should have the FirstName value Cindy. Only the Students table contains a field named FirstName so the database can figure out that the query is referring to the Students table. If you wanted, you could explicitly refer to this table's field as Students.FirstName. This part of the WHERE clause means a Students record will be selected only if its FirstName field has value Cindy.

Similarly, the second part of the WHERE clause makes the database select a Students record only if its LastName field has the value Smith.

The last part of the WHERE clause is called a *join condition* because it joins the Students and Scores tables. This statement makes the database select records from both tables where the

StudentId fields of the records match. Because both tables contain a StudentId field, the statement must prefix the fields with their table names so the database can tell which fields to use.

Taken all together, this query makes the database select fields from the Students and Scores table where the Students record is for Cindy Smith and the Scores records have a matching StudentId.

ORDERING DATA

The records in a relational database are not necessarily stored in any particular order. The physical layout of the records is up to the database and you should not rely on the records being stored in a specific order. If you want to ensure that the database returns data in some desired order, you can add an ORDER BY clause to the SQL SELECT statement. The following query selects the same data as the previous query, only the results are ordered by TestNumber:

```
SELECT TestNumber, Score
FROM Students, Scores
WHERE FirstName='Cindy'
  AND LastName='Smith'
  AND Students.StudentId = Scores.StudentId
ORDER BY TestNumber
```

Using SQL, you can make a relational database join more than two tables, sort in ascending or descending order on multiple fields, group related items, and calculate totals and other functions. Appendix A, "SQL," provides a tutorial on using SQL. For now you only need to know that relational databases provide these sorts of features.

INDEXES

Although conceptually a relational database holds data in an array-like table, the physical structure of the data may be very different. To make particular kinds of searches faster, you can create an index containing one or more key fields. The database can then build special lookup data structures to make searching for records using that key faster.

For instance, in the previous test score database you could create an index that combined the LastName and FirstName fields. Then queries with a SELECT clause that uses those fields can execute faster. Although the database can select records using those fields with or without the index, the index can improve performance.

Sometimes you may want to select records based on different criteria. For example, you might want to select a Students record using a pupil's name as in the previous example, or you might want to select all the records where the Period field has a certain value. In that case, you can build a second index with Period as its key field.

Some databases also provide their own automatic optimization. You can compose a query and ask the database to compile it. That prepares the database to make the query more quickly in the future.

STORED PROCEDURES

A typical database application uses a database to store data, but relational databases can also store program code. A *stored procedure* is a subroutine stored in the database itself. An application can invoke a stored procedure to perform complex tasks before returning results to the program. If the application accesses the database across a network, this can sometimes save a lot of communication time.

Placing code inside the database also lets you change the code without recompiling the application. If a business rule changes the way the program should perform a certain calculation and that calculation is performed by a stored procedure, you only need to update the stored procedure.

This can be a huge timesaver for large applications that are accessed by many users scattered across a network. Suppose you have several hundred users sharing a business application. Rather than recompiling the application and reinstalling it on every computer, you only need to make a single change in the shared database.

SECURITY

Different implementations of relational databases also provide different additional features. Most provide some level of security. An Access database can be password protected so a user cannot open it without giving the password. More sophisticated databases can require different users to have different passwords, and can restrict a user's access to specific tables and even to certain fields within a table.

For example, a data entry clerk might need access to the `Employees` table but not to the `Salary` field on that table. The clerk might not need any access to the `MarketPlanning` table.

The other data storage methods described previously have little or no built-in security. If you make a CSV or XML file available on a network, anyone can read it.

SPECIFIC RELATIONAL DATABASE ENGINES

Many vendors sell relational database products. Microsoft Access, Microsoft SQL Server, and Oracle are three of the most popular database products used by Visual Basic developers. Each provides its own assortment of database features and database management tools. The following sections provide a little more detail about these products.

MICROSOFT ACCESS

Access databases are relatively simple. Each database is stored in a separate file with a `.mdb` extension. A Visual Basic program accesses the database directly using data access routines built in to Visual Basic libraries as shown in Figure 1.6.

Figure 1.6
Visual Basic programs interact with Access databases directly through data access routines.

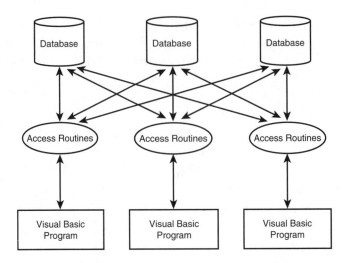

Because Access databases are file-based, they are subject to some limitations imposed by the computer's file system. Those limitations mean an Access database can hold at most roughly 2GB of data. The database file structure also means record locking is somewhat primitive in an Access database. Two users trying to manipulate the database at the same time may slow each other down.

For small desktop applications, these restrictions are often not a big deal. If the database only needs to serve a single user, record locking isn't an issue.

Many applications also never come close to the 2GB limit. If you need a huge amount of storage, you might be able to work around the limit. Sometimes you can store an application's data in more than one database, each holding less than 2GB. Other times you can reduce the size of the database by storing some data externally.

For example, pictures take up a lot of space. A 512×512 pixel image stored with 32 bits of color precision takes up 1MB of space. A database containing 2,000 images takes up 2GB of space. Instead of storing the images in the database, however, you could store them in normal disk files and then store only the filenames in the database. If the longest filename contains 256 characters, you could store more than 8 million pictures before you reached the database's size limit.

There is an important difference between an Access database and the Microsoft Access product. An Access database is the actual .mdb file holding the database. The Access product is a Microsoft Office application that lets you design, build, and use Access databases. It provides tools to let you manage Access databases interactively.

A Visual Basic program can open and manipulate an Access database. Using Visual Basic, you can create tables, add records, select records, and perform joins in the database. However, Visual Basic itself does not provide tools for interactively managing the database. You can write code to modify the database but Visual Basic will not help you manage the database interactively.

The Visual Data Manager Add-In included with Visual Basic 6 allows you to create and modify Access databases interactively. Although Visual Basic .NET does not include a similar tool, you can build your own database management programs without much difficulty. The RunScript example program described in Chapter 6, "Database Connections," can execute scripts that define a database's structure.

SQL SERVER

SQL Server (pronounced "sequel server") is Microsoft's premier database engine. Unlike Access databases, a SQL Server database is not subject to a 2GB size limit. SQL Server tables can each hold up to roughly 2GB of data and a database can hold up to 1TB (1 terabyte = 1,024 gigabytes). SQL Server comes with database design and development tools so you don't need to write your own.

SQL Server uses a centralized database server to manage access to the database as shown in Figure 1.7. In addition to managing databases that exceed the file system's normal limitations, the server provides much better record locking features than an Access database does. That means SQL Server can handle practically any number of concurrent users with minimal conflict.

Figure 1.7
A shared server process handles access to SQL Server databases.

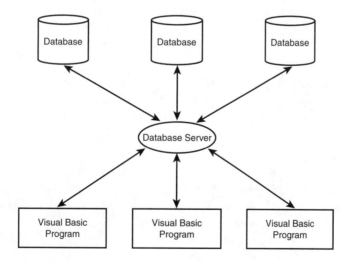

Because Access and SQL Server use such different data access models, Visual Basic programs that use these different kinds of databases must access data in significantly different ways. That means it can be difficult to upgrade a Visual Basic application if Access does not give good enough performance.

One major drawback to SQL Server is its price. Some SQL Server installations cost several thousand dollars. MSDE provides a compromise between Access and SQL Server databases that combines reasonable price with a data access model similar to the one used by SQL Server, making it much easier to upgrade if necessary.

MSDE

Microsoft Data Engine (MSDE) is a restricted subset of SQL Server. It has size limitations similar to those of Access databases, but the model it uses for accessing databases is similar to the one shown in Figure 1.7 and used by SQL Server. That means you can build an inexpensive Visual Basic program using MSDE. Later if you decide the performance is inadequate, you can upgrade to SQL Server with a minimum of hassle.

MSDE is available for free with a number of Microsoft products including Microsoft Access 2000, Microsoft Office 2000 (which includes Access), Visual Basic 6 Professional and Enterprise editions, and all Visual Basic.NET editions.

If you also have Access, you can use its tools to design MSDE databases. If you have the Visual Basic .NET Professional or Enterprise edition, you can use the Visual Data Tools provided by Visual Basic to design and build the database.

If you have Visual Basic .NET Standard edition and no copy of Access, you are in a situation similar to a developer trying to use Access databases without Access. You can write programs that manipulate MSDE databases, but you will not have any tools for managing them interactively.

For information on MSDE, including instructions for obtaining and installing it, visit Microsoft's MSDE Web site http://msdn.microsoft.com/vstudio/msde.

ORACLE

Oracle is another high-performance database product that is similar in many ways to SQL Server. It provides interactive tools for working with Oracle databases. Oracle also provides optional tools for data mining and warehousing, OLAP (online analytical processing), spatial databases, and enhanced security.

Oracle's data access strategy is similar to the one shown in Figure 1.7 and used by SQL Server, with a central database server providing access to the data. All Oracle products use this same approach so upgrading from the Personal Edition to the Standard or Enterprise Editions is relatively straightforward. The different Oracle editions range in price from a few hundred dollars to several thousand.

OTHERS

Other relational database products are also available. For example, the Informix product now owned by IBM provides features similar to SQL Server and Oracle.

Because they require the fewest additional components, this book assumes you will be using Access databases or MSDE. Later chapters talk briefly about the Access design tools available if you have Access.

However, most of the book focuses on writing programs that work with databases rather than on managing databases interactively. Working with databases is reasonably similar no matter which database product you use; as such, most of the book will be helpful whether you buy a $20,000 database or work with nothing more than MSDE.

MORE EXOTIC DATABASES

Besides relational databases, there are several other kinds of more exotic databases. This book focuses on relational databases, so these are only mentioned briefly here. If you think you could benefit from one of these more unusual types of database, you can search the Web for more information.

A *hierarchical database* stores data in a hierarchical, tree-like structure. A typical computer's file system is a form of a hierarchical database. A directory or folder contains files and other directories or folders. In some file systems, links or shortcuts allow relationships between directories and files that break the normal hierarchical model. For example, a shortcut in one directory might invoke a program stored in another. In some operating systems, a link in one directory can lead to another directory; therefore, a directory's links can make it seem to be a subdirectory of more than one parent directory.

An XML file is another example of a hierarchical database. The file includes tags that can include other tags in a tree-like arrangement. Visual Basic .NET provides tools that let a program perform such actions as reading XML files, manipulating their structure, searching for items with certain characteristics, and so forth.

An *object-oriented database* stores and retrieves objects. For example, an application can create an instance of the Customer class and use the database to store that object. The program can later retrieve the object using selection criteria much as a relational database does. For example, it might ask the database to create a Customer object for a customer with a certain name. This kind of database can be useful if your application architecture is very object-oriented. It is not too difficult to map object properties in and out of a relational database, but a truly object-oriented database can save you the effort.

A *data warehouse* is a collection of data gathered from a variety of sources and stored all in one place. An application can query the data warehouse instead of searching for data in the original data sources. For instance, suppose different organizations within your company have their own databases containing information about sales, inventory, planning, market forecasts, and finance. A data warehouse would gather all this data so you can easily perform queries that cross the organizational boundaries.

A *data mart* is a reprocessed data warehouse. It contains a filtered and rearranged copy of the information stored in the data warehouse. For example, a data mart might include information relating sales, advertising, and market forecasting data, ignoring the rest of the data in the data warehouse. You could use the data mart to analyze the results of different advertising campaigns on sales in different markets. Using the data mart lets you analyze the data more efficiently without having to work through the larger data warehouse.

A table in a relational database stores data logically in a two-dimensional array. A *data cube* stores data in an array of three or more dimensions. For example, suppose you have sales figures for three employees (Amy, Bob, and Cindy) in five states (CO, UT, NM, WY, and ID) over a four-year period (2000–2003). Figure 1.8 shows the way this data would be arranged in a data cube.

Figure 1.8
A data cube holds data defined by multi-dimensional axes.

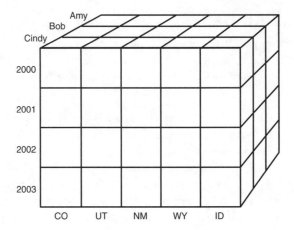

Data cubes also allow you to zoom in on a chunk of data and see more detail. For instance, in Figure 1.8 you could break the section defined by Amy's sales in CO for 2001 into a smaller cube that divides the data by county and month.

Conversely, you can zoom out and see the current data cube view aggregated on a larger scale. If you zoom out in this example, you might discover that the cube shown in Figure 1.8 is just one block in a larger cube with dimensions giving sales group, decade, and region.

Note also that a data cube can contain more than three dimensions. For example, this data might be further refined by product type and revenue. Visualizing higher dimensional arrays is difficult but using the data in a higher dimensional cube isn't too hard.

SUMMARY

If you can use one of the simpler data storage methods described in this chapter, by all means do so. Relational databases are not the best solution to every problem.

If your program needs to store a list of values that will never change, you can compile the data into the source code.

If your program needs to save and restore a limited number of simple values, consider using the Registry. This solution works well for user configuration settings as long as each computer has only one user. If users share computers or move from one computer to another, you need to store these settings in a more central location. The Registry is also less useful for information you want all users to share. For instance, if you want your program to display a message of the day when the user logs in, you need to store the message in a central location.

CSV files and files containing fixed-length records can store textual information. If you place these files in a shared directory, they are accessible to all users. Although loading these files isn't hard, Visual Basic doesn't provide a lot of support for them. If you have a lot of data in these files, you may want to convert them into XML files or load their data into a database so you can use Visual Basic's more powerful XML and database processing features.

INI files are obsolete so you should avoid using them. If you need to load data from an existing INI file, convert it into an XML file and use that instead.

XML files hold textual data in an extremely flexible, easy to understand format. Visual Basic. NET provides extensive support for XML. As is the case with other text file formats, if you store XML files in a shared directory, all users can access them.

One drawback to XML files is that they are relatively verbose. If you have a large number of records with a fixed format, all the repeated XML tags begin to add up. For example, consider the following CSV representation of three address records. This representation takes 139 bytes:

```
Rod,Stephens,1234 Programmer Way,Bugville,CO,80333
Snortimer,Canid,827 E Cat Chaser's Ct,Hoot,AZ,98765
Cobe,Cat,POB 12763,Reno,NV,90219
```

Compare that to this 640-byte XML representation:

```
<AllAddresses>
  <Address>
    <FirstName>Rod</FirstName>
    <LastName>Stephens</LastName>
    <Street>1234 Programmer Way</Street>
    <City>Bugville</City>
    <State>CO</State>
    <Zip>80333</Zip>
  </Address>
  <Address>
    <FirstName>Snortimer</FirstName>
    <LastName>Canid</LastName>
    <Street>827 E Cat Chaser's Ct</Street>
    <City>Hoot</City>
    <State>AZ</State>
    <Zip>98765</Zip>
  </Address>
  <Address>
    <FirstName>Cobe</FirstName>
    <LastName>Cat</LastName>
    <Street>POB 12763</Street>
    <City>Reno</City>
    <State>NV</State>
    <Zip>90219</Zip>
  </Address>
</AllAddresses>
```

The XML version takes more than 4.5 times as much space. You could squeeze a little space out of the file by abbreviating the tag names, but that would undercut XML's self-documenting nature.

In a small example such as this one, a few hundred wasted bytes is no big deal. If you have a much larger database containing hundreds of thousands of records, a better solution would be to load the data into a relational database.

Relational databases provide more flexibility and power than these simpler data storage schemes. They let you perform complex queries, joining data from multiple tables. They let you define indexes, build code into the database in the form of stored procedures, and provide at least limited security features.

This book focuses on using relational databases because that is the most powerful of the techniques listed in this chapter. It also spends some time on XML files because the tools in Visual Basic.NET let you treat them in the same way as relational databases, and they are a bit simpler than databases. You can also easily read XML files in a text editor so it can be easier to figure out what's going wrong in the early stages of application development when the program reads data from an XML file instead of a database.

DATABASE DESIGN

In some ways, building a database is a lot like building any complex application. You start with a set of requirements, analyze the requirements, build something, and then test and revise until what you built satisfies the requirements. Building a database is also similar to building an application in the sense that it's easy to build *something*, but building something that works well can be deceptively difficult. Often what you think will be a simple database becomes surprisingly complex as you work with it.

This chapter describes some of the steps you should take to design a database before you start building it. It discusses how to decide what tables the database needs, how the tables should interact, which fields belong in the tables, and which fields would make good indexes.

You use the application requirements to devise an initial database design, then you study the design looking for flaws and possible improvements. There are several standard data normalization steps you can take to ensure that the database provides some degree of flexibility while minimizing redundant data storage.

The following sections explain this process using a simple order-tracking example for illustration.

APPLICATION DESIGN APPROACHES

You can approach application design from many points of view. Two effective methods are *user-centric* and *data-centric*. A user-centric approach focuses on what the user needs to do and how the program can get it done. Understanding these helps define the application's user interface and how the program will work with the data. That in turn helps define the format of the data, and thus the database.

A data-centric approach concentrates on the data itself. It asks what data the program will need and what data is available. It then builds a design for the database and treats the application as a user interface for the data.

Although both of these approaches are effective, they work best when you use them together. Each focuses on different aspects of the application so they uncover different constraints that you need to handle. This chapter deals with data-centric design because it leads more directly to the design of the database.

REQUIREMENTS

Initially, an application's requirements are somewhat vague. In fact, they should be a little vague. They should focus on what needs to be done, not on how it should be done. That allows you the most flexibility in your design.

For instance, consider the requirements for a simple order tracking system, as demonstrated in the following example.

Example

The application should track customer orders. It should be able to list past orders by a given customer, display details for an order, and print an invoice for an order.

When the customer orders an item that is not in stock, the system should display a message so the user can order new inventory.

The system should produce reports giving order amounts. Optional report parameters should include customer, user, a date range, and specific items in an order. For example, it should be able to list orders entered between 1/1/2001 and 3/31/2001 by user Bill that contained item number 1001.

Other reports should list orders that have not shipped and were placed more than 10 days ago, and invoices that have not been paid by the customer 40 days after the order was shipped.

From these requirements, you can begin to pull out the definition of the database. After you've designed some databases, you will probably know what tables and fields you will need immediately, and then you can jump to something close to the final solution needed by the application. Even if you have no experience with database design, you can get started without too much trouble.

ENTITIES

The main purpose of this application is to track customer orders, and the database probably needs some sort of entity to hold order information. For now, call this object the CustomerOrders entity. This object is called an *entity* rather than a table because it does not necessarily represent an actual database table. Entities can model patterns that do not work directly in a relational database, so design usually begins with them. At some point, all the data in the entities will map into database tables.

The CustomerOrders entity holds information on past and present orders. To print an invoice, this entity needs to contain all the information that should be part of the invoice. That information includes the following values:

- CustomerName (the company's name)
- BillingAddress (street, city, state, ZIP code)
- ShippingAddress (street, city, state, ZIP code)
- ContactInformation (purchaser's name and phone number)
- InvoiceNumber

- `DateOrdered`
- `ItemsOrdered` (item number, description, quantity, unit price, total price)

Don't worry about the specific data types and subfields of these items just yet. They will come out as you refine the design.

To generate reports giving order amounts by customer, user, date, and items, `CustomerOrders` must also include the user ID of the person who entered the order. To generate reports showing orders not shipped and orders not paid, `CustomerOrders` must know when an order was shipped and when it was paid. This gives the entity these new values:

- `EnteredByUser`
- `DateShipped`
- `DatePaid`

The design so far knows nothing about inventory. One of the requirements says the application should display a message if the customer orders an item that is out of stock. This information should not be part of the `CustomerOrders` entity because it has to do with inventory, not customer orders. That means the design needs another entity.

The `Inventory` entity will hold the number of each item in stock. To identify an item and keep track of the number in stock, `Inventory` needs these values:

- `ItemNumber`
- `QuantityInStock`

If you think about how the application needs to use the `CustomerOrders` and `Inventory` entities, you will see that the entities must be related in some way. When the user creates a new `CustomerOrders` record, the program must be able to tell if the ordered items are in stock. That means the program must be able to use the information in the order to look up the correct `Inventory` records.

In this design, the item numbers of the ordered items connect the two tables. A `CustomerOrders` record contains a list of items ordered. The program can use the item numbers of those items to look up the corresponding records in the `Inventory` entity to see if the items are available.

One important categorization of this kind of relationship gives the number of related records in each entity. In this example, think about a single `CustomerOrders` record and ask yourself how many `Inventory` records might be related to it. The order could include one, two, or many more items so a single `CustomerOrders` record could be related to many `Inventory` records.

Now think about a single `Inventory` record and ask yourself how many `CustomerOrders` records might be related to it. Different customers might order the same item so a single item might appear in many orders. That means one `Inventory` record might be related to many `CustomerOrders` records.

Because a record from each entity might be related to many records in the other entity, these entities have a *many-to-many* relationship. As the example design progresses, you will see instances of other relationship types such as *one-to-many* relationships.

Figure 2.1 shows the relationship graphically. The infinity symbols (∞) over the ends of the relationship link indicate the number of records in that entity used in the relationship. In this case, both symbols are ∞ because this is a many-to-many relationship.

Figure 2.1
The CustomerOrder and Inventory tables have a many-to-many relationship.

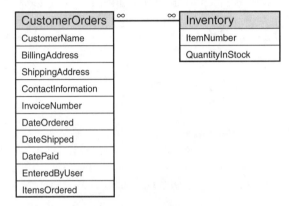

Because Figure 2.1 shows the relationships among database entities, it is called an *entity-relationship diagram* or *ER diagram*. This chapter covers only a small fraction of the full complexity of ER diagrams. For more information, see a book on data modeling such as *Data Modeling Essentials* (2000, Simsion, The Coriolis Group) or search the Web for "ER diagrams."

REFINING THE DESIGN

Consider the definition of the CustomerOrders entity shown in Figure 2.1 in more detail. Some of the items contained in the entity represent several data values. For example, CustomerAddress includes a street number, city, state, and ZIP code. Although they may be complicated, each item represents one chunk of information, except for ItemsOrdered. The CustomerAddress item contains several subfields, and you know exactly how many subfields every CustomerAddress contains. On the other hand, a single CustomerOrders record might need to hold many ItemsOrdered entries.

Figure 2.2 shows one attempt to model the CustomerOrders entity in more detail. In this version, the ItemsOrdered entity is broken into four separate entries. Each of these items provides information linking the order to one record in the Inventory entity. Now the relationship between the CustomerOrders and Inventory entities is really a case of several many-to-one relationships rather than a single many-to-many relationship.

Figure 2.2
This diagram attempts to model a many-to-many relationship as a series of many-to-one relationships.

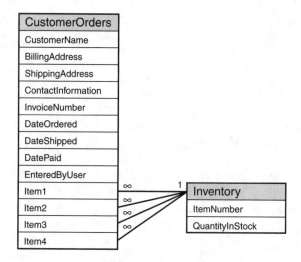

Unfortunately this attempt doesn't quite work. Although the new CustomerOrders design can handle up to four items, it cannot handle a fifth item. You can add an Item5 field to CustomerOrders, but the result will still not handle six items. No matter how many Item fields you add, this design cannot handle an unlimited number of order items.

The solution is to create a new entity that gives information about the items contained in an order. Figure 2.3 shows the new OrderItems entity. Each record in OrderItems contains information about a single item in a particular order.

The OrderId field links the CustomerOrders and OrderItems entities in a one-to-many relationship. A single CustomerOrders record might correspond to any number of OrderItems records but an OrderItems record corresponds to a single CustomerOrders record.

Figure 2.3 also shows that the order-inventory relationship should connect the OrderItems and Inventory entities. The main body of the order doesn't really have anything to do with the number of items in stock. It holds information about the customer's address, invoice number, and so forth. The OrderItems records contain the information about the items that are part of the order. Their ItemNumber fields provide the link to the Inventory entity.

Figure 2.3
This diagram allows an order to contain any number of items.

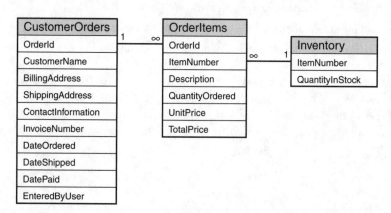

This version of the design makes two improvements over the previous version. First, it allows the program to handle any number of items in a single order. Second, it converts a many-to-many relationship into two one-to-many relationships connected via a new entity. This is important because relational databases do not easily represent general many-to-many relationships directly.

To see why relational databases don't model these relationships well, suppose a database has two tables connected with a single field. One record in the first table might correspond to many records in the second. However, each of the records in the second table might correspond to many records in the first. If you follow the relationship from the first table to the second and back to the first, a record in the first table can be related to many records that are also in the first table. Usually that doesn't make much sense. If enough records in the two tables are related, every record is indirectly related to every other record in both tables. In that case, every record must have the same value for the linking field, and it doesn't tell you anything new.

In cases like this, it's better to replace the many-to-many relationship with two one-to-many relationships connected via a new entity as shown in Figure 2.3.

MASTER-DETAIL RELATIONSHIPS

Most many-to-one relationships also define master-detail relationships. In a *master-detail* relationship, a record in one entity defines the main body of the data and one or more records in another entity provide additional detail. In Figure 2.3, the CustomerOrders record defines the main body of data. For each CustomerOrders record, one or more OrderItems records provide additional detail.

The master-detail relationship is conceptual and does not automatically apply to all many-to-one relationships in the same way. For instance, the relationship between OrderItems records and Inventory records is in some sense the opposite of the relationship between CustomerOrders records and OrderItems records. You can think of the Inventory record as providing detail about an item in an OrderItems record. To display a customer's order, you would follow these steps:

1. Find the CustomerOrders record.
2. Get details about the items from the OrderItems entity.
3. For each item, get details (QuantityInStock) about the item from the Inventory table.

Working the other way makes less sense. If you want to list information about a particular inventory item, you can look up the Inventory record. It would make little sense to then find all the OrderItems records that are related to that Inventory record. You certainly wouldn't consider those records to be giving more information about the Inventory record.

NORMALIZATION

At this point, you could build `CustomerOrders`, `OrderItems`, and `Inventory` tables in a relational database and you could probably make the application run. Before you do that, there are several steps you can take to increase the database's flexibility and to remove redundant data. This process is called *normalization*. There are several different levels of normalization that provide different benefits. The following sections describe first, second, and third level normalization.

FIRST NORMAL FORM

In *first normal form* (*1NF*), the database entities do not contain fields representing the same kind of data. In Figure 2.3, the `CustomerOrders` entity contains a couple of fields that have the same data type. The `BillingAddress` and `ShippingAddress` both contain addresses. There isn't really anything wrong with that until the project manager decides the application should also be able to send a copy of the invoice to a contact address. At that point, you could extend `CustomerOrders` to add the new address, but then what happens when someone decides you need to store another address?

When you encounter this situation, you should think of the adage, "Fool me once, shame on you. Fool me twice, shame on me." After you know the `CustomerOrders` entity needs to store two addresses, you should wonder if it might need to store more. Every time you need to add a new kind of address, you will need to rebuild the database, rewrite the related program source code, recompile the application, and distribute it to all of the users. To avoid this, you can pull out the repeated address fields into their own `OrderAddresses` entity and link them to the original entity with a master-detail relationship.

Similarly, the `CustomerOrders` entity contains several date fields. There's nothing wrong with that as long as you are certain you will not need to add other date fields later. If someone decides the program should send customers warning letters when payment is overdue, you will probably need to keep track of the date that letter was sent. If the customer still doesn't pay after you send the warning letter, you may want to suspend the customer's account and you will need to keep track of the suspension date. You can prevent problems with these issues by pulling the dates out into their own `OrderDates` entity.

Figure 2.4 shows a new design with separate `OrderAddresses` and `OrderDates` detail entities.

BEYOND 1NF

Pulling out repeated types of data into detail entities makes the database more flexible, but you can carry this idea too far. For example, you might now notice that the `CustomerName` and `EnteredByUser` values are both strings. You could create an `OrderStrings` entity and pull them out. That entity would hold the data values `OrderId`, `StringType`, and `StringValue`.

This scheme works and provides great flexibility. It allows you to add new strings of any type to a customer's order. However, this is needlessly complex. If the application design calls for a completely new piece of data, chances are you will need to redesign the program's user interface to display the new data and validate its format. At that point, you can modify the database to add the new field to the CustomerOrders table directly.

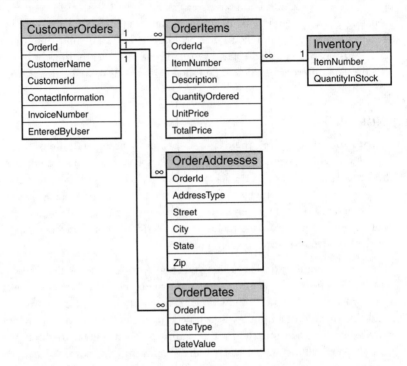

Figure 2.4
This design puts addresses and dates in their own entities.

If you are still tempted to add an OrderStrings table, think about how a program normally displays information in a detail table. Because the program cannot know how many instances of the data it will need to display, it must put them in a scrolling window, grid, list box, or some other open-ended control. Letting the user select addresses using a combo box makes sense. Displaying basic order information, such as the company name in a grid, does not.

Before you create a detail table, think about whether you need its flexibility. Will you need to add more addresses in the future? Possibly. Will you need to add more strings of an unknown type? Perhaps, but if you do, you will almost certainly need to modify the application as well.

SECOND NORMAL FORM

A database in *second normal form* (2NF) is in first normal form and every field in each record in an entity is directly related to the record's primary key. In other words, the fields in a record each add new information to the record. If two records have different keys, they should have different field values.

That doesn't mean two records can never have fields containing the same values. If two orders happen to have been ordered on the same date, the OrderDates entity will contain records that differ only in their OrderId values.

However, two records should not contain the same logical value. For instance, in Figure 2.4 the CustomerOrders entity stores the name of the company placing the order. If a company places two orders, both records will have the same value for CustomerName. Those values don't just happen to be the same by coincidence, as is the case for the previous order date example. The CustomerName values are the same because the same company is placing the orders.

A more obvious example occurs in the OrderItems entity. If two orders include the same item, they will create two very similar OrderItems records. The OrderId, QuantityOrdered, and TotalPrice values will be different, but the ItemNumber, Description, and UnitPrice will all be the same. ItemNumber determines the kind of object ordered, so you cannot remove it from the entity, but you can remove Description and UnitPrice. You can pull these values into a new entity and connect it to the OrderItems record using a many-to-one relationship. In this design, the Inventory entity already provides detail for the OrderItems records, so you can simply add these fields to the Inventory records.

Figure 2.5 shows the new database design with a separate Customers entity and with item information pulled into the Inventory entity.

Figure 2.5
A separate
Customers entity
and moving item
data into the
Inventory entity
reduces redundancy.

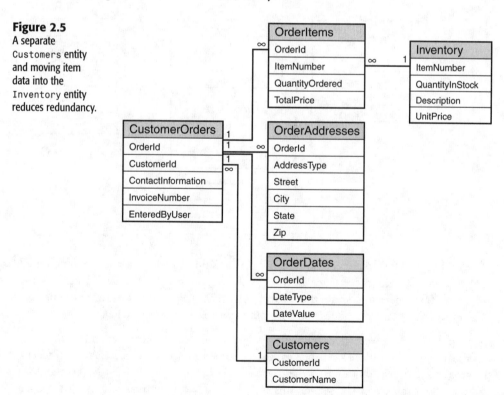

The OrderAddresses entity provides a trickier problem. It is very likely that different orders by the same customer will have the same shipping and billing addresses. This means that

`OrderAddresses` records will contain a lot of redundant information. To state the problem in terms of the definition of second normal form, many `OrderAddresses` records with different `OrderId` values will have the same address values. This is not simply coincidence because the same company placed the different orders.

This problem is caused by the fact that the addresses are not really features of specific orders. Instead they are closely related to the customer. This presents two likely solutions.

First, if you want to allow different orders from the same company to have different shipping and billing addresses, you can move the address information into a new entity, much like Figure 2.5 moves customer information into a new `Customers` entity. Figure 2.6 shows the result.

Figure 2.6
Moving address information into the `Addresses` entity removes redundant information from `OrderAddresses`.

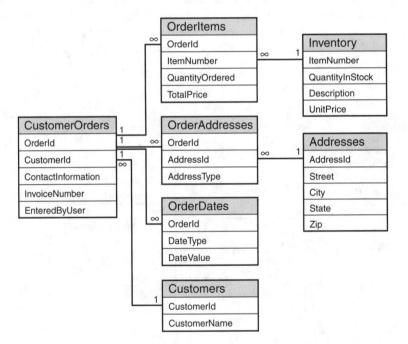

A second approach is to require that the billing and shipping addresses be the same for all orders placed by a given customer. In that case, you can replace the `OrderAddresses` entity with a `CustomerAddresses` entity that provides detail for `Customers` as shown in Figure 2.7. The rest of this chapter assumes you have opted for this second approach.

Now to find a particular order's billing and shipping addresses, the program looks up the `CustomerOrders` record and uses the `CustomerId` value to find the correct `CustomerAddresses` records. Because this solution uses the `CustomerId` value to tie the `CustomerOrders` and `CustomerAddresses` records together, this appears to create an unusual situation. If you diagram these entities separately, the `CustomerId` value creates a many-to-many relationship.

Figure 2.7
Making
`CustomerAddresses`
a detail entity for
`Customers` removes
redundant address
information.

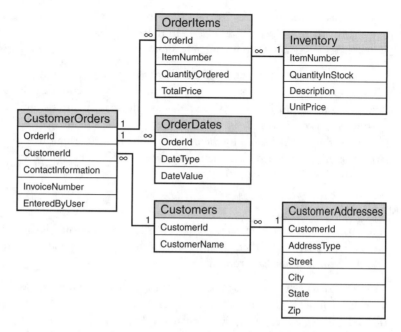

In this case, that is not a problem because all the records in the `CustomerOrders` and `CustomerAddresses` entities that share the same `CustomerId` are related. They form a *clique* or a group of closely related objects. The presence of a many-to-many relationship can still be confusing, however, so it is better to think of this relationship as the `CustomerOrders` and `CustomerAddresses` entities providing detail for the master `Customers` record. Figure 2.7 shows the relationship drawn in this way.

BEYOND 2NF

Just as you can go too far while putting a database in first normal form, you can go overboard putting it in second normal form. For instance, you might notice that many records in the `CustomerAddresses` entity have the same city, state, and ZIP code values, particularly if your customers all live in the same area. You could create a new `Cities` entity and link it to `CustomerAddresses` with a `CityId` value. This would save some space in the database but it would make searching for an order's addresses much more complicated. Before you take this additional step, you should perform a rough calculation of the amount of space you would save. To do that, you need to assume some numbers.

Suppose you are working for a computer parts supplier and you have 100 customers who have placed an average of 200 orders each. Also suppose most of the customers' shipping and billing addresses are different, and that an address uses 150 bytes of storage. The database design shown in Figure 2.5 stores each address separately for each order, so the database contains $100 \times 200 \times 2 \times 150 = 6$ million bytes or roughly 5.7MB of address information.

The designs shown in Figures 2.6 and 2.7 store only two addresses per customer, no matter how many orders each customer places. In those designs, the database contains $100\times2\times150 = 30{,}000$ bytes, a savings of approximately 5.69MB.

Now assume the city, state, and ZIP code parts of the address information take up 50 of the 150 bytes used by an address and that every address in the entire database uses the exact same city, state, and ZIP code. If you pull this information into its own table, the address information takes up $100\times2\times50 = 10{,}000$ bytes, a savings of about 20KB. This pales in comparison to the 5.69MB saved by the optimizations shown in Figures 2.6 and 2.7. With the large disk drives provided by modern computers, 20KB is negligible and it's almost certainly not worth the added complication.

THIRD NORMAL FORM

A database is in *third normal form (3NF)* if it is in second normal form and the entities' fields do not depend on each other. Another way to think of this is that no field contains information that you can calculate from other fields.

The TotalPrice is an obvious violation of this rule because it is the product of QuantityOrdered in the OrderItems entity and UnitPrice in the Inventory entity. Eliminate this redundancy by removing the calculated value, in this case TotalPrice. Figure 2.8 shows the design with this minor correction.

Figure 2.8
This design removes the TotalPrice value because the application can easily calculate it from the QuantityOrdered and UnitPrice values.

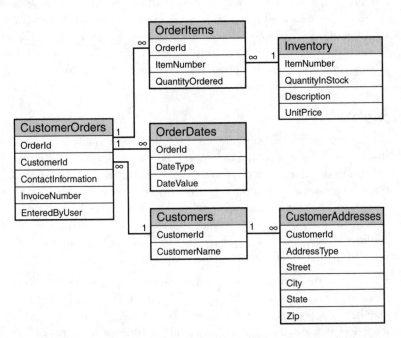

Here it is obvious that TotalPrice = QuantityOrdered×UnitPrice but in some cases it is harder to decide which value is the one calculated from the others. For instance, suppose an application works with temperatures in both degrees Fahrenheit and Celsius. You can calculate either value from the other so it doesn't matter which one you remove. Save the value that seems most natural for the application and remove the other one.

BEYOND 3NF

Once again, it is possible to get carried away and apply the third normal form rule too aggressively. In the design shown in Figure 2.8, there is some redundancy among the Street, City, State, and Zip values. If you know the Street, City, and State values, you can look up the Zip code. Conversely if you know the Street and Zip code, you can look up the City and State.

If you ruthlessly apply the rules for third normal form, you would need to remove either Zip or City and State. That would save a few kilobytes of space in the database, but it would make decoding an address much more complicated. It would also require the database to include a table relating ZIP code with City and State. That table would be large enough to more than offset this method's savings unless the customer database was enormous.

DENORMALIZATION

Rigidly following the rules of normalization does not always lead to the best solution. Removing the City and State fields and calculating them from the Zip field would make the database more complex, harder to understand, and probably larger.

Sometimes it is better to ignore the rules in specific instances to keep the design simple. The previous sections discussed some of these cases as they arose so you could see how they violate different rules of normalization. You might also apply the rules in their entirety and then denormalize the database when you are finished. Denormalizing at the end may let you see more of the database's detailed structure so you can make better decisions. On the other hand, it may make the intermediate designs too confusing to understand.

A REFORMATTED DATABASE DIAGRAM

As far back as Figure 2.5, you might have noticed that the Customers and CustomerOrders tables have a master-detail relationship. For a given record in the Customers table, the CustomerOrders table provides details about the orders placed by that customer. One hint that this might be a master-detail relationship is the one-to-many relationship between these entities. One-to-many and master-detail relationships often go hand-in-hand.

As is mentioned earlier in this chapter, a master-detail relationship depends on your point of view. If your focus is customers, the CustomerOrders table clearly provides detail. If your focus is on orders, that might not be as obvious. You might choose to regard the Customers records as providing the address and other details for a particular CustomerOrders record. The requirements statement for this application focuses on order tracking, so that would be reasonable.

However, the system's broader functionality also needs to work with customer records. To create a new order, for example, the program must be able to locate the customer's account record. In that case, it makes more sense to think of `CustomerOrders` as providing detail for the `Customers` records.

Figure 2.9 shows a slightly rearranged database design with the `Customers` entity on the left. In this version, the master-detail relationships all flow from left to right and entities that represent higher-level objects appear on the left. This arrangement isn't necessary to describe the database accurately but it makes understanding the structure a little easier.

Figure 2.9
Rearranging the entities in Figure 2.8 makes master-detail relationships flow from left to right.

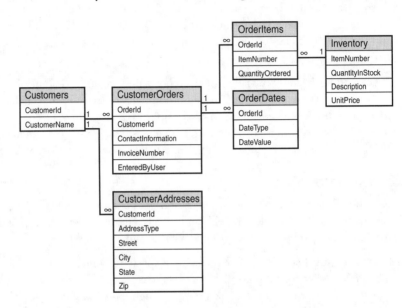

KEYS

A *key* is a set of one or more fields that you use to connect two tables. Usually the keys in a relationship are single fields, but you could use more than one field in a record to link to one or more fields in another table. For instance, you could use the `FirstName` and `LastName` fields in two tables to link the tables. The tables might contain many customers with the same first names or the same last names, but only those with the same first and last name would be related.

There are two types of keys: primary and foreign. A *primary key* defines the relationship in the master or home table. The corresponding key in the related table is a *foreign key*.

The values for a primary key in a table must always be unique. In other words, no two records in the table can have the same value for their primary key fields. For instance, Social Security number would make a good primary key for an `Employees` table because it is impossible for two employees to have the same Social Security number. Last name would be a bad value to use as a primary key because you might easily have two employees with the same last name. The combination of first name and last name would be better because it is less likely that two employees would have the same first and last names, but that is still possible.

Relational database engines like Access let you give a field an autonumber data type. When you insert a new record into the table, the database automatically gives this field the next available number. For instance, if you add a series of new Customers records, the database could assign the autonumbered CustomerId field the values 1, 2, 3, and so forth.

> **Tip**
>
> Autonumbered fields make good choices for primary keys because the database guarantees that they are all unique.

A *foreign key* links one record in the home table to one or more records in another table. Often this link defines a master-detail one-to-many relationship. Because primary key values must be unique, the table with the primary key is on the "one" side of the one-to-many relationship. You can also define a one-to-one relationship using the primary keys from two tables.

INDEXES

An *index* is a set of one or more fields that you will frequently use for locating records. For example, you might want to locate records in the Customers table using the customers' names. To make that easier, you could make the CustomerName field an index.

Sometimes you might also want to locate records using a customer's address. To make that easier, you could designate the Street, City, State, and Zip fields as an index.

When you define an index, the database builds special data structures that make searching the table using the index faster. For example, this data structure might be a tree holding the values in the indexed field. To find a record with a particular value, the database would search the tree. The result would point to the record in the table data.

Depending on the size of the database and the nature of the data, an index can make searching much faster. On the other hand, the data structures that hold the indexing information take up extra space. When you add, modify, and delete records from the table, the database must also update its index structures, so those operations are a bit slower than they would be if the table had no indexes.

Because of this overhead, you should use a little restraint when creating indexes. Make as many indexes as you need, but no more. Adding an index to a table is relatively easy; as such, you can add more indexes later if you discover you have performance problems with certain queries. It is usually easier to start with few indexes and add more later rather than to start with many indexes and remove them later.

GOOD AND BAD INDEXES

You should generally index fields that you will use frequently in searches, but some fields are inherently better choices for indexing than others. For example, suppose you want to list all your female customers. Without an index, the database would need to examine every record in the Customers table and list those with Gender = F.

If you place an index on the Gender field, the database would search the index for the first record with Gender = F. It would then list the customers in gender order until it found one where Gender = M. Even with the index, the database still needs to list roughly half of the records in the database (assuming there are about the same number of men as women). This is slightly faster than examining every record, but it will not give you an order of magnitude improvement.

Contrast this with a case where you want to find the customer with a particular CustomerId value. Without an index, the database would need to search through the entire table one record at a time searching for the CustomerId. Even if that record happened to be first, the database would not be sure there is only one such record so it would need to examine every record.

If you index the CustomerId field, the database can quickly locate the right record. If the database is large, the index can make the difference between a query that takes several seconds and one that returns almost instantly.

A good candidate for an index field should narrow the search significantly. Gender is a bad choice because searching with Gender eliminates only half of the records in the table. CustomerId is a good choice for an index because it narrows the search to a single record.

COMPOSITE INDEXES

A *composite index* is an index built from a combination of several fields. One field might not do a good job of narrowing the search but a combination of fields might. For instance, FirstName might be a reasonable index but FirstName plus LastName would probably be better.

Similarly Street, City, State, and Zip might make a reasonable index.

Relational databases can also provide additional benefits when you use a prefix of an index. If you know the first part of an index value, the database may still be able to locate the record quickly.

For example, suppose you index the Customers table's LastName field. Then searching for records where LastName = Stephens is quick. Searching for records where LastName begins with the string Ste is also faster than it would be without the index. Finding records where LastName starts with S will also be faster than it would be without the index, though that query would return a lot more records than one looking for Stephens.

An index can only help you with prefixes, not with other parts of the index values. The LastName index will not make finding names that end with "ens" or that contain "ph" in the middle any faster. The database will need to examine every record in the table looking for those matches.

Prefixes also work for composite indexes. If you know the values for some of the first fields in the index, the database can use the index. For instance, suppose the Customers table contains an index that includes the Street, City, State, and Zip fields. The database can use the index to speed up searches for the following addresses:

123 Bug St, Programmerville, CO 80500

123 Bug St, Programmerville

123 Bug St

Index prefixes can also help the database in ordering query results. If you select a group of customer records and want them ordered by Street and City, the index may help the database order the results more quickly. The index will not help the database order the results using some other part of the index. For example, it will not make ordering the results by City faster.

When you build composite indexes, you might want to think about how you will use them in your queries and result orderings. For example, suppose you often want to list all the customers in a particular state or city. Then you might want to make the previous index include its fields in this order: State, City, and Street. Because State and City come first, you can use the index's prefix capabilities to quickly find all the customers in a particular state or city.

This index will not help you locate a customer by Street unless you also know the customer's state and city. That is probably a good assumption, but you can make Street its own index if you think you won't have all the information. For example, if you know a customer has street number 698 but you don't remember anything else, an index on the Street field would let you quickly find all records with Street values that start with 698.

Keep in mind, however, that indexes take extra resources and make some operations slower. Add indexes only to the fields you think will be used most often in searches and ordering operations. You can add more indexes later if necessary.

DUPLICATES IN INDEXES

When you define an index, you can tell the database whether the index should allow duplicate values. If you prohibit duplicates, the database can use a slightly more efficient data structure so you may get slightly better performance. More importantly from a development standpoint, the database will raise errors if an application tries to insert a duplicate value in the index so you can catch bugs sooner.

CONSTRAINTS

A *constraint* is a condition placed on the fields in a database table. For example, you might require that the value in a certain numeric field be between 1 and 100.

A *referential constraint* is one where a field is related to another field. For example, you might require that the CustomerId field in a new Orders record have a value that matches the

`CustomerId` field in some record in the `Customers` table. In other words, the database cannot use a `CustomerId` in the `Orders` table unless that `CustomerId` has already been defined in the `Customers` table. That is sensible because it would be illogical to allow an order without a customer to place the order.

Referential constraints protect the database from garbage data. The user interface you build using Visual Basic should also protect the data. For example, rather than making the user type in the `State` field's value, you could let the user pick a value from a combo box. In that case, the user cannot enter an incorrect value so you might think you don't need a referential constraint on the database tables themselves.

To an extent, that is correct. If the software worked perfectly and no one modified the database except through your application, you would not need the database constraints. However, constraints are handy for a couple of reasons. First, if someone tries to modify the data using some method other than your program (such as Access or another program), the database can protect itself from some kinds of errors.

Second, during development the application may not work perfectly. If the database uses a lot of constraints, it will uncover programming errors quickly while they are still easy to fix. If bad data creeps into the database while the application is still under development, it may take quite a bit of work to fix the database later.

RANGE TABLES

A special kind of referential integrity constraint involves *range tables*. A range table contains a list of values that are used primarily for verifying some other field in a referential constraint. For example, suppose the `States` table contains a list of state abbreviations. The `CustomerAddresses` table might contain a `State` field linked to the `States` table. The database would not allow a `CustomerAddresses` record to hold a `State` field value that does not appear in the `States` table. That means you could not create an address with `State` equal to `ZX`.

A *lookup table* is similar to a range table but it also contains some extra information about the values it defines. For example, the `States` table might contain two fields: `Name` and `Abbreviation`. Given a state's abbreviation, an application can use the table to look up its name and vice versa.

Typically a range table isn't used for much except to enforce a constraint, but you can use these tables to make your Visual Basic application's user interface more robust. For example, rather than making the user type in a state's abbreviation, you let the user select a value from a combo box. When the application starts, it can read the `States` range table to build the combo box's choices. That ensures that the program's list allows only choices that will satisfy the referential integrity constraint.

This trick also makes it easier to modify the application. If you need to allow a new state abbreviation, you can simply add a new record to the `States` table. The program automatically adds the new value to its combo box the next time it starts.

You could easily add a few range tables to the design shown in Figure 2.9. Some good candidates would include:

- A `States` table giving the values allowed in the `CustomerAddresses` table's `State` field.
- An `AddressTypes` table listing allowed values for the `CustomerAddresses` table's `AddressType` field.
- A `DateTypes` table listing allowed values for the `OrderDates` table's `DateType` field.
- A `Users` table listing allowed values for the `CustomerOrders` table's `EnteredByUser` field.

If you knew your customers came from a small geographic area, you could also build range tables to list allowed values for the `CustomerAddresses` table's `City` and `Zip` fields. Figure 2.10 shows the new database design with range and lookup tables `DateTypes`, `Users`, `AddressTypes`, `Cities`, `States`, and `Zips`.

Figure 2.10
Range tables ensure
that data entries are
correct.

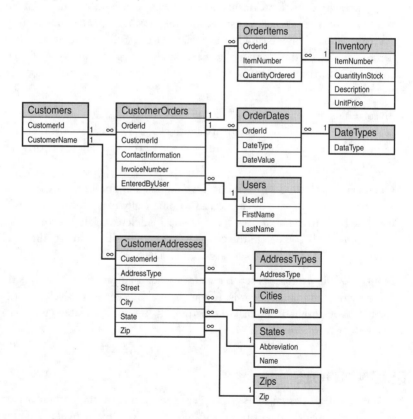

CASCADING UPDATES AND DELETES

If you have an intricate series of referential integrity constraints, updating and deleting values can be complicated. If you don't update every record properly, a record may become orphaned. An *orphaned* record is one where the relationship linking the record to another record has been broken.

For example, suppose the CustomerAddresses and CustomerOrders tables both have CustomerId fields that must match a CustomerId value in the Customers table as shown in Figure 2.10. If you delete a record in the Customers table, all the CustomerAddresses and CustomerOrders records using that CustomerId value are orphaned. The database no longer contains a Customers record that links to those records, so the records violate the tables' referential constraints.

To make this change legally, you would need to track down all the CustomerAddresses and CustomerOrders records and delete them first. Then you could delete the main Customers record. You can certainly do this, but it is extra work.

Updating a value used for referential integrity is even more confusing. Suppose you need to change the CustomerId value in the Customers table. If you change that value, all the CustomerAddresses and CustomerOrders records using the old value would violate the referential integrity constraint. In this case, however, you cannot update the CustomerAddresses and CustomerOrders records first because the new CustomerId value is not yet present in the Customers table. You are caught in a vicious circle: You cannot change the Customers record before you update the CustomerAddresses and CustomerOrders records, but you cannot change the CustomerAddresses and CustomerOrders records until you update the Customers record.

To solve this problem, you need to create a copy of the Customers record but with the new CustomerId. Then you can safely update the CustomerAddresses and CustomerOrders records. When you have updated those records, you can delete the original Customers record.

Once again, you can do all this but it would be a fair amount of extra work. Fortunately, relational databases such as Access can automatically make these changes for you. If the database is set to *cascade deletes*, it automatically deletes related records when you delete the master record. If you delete the Customers record in this example, the database automatically deletes the related CustomerAddresses and CustomerOrders records.

Similarly if the database is set to *cascade updates*, it automatically updates the referential integrity field in related records. If you change the CustomerId value in a Customers record, the database automatically makes the same change to the related CustomerAddresses and CustomerOrders records.

DESIGN TOOLS

Several database design tools are available depending on the particular database product you use. If you use SQL Server or Oracle, Visual Basic .NET provides an integrated set of Visual Database Tools to help you model and construct the database. These tools are disabled if you do not use either SQL Server or Oracle. For example, you cannot use the Visual Database Tools if you use Access databases or the Microsoft Data Engine (MSDE) even though MSDE is a subset of SQL Server.

Specific database engines also provide their own design and maintenance tools. Oracle and Microsoft Access each provide their own set of tools for designing and building databases.

Unfortunately, if you do not have one of these products, you are on your own. You can still design the database, however, using a drawing program or even pencil and paper. Then you can use a Visual Basic program to build an MSDE database from scratch. The RunScript application described in Chapter 6, "Database Connections", executes scripts. Using this program, you can create and modify database structures without any additional tools.

Although the design tools provided by Oracle, SQL Server, and Access are not absolutely necessary to build a database, they do make some operations a little easier. The following section explains how you can use Access to design the database shown in Figure 2.9.

PART

I

CH

2

DESIGNING DATABASES WITH MICROSOFT ACCESS

When you first start Access, it displays the dialog shown in Figure 2.11. This dialog lets you open an existing database, create a new database using a wizard, or build a database by hand. The following section briefly describes how the Database Wizard creates an Order Entry database. The section after that tells how you can use Access to build the database shown in Figure 2.9 by hand.

Figure 2.11
When Microsoft Access starts, you can open an existing database, or build a new one either using a wizard or by hand.

USING THE DATABASE WIZARD

If you select the "Access wizards, pages, and projects" option in Figure 2.11 and click OK, Access displays the dialog shown in Figure 2.12. Select one of the database types and click OK to start the Access Database Wizard. The wizard automatically creates a series of tables that are usually appropriate for the kind of database you selected.

Figure 2.12
Access Database Wizards let you quickly build several standard kinds of databases.

Keep in mind that Access is more than a simple database engine. It also lets you build data entry forms, reports, and other user interface elements. The Database Wizard automatically builds user interface elements for the database it creates. It builds forms to let you enter and modify data, and reports to display standard summaries that make sense for that type of database. All this can be a huge timesaver if you just want to get a database application up and running quickly. Even if you want to implement the final application in Visual Basic rather than as an Access project, the Wizard's version can act as a prototype and give you a big head start in designing the final application.

If you select the Order Entry item highlighted in Figure 2.12, the Wizard displays the choices shown in Figure 2.13. Click on a table in the left column to see the fields the wizard creates. Use the check boxes to tell the wizard which fields to include. You can see from Figure 2.12 that the database design created by this wizard is similar, but not identical, to the one shown in Figure 2.9.

Figure 2.13
Use the Database Wizard to select the fields that should be included in the Order Entry database.

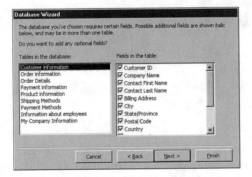

The rest of the Wizard's screens let you specify the format for the forms and reports that the Wizard builds. The following screens let you pick styles for screen displays and reports. They also let you define a picture to include on all the project's reports.

When you have entered all this information, the Wizard builds the database tables and automatically connects them using relationships that make sense for the kind of database you are building.

Figure 2.14 shows the relationships automatically created by the Database Wizard for an Order Entry database. This diagram clearly shows the one-to-many relationships linking the Customers, Orders, Order Details, Products, and Payments tables. These links are relational constraints with cascading updates and deletes.

Figure 2.14
The Database Wizard automatically creates suitable relationships among the database tables.

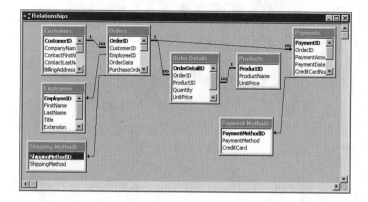

For example, the link between Customers and Orders is a relational constraint. You cannot create an Order record with a CustomerID field that does not already exist in the Customers table. If you change the CustomerID value in a Customers record, the database automatically updates the corresponding CustomerID values in the Orders table to match. If you delete a record in the Customers table, the database automatically deletes the related Orders records.

The other links shown in Figure 2.14 represent one-to-many relationships that are not referential constraints. They define relationships between fields but the database does not ensure that the relationships are enforced.

For instance, the Orders table and Employees table have a one-to-many relationship defined by their EmployeeID fields. One record in the Employees table can correspond to many records in the Orders table. That makes intuitive sense because an employee can be assigned to many orders. This relationship is not enforced by the database, however.

If you want, you can right-click on a link and modify its properties. If you right-click on a link, Access displays the dialog shown in Figure 2.15. Check the Enforce Referential Integrity box if you want the database to automatically enforce the constraint. When that box is checked, Access enables the Cascade Update Related Fields and Cascade Delete Related Records boxes. Use those boxes to determine whether the database automatically cascades updates and deletes.

BUILDING A DATABASE BY HAND

To build a database by hand using Microsoft Access, choose File, New. On the General tab shown in Figure 2.16, select the Database item and click OK. When Access prompts you, enter the name of the file that should hold the new database. Figure 2.17 shows a newly created database in the file OrderEntry.mdb.

Figure 2.15
Access lets you determine whether a link should enforce referential integrity, cascade updates, and cascade deletes.

Figure 2.16
To create a new Access database, select the Database item and click OK.

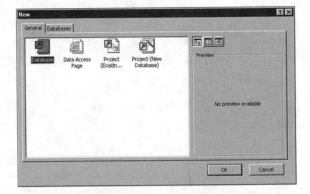

Figure 2.17
Initially a new database contains no tables.

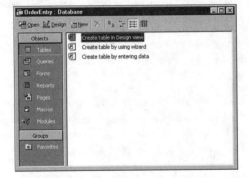

If you double-click the Create table in the Design view entry, Access displays the form shown in Figure 2.18. Enter the names of the fields in the left column. When you click the middle column, a drop-down list appears that lets you select the field's data type. You can enter comments in the right column to document the fields.

Right-click on a row and select Primary Key to make the corresponding field the table's primary key. In Figure 2.18, the OrderId field is marked as the primary key with a little key symbol on the left.

When you click a field, Access displays the field's additional properties on the bottom of the form. Use the text controls in this area to modify the field's characteristics. For instance, here you can set the Required value to Yes or No. Similarly, you can set the Indexed value to No, Yes (Duplicates OK), or Yes (No Duplicates).

Figure 2.18
The design view lets you build a database table.

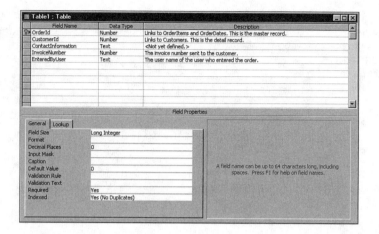

When you have finished defining the table's fields, close the design view. Access will ask if you want to save your changes. If you click Yes, Access asks what you want to name the new table. When you enter the name and click OK, Access creates the table and adds it to the display as shown in Figure 2.19.

Figure 2.19
After you create a new table, it appears in the database table list.

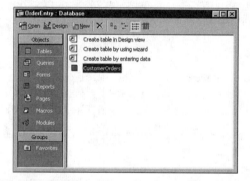

Create the other tables similarly. Then right-click on the list of tables shown in Figure 2.19 and select the Relationships command. At that point, Access displays a table selection dialog. Select all the tables and click Add to add the tables to the Relationships editor. Then click Close to make the table selection dialog disappear. Figure 2.20 shows the Relationships editor displaying the tables before any relationships are defined.

Click and drag the tables' title bars to arrange the tables in positions more or less like those used by the database diagram shown in Figure 2.9. Next click and drag a field from one table onto a field in another to define a relationship using those two fields. Use the Edit Relationships dialog shown in Figure 2.15 to define the relationship. In this example, check the Enforce Referential Integrity, Cascade Update Related Fields, and Cascade Delete Related Records check boxes.

Figure 2.20
This view of the Relationships editor shows the database's tables before relationships are defined.

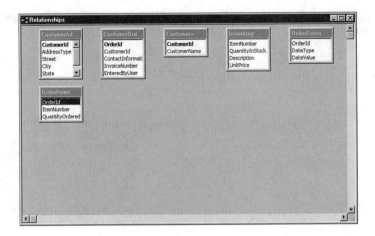

This is one of the places where the Access design tools come in handy. If you try to define a relationship between two fields that don't make sense, the editor will either refuse to allow the relationship or you will get a result that you don't expect. You can then take a closer look at the fields to see what is wrong.

For example, a field that is a primary key or that is indexed but does not allow duplicates cannot be on the "many" side of a one-to-many relationship. If you try to create a one-to-many relationship using a field that has the wrong type of indexing, the editor will make the error immediately obvious.

You can then right-click on the table containing the incorrect end of the relationship to open the table's design view. You can examine the field, fix its indexing properties, close the design view, and try to build the relationship again in the Relationships editor.

When you have finished defining the table's relationships, you should see a diagram similar to the one shown in Figure 2.21.

Figure 2.21
The Relationships editor lets you drag and drop fields to define relationships.

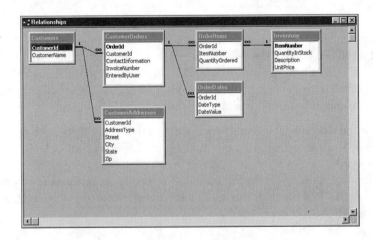

BUILDING A DATABASE WITH SQL

Access, SQL Server, Oracle, and other database design tools build databases for you. When you design tables and relationships in Access, Access modifies the database accordingly.

One problem with these design tools is that they are all different. You need to use different methods to define tables and relationships.

Another potentially more important problem is that to use these tools you need to own them. If you want to build a small database using MSDE, you may not want to spend a few hundred dollars buying Access.

Fortunately, relational databases support SQL (Structured Query Language), an industry standard language for building and manipulating relational databases and their content. SQL includes statements for adding, selecting, ordering, and deleting records. It also contains statements for defining the database structure.

You can write a SQL script that creates the database's tables and defines the relations between them. You can even add statements to populate range tables and fill other tables with test data. Then you can connect to the database using whichever engine you prefer and execute the SQL statements.

If you stick to standard SQL statements, you can run your scripts using different database engines. If you decide to switch engines for some reason, you can execute your scripts using the new engine to rebuild the database.

SQL scripts also serve as documentation for the database structure. Entity-relationship diagrams and database design pictures similar to those shown earlier in this chapter are often more intuitive than SQL scripts, however. One good approach to documenting the database is to use a design tool or even a simple drawing tool to design the database. Then use the design pictures to develop the database creation scripts. When you run the scripts, be sure to update the design drawings if you need to make any changes to get the scripts to work. When you are finished, the drawings and scripts together make excellent documentation.

Appendix A, "SQL," describes many of the most useful SQL commands. If you are unfamiliar with SQL, take a look at Appendix A. For building databases, you should focus on these SQL statements:

CREATE DATABASE	DROP DATABASE	ALTER DATABASE
CREATE TABLE	DROP TABLE	ALTER TABLE
CREATE INDEX	DROP INDEX	
CREATE VIEW	DROP VIEW	

Once you get used to it, SQL is fairly intuitive and you should not have much trouble reading SQL scripts.

The script OrderEntryDBCreate.sql shown in Listing 2.1 creates the Order Entry database described in this chapter and diagrammed in Figure 2.10. This script builds master tables before it builds other tables that refer to the master tables. For example, the EnteredByUser field in the CustomerOrders table references the UserId field in the Users table. The script must create the Users table first so the definition of the CustomerOrders table can refer to that field.

LISTING 2.1 THIS SCRIPT BUILDS A DATABASE SIMILAR TO THE ONE SHOWN IN FIGURE 2.10

```
# Create the order entry database's tables.
# Be sure to create the tables in the right order
# so you can create their referential constraints.

# Create the database.
# Comment this statement out if the database already exists
# or if you are using an Access database.
CREATE DATABASE OrderEntry
ON
    (NAME = oe_data,
     FILENAME = 'C:\Temp\OrderEntry.mdf',
     SIZE = 2MB,
     MAXSIZE = 10MB,
     FILEGROWTH = 2MB
)
LOG ON
    (NAME = oe_log,
     FILENAME = 'C:\Temp\OrderEntry.ldf',
     SIZE = 1MB,
     MAXSIZE = 5MB,
     FILEGROWTH = 1MB
);

# Use the new database.
# Comment this statement out if you are using an Access database.
USE OrderEntry;

###############
# Range Tables #
###############
# Range table for Zip codes in our operating area.
# The Zip code must have format 12345 or 12345-6789.
CREATE TABLE Zips (
    Zip VARCHAR(10) UNIQUE NOT NULL
        CHECK ((Zip LIKE '[0-9][0-9][0-9][0-9][0-9]') OR
               (Zip LIKE '[0-9][0-9][0-9][0-9][0-9]-[0-9][0-9][0-9][0-9]'))
);

# Range table for states in our operating area.
CREATE TABLE States (
    Abbreviation CHAR(2)     UNIQUE NOT NULL,
    Name         VARCHAR(20) UNIQUE NOT NULL
);

# Range table for cities in our operating area.
CREATE TABLE Cities (
    Name         VARCHAR(40) UNIQUE NOT NULL
);
```

LISTING 2.1 CONTNUED

```
# Range table for address types.
CREATE TABLE AddressTypes (
    AddressType  VARCHAR(20) UNIQUE NOT NULL
);

# Range table for date types.
CREATE TABLE DateTypes (
    DateType     VARCHAR(20) UNIQUE NOT NULL
);

####################
# Main Data Tables #
####################
# Inventory.
CREATE TABLE Inventory (
    ItemNumber      INT             IDENTITY(1,1) PRIMARY KEY,
    QuantityInStock INT             NOT NULL,
    Description     VARCHAR(40)     NOT NULL,
    UnitPrice       SMALLMONEY      NOT NULL
);

# Users.
CREATE TABLE Users (
    UserId          VARCHAR(12)     UNIQUE NOT NULL,
    FirstName       VARCHAR(40)     NOT NULL,
    LastName        VARCHAR(40)     NOT NULL
);

# Customers.
CREATE TABLE Customers (
    CustomerId      INT             IDENTITY(1,1) PRIMARY KEY,
    CustomerName    VARCHAR(40)     UNIQUE NOT NULL
);

# CustomerAddresses.
CREATE TABLE CustomerAddresses (
    CustomerId      INT             REFERENCES Customers (CustomerId),
    AddressType     VARCHAR(20)     REFERENCES AddressTypes (AddressType),
    Street          VARCHAR(40)     NOT NULL,
    City            VARCHAR(40)     REFERENCES Cities (Name),
    State           CHAR(2)         REFERENCES States (Abbreviation),
    Zip             VARCHAR(10)     REFERENCES Zips (Zip)
);

# CustomerOrders.
CREATE TABLE CustomerOrders (
    OrderId         INT             IDENTITY(1, 1) PRIMARY KEY,
    CustomerId      INT             REFERENCES Customers (CustomerId),
    ContactName     VARCHAR(80),
    InvoiceNumber   VARCHAR(10),
    EnteredByUser   VARCHAR(12)     REFERENCES Users (UserId)
);

# The following tables reference the CustomerOrders table.
# They are essentially detail for CustomerOrders.
# OrderItems.
```

LISTING 2.1 CONTNUED

```
CREATE TABLE OrderItems (
     OrderId          INT              REFERENCES CustomerOrders (OrderId),
     ItemNumber       INT              REFERENCES Inventory (ItemNumber),
     QuantityOrdered INT               NOT NULL
);

# OrderDates.
CREATE TABLE OrderDates (
     OrderId          INT              REFERENCES CustomerOrders (OrderId),
     DateType         VARCHAR(20)      REFERENCES DateTypes (DateType),
     DateValue        SMALLDATETIME NOT NULL
);
```

The script OrderEntryDBPopulate.sql fills the database with test data. It is quite long and not spectacularly interesting so it is not shown here.

When you build a script to fill database tables, you must create master records before you create records that refer to them. For example, in this database the CustomerAddress table's State field contains a reference to the States table's Abbreviation field. You must create a record in the States table before you can create a record in the CustomerAddresses table that uses the value from the States table. If you have not yet created a States record for CO, you cannot make an address record that uses the state CO.

If you fill the tables in the order in which script OrderEntryDBCreate.sql built them, this is not a problem. The script would create all the valid States table entries before creating any CustomerAddresses records.

The script OrderEntryDBDrop.sql shown in the following code drops the tables that OrderEntryDBCreate.sql builds. Remember that you cannot drop a table if another table has a reference to its fields. This script drops the tables in the reverse of the order in which OrderEntryDBCreate.sql created them. To make the references, that script had to build the tables in order so a master table is created before it is referenced. This script reverses the order, so the referencing table is removed before the master table:

```
# Drop all the tables in reverse order.
DROP TABLE OrderDates;
DROP TABLE OrderItems;
DROP TABLE CustomerOrders;
DROP TABLE CustomerAddresses;
DROP TABLE Customers;
DROP TABLE Users;
DROP TABLE Inventory;
DROP TABLE DateTypes;
DROP TABLE AddressTypes;
DROP TABLE Cities;
DROP TABLE States;
DROP TABLE Zips;
```

If you are using SQL Server, MSDE, Oracle, or some other server-based system, you can probably drop all the tables more quickly by dropping the entire database using the following code:

```
# Stop using the new database. We can't drop it while is it in use.
USE master;

# Drop the database.
DROP DATABASE OrderEntry;
```

The script `OrderEntryDBDelete.sql` shown in the following code deletes all the records from all the tables in the database. It is the same as the script `OrderEntryDBDrop.sql` except it uses `DELETE FROM` statements instead of `DROP TABLE` statements:

```
# Delete all of the records from all of the tables in reverse order.
DELETE FROM OrderDates;
DELETE FROM OrderItems;
DELETE FROM CustomerOrders;
DELETE FROM CustomerAddresses;
DELETE FROM Customers;
DELETE FROM Users;
DELETE FROM Inventory;
DELETE FROM DateTypes;
DELETE FROM AddressTypes;
DELETE FROM Cities;
DELETE FROM States;
DELETE FROM Zips;
```

Deleting all the data from the database may not be sufficient to reset the database. If a table's field is marked with the `IDENTITY` keyword, the database automatically generates a value for that field when you insert a new record in the table.

For example, in this database the `CustomerId` field in the `Customers` table is an `IDENTITY` field. When you create a series of records in that table, the database automatically assigns the records the `CustomerId` values 1, 2, 3, and so forth.

The script `OrderEntryDBPopulate.sql` that loads test data into the database needs to know which values for `CustomerId` are present in the database so it can refer to those values. If you delete all the records in the `CustomerOrders` table, the database does not reset the table's `IDENTITY` field values. If you previously added 10 records, when `OrderEntryDBPopulate.sql` runs again the database will assign the `CustomerId` values 11, 12, 13, and so on. When the script tries to create `CustomerOrders` records referring to the `CustomerId` values 1, 2, and 3, it will fail.

To prevent this kind of mismatch, you may need to drop some of the tables and re-create them. You can break the record insertion and deletion scripts into tables that must be re-created and those that only need to be emptied, but it may be easiest to just drop every table and re-create them from scratch.

You can download all four scripts for this database from this book's Web page at www.vb-helper.com/vbdb.html.

SUMMARY

Building a database is easy. Building a database that works efficiently takes some practice.

Start by analyzing your requirements. Identify the objects that will store data and define the relationships among them. Then normalize the data model, transforming it into first, second, and third normal forms, possibly denormalizing some parts of the database where that makes sense. Finish the design by adding range tables to validate as many fields as possible.

Now create the database. If you have a database product such as Oracle, SQL Server, or Access, you can use the built-in design tools. If you want to work with MSDE or Access databases without one of these products, build scripts to define the database. Then you can use the RunScript program described in Chapter 6 to execute the scripts and build the database.

Even if you have one of these products, you may want to define the databases using scripts so you can easily make changes and rebuild the database later if necessary.

CHAPTER 3

SECURITY

Security is an important consideration in many database applications. Unfortunately, it is also one of the more vendor-specific aspects of database programming. Access, SQL Server, and Oracle databases all handle security differently, so you cannot work out all the details until you know which database you are using.

This chapter discusses some general security issues. It then focuses on Microsoft Data Engine (MSDE). MSDE is a subset of SQL Server, so whatever security you implement with MSDE should work in SQL Server. That gives you the easiest migration path when you may need to move to a larger, higher performance database. You can start with MSDE and if you need features MSDE doesn't provide, you can move to SQL Server without too much difficulty.

DEGREES OF SECURITY

Not every application needs to be the database equivalent of Fort Knox. A simple one-user address book doesn't need the same level of security as an accounting system or a medical database that contains confidential patient information. Before you lose sleep worrying about how to secure your data against attacks from sophisticated information spies, you should consider your actual security needs and pick an appropriate solution. Often a simple solution provides adequate security with a lot less work than a more robust system.

NO SECURITY

Many one-user desktop applications need little or no database security. If you think about the programs you use throughout the day, you will probably find that very few of them ask you to enter passwords. Word processors, spreadsheets, drawing packages, and even desktop tax preparation packages rarely require passwords. These applications typically assume your computer is reasonably safe from hackers so they dodge this whole issue. Even when an application is available on a local area network, security is often minimal. If you trust the people on the network, you don't need to worry that they will actively try to destroy your database.

All database engines can work without security. Few Access databases use security and you can easily grant all privileges to every user in a SQL Server or Oracle database. If this is good enough for you, skip to the next chapter and call it a job well done.

On the other hand, if your data is sensitive, exposed to a network containing people you cannot trust completely (particularly the Internet), or available to users who may make disastrous mistakes, you should consider at least some level of security.

Some take the stand that any access to your data by someone other than yourself is a security risk. If you think someone on your network will eventually mess up your data, you may want to err on the side of caution and implement a greater level of security.

DATABASE PASSWORDS

You can place a password on an Access database so a user or application cannot open the database without giving the password. There are two ways a program might gain access to the data. First, it can prompt the user for the password and then use it to open the database. In that case, if you are the only one who knows the password, you are the only one who can use the program to access the data.

In an alternative strategy, the program contains the password embedded in its code. Then any user can access the data indirectly through the program. This prevents a casual user, wandering aimlessly through the system, from opening the database and making unsupervised changes.

This second method works well when you know that the people who have access to the database will not try to do anything malicious but you don't want them poking around randomly in the data. It provides no real protection against a determined attacker, however. Because your program contains the password, a hacker could pick the code apart and recover the password. You can try to hide the password in the program but a determined hacker will eventually find it. Even this level of protection is better than nothing, however, and is good enough to prevent accidental damage.

To set a database password in Access, use the File menu's Open command to select the database. Click the drop-down arrow by the file selection dialog's Open button and choose Open Exclusive. Next select the Tools menu's Security submenu and choose the Set Database Password command. Enter the new database password and click OK. Now you can include the password information in the database connect string.

Although SQL Server and Oracle do not use database passwords, you can make them behave as if the database is protected by a single password. Create a new user ID for your program to use, and then code the user ID and its password into the code so the program can log in as that user.

USER PASSWORDS

If your data is sensitive or may be exposed to determined attackers as it is on the Internet, database-level security is not good enough. To avoid putting a password in your application's code, you must ask the user to enter the password. You shouldn't give every user the database password, however, because from the program's point of view that would make the users indistinguishable. That can be particularly troublesome if different groups of users should have different privileges. Giving all users the same password means anyone can log on as a supervisor or database administrator and view and modify sensitive data.

You could add a second layer of security by creating a password table in the database. You could then require the user to enter the database password and a second password. This places an extra burden on the user and is needlessly complex.

After you get this sort of two-password system working, a database password provides no further security once the user is connected to the database. After opening the database with Access, for example, the user could delete records, drop tables, and wreak all kinds of havoc.

Even if you trust your users not to intentionally do this sort of thing, adding further levels of security can prevent your application from accidentally doing something dangerous. If the user doesn't have the privileges necessary to drop a table, your program cannot do it by mistake.

This sort of defensive security is particularly useful when different groups of users employ the same program. For example, suppose order entry clerks create new service orders, customer service representatives enter and modify account information, and supervisors view and edit just about every part of the database, including configuration tables. Giving each of these groups of users a different set of privileges helps protect the data from accidental changes. If the order entry clerks don't have permission to modify customer account information, they cannot mess up those tables even if your program has a bug.

To add this level of security, you can give each user a user ID and password. When the program starts, it asks the user for an ID and password. It then tries to connect to the database using those values. If the user ID and password are valid, the program connects successfully to the database. If the values are incorrect, the program fails to connect to the database. It can then exit or give the user another chance.

After you have created user passwords, your program can use them to connect to the database. The Login example program, shown in Figure 3.1, shows how to do this. Enter a valid server username and password and click OK. The program connects to the database using that username and password, displays a success message, and exits.

PART

I

CH

3

Figure 3.1
Program Login uses the username and password entered by the user to connect to the database.

Program Login uses the following code to connect to the database. The secret is in composing the connection string. The string has User ID and Password sections containing the values you entered on the form. If the values are correct, the call to the SqlConnection object's Open method succeeds.

If you enter an incorrect username/password pair, the call to open generates an error. The program displays an error message and lets you try again. This program lets you try to connect to the database three times before it exits:

```
Private m_Attempts As Integer

' Try to connect to the database.
Private Sub btnOk_Click(ByVal sender As System.Object, _
    ByVal e As System.EventArgs) Handles btnOk.Click
    Dim connect_string As String
    Dim db_conn As SqlConnection

    connect_string = _
        "Data Source=" & txtServer.Text & ";" & _
        "User ID=" & txtUserName.Text & ";" & _
        "Password=" & txtPassword.Text
    db_conn = New SqlConnection(connect_string)

    Try
        db_conn.Open()

        ' We succeeded. Tell the user.
        db_conn.Close()
        MsgBox("Connected to database. Press OK to exit.")
        Me.Close()
    Catch exc As Exception
        ' We failed.
        MsgBox("Error connecting to database")

        ' If the user has failed 3 times, exit.
        m_Attempts = m_Attempts + 1
        If m_Attempts >= 3 Then
            Me.Close()
        End If
        txtPassword.Focus()
        txtPassword.SelectAll()
    End Try
End Sub

Private Sub btnCancel_Click(ByVal sender As System.Object, _
    ByVal e As System.EventArgs) Handles btnCancel.Click
    Me.Close()
End Sub
```

Notice that this program displays the same error message no matter why you failed to connect to the database. If the server does not exist, the Open statement generates the error SQL Server does not exist or access denied. If you enter the correct server name but an incorrect username or password, the Open statement generates the error Login failed for user 'merlin', assuming merlin is the username you entered. In both cases, the program displays a generic login failure message to give a potential hacker less information. With this message, the hacker doesn't know whether he has the server name, username, or password incorrect.

A clever hacker might realize that the database returns an error faster when the username or password is incorrect than it does when the server name is wrong. To avoid giving information away, you could modify the program to wait a certain amount of time if there is an error making the connection. The following code waits roughly 20 seconds before displaying an error message no matter why the connection fails:

```
' Try to connect to the database.
Private Sub btnOk_Click(ByVal sender As System.Object, _
  ByVal e As System.EventArgs) Handles btnOk.Click
    Dim connect_string As String
    Dim db_conn As SqlConnection
    Dim wait_until As Date

    connect_string = _
        "Data Source=" & txtServer.Text & ";" & _
        "User ID=" & txtUserName.Text & ";" & _
        "Password=" & txtPassword.Text
    db_conn = New SqlConnection(connect_string)

    ' Pause 20 seconds if we fail to connect.
    wait_until = DateAdd( _
        DateInterval.Second, 20, Now)
    Try
        db_conn.Open()

        ' We succeeded. Tell the user.
        db_conn.Close()
        MsgBox("Connected to database. Press OK to exit.")
        Me.Close()
    Catch exc As Exception
        ' We failed. Wait a bit.
        Do While Now < wait_until
            Application.DoEvents()
        Loop

        ' Display a generic error message.
        MsgBox("Error connecting to database")

        ' If the user has failed 3 times, exit.
        m_Attempts = m_Attempts + 1
        If m_Attempts >= 3 Then
            Me.Close()
        End If
        txtPassword.Focus()
        txtPassword.SelectAll()
    End Try
End Sub
```

This code also slows down a hacker so he cannot try incorrect passwords quickly. That effectively prevents an attacker from writing a program to automatically try hundreds of username and password combinations per minute.

PHYSICAL SECURITY

An issue that many database administrators forget is physical security. They spend endless hours tweaking database passwords and access controls but don't consider the physical location of the database and the network. This is like locking an expensive computer in a briefcase and then leaving the briefcase on a park bench—anyone who walks by can simply take it.

Computers today are so small that a large database can sit on a desktop system that anyone could pick up and carry away. It could even sit on a removable disk drive that could be carried out in someone's pocket. In these cases, the thief could take the database home and attack it at his leisure. Meanwhile, your application is unavailable to you.

An attacker can gain even more information by connecting to your network. A network packet analyzer may show valid usernames and passwords flowing from your users' desktop applications to the database. The hacker can simply read those values and then connect to the database.

In many cases, the users form the weakest link in the security chain. It is usually easier to peek over someone's shoulder while they enter their password than it is to try to break into the database. Users do not always select good passwords either. In a test, I once attacked a 600-user password file and in a few hours managed to guess almost 200 passwords. At one service center I visited, the users had written their passwords on notes taped to their desks and the supervisor's password was written on the whiteboard at the front of the room.

These stories are enough to make the most trusting soul paranoid. Unless you have extremely sensitive or valuable data, however, chances are slight that anyone will use a telescope to peer through a window at your users as they type their passwords. Take a few moments to ensure your database server is in a reasonably secure room.

Explain to your users how to pick good passwords and ask that they keep their passwords secret. Tell users to pick passwords that are not names, dates, Social Security numbers, phone numbers, license plate numbers, driver's license numbers, or other pieces of information an attacker could discover. Much better passwords include both letters and non-letters (867gpf12#), a series of misspelled words that make no sense taken together (Who8DaWatre?), or just plain gibberish. Invent a bizarre rule that makes it easy for you to remember the password but that no attacker would ever guess. After you've selected a good password, don't write it down anywhere and never tell it to anyone under any circumstances. Ever.

After you've added user passwords to the database and taught the users how to selected good passwords, briefly consider physical security. If you see someone you don't know connecting strange equipment to your local area network, ask what he is doing.

CONTROLLING PRIVILEGES

If your application employs user passwords, it connects to the database with a particular login name that tells the database which user is running the program. The database uses that login name's privileges to determine what access it should grant to your application.

As the database administrator, you can grant or deny privileges to individual users. For example, if you deny the CREATE TABLE privilege for the user Crissy, then while Crissy is using your program the program cannot create tables in the database.

The owner of a database object can also grant privileges for that object. For instance, if you created the Students database, you can grant and revoke privileges in that database.

Besides user logins, SQL Server provides *roles*. Roles are described in more detail later in this chapter but, briefly, a role represents a collection of related users who share some privileges. If Crissy is a member of the Supervisor role, and that role has privilege to delete records from the Employees table, then your program can delete records from that table while Crissy is using it.

The SQL GRANT, DENY, and REVOKE statements let you give and remove privileges for users and roles. You can execute those statements using a database development tool that executes scripts. You can also write your own Visual Basic program to execute these statements. The RunScript program described in Chapter 6, "Database Connections", can execute these statements, as well as the SQL Server system stored procedures described later in this chapter.

PART
I
CH
3

Naturally you need to have appropriate permissions yourself to give or remove privileges. If you don't have permission to view a table, you cannot grant yourself that permission. Usually only the database administrator needs to manage privileges. Your program will probably not need to change privileges itself.

The following sections describe the SQL GRANT, DENY, and REVOKE statements. The rest of the chapter explains SQL Server stored procedures you can use to manage user accounts. Other databases such as Oracle use the same GRANT, DENY, and REVOKE statements but will provide a different set of stored procedures for managing users.

GRANT

The GRANT statement explicitly gives permissions to a user or role. The basic syntax for the GRANT statement is simple:

```
GRANT privilege1, privilege2, ... TO account_id
```

The account_id parameter gives the user or role name that should get the new privileges. The list of privileges can include those shown in Table 3.1.

TABLE 3.1   GRANT STATEMENT PRIVILEGES

Privilege	Description
CREATE DATABASE	Creates a new database
CREATE DEFAULT	Creates a default object used to give a table's column a default value
CREATE FUNCTION	Creates a stored function (such as a stored procedure that returns a value)

TABLE 3.1 CONTINUED

Privilege	Description
CREATE PROCEDURE	Creates a stored procedure
CREATE TABLE	Creates a new table
CREATE VIEW	Creates a view or virtual table
BACKUP DATABASE	Backs up a database
BACKUP LOG	Backs up a database log

Setting the privilege to ALL grants all the privileges possible.

To grant privileges that apply to a specific database, you must first connect to the database. For example, if you want to grant the CREATE TABLE privilege, you must first open the database where you want to grant the privilege. The following script allows the user Mike to create tables in the OrderProcessing database:

```
USE OrderProcessing;
GRANT CREATE TABLE TO Mike;
```

To grant the CREATE DATABASE privilege, you must first connect to the master database. The following script grants the CREATE DATABASE privilege to the user Candy:

```
USE Master;
GRANT CREATE DATABASE TO Candy;
```

In all GRANT statements, the user must exist in the database where you are granting the privilege. If you want to give Ernie the CREATE TABLE permission in the OrderProcessing database, the user Ernie must have permission to connect to that database. If you want to grant Ernie the CREATE DATABASE permission, Ernie must have permission to connect to the master database. Later sections describe the SQL Server stored procedures sp_grantlogin, sp_addlogin, and sp_grantdbaccess that you can use to give a user access to a database.

A more complicated form of the GRANT statement gives privileges that apply to a specific database object such as a table or stored procedure. The syntax is

```
GRANT privilege1, privilege2, ...
ON database_object
TO account_id
```

The account_id parameter is a user or role as before. The database_object parameter can be a stored procedure, user-defined function, table, or view.

For tables and views, the privileges list can include those listed in Table 3.2.

TABLE 3.2 PRIVILEGES FOR TABLES AND VIEWS

Privilege	Description
DELETE	Allows the user to delete records
INSERT	Allows the user to insert records

TABLE 3.2   CONTINUED

Privilege	Description
REFERENCES	Allows the user to create a foreign key constraint that references the table
SELECT	Allows the user to select records
UPDATE	Allows the user to update records

When you use the SELECT or UPDATE privilege, you can opt to include a list of columns indicating the table's columns to which the privilege applies. For example, the following statement gives the role Clerks permission to select the FirstName, LastName, and PhoneNumber fields from the Employees table. Other Employees table columns such as Salary and HomePhone are hidden from the Clerks role and if a user with only Clerks privileges tries to select those fields, the database generates an error:

```
GRANT SELECT
ON Employees (FirstName, LastName, PhoneNumber)
TO Clerks
```

The only privilege you can grant for stored procedures is EXECUTE.

If you grant privileges to the special role named public, the privileges apply to all users. For example, the following statement allows all users to select records from the Customers table in the current database:

```
GRANT SELECT ON Customers TO public
```

You should not grant powerful privileges such as CREATE DATABASE or CREATE TABLE to public.

DENY

The DENY statement explicitly prohibits a user or role from performing an action. The syntax and parameters are the same as those used by the GRANT statement.

Denied privileges have precedence over granted privileges, so a user who is denied a privilege cannot use that privilege even if a role would normally grant it. For example, suppose the role OrderEntryClerks is a member of the role Clerks. The following SQL script code lets the Clerks role select records from the Customers table. It then prohibits the OrderEntryClerks role from looking at that table's AccountBalance field:

```
GRANT SELECT ON Customers TO Clerks;
DENY SELECT ON Customers (AccountBalance) TO OrderEntryClerks;
```

Users who are members of the OrderEntryClerks role can view all the table's columns except AccountBalance. Users who are members of the Clerks role and not members of the OrderEntryClerks role can see all the table's columns.

Part
I

Ch
3

REVOKE

The REVOKE statement removes a privilege entry that either grants or denies a privilege. Depending on the other security entries, this may either prevent or allow a user to perform an action.

For example, suppose you have a fresh database with no security records and you grant Ben the SELECT privilege on the Customers table. The following statement then revokes Ben's SELECT privilege. After you execute this statement, Ben cannot select records from the Customers table. In this case, the REVOKE statement stops Ben from selecting records:

```
REVOKE SELECT ON Customers TO Ben
```

Next, suppose you have explicitly denied Ben access to the Customers table with the following statement:

```
DENY SELECT ON Customers TO Ben
```

Now when you execute the REVOKE statement, the database removes the security record prohibiting Ben from selecting records so Ben can now see the Customers table. In this case, the REVOKE statement allows Ben to select records again.

Finally, suppose Ben is a member of the Clerks role and that role has the SELECT privilege on the Customers table. Revoking Ben's SELECT privilege from the table does not affect his ability to select records. Although he personally no longer has the privilege, the Clerks role does. In this case, the REVOKE statement has no practical effect on Ben's capability to select records.

If you really want to prevent a user or role from doing something, use DENY. If you use REVOKE, you need to examine the other privileges granted by other roles.

CONTROLLING ACCESS WITH VIEWS

Using privileges and roles, you can control exactly which users have access to which columns in a table. Another common method for controlling access to data is to create a view that selects specific fields from one or more tables. Then you can grant permission to use the view without granting permission to use the underlying table.

For example, suppose the Clerks role needs to view the Customers table's CompanyName field but nothing else. The following SQL script code creates a view named CustomerNames that selects only that field. It then grants select access to the view for the Clerks role:

```
# Create the view.
CREATE VIEW CustomerNames AS
SELECT CompanyName FROM Customers;

# Give Clerks permission to select the view.
GRANT SELECT ON CustomerNames TO Clerks;
```

Now a user who is a member of the Clerks role can select data using the CustomerNames view but not the underlying Customers table. When a Clerks member executes the following SQL script, the first query works but the second one fails:

```
# This works.
SELECT * FROM CustomerNames
ORDER BY CompanyName;

# This fails.
SELECT CompanyName FROM Customers
ORDER BY CompanyName;
```

Besides determining the columns it returns, a view can also filter the rows it selects. For instance, suppose the role OrderEntryClerks should be able to work only with Customers records where the AccountStatus field has value Active. The following statement creates a view that selects only those records. If you grant the OrderEntryClerks role privileges to select this view but not the Customers table, those users cannot access any other records:

```
CREATE VIEW ActiveCustomers AS
SELECT * FROM Customers
WHERE AccountStatus = 'Active'
```

Views not only give you more options for controlling access to the data, they also hide some of the database's structure from the user. If you deny access to a table's column and the user tries to access that column, the database returns an error that describes the restricted column. The following error message means the user does not have permission to view the Customer table's AccountBalance column. That tells the user that the AccountBalance column exists:

```
SELECT permission denied on column 'AccountBalance' of object 'Customers',
database 'OrderEntry', owner 'dbo'.
```

On the other hand, suppose you allow access to the AccountBalance column through a view and you do not allow any direct access to the Accounts table. Then if the user tries to access the table directly, the database produces this error:

```
SELECT permission denied on object 'Customers', database 'OrderEntry',
owner 'dbo'.
```

This doesn't tell the user anything about the structure of the Customers table. This may not seem like a big deal, but this extra layer of protection can be useful if your database is exposed to possible hackers. The less a potential attacker knows about the structure of your database, the better.

SQL SERVER SECURITY PROCEDURES

SQL Server provides a large assortment of stored procedures that you can use to manage security. You can use SQL Server tools to execute these procedures or you can write a Visual Basic program to execute them. The RunScript program described in Chapter 6, "Database Connections," can execute these statements, as well as standard SQL commands.

The following sections describe the SQL Server stored procedures that are most useful in managing server and database access.

PART

I

CH

3

SQL SERVER ACCESS

A database login allows a user to connect to SQL Server. This does not automatically allow the user to connect to a database served by SQL Server. The next section explains how to allow access to a database.

SQL Server can use two kinds of user authentication: integrated Windows NT Authentication and SQL Server Authentication.

WINDOWS AUTHENTICATION

SQL Server can integrate with Windows NT security to control access. The sp_grantlogin stored procedure allows a Windows NT user or group to connect to SQL Server using Windows Authentication. Its single parameter is the domain-qualified name of the Window NT user or group that should be allowed access to the database:

```
sp_grantlogin 'Bender\Rod'
```

The sp_denylogin procedure flags the login record created by sp_grantlogin so access is disallowed. If the login record does not exist, sp_denylogin creates it and then flags it to prevent access:

```
sp_denylogin 'Bender\Rod'
```

The sp_revokelogin procedure removes a login entry created by sp_grantlogin or sp_deny-login:

```
sp_revokelogin 'Bender\Rod'
```

Removing the login entry takes away the information about this login's access. If the login was flagged by sp_denylogin to prevent access, that prohibition is now removed. If the user belongs to a group that has access permission, the user can connect to the server again.

To prevent a user from connecting to the server, you must use one of the following two methods:

- Use sp_revokelogin to remove the login entries for the user and all groups to which the user belongs.
- Use sp_denylogin to explicitly disallow access to the user.

SQL SERVER AUTHENTICATION

SQL Server can also use its own authentication scheme to control access. The previous method of controlling access uses the Windows NT login system so that the system manages user IDs and passwords. When you use SQL Server Authentication, you must manage the user IDs and passwords.

The sp_addlogin procedure creates a new SQL Server login. The syntax is

```
sp_addlogin user_id
     [, password]
     [, default_database]
```

```
[, default_language]
[, security_id]
[, encryption_option]
```

Table 3.3 describes this procedure's parameters.

TABLE 3.3 sp_add_login **PARAMETERS**

Parameter	Description
user_id	The user's login ID.
password	The user's initial password. The sp_addlogin procedure encrypts the password and stores it in the system tables.
default_database	The user's default database. When this account logs in, it is initially attached to this database.
security_id	The account's *security identification number* (SID). If this is NULL, the system automatically generates a new SID. The SID is a unique number used to identify the user for the security system.
encryption_option	Tells sp_addlogin how to encrypt the password. The default value NULL tells sp_addlogin to encrypt the password as usual. The value skip_encryption tells the procedure that the password parameter is already encrypted and it should not encrypt it again.

PART

I

CH

3

The following statement creates a login entry for the user merlin with password prestochangeo:

```
sp_addlogin 'merlin', 'prestochangeo'
```

The sp_droplogin procedure removes the login record created by sp_addlogin:

```
sp_droplogin 'merlin'
```

DATABASE ACCESS

After a user has access to the server, he still needs access to any databases he must use. The sp_grantdbaccess procedure creates a record in the current database allowing access to the database. The following script statement selects the Accounting database. The second statement gives access to the database to the user Bender\rod. Within the database, this user is known as Rod. For example, an SQL GRANT statement would use the username Rod, not Bender\rod:

```
USE Accounting;
sp_grantdbaccess 'Bender\rod', 'Rod';
```

The following script statements grant access to the Accounting database to the user merlin. SQL Server Authentication manages the merlin login so it doesn't have a qualified Windows NT name. Because the sp_grantdbaccess statement does not specify the login's name in the database, this account is known as merlin within the database:

```
USE Accounting;
sp_grantdbaccess 'merlin';
```

The sp_revokedbaccess procedure removes a database's security record for a login, preventing access in the future:

```
sp_revokedbaccess 'merlin'
```

Note that you cannot remove access to the server on a login that has access to a database. You must use sp_revokedbaccess to remove the login's database access before you can use sp_revokelogin or sp_droplogin.

CHANGING LOGIN INFORMATION

SQL Server provides several stored procedures for modifying a login.

sp_password

The sp_password procedure changes a user's password. The following statement changes the password for the merlin login from old_password to new_password:

```
sp_password 'old_password', 'new_password', 'merlin'
```

sp_defaultdb

The sp_defaultdb procedure changes a user's default database. When a login connects to the server, it is automatically attached to this database just as if the program had executed the SQL statement USE database_name.

The following example sets the merlin login's default to the Customers database:

```
sp_defaultdb 'merlin', 'Customers'
```

The sp_addlogin procedure assigns the login an initial default database. If you do not specify a default database in the call to sp_addlogin, the login's initial default database is master.

sp_defaultlanguage

The sp_defaultlanguage procedure changes a login's default language. The following example changes merlin's default language to German:

```
sp_defaultlanguage 'merlin', 'German'
```

The sp_addlogin procedure assigns the login an initial default language. If you do not specify a default language in the call to sp_addlogin, the login's initial default language is the default for the server.

DEFINING ROLES

A role represents a set of privileges in a particular database. You can think of a database role as representing a role played by a group of users. For example, an order processing system might have users that take on three roles: clerks, supervisors, and database administrators. A clerk works with customers over the phone to enter orders, generate bills, and record payments.

A supervisor can to do everything a clerk does and more. The supervisor might have authority to waive fees and shipping charges, and to modify parameter tables that determine values such as the number of days late a payment should be before the customer's account is deactivated.

A database administrator has permission to do just about anything to the database.

You could explicitly grant and deny the appropriate privileges for each user. The section "Controlling Privileges" later in this chapter explains how to do this. For now, just assume you can grant and revoke privileges to do things like create tables, view records, and update data.

Although you could manage each user's privileges individually, that would be a lot of work. An easier solution is to create three roles named Clerks, Supervisors, and DBAs. You would assign the appropriate privileges to these roles and then add the users to the roles.

For example, if the user Andy is a member of the Clerks role, Andy inherits the privileges defined by Clerks. If the Clerks role has permission to view but not update the SystemParameters table, then Andy can view, but not update that table.

A user can be a member of more than one role so you do not need to overlap the privileges of these roles. In this example, the Supervisors role need not include all the privileges that are held by the Clerks role. If Betty is a supervisor, you can make her a member of the Clerks and Supervisors roles so she inherits the privileges of both roles.

Note that roles provide live views of privileges. If you change a role's privileges, the privileges inherited by its members are automatically changed as well.

CREATING ROLES

A role applies to a particular database, not to the whole server. To create a role, open the database that you want to hold it. Then use the sp_addrole stored procedure to create the role. You can use the sp_addrole procedure's optional second parameter to indicate the login that should own the role.

The following script code selects the OrderProcessing database and uses sp_addrole to create the Clerks role in it. It then uses sp_addrolemember to add the user Andy to the role. It finishes by denying the role's ability to create tables:

```
USE OrderProcessing;
sp_addrole 'Clerks';
sp_addrolemember 'Clerks', 'Andy';
DENY CREATE TABLE TO Clerks;
```

After this script is run, Andy is unable to create tables in the OrderProcessing database. Note that the user Andy must already have been created and granted access to the OrderProcessing database with the sp_grantdbaccess procedure for this to work.

As you would probably guess, the sp_droprolemember procedure removes a member from a role. The following statement removes Andy from the Clerks role:

```
sp_droprolemember 'Clerks', 'Andy'
```

The sp_droprole procedure removes a role from the current database. The following statement removes the Clerks role:

```
sp_droprole 'Clerks'
```

You cannot drop a role if it has any members. Use sp_droprolemember to remove the role's members first, and then use sp_droprole to remove the role itself.

OBTAINING INFORMATION

To make managing users and roles less confusing, SQL Server provides several stored procedures that give you information about server and database access and privileges. The following sections describe some of the most useful of these procedures.

sp_helplogins

The sp_helplogins procedure lists logins that have access to the server. The following output shows some of the logins on one server. In this output, you can see the Windows NT user Bender\rod is mapped to the user name rod. The SQL Server Authentication login merlin has user name merlin. The second row means the login merlin is a member of the role clerks:

LoginName	DBName	UserName	UserOrAlias
Bender\rod	Numbers	rod	User
merlin	TestRoles	clerks	MemberOf
merlin	TestRoles	merlin	User
sa	ContactsDB	db_owner	MemberOf
sa	ContactsDB	dbo	User
sa	master	db_owner	MemberOf
sa	master	dbo	User

...

sp_helpuser

The sp_helpuser procedure lists the users that have access to the current database. The following output shows that two logins, sa and merlin, have access to this database. The user merlin belongs to two roles: clerks and supervisors:

UserName	GroupName	LoginName	DefDBName	UserID	SID
dbo	db_owner	sa	master	1	<byte>
merlin	clerks	merlin	master	5	<byte>
merlin	supervisors	merlin	master	5	<byte>

sp_helprole

The sp_helprole procedure lists the current database's roles. The following output lists the SQL Server fixed roles db_owner, db_accessadmin, and so forth. It then lists two custom roles: clerks and supervisors:

RoleName	RoleId	IsAppRole
public	0	0

```
db_owner            16384           0
db_accessadmin      16385           0
db_securityadmin    16386           0
db_ddladmin         16387           0
db_backupoperator   16389           0
db_datareader       16390           0
db_datawriter       16391           0
db_denydatareader   16392           0
db_denydatawriter   16393           0
clerks              16400           0
supervisors         16401           0
```

sp_helprolemember

The sp_helprolemember procedure lists the members of a role in the database, or of all roles in the database. The following output shows that merlin is the only member of the clerks role:

```
DbRole MemberName MemberSID
====== ========== =========
clerks merlin        <byte>
```

sp_helplanguage

The sp_helplanguage procedure gives information about a particular language or all the languages available on the server. The result lists values such as the language's name (English), date format (mdy), month names (January, February, March), short month names (Jan, Feb, Mar), and days of the week (Monday, Tuesday, Wednesday).

sp_table_privileges

The sp_table_privileges procedure lists a table's privileges. The following statement lists the privileges granted on the CompanyAccounts table:

```
sp_table_privileges CompanyAccounts
```

This statement produced the following results. Most of the entries apply to the database owner (dbo). The third and sixth rows show that the user merlin was granted the INSERT and SELECT privileges by dbo for the TestRoles database's CompanyAccounts table:

TABLE_QUALIFIER	TABLE_OWNER	TABLE_NAME	GRANTOR	GRANTEE	PRIVILEGE	IS_GRANTABLE
TestRoles	dbo	CompanyAccounts	dbo	dbo	DELETE	YES
TestRoles	dbo	CompanyAccounts	dbo	dbo	INSERT	YES
TestRoles	dbo	CompanyAccounts	dbo	merlin	INSERT	NO
TestRoles	dbo	CompanyAccounts	dbo	dbo	REFERENCES	YES
TestRoles	dbo	CompanyAccounts	dbo	dbo	SELECT	YES
TestRoles	dbo	CompanyAccounts	dbo	merlin	SELECT	NO
TestRoles	dbo	CompanyAccounts	dbo	dbo	UPDATE	YES

`sp_column_privileges`

The `sp_column_privileges` procedure lists privileges granted to a table's columns. The result is similar to those produced by `sp_table_privileges` except each row has an additional `COLUMN_NAME` column and the result contains more rows to represent the privileges for each column.

STORED PROCEDURE SUMMARY

Keeping track of all the SQL Server security stored procedures can be confusing, particularly for `sp_grantlogin`, `sp_denylogin`, `sp_revokelogin`, `sp_addlogin`, `sp_droplogin`, `sp_grantdbaccess`, and `sp_revokedbaccess`, which have similar purposes. Table 3.4 summarizes these procedures so you can easily find the one you need.

TABLE 3.4   USEFUL SQL SERVER STORED PROCEDURES

Procedure	Purpose
`sp_grantlogin`	Creates a new SQL Server login for a user or group using Windows NT Authentication
`sp_denylogin`	Prohibits SQL Server access to a Windows NT user or group
`sp_revokelogin`	Removes a SQL Server login entry created by `sp_grantlogin` or `sp_denylogin`
`sp_addlogin`	Creates a new SQL Server login using SQL Server Authentication
`sp_droplogin`	Removes a SQL Server login entry created by `sp_addlogin`
`sp_grantdbaccess`	Allows a user to connect to a database
`sp_revokedbaccess`	Removes a user's access to a database
`sp_password`	Changes a user's SQL Server password
`sp_defaultdb`	Changes a user's default database
`sp_defaultlanguage`	Changes a user's default language
`sp_addrole`	Adds a new role to the current database
`sp_droprole`	Removes a role from the current database
`sp_addrolemember`	Adds a user or role to a role.
`sp_droprolemember`	Removes a user or role from a role.
`sp_helplogins`	Lists logins that have access to the server.
`sp_helpuser`	Lists users with access to the current database.
`sp_helprole`	Lists the current database's roles.
`sp_helprolemember`	Lists the members of a role in the database, or of all roles in the database.
`sp_helplanguage`	Lists information about a particular language or all languages on the server.
`sp_table_privileges`	Lists users' privileges for a table.
`sp_column_privileges`	Lists users' privileges for a table's columns.

SUMMARY

Using SQL Server stored procedures, you can create user logins and give the users access to different databases. Using the SQL statements GRANT, DENY, and REVOKE, you can control which users can perform what actions. Roles and views give you methods for controlling access to groups of users without forcing you to manage each user individually.

Using these techniques, you can give as much or as little access to the data as you want. A standard rule of thumb is to grant the fewest privileges possible to get the job done. That gives the server and the database as much protection as possible against damaging changes, whether accidental or malicious. If you later discover that a user needs an additional privilege, you can add it then. It is easier to find missing privileges that are needed than it is to find granted privileges that are unnecessary.

## CHAPTER 4

OFF TO SEE THE WIZARD

A *wizard* is a program that asks you a series of questions and then produces some sort of hopefully useful output. The output might be the text of a SQL SELECT statement, a new form that automatically displays data from a database, or even an entire database application.

This chapter describes four of the more useful database-related wizards provided by Visual Basic. The Data Link Properties dialog, Query Builder, and Data Adapter Configuration Wizard provide relatively small services that can help you configure the components you will use in your application.

The Data Form Wizard is a much more complicated wizard that helps you build a complete data access form. This wizard doesn't produce a perfect result. The form layout it makes is fairly ugly and the code it generates is confusing and uncommented. Although its results are less than perfect, the Data Form Wizard lets you get an application up and running quickly. Even if you don't want to use the wizard-generated code in your final application, you might be able to use it to define what you want the final application to do.

Although these wizards won't do all your work for you, they can help get you started.

DATA LINK PROPERTIES

The Data Link Properties dialog helps you configure a connection to a database. Many of the other wizards use this dialog to let you build a connection if you have not already built one.

To start this dialog by itself, open a new form, click the Toolbox's Data tab, and double-click the SqlConnection tool. If you are using Access instead of SQL Server, double-click the OleDbConnection tool.

Below the form's design area, you should see the new SqlConnection object with a name such as SqlConnection1. Click this object and then click the ConnectionString property in the Properties window. When the drop-down arrow appears, click it, and select <New Connection...> from the drop-down list. The Data Link Properties dialog shown in Figure 4.1 appears.

Figure 4.1
The Data Link
Properties dialog
helps you to configure
a data connection.

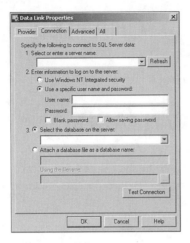

Initially the dialog assumes you want to use the Microsoft OLE DB Provider for SQL Server to connect to the database. The Connection tab shown in Figure 4.1 contains fields in which you can enter SQL Server configuration information. If you want to use SQL Server, enter the connection information as shown in Figure 4.2. Enter the data server name or select it from the drop-down list. Enter the user name and password that the wizard should use to connect to the database. If you haven't established passwords for the database, use "sa" (system administrator) for the user and a blank password.

If you entered the server name, user name, and password correctly, the drop-down in the dialog's third step will show the databases provided by the server. Select the name of the database that you want to use from the list.

Figure 4.2
To use SQL Server,
enter the server
name, user name,
password, and data-
base name.

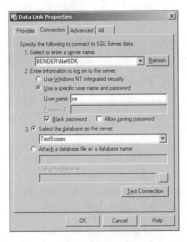

If you do not want to use the Microsoft OLE DB Provider for SQL Server, click the Provider tab. Select the provider you want to use from the dialog shown in Figure 4.3. For example, to open an Access database select the Microsoft Jet 4.0 OLE DB Provider. After you have made your selection, return to the Connection tab.

Figure 4.3
Select the data
provider you want to
use.

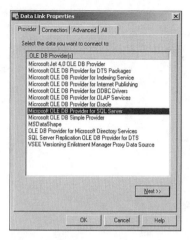

The Connection tab asks for information related to the provider you selected. Figure 4.4 shows what the dialog looks like if you select the Microsoft Jet 4.0 OLE DB Provider. Enter the database's filename or click the ellipsis (...) button on the right to browse for the database file.

Figure 4.4
Enter information for
the Microsoft Jet 4.0
OLE DB Provider.

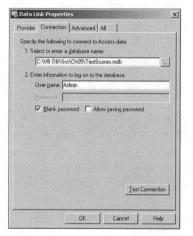

PART

I

CH

4

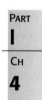

After you have finished entering connection information for the data provider you selected, click the Test Connection button. The Data Link Properties dialog tries to connect to the database to verify that everything is okay. If the test succeeds, click OK to finish configuring the data connection object.

Return to the form's design view, click the connection object, and look at the ConnectionString property in the Properties window. The following value shows a typical ConnectionString value for a SqlConnection object. This value appears on one line in the Properties window:

```
data source=BENDER\NetSDK;initial catalog=ContactsDB;persist security
info=False;user id=sa;workstation id=BENDER;packet size=4096
```

The following text shows a typical ConnectionString for an OleDbConnection object. Again, this value is all on one line in the Properties window. It is shown here with each command parameter on a separate line to make it easier to read:

```
Provider=Microsoft.Jet.OLEDB.4.0;
Password="";
User ID=Admin;
Data Source=C:\VB DB\Src\Ch04\TestScores.mdb;
Mode=Share Deny None;
Extended Properties="";
Jet OLEDB:System database="";
Jet OLEDB:Registry Path="";
Jet OLEDB:Database Password="";
Jet OLEDB:Engine Type=5;
Jet OLEDB:Database Locking Mode=1;
Jet OLEDB:Global Partial Bulk Ops=2;
Jet OLEDB:Global Bulk Transactions=1;
Jet OLEDB:New Database Password="";
Jet OLEDB:Create System Database=False;
Jet OLEDB:Encrypt Database=False;
Jet OLEDB:Don't Copy Locale on Compact=False;
Jet OLEDB:Compact Without Replica Repair=False;
Jet OLEDB:SFP=False
```

Usually you can omit most of the OLE DB connection string. If you are opening an Access database without a password, you can usually trim this to the following value, again all on one line, but shown on separate lines here for readability:

```
Provider=Microsoft.Jet.OLEDB.4.0;
Data Source=C:\VB DB\Src\Ch04\TestScores.mdb
```

The Data Link Properties dialog is useful for configuring connection objects you place on a form, but you can also use it to help build connection strings for use within your code. Add a connection object to a form and use the dialog to initialize it, then copy the ConnectionString property into your code. For example, the following code shows how a Visual Basic application can use the previous ConnectionString to open a connection to an Access database:

```
Dim ole As New OleDb.OleDbConnection( _
    "Provider=Microsoft.Jet.OLEDB.4.0;" & _
    "Data Source=C:\VB DB\Src\Ch04\TestScores.mdb")
ole.Open()
```

Many of the wizards described in the following sections use the Data Link Properties dialog as one step in their configuration process.

THE DATA FORM WIZARD

The Data Form Wizard helps you build forms to display and modify data. It is good at building simple forms that show one table. It can also build forms that display simple master-detail relationships, although those forms don't manage detail data very well.

To start the Data Form Wizard, begin a new Windows application. Open the Project menu and select the Add Windows Form command. On the dialog shown in Figure 4.5, enter the name you want to give the form, select the Data Form Wizard template, and click Open.

Figure 4.5
Select the Data Form Wizard template to launch the wizard.

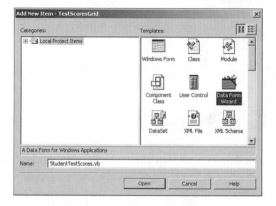

When the wizard presents its welcome screen, click Next. When the wizard presents the dialog shown in Figure 4.6, enter the name you want to give the DataSet that will contain the form's data. You can give the DataSet any name you want but the code will be less confusing if you give it a meaningful name. You may want to start the name with "ds" to remind you later that it is a DataSet.

Figure 4.6
Enter the DataSet name you want to use.

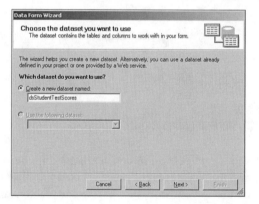

After you enter the DataSet name and click Next, the wizard asks you to select a data connection on the dialog shown in Figure 4.7. If you have already added connections to this form, pick one from the drop-down list.

If you did not add any connections to the form, click the New Connection button to launch the Data Link Properties dialog. Use the dialog to create a new database connection as described in the previous section, "Data Link Properties."

Figure 4.7
Select a data connection or click the New Connection button to make a new one.

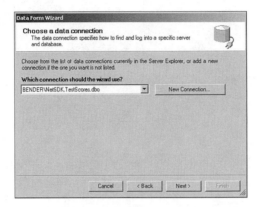

After you have selected the data connection, click OK to move to the next step shown in Figure 4.8. In the list on the left, select the tables and views you want to use on the form. Click the > button to move those tables to the list on the right. In Figure 4.8, the tables Students and TestScores have been selected. The example database doesn't hold any other tables and contains no views, so the list on the left is empty.

Figure 4.8
Select the tables that hold the data you want to display.

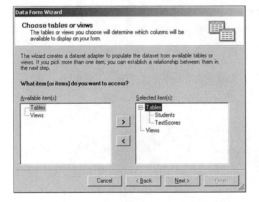

After you select the tables to use, click Next to define relationships between the tables as shown in Figure 4.9. Enter a name for the relationship. From the Parent Table drop-down list, select the table you want to use as the master table in the relationship. From the Child Table drop-down list, select the detail table.

Use the drop-down lists in the Keys section to pick the fields that relate the parent and child tables. In Figure 4.9, the StudentId field in the Students table is related to the StudentId field in the TestScores table.

After you finish defining the relationship, click the > button to add it to the list on the right. After you have created all the relationships you want, click Next.

Figure 4.9
Define relationships between the tables you selected.

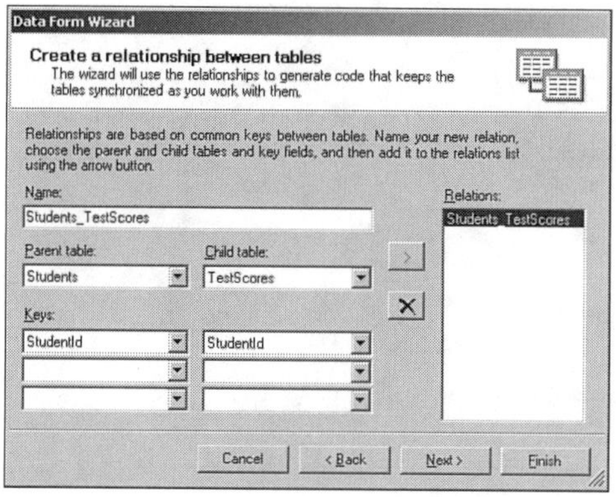

In the next step, shown in Figure 4.10, the Data Form Wizard lets you select the fields you want to display. Use the drop-down lists to select the master and detail tables. Use the check boxes to pick the fields you want to display on the form.

In Figure 4.10, the StudentId field is not selected. That field links the Students and TestScores tables and its value is not very interesting to the user. Linking fields like this one are often not displayed in master-detail relationships. If you do want to display the field's value, you probably won't want to display it both in the master and detail data.

Figure 4.10
Pick the fields you want to display.

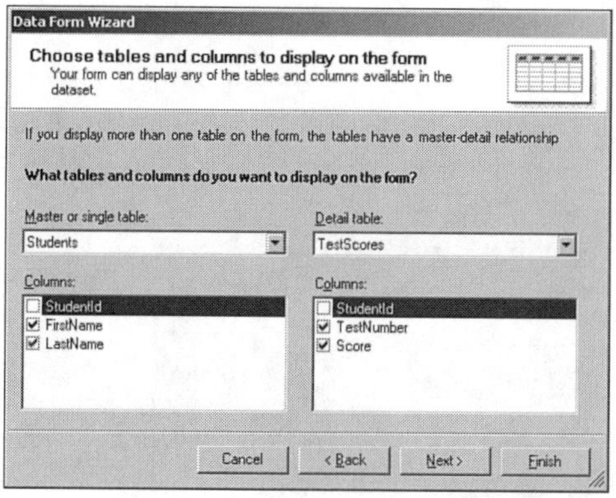

After you have chosen the fields to display, click Next. Now the Data Form Wizard lets you pick the final form's display style. If you select the All records in a grid option, as shown in Figure 4.11, the form displays the master and detail records in the grids shown in Figure 4.12. The user changes records by typing into the grids. If you check the Cancel All box shown in Figure 4.11, the wizard adds a Cancel All button to the form to let the user cancel all of the changes.

PART
I

CH
4

Figure 4.11
The "grid" display style lets you decide whether to include a Cancel All button.

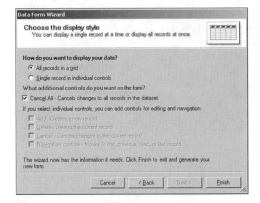

Figure 4.12
In the "grid" display style, users can add, modify, and delete master and detail data using grids.

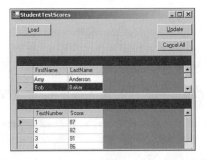

If you select the Single record in the individual controls option as shown in Figure 4.13, the form displays the master data one record at a time. When you move to a new master record, the form displays the corresponding detail records as shown in Figure 4.14.

Figure 4.13
The "single record" display style lets you decide whether to include Add, Delete, Cancel, and navigation buttons.

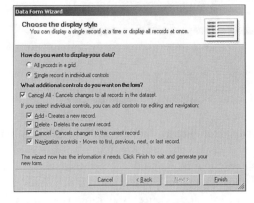

Figure 4.14
In the "single record" display style, users view and manipulate master records using buttons and detail records using a grid.

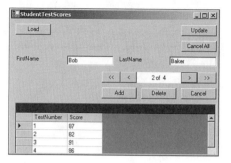

CUSTOMIZING DATA FORMS

As you can see from Figures 4.12 and 4.14, the Data Form Wizard doesn't produce a dazzlingly esthetic result. The forms demonstrate a generally useful design, but they are cumbersome and they look terrible. You need to click the Load button to display anything. You can probably rationalize this because the DataSet underlying the form only takes a snapshot of the data rather than providing a live view. Making the user click Load emphasizes the fact that the data is valid only at that time. Of course, the user can't do anything useful until he clicks the Load button, so the button seems rather silly no matter why it is there.

The form also has a poor layout. Imagine how cluttered Figure 4.13 would be if the master record had a lot of fields spaced widely across the form. Finally, the form's controls are not tied to its size. If you resize the form, the grids stay put and you get a big piece of unused form.

The good news is that these problems are easy to fix. The bad news is once you have modified the form, you cannot rerun the Data Form Wizard because it will remove any changes you have made. If you later add a field to the master table, you'll need to manually modify the form to add the new field. Alternatively, you can rerun the wizard and then make your modifications again.

CUSTOMIZING GRID FORMS

To really understand what the form does, you would need to study the code that the Data Form Wizard generates. To get rid of the Load button, however, all you need to do is copy its code into the form's Load event handler.

Open the form in design mode and double-click the Load button. You will see the following code:

```
Private Sub btnLoad_Click(ByVal sender As System.Object, _
  ByVal e As System.EventArgs) Handles btnLoad.Click
    Try
        Me.LoadDataSet()
    Catch eLoad As System.Exception
        System.Windows.Forms.MessageBox.Show(eLoad.Message)
    End Try

End Sub
```

PART

I

CH

4

Select the code from the Try statement to the End Try statement and press ^X to cut out the code and put it in the Clipboard. In the code window's left drop-down, select (Base Class Events). Then in the right drop-down, select Load. Paste the code you copied into the Load event handler as shown in the following code:

```
Private Sub StudentTestScores_Load(ByVal sender As Object, _
  ByVal e As System.EventArgs) Handles MyBase.Load
    Try
        Me.LoadDataSet()
    Catch eLoad As System.Exception
        System.Windows.Forms.MessageBox.Show(eLoad.Message)
    End Try
End Sub
```

Now return to the form's design view, select the Load button, and delete it. If you run the program now, the form automatically loads its data as soon as it starts.

If you want, you can remove the Update button in the same way. Double-click the button and cut out its code. Select (Base Class Events) in the left drop-down, pick Closing in the right, and paste the code into the form's Closing event handler. Now the form will automatically save any changes the user made when it closes. If you like, you can remove the Update button from the form.

To make better use of the form's space, remove the Cancel All button. This removes the user's ability to cancel changes and gives the form a more "what you see is what you get" (WYSIWYG, pronounced *wizzy-wig*) function. You could create a menu command to let the user cancel changes and still let the grids fill the entire form.

Next drag a Splitter control onto the form. Set its Dock property to Top and its Size.Height property to 5.

Set the master grid's Dock property to Top by opening the Dock property's drop-down and clicking the upper rectangle. Set the child grid's Dock property to Fill by opening the drop-down and clicking the middle rectangle.

To put the controls in the right order, right-click the master grid and select Send to Back. Then right-click the child grid and select Bring to Front.

Figure 4.15 shows the newly designed form. This form automatically fetches its data when it loads and automatically saves any changes you make when it closes[1]. You can click and drag the splitter to give more or less room to the master and child grid controls. If you resize the form, the controls stretch to fit.

---

[1] *Actually the Beta version of the Data Form Wizard used to test this code doesn't update the child table properly. It does update the parent table.*

Figure 4.15
Removing the buttons and adding a splitter makes the grid-style data form more useful.

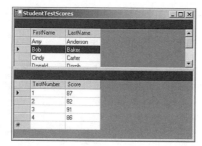

CUSTOMIZING SINGLE RECORD FORMS

When the Data Form Wizard builds a single-record style form, it arranges the labels and text boxes in rows and columns in the order in which the fields appear in the master table. It makes all the labels the same size and all the text boxes the same size. Often that doesn't make much sense. It seems silly to give as much room to a 2-character state abbreviation as to an 80-character name field.

Start customizing the form by dragging the form's controls into a more reasonable arrangement. If you change the order of the text boxes, you may need to change their TabIndex properties to let the user tab between them in their new order.

Remove the Load, Update, and Cancel All buttons as described in the previous section. Then add a panel control to the form and set its Dock property to Top. Cut and paste the master table controls into the panel so they appear at the top of the form.

Set the Dock property of the child table's grid control to Fill so it fills the rest of the form. To put the controls in their proper order, right-click on the panel and select Send to Back. Figure 4.16 shows the results.

Figure 4.16
The Data Form Wizard's single-record style form makes more sense after a little rearrangement.

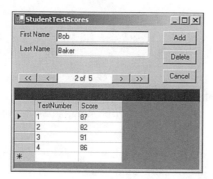

QUERY BUILDER

With a little practice, building SQL SELECT statements is easy. If you don't want to compose queries yourself, however, Visual Basic includes a Query Builder to help you build them graphically. Other wizards provide access to Query Builder to help you enter SELECT statements for their own purposes. For example, at one point the Data Adapter Configuration Wizard needs you to enter a SELECT statement. If you click the Query Builder button, the wizard launches Query Builder so you can build the statement graphically.

A relatively easy way to run Query Builder is to create a new database command object. Open a new form. From the Toolbox's Data tab, double-click the SqlCommand tool if you are using a SQL Server database or the OleDbCommand tool if you are using an Access database.

Select the new command object. Then in the Properties window, assign the object's Connection property to a SqlConnection or OleDbConnection object. For information on creating those objects, see the section "Data Link Properties" at the beginning of this chapter.

Now select the command object's CommandText property and click the ellipsis (...) to the right. Query Designer appears.

In the Add Table dialog shown in Figure 4.17, select the tables you want to add to the query and click Add. Query Builder gets its list of tables from the connection object you assigned to the Connection property. That's why you need to create the connection object before you can use Query Builder. If it doesn't have a connection to the database, Query Builder doesn't know what tables and fields it can use.

After you have added all the tables you want, click Close.

Figure 4.17
Select the tables from which Query Builder will select data.

Figure 4.18 shows the Query Builder with the Contacts table selected. Had you selected more than one table, the tables would be shown with lines connecting the fields that link them.

Use the check boxes in the Contacts window to select the fields you want to display from that table. If you select the fields individually rather than by checking the (All Columns) box, the fields are listed in the SQL SELECT statement in the order in which you pick them.

To add a field to the SELECT statement's ORDER BY clause, right-click the field and select Sort Ascending or Sort Descending. The fields are added to the ORDER BY clause in the order in which you select them. If you want to change the order, right-click and select Sort Ascending or Sort Descending again to remove the fields from the clause, then reselect the fields in the correct order.

Figure 4.18
Select the tables from which Query Builder will pull data.

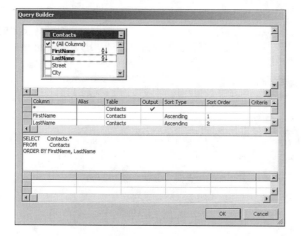

After you have finished building the query, click OK. Query Builder inserts the SELECT statement it composed in the wizard that invoked it. If you are configuring a database command object, the Query Builder copies the select string into the object's CommandText property.

If you want to use the query in your code, copy and paste it from the Query Builder or from the command object's CommandText property.

DATA ADAPTER CONFIGURATION WIZARD

A *data adapter* connects a DataSet object to a database. It pulls data into the DataSet and saves changes back to the database as shown in Figure 4.19. Your program manipulates the DataSet object to read, modify, and delete data values.

Figure 4.19
A data adapter moves data between a database and a DataSet.

If you add a data adapter to a form, the Data Adapter Configuration Wizard will help you initialize it. The wizard helps you connect the adapter to a database and prepare it for use. If you add a DataGrid or other data bound control to your form, you can build a functional database application with surprisingly little code.

To start the wizard, open a new form, click the Toolbox's Data tab, and double-click the SqlDataAdapter tool. If you want to use an Access database instead of a SQL Server database, double-click the OleDbDataAdapter tool. When the wizard presents its welcome screen, click Next to get started.

The first step in configuring the data adapter is selecting a database connection. Pick a connection from the drop-down list or click the New Connection button to build a new one. For detailed information on building a new database connection, see the "Data Link Properties" section at the beginning of this chapter.

After you select a database connection, click Next to see the screen shown in Figure 4.20. You can make the adapter use SQL statements or stored procedures to select, insert, update, and delete records in the database. This example uses SQL statements.

Figure 4.20
A data adapter can use SQL statements or stored procedures to select, insert, update, and delete records.

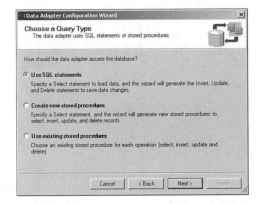

When you click Next, the wizard displays the screen shown in Figure 4.21. Enter the SQL statement you want the adapter to use to select database records. Later the wizard will derive the insert, update, and update statements the adapter needs.

Figure 4.21
Enter the SQL SELECT statement the adapter should use to select records.

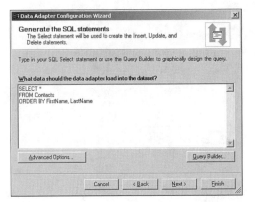

If you are not comfortable building SQL SELECT statements yourself, you can click the Query Builder button to build the query graphically. See the previous section, "Query Builder," for information on how to use Query Builder.

After you enter or build the SELECT statement, click Next to make the Data Adapter Configuration Wizard display a summary similar to the one shown in Figure 4.22. Depending on the tables and the SELECT statement you selected, the wizard may not generate all of the statements. For instance, if you selected fields from multiple tables, the wizard will not generate UPDATE or DELETE statements.

Figure 4.22
The wizard displays a summary when it finishes.

Click Finish to close the wizard and configure the data adapter.

USING THE DATA ADAPTER

Using the data adapter, you can build a functional database form with very little code. Open the form in design mode and click the new data adapter. In the Properties window, give it a meaningful name, such as daContacts.

Next, add a DataSet for the adapter to connect to the database. Click the adapter and look at the Properties window. Below all the properties, there are several commands, shown in Figure 4.23. Later if you want to change the data adapter's settings, click the Configure Data Adapter command to start the Data Adapter Configuration Wizard again. For now, click the Generate Dataset command.

Figure 4.23
The Generate Dataset command attaches the data adapter to a new DataSet.

In the dialog shown in Figure 4.24, enter the name for the new DataSet type and click OK. The dialog defines a new DataSet type with the name you entered and adds an instance of that type to the form. In the example shown in Figure 4.24, the DataSet type is called dsContacts and the new instance is named DsContacts1.

PART

I

CH

4

Figure 4.24
Enter the new DataSet
class name and click
OK.

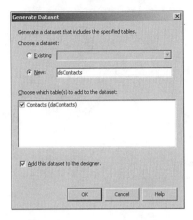

At this point, the form contains objects to select and manipulate data but nothing to display it. Add a DataGrid control to the form. In the Properties window, set its Dock property to Fill so the control fills the form. Select the DataSource property, click the drop-down arrow to the right, and select the DsContacts1.Contacts entry. That binds the DataGrid control to the Contacts table selected by the DsContacts1 DataSet.

Figure 4.25 shows the form in design mode. The DataGrid control fills the form. Below the form, you can see the database connection named SqlConnection1, the data adapter named daContacts, the adapter's four SQL command objects, and the DataSet DsContacts1.

Figure 4.25
The form now con-
tains a database con-
nection, data adapter,
four database com-
mand objects, and a
DataSet.

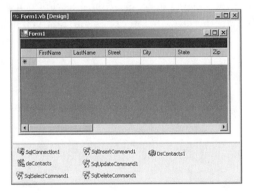

At this point, the form has all the objects it needs to display the data but it still needs to load and save the data. Figure 4.26 shows how the data will flow between the database and the DataGrid control. The link between the DataGrid control and the DataSet is automatic. You created that link when you set the DataGrid control's DataSource property.

The link between the database and the data adapter is also automatic. You defined that link when you created the data adapter.

Figure 4.26
Data flows between the database and DataGrid control almost automatically.

You still need to create the link between the DataSet and the data adapter. Although the data adapter contains all the tools it needs to move data in and out of the DataSet, the project doesn't contain any code that calls those tools.

Open the form's code window and add the following code. The form Load event handler uses the data adapter's Fill method to load the DsContacts1 DataSet. The form's Closing event handler uses the data adapter's Update method to save changes in the DataSet back to the database:

```
Private Sub Form1_Load(ByVal sender As System.Object, _
  ByVal e As System.EventArgs) Handles MyBase.Load
    ' Fill the DataSet.
    daContacts.Fill(DsContacts1)
End Sub

Private Sub Form1_Closing(ByVal sender As Object, _
  ByVal e As System.ComponentModel.CancelEventArgs) Handles MyBase.Closing
    ' Update the database.
    daContacts.Update(DsContacts1)
End Sub
```

Figure 4.27 shows the final form in action. When the form loads, its Load event handler automatically loads the data and displays it. Click a grid cell and type to enter a new value. When you close the form, the Closing event handler automatically saves any changes you made. If you run the program again, you will see the changes.

PART

I

CH

4

Figure 4.27
This program automatically loads data when it starts and automatically saves any changes when it closes.

FirstName	LastName	Street	City	State	Zip	HomePhone	Hom
Amy	Anderson	1243 Left Ha	Boxcar	CO	80300	303-987-654	[null]
Ben	Baker	7643 Progra	Bugsville	AZ	90102	858-987-837	[null]
Candy	Cameron	#9 Ninth Ave	Recursive	WY	79010	[null]	[null]
Danforth 'Dic	Dickleson III	1 Posh Place	Manageria	KS	75048	858-987-837	213
Edna	Evenson	847 Table Me	Idle Hands	NV	90874	374-498-347	[null]
Frank	Finney	654 Platt Ave	Denver	CO	81376	303-983-439	[null]
Gina	Galagher	89749 South	Hannover	CA	92398	[null]	[null]

Now that the form contains objects to connect to the database, you can modify it to provide other features. For instance, you could add a Cancel Changes menu item that removed any changes the user had made to the data. The following code shows how this menu item could call the DataSet's RejectChanges method to remove the changes:

```
Private Sub mnuDataCancelChanges_Click(ByVal sender As System.Object, _
  ByVal e As System.EventArgs) Handles mnuDataCancelChanges.Click
    ' Cancel any changes.
    DsContacts1.RejectChanges()
End Sub
```

SUMMARY

The Data Link Properties dialog, Query Builder, and Data Adapter Configuration Wizard help you initialize database connections, compose queries, and perform other small database-related chores. They can help you get your database application up and running quickly with a minimum of fuss.

The Data Form Wizard is much more ambitious. After gathering information, it generates a complete data access form. The layout and source code leave much to be desired, but the wizard lets you get something running with relatively little effort. Even if you don't use the wizard's form, you may be able to use it for prototyping purposes.

## CHAPTER 5

THE DATASET FAMILY OF OBJECTS

ADO.NET includes a bewildering assortment of objects including DataSets, DataTables, DataRows, DataColumns, DataRelations, DataViews, and Constraints. Using these objects, you can model practically every aspect of a database's content and structure. You can filter the data and build objects representing subsets of the data you have selected. You can add, modify, and delete data.

This chapter explains these objects and shows how you can use them to view, modify, add, and delete data. Chapter 6, "Database Connections," explains how you can move data between these objects and a database.

DATASET

If you've done any database programming using previous versions of ADO, you are probably familiar with the Recordset object. A Recordset object represents the results of a query returned by the database. Its properties and methods let you move through the returned data record-by-record, examining and modifying individual fields, and inserting and deleting records. In ADO, the Recordset provides a program's main point of interaction with the database. You can perform some operations using other objects, such as using the Connection object to execute SQL statements to create and drop tables, but programs use the Recordset to fetch large amounts of data.

In ADO.NET, the DataSet object is positioned to be the program's main access to the database. The DataSet is not really the equivalent of the Recordset, however, and its similarity of name can be a little misleading. While a Recordset object manipulates the records in a single table or is selected by a single query, the DataSet object can represent the results of multiple tables or queries. If a Recordset models a database table, the DataSet models a database.

The DataSet models a database using two key collections: Tables and Relations. The DataSet's Tables collection contains a group of DataTable objects. Those objects represent a table or the results of a query, and they more closely resemble the Recordset objects of old than the DataSet object does. The DataTable's properties and methods let a program manipulate records in a table or returned by a query. They let the program examine and modify values, and add and delete records from the DataTable.

The DataSet's Relations collection holds a series of DataRelation objects that define the relationships among the tables loaded by the DataSet. These are analogous to the relational constraints you can define in the database itself.

Later sections in this chapter define these objects in greater detail. The next sections describe some of the DataSet's more useful properties and methods.

Many of these methods delegate their functions to the DataTable objects in the DataSet's Tables collection. For example, Clear, HasChanges, AcceptChanges, RejectChanges, and HasErrors simply call the corresponding method for each of the DataTables. The DataSet methods give you an easy place to apply these operations to all the DataTables at once.

Clear

The Clear method removes all the data from all the DataSet's tables. The table definitions and any constraints defined by the DataSet remain. If you also want to remove the tables and constraints, simply re-create the DataSet as in this code:

```
dsEmployees = New DataSet()
```

HasChanges

The DataSet keeps track of whether any changes have been made to its data. The HasChanges method returns True if the data has been modified.

When a program initially loads data into the DataSet, the data has not been changed and HasChanges returns False. If the program modifies any of the tables' data, the DataSet flags itself as modified and HasChanges returns True. Later, if the program calls AcceptChanges or RejectChanges, the DataSet resets the modified flag to indicate that the data is not modified.

HasChanges can take an optional parameter indicating the kinds of changes that interest you. You can use HasChanges to see if records have been added, modified, or deleted. For example, the following code determines whether new rows have been added to the DataSet's tables:

```
If dsEmployees.HasChanges(DataRowState.Added) Then
    ' Do something with the new rows.
    ...
End If
```

AcceptChanges AND RejectChanges

RejectChanges cancels any changes made to the data since the data was loaded or since the last call to AcceptChanges. It removes any newly added rows, restores recently deleted rows, and resets modified rows to their previous values. RejectChanges also resets the DataSet's modified flag to indicate that the data has not been modified, making future calls to HasChanges return False (until the program modifies the data again).

AcceptChanges resets the DataSet's changed flag to indicate that the data has not been modified. It is extremely important to realize that AcceptChanges does not actually update the database. It merely resets the DataSet's changed flag so HasChanges returns False (until the program modifies the data again). Typically a program will save any changes to the database and then call AcceptChanges immediately afterward.

AcceptChanges also removes information about the previous state of the data so you cannot use RejectChanges to restore earlier data values. A call to RejectChanges restores the data to the state it had after the most recent call to AcceptChanges.

HasErrors

A program can flag rows or columns in a DataTable with an error message. For instance, suppose the user enters the value 987-654-321 in a phone number field. The program can flag this field in this particular record as invalid. Later, just before it updates the database, the program can use the DataSet's HasErrors method to determine whether the data has errors that the user must fix.

You might wonder why the program doesn't tell the user about the error immediately. Sometimes it is useful to defer error handling in this way. For example, one field's value might depend on the value of another that has not yet been entered. In that case, the program must wait until it has both values before it can determine whether there is a problem. For another example, suppose the program is loading many records from a file. It could wait until it has loaded all the new data and then examine the DataSet and its DataTable objects to give the user a summary of all the errors at the same time.

GetChanges

The GetChanges method builds a new DataSet object with the same structure as the original but containing only records representing changes to the data. An optional parameter tells GetChanges whether it should return records that were added, modified, deleted, or left unchanged. The following code shows how a program might create a DataSet containing records that were added. It uses that DataSet to tell the user how many rows are new.

```
' Get added records.
ds_added = dsEmployees.GetChanges(DataRowState.Added)

' Tell how many records were added.
MsgBox(ds_added.Table(0).Rows.Count & " records added")
```

You can combine DataRowState values to select more than one type of change. For example, the following code tells the user the number of rows added or deleted:

```
' Get added or deleted records.
ds_added = dsEmployees.GetChanges(DataRowState.Added Or DataRowState.Deleted)

' Tell how many records were added or deleted.
MsgBox(ds_added.Table(0).Rows.Count & " records added or deleted")
```

If you want to select all the rows that have not been changed since the data was loaded or since the last call to AcceptChanges or RejectChanges, pass GetChanges the value DataRowState.Unchanged. To select all the changed rows, whether added, deleted, or modified, omit the parameter entirely.

A program uses a DataAdapter object (described later in this chapter) to save changes in a DataSet back to the database. The DataAdapter's Update method looks through the DataSet for changes and saves them one at a time. Saving the changes is faster if they are grouped by change type. In other words, the Update method gives better performance if you save all the modifications first, all the additions next, and all the deletions last.

Listing 5.1 shows one way a program could save changes grouped by type. Ignore the parts you don't understand. They will become clear when you learn about the other objects described in this chapter.

The code begins by using the HasChanges method to see if the DataSet dsContacts has any changes. If there are changes to save, the subroutine uses the DataSet's GetChanges method with no parameter to make a new DataSet containing all the changes.

Next the routine uses the new DataSet's GetChanges method to create another DataSet holding only the row modifications. If that DataSet is not Nothing, the code calls the data adapter's Update method, passing it that DataSet. The code repeats these steps for the newly added and deleted records.

When it has saved all the changes, the subroutine calls the main DataSet's AcceptChanges method to indicate that the DataSet's current data matches the data in the database.

LISTING 5.1 SAVING DATA IS FASTER WHEN CHANGES ARE GROUPED BY TYPE

```
' Save changes to the database.
Private Sub SaveChanges()
    Dim ds_changes As DataSet
    Dim ds_subset As DataSet

    ' Finish the current edit.
    m_CurrencyManager.EndCurrentEdit()

    ' See if there are any changes to save.
    If dsContacts.HasChanges Then
        ' Get a DataSet holding the changes.
        ds_changes = dsContacts.GetChanges()

        ' Save the changes grouped by type.
        ds_subset = ds_changes.GetChanges(DataRowState.Modified)
        If (Not (ds_subset) Is Nothing) Then daContacts.Update(ds_subset)

        ds_subset = ds_changes.GetChanges(DataRowState.Added)
        If (Not (ds_subset) Is Nothing) Then daContacts.Update(ds_subset)

        ds_subset = ds_changes.GetChanges(DataRowState.Deleted)
        If (Not (ds_subset) Is Nothing) Then daContacts.Update(ds_subset)

        ' Mark the modified records as not modified.
        dsContacts.AcceptChanges()
    End If

    ' Update the form's caption to show the data is unmodified.
    Me.Text = APP_TITLE
End Sub
```

If the DataSet contains a lot of changes, grouping the changes by modification type can save some time. If there are only a few changes, you can greatly simplify the code by saving the original DataSet's changes directly. You can remove the HasChanges test because the Update and AcceptChanges methods do nothing if there are no changes to save.

```
' Save changes to the database.
Private Sub SaveChanges()
    ' Finish the current edit.
    m_CurrencyManager.EndCurrentEdit()

    ' Save the changes.
    daContacts.Update(dsContacts)

    ' Mark the modified records as not modified.
    dsContacts.AcceptChanges()

    ' Update the form's caption to show the data is unmodified.
    Me.Text = APP_TITLE
End Sub
```

Sometimes a program might need to save changes in a particular order to satisfy the database's relational constraints. For instance, it might need to remove records in one table that reference values in another table before it can modify the referenced values. Sometimes you can use similar code and GetChanges to perform the operations in the necessary order.

For example, suppose the Customers and CustomerOrders tables are linked by a common CustomerId field. The CustomerOrders table specifies Customers.CustomerId as a relational constraint so you cannot create a CustomerOrders record until a corresponding Customers record exists. Similarly, you cannot delete a Customers order until after you delete any CustomerOrders records with the same CustomerId.

Listing 5.2 shows how a program might create and delete Customers and CustomerOrders records. To satisfy the relational constraint, it creates Customers records before CustomerOrders records and then deletes CustomerOrders records before Customers records.

LISTING 5.2   SOMETIMES A PROGRAM MUST USE GetChanges TO SATISFY RELATIONAL CONSTRAINTS

```
' Save changes to the database.
Private Sub SaveChanges()
    ' Finish the current edit.
    m_CurrencyManager.EndCurrentEdit()

    ' Create new Customers records (before creating CustomerOrders records).
    ds_subset = dsCustomers.GetChanges(DataRowState.Added)
    If (Not (ds_subset) Is Nothing) Then daCustomers.Update(ds_subset)

    ' Create new CustomerOrders.
    ds_subset = dsCustomerOrders.GetChanges(DataRowState.Added)
    If (Not (ds_subset) Is Nothing) Then daCustomerOrders.Update(ds_subset)

    ' Delete CustomerOrders records (before deleting Customers records).
    ds_subset = dsCustomerOrders.GetChanges(DataRowState.Deleted)
```

LISTING 5.2   CONTINUED

```
    If (Not (ds_subset) Is Nothing) Then daCustomerOrders.Update(ds_subset)

    ' Delete Customers records.
    ds_subset = dsCustomers.GetChanges(DataRowState.Deleted)
    If (Not (ds_subset) Is Nothing) Then daCustomers.Update(ds_subset)

    ' Mark the modified records as not modified.
    dsContacts.AcceptChanges()

    ' Update the form's caption to show the data is unmodified.
    Me.Text = APP_TITLE
End Sub
```

Merge

The `Merge` method adds the data in another DataSet, DataTable, or array of DataRow objects to the current DataSet. Usually the object being merged has a similar structure to the DataSet. For example, if the new object is another DataSet, it may contain the same tables as the first DataSet.

In particular, a DataSet generated by the `GetChanges` method is compatible with the original DataSet. The program can use `GetChanges` to get a DataSet containing only the changes. It can then validate the changes, possibly modifying some data values, and save the changes to the database. When it is finished updating the database, the program can merge the changes back into the original DataSet so it is synchronized with the database.

The `Merge` method takes two optional parameters that tell it how to merge the changes. The first is a Boolean value that tells the method whether changes in the original DataSet should be maintained. The second parameter tells what action the method should take if a table or column in the new data source is missing in the original DataSet. The value `MissingSchemaAction.Add` makes the method add the new table or column.

The value `MissingSchemaAction.AddWithKey` makes the method add new columns and primary key information as necessary. This value is rather complicated so it is not described in detail here. See the online documentation for more information on creating primary keys automatically.

The value `MissingSchemaAction.Error` makes `Merge` raise an error if it cannot match the incoming data to the original DataSet's structure. The value `MissingSchemaAction.Ignore` makes the `Merge` method ignore the new data if it won't fit into the original DataSet.

Clone AND Copy

The `Clone` method makes a new DataSet with the same structure as the current one. It has all the same tables and constraints.

The `Copy` method makes a new DataSet with the same structure and data as the current one. `Copy` is similar to `Clone` but includes the data.

GetXml, WriteXml, AND ReadXml

The DataSet object provides several methods for reading and writing XML data. The GetXml method returns a string containing an XML representation of the DataSet. For example, Listing 5.3 shows an XML representation of a DataSet containing one DataTable named Contacts. That table contains two records.

LISTING 5.3   A DataSet's GetXml Method Returns an XML Representation of the Data

```
<NewDataSet>
  <Contacts>
    <LastName>Canid</LastName>
    <FirstName>Snortimer</FirstName>
    <Street>8723 Bad Spelling Way</Street>
    <City>Bee</City>
    <State>UT</State>
    <Zip>87647</Zip>
    <HomeFax>387-498-3849</HomeFax>
    <WorkPhone>387-398-3287</WorkPhone>
    <SnapshotFile>C:\VB DB\Src\Tests\RunScript\pic08.jpg</SnapshotFile>
  </Contacts>
  <Contacts>
    <LastName>Cats</LastName>
    <FirstName>Merlin &amp; Cobe</FirstName>
    <Street>1 Posh Place</Street>
    <City>Manageria</City>
    <State>KS</State>
    <Zip>75048</Zip>
    <Email>cats@vb-helper.com</Email>
    <HomePhone>858-987-8375</HomePhone>
    <HomePhoneExtension>213</HomePhoneExtension>
    <HomeFax>858-987-8375</HomeFax>
    <HomeFaxExtension>7000</HomeFaxExtension>
    <SnapshotFile>C:\VB DB\Src\Tests\RunScript\pic04.jpg</SnapshotFile>
  </Contacts>
</NewDataSet>
```

The WriteXml method writes an XML representation of the DataSet into a file. This method's first parameter gives the object that should receive the XML output. This object can be a stream, TextWriter, XmlWriter, or string containing the output file's name.

The method's optional second parameter tells WriteXml what to include in the output. The value XmlWriteMode.DiffGram makes the method create an XML file that includes both the current and original data. If you want to see only the changed data, use GetChanges to make a new DataSet containing the changes and use its WriteXml method to create the XML file.

The value XmlWriteMode.IgnoreSchema writes an XML file containing the data very similar to the results produced by the GetXml method.

The value XmlWriteMode.WriteSchema makes WriteXml save the DataSet's schema information in the XML file as well as the data. Listing 5.4 shows the schema output for a DataSet containing one table named Contacts holding two records.

LISTING 5.4   THE DATASET'S WriteXml METHOD CAN INCLUDE THE DATA'S SCHEMA IN AN
XML FILE

```xml
<?xml version="1.0" standalone="yes"?>
<NewDataSet>
  <xsd:schema id="NewDataSet" targetNamespace="" xmlns=""
xmlns:xsd="http://www.w3.org/2001/XMLSchema" xmlns:msdata="urn:schemas-microsoft-
com:xml-msdata">
    <xsd:element name="NewDataSet" msdata:IsDataSet="true">
      <xsd:complexType>
        <xsd:choice maxOccurs="unbounded">
          <xsd:element name="Contacts">
            <xsd:complexType>
              <xsd:sequence>
                <xsd:element name="LastName" type="xsd:string" minOccurs="0" />
                <xsd:element name="FirstName" type="xsd:string" minOccurs="0" />
                <xsd:element name="Street" type="xsd:string" minOccurs="0" />
                <xsd:element name="City" type="xsd:string" minOccurs="0" />
                <xsd:element name="State" type="xsd:string" minOccurs="0" />
                <xsd:element name="Zip" type="xsd:string" minOccurs="0" />
                <xsd:element name="Email" type="xsd:string" minOccurs="0" />
                <xsd:element name="Notes" type="xsd:string" minOccurs="0" />
                <xsd:element name="HomePhone" type="xsd:string" minOccurs="0" />
                <xsd:element name="HomePhoneExtension" type="xsd:string"
minOccurs="0" />
                <xsd:element name="HomeFax" type="xsd:string" minOccurs="0" />
                <xsd:element name="HomeFaxExtension" type="xsd:string"
minOccurs="0" />
                <xsd:element name="WorkPhone" type="xsd:string" minOccurs="0" />
                <xsd:element name="WorkPhoneExtension" type="xsd:string"
minOccurs="0" />
                <xsd:element name="WorkFax" type="xsd:string" minOccurs="0" />
                <xsd:element name="WorkFaxExtension" type="xsd:string"
minOccurs="0" />
                <xsd:element name="SnapshotFile" type="xsd:string" minOccurs="0"
/>
              </xsd:sequence>
            </xsd:complexType>
          </xsd:element>
        </xsd:choice>
      </xsd:complexType>
    </xsd:element>
  </xsd:schema>
  <Contacts>
    <LastName>Canid</LastName>
    <FirstName>Snortimer</FirstName>
    <Street>8723 Bad Spelling Way</Street>
    <City>Bee</City>
    <State>UT</State>
    <Zip>87647</Zip>
    <HomeFax>387-498-3849</HomeFax>
    <WorkPhone>387-398-3287</WorkPhone>
    <SnapshotFile>C:\VB DB\Src\Tests\RunScript\pic08.jpg</SnapshotFile>
  </Contacts>
  <Contacts>
    <LastName>Cats</LastName>
    <FirstName>Merlin &amp; Cobe</FirstName>
```

LISTING 5.4   CONTINUED

```
      <Street>1 Posh Place</Street>
      <City>Manageria</City>
      <State>KS</State>
      <Zip>75048</Zip>
      <Email>cats@vb-helper.com</Email>
      <HomePhone>858-987-8375</HomePhone>
      <HomePhoneExtension>213</HomePhoneExtension>
      <HomeFax>858-987-8375</HomeFax>
      <HomeFaxExtension>7000</HomeFaxExtension>
      <SnapshotFile>C:\VB DB\Src\Tests\RunScript\pic04.jpg</SnapshotFile>
   </Contacts>
</NewDataSet>
```

The DataSet's `ReadXml` method reads an XML file's data into a DataSet. This method takes as a parameter an object of a class that inherits from the `XmlReader` class and that is attached to the XML file to read. The following code fragment shows how a program might read an XML file's data into a DataSet:

```
' Create a FileStream to read the file.
Dim file_stream As New FileStream(file_name, FileMode.Open)

' Attach an XmlTextReader to the FileStream.
Dim xml_text_reader As New XmlTextReader(file_stream)

' Load the DataSet's data.
data_set.ReadXml(xml_text_reader)

' Close the XmlTextReader.
xml_text_reader.Close
```

GetXmlSchema, WriteXmlSchema, AND ReadXmlSchema

A schema describes an XML file's structure. The first part of the XML file shown in Listing 5.4 contains a schema describing the fields in the `Contacts` table.

The `GetXmlSchema`, `WriteXmlSchema`, and `ReadXmlSchema` methods are analogous to the `GetXml`, `WriteXml`, and `ReadXml` methods described in the previous section except they work with the DataSet's structure rather than its data. `GetXmlSchema` returns a string containing the DataSet's schema, `WriteXmlSchema` saves the DataSet's schema into a file, and `ReadXmlSchema` defines a DataSet's structure by reading a schema from an XML file.

DATATABLE

The DataTable object represents a database table or the results of a query. In many ways, the DataTable class more closely corresponds to the Recordset class used in previous versions of ADO than the DataSet class does.

The following sections describe some of the DataTable's most useful properties, methods, and events.

TableName

As its name implies, the `TableName` property simply returns the table's name. This is not a complicated property but it is useful so it is listed here. The only surprising thing about this property is that you can set its value to change the DataTable's name. The name is used as a key in the DataSet's `Tables` collection, so if you give a DataTable the same name as another DataTable, the program raises an error.

Columns

The `Columns` collection contains DataColumn objects describing the DataTable's columns. These objects determine the column's database field name, display name, data type, and so forth. See the section "DataColumn" later in this chapter for more information.

Rows

The `Rows` collection holds DataRow objects representing each row of data in the table. The DataRow object gives access to the row's field values, child and parent rows related to the row, and the row's state (modified, added, deleted, or unchanged). The DataRow's `Delete` method deletes the row from its DataTable, although you could restore it by calling the DataTable's `RejectChanges` method.

When a program needs to manipulate data directly, it usually does so through the DataRow's `Item` property. For example, the following code uses the `dsEmployees` DataSet. It locates the DataTable named `Managers` in the `Tables` collection. It then selects the first DataRow object and changes the value of its `LastName` item to `Stephens`.

```
dsEmployees.Tables("Managers").Rows(0).Item("LastName") = "Stephens"
```

See the section "DataRow" later in this chapter for more information on DataRow objects.

CaseSensitive AND Select

The `CaseSensitive` property determines whether string comparisons made by the DataTable should be case-sensitive. The `Select` method uses a selection criterion to select records from the DataTable in a manner that is somewhat similar to a SQL SELECT statement. The value of `CaseInsensitive` affects the results returned by `Select`.

`Select` returns an array of references to DataRow objects that meet a certain condition. Its first parameter gives an expression that specifies the condition. This expression is quite similar to the expressions you can use in a SQL SELECT statement's WHERE clause. For example, the expression `"Price > 100"` selects rows where the `Price` field has a value greater than 100.

For another example, the expression `"PhoneNumber LIKE '800%'"` selects rows where the `PhoneNumber` field begins with 800. In other words, it selects the rows where the `PhoneNumber` field has the area code 800.

One restriction on the LIKE operator is that you cannot use wildcards in the middle of the expression. You can use wildcards at the beginning or end of the expression or both, but you cannot use them in the middle. You can say `"PhoneNumber LIKE '800%'"`, and you can say `"PhoneNumber LIKE '%1234'"`, but you cannot say `"PhoneNumber LIKE '800%1234'"`.

The `Select` method takes an optional third parameter that tells it the state of the DataRows it should return. Table 5.1 lists the values this parameter can take.

TABLE 5.1   `DataViewRowState` **VALUES**

Value	Meaning
`DataViewRowState.Added`	New rows.
`DataViewRowState.CurrentRows`	The current values in the DataTable, including new and modified rows, excluding deleted rows.
`DataViewRowState.Deleted`	Deleted rows.
`DataViewRowState.ModifiedCurrent`	The modified values of modified rows.
`DataViewRowState.ModifiedOriginal`	The original values of modified rows.
`DataViewRowState.None`	No rows.
`DataViewRowState.OriginalRows`	The original rows, including original values of modified and deleted rows.
`DataViewRowState.Unchanged`	Original rows that have not been modified or deleted.

Note that the `Select` method returns an array of references to DataRow objects matching the selection expression. If you modify one of those objects, you modify the underlying object in the DataTable. For example, if you change a field's value in the DataRow and the DataTable is bound to a DataGrid control, the control immediately shows the new value.

The `Select` method returns an array of objects. If you want to store the DataRows in a DataTable instead of an array, use a DataView object. See the section "DataView" later in this chapter for more information on DataViews.

ImportRow

The `ImportRow` method copies a DataRow object into the DataTable. Note that the DataRow object has no callable constructors so you cannot create a DataRow directly. That means the program must have used another DataTable or some other data source to create the new DataRow and hence the word *import*.

`ImportRow` copies the entire DataRow, including its original and modified values, its row state (added, modified, deleted, or unchanged), and any errors associated with it.

LoadDataRow

The `LoadDataRow` method takes as a parameter an array of values. It searches the table for a row with matching primary key columns. If it finds such a record, it uses the other values in the array to update the record. If it doesn't find a matching record, `LoadDataRow` uses the array's values to add a new row to the table.

This routine could be used to merge two related sets of data. For instance, suppose you have one database containing information about customers who have made purchases and another database that holds information about a product information mailing list. You could open the customer database and then use LoadDataRow to load the information in the mailing list database. If the customer database uses the customers' names as its primary key, then LoadDataRow will add the mailing list information to the customer data if it finds a matching name. If it doesn't find a mailing list record's name in the customer database, it creates a new record.

NewRow

The NewRow method creates a new DataRow object using the DataTable's schema. The program can then set the row's item values and add it to the DataTable's Rows collection.

Note that the Rows collection's Add method can also take an array of values as a parameter. In that case, it creates a new row using the values in the array to initialize the row's fields. If you don't need to manipulate the new row more directly, this method may be easier. The following code shows both methods:

```
' Get a reference to the DataTable.
Dim data_table As DataTable
data_table = dsEmployees.Tables("Managers")

' Add a new row using NewRow.
Dim new_row As DataRow
new_row = data_table.NewRow()
new_row.Item("LastName") = "Appleby"
new_row.Item("FirstName") = "Andrew"
dt.Rows.Add(new_row)

' Add a new row using an array of values.
Dim data_values() As String = {"Benny", "Barbara"}
data_table.Rows.Add(data_values)
```

PrimaryKey

The PrimaryKey property gets or sets an array of DataColumn objects that describe the fields the DataTable should use as its primary key. This property is an array because the primary key can include more than one column. For instance, the following code makes the primary key for the Managers DataTable include the fields LastName and FirstName:

```
Dim data_table As DataTable
Dim primary_key_columns(1) As DataColumn

data_table = dsEmployees.Tables("Managers")
primary_key_columns(0) = data_table.Columns("LastName")
primary_key_columns(1) = data_table.Columns("FirstName")
dt.PrimaryKey = primary_key_columns
```

Primary key values must be unique for each record. If you try to insert two records with the same primary key values, the program raises an error.

For the same reason, if you try to set the PrimaryKey property and the table's records do not currently have unique values for the primary key columns, the program raises an error.

ChildRelations **AND** ParentRelations

The ChildRelations and ParentRelations methods return collections of DataRelation objects that define the relationships between this table and others. For instance, suppose the Customers table lists customer information. The CustomerAddresses table holds address information for the customers. A common CustomerId field links the two tables. In this example, the Customers table is the parent and the Addresses table is the child in the relationship.

A DataRelation object holds references to the DataColumn objects representing the related fields in the two tables. The relation can cascade changes from a parent row to child rows depending on the constraints on the child table. The next section has a bit more to say about this.

Constraints

The Constraints collection contains references to Constraint objects that restrict the table's behavior. The Constraint class has two subclasses: UniqueConstraint and ForeignKeyConstraint.

UniqueConstraint

The UniqueConstraint is relatively simple. It defines a set of columns in the table that must have a unique combination of values. Example program Unique, shown in Figure 5.1, adds a unique constraint to the LastName and FirstName fields in the People table. If you try to create a new record that has the same LastName and FirstName values as an existing record, the UniqueConstraint object raises an error.

Figure 5.1
Program Unique requires that all People records have unique LastName and FirstName values.

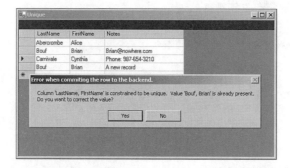

PART I CH 5

Program Unique uses the code shown in Listing 5.5 to build its UniqueConstraint. The form's Load event handler begins by creating the People table. It creates a new UniqueConstraint object that refers to the LastName and FirstName fields, and adds the constraint to the table's Constraints collection.

The routine then creates some People records and attaches the People DataTable to the dgPeople DataGrid control for easy viewing. If you try to add a new record to the DataGrid that has the same `LastName` and `FirstName` values as an existing record, the constraint raises an error and you see the message shown in Figure 5.1.

LISTING 5.5   A `UniqueConstraint` OBJECT REQUIRES FIELDS TO HOLD UNIQUE VALUES

```
Private m_DataSet As DataSet
Private m_dtPeople As DataTable

Private Sub Form1_Load(ByVal sender As Object, _
  ByVal e As System.EventArgs) Handles MyBase.Load
    ' Build the DataSet.
    m_DataSet = New DataSet()

    ' Build the People table.
    m_dtPeople = New DataTable("People")
    m_DataSet.Tables.Add(m_dtPeople)
    m_dtPeople.Columns.Add("LastName", GetType(String))
    m_dtPeople.Columns.Add("FirstName", GetType(String))
    m_dtPeople.Columns.Add("Notes", GetType(String))

    ' Make the UniqueConstraint on LastName
    ' and FirstName.
    Dim data_columns(1) As DataColumn
    Dim unique_constraint As UniqueConstraint

    data_columns(0) = m_dtPeople.Columns("LastName")
    data_columns(1) = m_dtPeople.Columns("FirstName")
    unique_constraint = New UniqueConstraint(data_columns)
    m_dtPeople.Constraints.Add(unique_constraint)

    ' Populate the People table.
    Dim people_data(2) As String
    people_data(0) = "Abercrombe"
    people_data(1) = "Alice"
    people_data(2) = ""
    m_dtPeople.Rows.Add(people_data)

    people_data(0) = "Bouf"
    people_data(1) = "Brian"
    people_data(2) = "Brian@nowhere.com"
    m_dtPeople.Rows.Add(people_data)

    people_data(0) = "Carnivale"
    people_data(1) = "Cynthia"
    people_data(2) = "Phone: 987-654-3210"
    m_dtPeople.Rows.Add(people_data)

    ' Attach the DataGrid to the DataTable.
    dgPeople.DataSource = m_dtPeople
End Sub
```

ForeignKeyConstraint

A `ForeignKeyConstraint` is more complex than a `UniqueConstraint`. . A foreign key is a value in one table on which a value in another table depends. For instance, suppose the

States table lists states and their abbreviations. The Addresses table contains address information and includes a State field. A foreign key constraint could require that every entry in the Addresses.State field be present in the States.Abbreviation field. If the program tried to create an Addresses record where the State field was AA, the ForeignKeyConstraint object would raise an error because that value is not in the States table.

The ForeignKeyConstraint object has several properties that determine its behavior. The DeleteRule and UpdateRule properties are both enumerations of type Rule. The Rule enumeration has the values listed in Table 5.2.

TABLE 5.2   Rule ENUMERATION VALUES

Value	Meaning
Cascade	Deletes or updates the related rows.
None	Related rows are unchanged.
SetDefault	Values in related rows are set to their default values.
SetNull	Values in related rows are set to NULL.

Changes to a DataTable are not final until the program calls AcceptChanges. At that time, the ForeignKeyConstraint object can take further action. If the AcceptRejectRule property is set to Cascade, the changes cascade to the child table. If this property is set to None, the object takes no further action.

For example, suppose the Addresses and States tables are related with a ForeignKeyConstraint object with UpdateRule property set to Rule.Cascade. If the program changes the States.Abbreviation value WY to WX, any Addresses records that use the value WY are also automatically changed to WX. Example program ForeignKey, shown in Figure 5.2, demonstrates this kind of foreign key constraint.

Figure 5.2
When you change a States.Abbreviat ion value in program ForeignKey, the ForeignKeyConstr aint cascades the change to the child table Addresses.

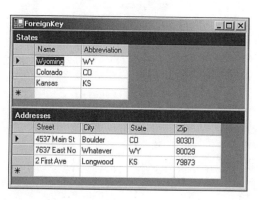

Program ForeignKey uses the code shown in Listing 5.6 to demonstrate foreign keys. When the program's form loads, the Load event handler executes. It starts by creating a new DataSet and by defining the States and Addresses tables.

It then creates a ForeignKeyConstraint object linking the States.Abbreviation column to the Addresses.State column. The States.Abbreviation column determines the values allowed for the Addresses.State column so it is the parent and is listed first in the ForeignKeyConstraint constructor. The Addresses.State column is the dependant or child field so its column is listed second.

> **Note**
>
> One way to remember which row is the parent and which is the child is to realize that a parent can have many children but a child can usually have only one parent (speaking in the sense of tree data structures not human reproduction). One States record can correspond to many Addresses records, so the States record is the parent and the Addresses records are the children.

After making the new constraint, the code adds the constraint to the child table's Constraints collection.

Next the program populates the States table and adds records to the Addresses table. At this point, the ForeignKeyConstraint is in effect and the new Addresses records must have State values that are present in the States table.

After it has loaded all the data, the program attaches the m_dtStates and m_dtAddresses DataTable objects to two DataGrids so you can see the tables' values.

LISTING 5.6   THIS CODE DEMONSTRATES ForeignKeyConstraint OBJECTS

```
Private m_DataSet As DataSet
Private m_dtStates As DataTable
Private m_dtAddresses As DataTable

Private Sub Form1_Load(ByVal sender As Object, _
    ByVal e As System.EventArgs) Handles MyBase.Load
    ' Build the DataSet.
    m_DataSet = New DataSet()

    ' Build the States table.
    m_dtStates = New DataTable("States")
    m_DataSet.Tables.Add(m_dtStates)
    m_dtStates.Columns.Add("Name", GetType(String))
    m_dtStates.Columns.Add("Abbreviation", GetType(String))

    ' Build the Addresses table.
    m_dtAddresses = New DataTable("Addresses")
    m_DataSet.Tables.Add(m_dtAddresses)
    m_dtAddresses.Columns.Add("Street", GetType(String))
    m_dtAddresses.Columns.Add("City", GetType(String))
    m_dtAddresses.Columns.Add("State", GetType(String))
    m_dtAddresses.Columns.Add("Zip", GetType(String))
    ' Make the ForeignKeyConstraint linking
    ' Addresses.State to States.Abbreviation.
    Dim foreign_key As ForeignKeyConstraint
    foreign_key = New ForeignKeyConstraint( _
```

LISTING 5.6   CONTINUED

```
        m_dtStates.Columns("Abbreviation"), _
        m_dtAddresses.Columns("State"))
    foreign_key.AcceptRejectRule = AcceptRejectRule.Cascade
    foreign_key.DeleteRule = Rule.Cascade
    foreign_key.UpdateRule = Rule.Cascade
    m_dtAddresses.Constraints.Add(foreign_key)

    ' Populate the States table.
    Dim state_data(1) As String
    state_data(0) = "Wyoming"
    state_data(1) = "WY"
    m_dtStates.Rows.Add(state_data)

    state_data(0) = "Colorado"
    state_data(1) = "CO"
    m_dtStates.Rows.Add(state_data)

    state_data(0) = "Kansas"
    state_data(1) = "KS"
    m_dtStates.Rows.Add(state_data)

    ' Populate the Addresses table.
    Dim address_data(3) As String
    address_data(0) = "4537 Main St"
    address_data(1) = "Boulder"
    address_data(2) = "CO"
    address_data(3) = "80301"
    m_dtAddresses.Rows.Add(address_data)

    address_data(0) = "7637 East North St #4"
    address_data(1) = "Whatever"
    address_data(2) = "WY"
    address_data(3) = "80029"
    m_dtAddresses.Rows.Add(address_data)

    address_data(0) = "2 First Ave"
    address_data(1) = "Longwood"
    address_data(2) = "KS"
    address_data(3) = "79873"
    m_dtAddresses.Rows.Add(address_data)

    ' Attach the DataGrids to the DataTables.
    dgStates.DataSource = m_dtStates
    dgAddresses.DataSource = m_dtAddresses
End Sub
```

Click on an Abbreviation field in the States grid and change its value. The ForeignKeyConstraint automatically updates the Addresses table and the DataGrid shows the change.

HasErrors, AcceptChanges, RejectChanges, Clear, AND GetChanges

The DataTable's HasErrors, AcceptChanges, RejectChanges, Clear, and GetChanges methods mirror those of the DataSet class. A DataSet object simply passes requests for these methods on to its DataTable objects. For example, the DataSet's `HasChanges` method calls the `HasChanges` method for each of the DataTable objects in the `Tables` collection. If any of those calls returns `True`, the original call to `HasChanges` returns `True`.

See the sections earlier in this chapter describing these methods for the DataSet object for details about what they do.

GetErrors

The `GetErrors` method returns an array of DataRow objects representing the DataTable rows that have errors. This includes rows with a row error set by the DataRow's `RowError` property, and rows with column errors set by the DataRow's `SetColumnError` method.

The program can loop through this array taking action on the rows with problems. Program DataErrors, shown in Figure 5.3, shows how to create, display, and remove errors. Select a DataGrid cell, enter an error message in the upper TextBox, and click Row Error to place an error on that row. Select a cell, enter a message in the lower TextBox, and click Column Error to place an error on that row's column. When you add errors to the rows, the DataGrid control automatically displays the exclamation mark icons shown in Figure 5.3.

When you click the List Errors button, the program uses the `GetErrors` method to retrieve an array containing rows with errors. It loops through the array, building a string that displays all the rows' error messages.

When you click the Clear Errors button, the program also uses the `GetErrors` method to fetch the rows with errors. It loops through this array calling each row's `ClearErrors` method to remove its row and column errors.

Figure 5.3
Program DataErrors
shows how to set,
read, and clear row
and column errors.

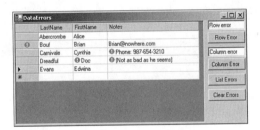

Program DataErrors uses the code shown in Listing 5.7 to set, display, and clear errors. The Row Error button finds the DataRow corresponding to the DataGrid's current row and sets its `RowError` property.

The Column Error button finds the DataRow corresponding to the DataGrid's current row. It uses that object's `SetColumnError` method to assign an error message to the field corresponding to the DataGrid's current cell.

The List Errors button uses `GetErrors` to fill an array with the DataRow objects for the rows that have errors. For each DataRow in the array, the program adds the row's error to the output text. It then calls the DataRow's `GetColumnsInError` method to fill an array with

DataColumn objects corresponding to the row's columns that have errors. It loops through the columns adding the column error messages to the output text. When it has finished looping through all of the DataRow objects, the program displays the combined list of error messages.

The Clear Errors button uses GetErrors to fill an array with DataRow objects corresponding to rows with errors much as the List Errors button does. The program then loops through the DataRows, calling their ClearErrors methods. The button finishes by calling the DataGrid control's Refresh method to make it remove the error icons it is displaying.

LISTING 5.7 PROGRAM DATAERRORS DEMONSTRATES ROW AND COLUMN ERRORS

```
' Place a row error on the current row.
Private Sub btnRowError_Click(ByVal sender As System.Object, _
   ByVal e As System.EventArgs) Handles btnRowError.Click
    Dim data_row As DataRow

    data_row = m_dtPeople.Rows(dgPeople.CurrentCell.RowNumber)
    data_row.RowError = txtRowError.Text
End Sub

' Place a column error on the current field.
Private Sub btnColumnError_Click(ByVal sender As System.Object, _
   ByVal e As System.EventArgs) Handles btnColumnError.Click
    Dim data_row As DataRow

    data_row = m_dtPeople.Rows(dgPeople.CurrentCell.RowNumber)
    data_row.SetColumnError(dgPeople.CurrentCell.ColumnNumber,
txtColumnError.Text)
End Sub

' List the errors.
Private Sub btnListErrors_Click(ByVal sender As System.Object, _
   ByVal e As System.EventArgs) Handles btnListErrors.Click
    Dim rows_in_error() As DataRow
    Dim cols_in_error() As DataColumn
    Dim data_row As DataRow
    Dim r As Integer
    Dim c As Integer
    Dim txt As String

    ' Get the rows with errors.
    rows_in_error = m_dtPeople.GetErrors

    ' Loop through the rows.
    For r = 0 To rows_in_error.GetUpperBound(0)
        ' Get the next row with an error.
        data_row = rows_in_error(r)
        txt = txt & data_row.Item(0) & ": " & data_row.RowError & vbCrLf

        ' Get the columns in error for this row.
        cols_in_error = data_row.GetColumnsInError

        ' Loop through the columns.
        For c = 0 To cols_in_error.GetUpperBound(0)
```

LISTING 5.7   CONTINUED

```
                txt = txt & "   (" & cols_in_error(c).ColumnName & ") " & _
                    data_row.GetColumnError(cols_in_error(c)) & vbCrLf
            Next c
        Next r

        ' Display the results.
        MsgBox(txt)
    End Sub

    ' Clear all errors.
    Private Sub btnClearErrors_Click(ByVal sender As System.Object, _
      ByVal e As System.EventArgs) Handles btnClearErrors.Click
        Dim rows_in_error() As DataRow
        Dim r As Integer

        ' Get the rows with errors.
        rows_in_error = m_dtPeople.GetErrors

        ' Loop through the rows.
        For r = 0 To rows_in_error.GetUpperBound(0)
            ' Clear this row's errors.
            rows_in_error(r).ClearErrors()
        Next r

        ' Remove the error icons from the DataGrid.
        dgPeople.Refresh()
    End Sub
```

Clone AND Copy

The Clone method creates a new DataTable object with the same structure as the current DataTable. The Copy method makes a new DataTable object with the same structure and data as the current DataTable.

DATATABLE EVENTS

The DataTable object provides several events that can help you keep track of changes to the data. The ColumnChanging event fires when a DataRow's column value is about to change. The program can use the event handler's DataColumnChangeEventArgs parameter to examine the column's current and proposed values. The event handler cannot cancel the change, but it can reset the column's proposed value to be the same as its current value, effectively negating the change.

The ColumnChanged event handler fires after a column's value has been changed. This event fires even if you set the column's proposed value equal to its current value in the ColumnChanging event handler. When ColumnChanged fires, the proposed value and current value both contain the new value and changing the proposed value doesn't affect the column's new value.

The RowChanging, RowChanged, RowDeleting, and RowDeleted events are informative. They tell you that one of the DataTable's rows is changing or has just changed, but they do not let you cancel or modify the change.

Example program DataEvents uses the code shown in Listing 5.8 to demonstrate these event handlers. Click on the DataGrid's cells and make changes. When you move to a new field, the appropriate events fire.

If you modify a cell's value and move to a new cell, the program's ColumnChanging event handler asks if you want to accept the change. If you do not accept the changes, the event handler sets the column's proposed value to its current value. The ColumnChanged, RowChanging, and RowChanged event handlers still fire, however, and the data is flagged as modified so the DataSet's HasChanges property returns True.

LISTING 5.8 PROGRAM DATAEVENTS DEMONSTRATES DATATABLE EVENTS

```
Private m_DataSet As DataSet
Private WithEvents m_dtPeople As DataTable

Private Sub Form1_Load(ByVal sender As Object, _
   ByVal e As System.EventArgs) Handles MyBase.Load
      ' Build the DataSet.
    m_DataSet = New DataSet()

    ' Build the People table.
    ...

    ' Populate the People table.
    ...

    ' Attach the DataGrid to the DataTable.
    dgPeople.DataSource = m_dtPeople

    ' Mark all the new data as permanent.
    m_dtPeople.AcceptChanges()
    Debug.WriteLine("*** Data loaded. Accepted changes")
    Debug.WriteLine("HasChanges: " & m_DataSet.HasChanges.ToString)
End Sub

' See if the user wants to allow this change.
Private Sub m_dtPeople_ColumnChanging(ByVal sender As Object, _
   ByVal e As System.Data.DataColumnChangeEventArgs) _
   Handles m_dtPeople.ColumnChanging
     Dim from_value As String = "" & e.Row.Item(e.Column)
     Dim to_value As String = "" & e.ProposedValue

     Debug.WriteLine("ColumnChanging: From '" & _
       from_value & "' to '" & to_value & "'")
     If MsgBox("ColumnChanging: Allow change from '" & _
       from_value & "' to '" & to_value & "'?", MsgBoxStyle.YesNo) = _
       MsgBoxResult.No _
     Then
         e.ProposedValue = e.Row.Item(e.Column)
     End If
```

LISTING 5.8 CONTINUED

```
      Debug.WriteLine("HasChanges: " & m_DataSet.HasChanges.ToString)
End Sub

' Tell the user the value has changed.
Private Sub m_dtPeople_ColumnChanged(ByVal sender As Object, _
  ByVal e As System.Data.DataColumnChangeEventArgs) _
  Handles m_dtPeople.ColumnChanged
    Debug.WriteLine("ColumnChanged")
    Debug.WriteLine("HasChanges: " & m_DataSet.HasChanges.ToString)
End Sub

' Tell the user the row is changing.
Private Sub m_dtPeople_RowChanging(ByVal sender As Object, _
  ByVal e As System.Data.DataRowChangeEventArgs) Handles m_dtPeople.RowChanging
    Debug.WriteLine("RowChanging: Action " & e.Action.ToString)
    Debug.WriteLine("HasChanges: " & m_DataSet.HasChanges.ToString)
End Sub

' Tell the user the row changed.
Private Sub m_dtPeople_RowChanged(ByVal sender As Object, _
  ByVal e As System.Data.DataRowChangeEventArgs) Handles m_dtPeople.RowChanged
    Debug.WriteLine("RowChanged: Action " & e.Action.ToString)
    Debug.WriteLine("HasChanges: " & m_DataSet.HasChanges.ToString)
End Sub

' Tell the user the row is being deleted.
Private Sub m_dtPeople_RowDeleting(ByVal sender As Object, _
  ByVal e As System.Data.DataRowChangeEventArgs) Handles m_dtPeople.RowDeleting
    Debug.WriteLine("RowDeleting")
    Debug.WriteLine("HasChanges: " & m_DataSet.HasChanges.ToString)
End Sub

' Tell the user the row was deleted.
Private Sub m_dtPeople_RowDeleted(ByVal sender As Object, _
  ByVal e As System.Data.DataRowChangeEventArgs) Handles m_dtPeople.RowDeleted
    Debug.WriteLine("RowDeleted")
    Debug.WriteLine("HasChanges: " & m_DataSet.HasChanges.ToString)
End Sub
```

DataRow

The DataRow object represents a record in the DataTable. Its Item method provides access to its field values.

You have already seen some of the more useful DataRow properties and methods in the previous sections. The following sections review some of those methods and refer to the earlier sections for examples.

Item

The Item method gives access to the row's field values. The most common ways to find a value in the Item collection are by field name and by number. For example, the following code sets the value of a DataRow's LastName field and then displays the value of its first field:

```
data_row.Item("LastName") = "Stephens"
MsgBox(data_row.Item(0))
```

The Item method can also take a DataColumn object as an index. Because the DataColumn's ColumnName property gives the column's name, the following two statements are roughly equivalent:

```
MsgBox(data_row.Item(data_column))
MsgBox(data_row.Item(data_column.ColumnName))
```

The Item method can also take a second parameter indicating the row version it should access. For example, the following code displays the original value of the row's LastName parameter:

```
MsgBox(data_row.Item("LastName", DataRowVersion.Original))
```

In addition to the DataRowVersion value Original, this parameter can take the values Default, Current, and Proposed.

ItemArray

The ItemArray method returns or defines the DataRow's field values using an array. The following code defines a DataRow's fields using an array of values:

```
Dim data_values() As Object = {"Johnson", "Wendy", "wendyj@vb-helper.com"}

data_row.ItemArray = data_values
```

The following code reads a DataRow's field values into an array and then prints them in the Debug window:

```
Dim data_values() As Object
Dim c As Integer

data_values = data_row.ItemArray
For c = 0 To data_values.GetUpperBound(0)
    MsgBox(data_values(c))
Next c
```

PART

I

CH

5

ERROR METHODS

The DataRow object provides several error-related methods. The RowError property gets or sets an error string for the DataRow. You can use this property to note a problem with the row.

The SetColumnError method sets error text for a specific column in the DataRow. GetColumnError retrieves the error. The GetColumnsInError method returns an array of DataColumn objects representing the columns with errors. A program can loop through this array to examine the errors without examining all the DataRow's fields.

The DataRow's HasErrors method returns True if the row's RowError property is set, or if any of its columns has an error set. The ClearErrors method clears all the row's errors, including the RowError property and any errors set on the row's columns.

The DataErrors example program described in the "GetErrors" section earlier in this chapter demonstrates these methods.

RowState

The RowState property indicates the row's current state. Table 5.3 lists the values this property can have.

TABLE 5.3 ROW STATES

State	Meaning
Added	The row was added.
Deleted	The row was deleted.
Detached	The row was created by the DataTable's NewRow method but has not yet been added to the DataTable's Rows collection.
Modified	The row's data has been modified.
Unchanged	The row has not been changed since the data was loaded or the last call to AcceptChanges or RejectChanges.

If you call the DataTable's AcceptChanges method, any pending changes are made permanent. After that point, all the table's DataRow objects have a RowState of Unchanged.

Similarly if you call a DataTable's RejectChanges method, any pending changes are discarded and the remaining DataRow objects have a RowState of Unchanged.

AcceptChanges AND RejectChanges

The AcceptChanges method makes permanent any changes that have been made to the row since the data was loaded or since the last call to AcceptChanges or RejectChanges. If the row was added or modified, its RowState is changed to Unmodified. If the row was deleted, it is permanently removed from the DataTable's Rows collection.

The RejectChanges method removes any changes made to the row since the data was loaded or since the last call to AcceptChanges or RejectChanges. If the row was deleted or modified, its original data is restored and its RowState is reset to Unchanged. If the row was added, it is permanently removed.

BeginEdit, CancelEdit, AND EndEdit

The BeginEdit method puts the DataRow in a *temporary editing mode*. While it is in this mode, the object does not raise its normal editing events. That lets you make changes to more than one DataRow, temporarily bypassing data validation.

The CancelEdit method cancels the edit operation, ends the temporary editing mode, and restores the DataRow's original values. EndEdit accepts the DataRow's new values and ends the temporary editing mode.

Delete

The `Delete` method removes the DataRow from its parent DataTable. You can recover the original value by calling the `RejectChanges` method. You make the change permanent by calling `AcceptChanges`.

GetChildRows, GetParentRow, GetParentRows, AND SetParentRow

The `GetChildRows` method takes as a parameter a DataRelation object defining a relation between this DataRow and others. It returns an array of DataRow objects that are children of the current row under this relation.

The `GetParentRow` method also takes a DataRelation object as a parameter. It returns the row's parent row under the relation.

If the row has more than one parent, the `GetParentRow` method raises an error. In that case, you need to use the `GetParentRows` method to retrieve an array containing the row's parents.

The `SetParentRow` method sets a row's parent under a relation. This effectively changes the row's fields that define the `DataRelation`. For instance, suppose the database contains two tables: `States` and `Addresses`. A `DataRelation` connects the `States.Abbreviation` parent field with the `Addresses.State` child field. Now suppose an `Addresses` record has `State` value `CO`. That row's parent row is the `States` record with `Abbreviation` value `CO`. You can use the `Addresses` row's `SetParentRow` method to change the row's parent to the `States` row with `Abbreviation` value `KS`. When it does this, `SetParentRow` changes the `Addresses.State` field's value to `KS`.

Example program Relations, shown in Figure 5.4, demonstrates the `GetChildRows` and `GetParentRows` methods.

Figure 5.4
Program Relations demonstrates parent and child relations between records.

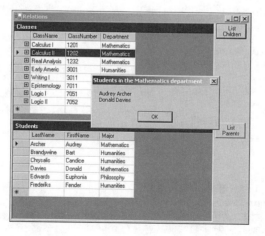

In this example, the `Classes` table's `Department` field is related to the `Students` table's `Major` field. Because these fields contain duplicate values in both tables, this is a many-to-many relationship. For example, the three classes with a Department value of Mathematics are related to the two student records with a Major value of Mathematics.

Select a row in the upper DataGrid and click List Children to see a list of the row's children. In Figure 5.4, the Calculus II row was selected so the program is showing the student records where Major is Mathematics. Select a row in the lower DataGrid and click List Parents to show the row's parents.

Listing 5.9 shows the most interesting parts of program Relations. The form's Load event handler defines the tables, creates a DataRelation to tie them together, and creates some sample records.

The List Children button's Click event handler finds the Classes DataRow corresponding to the upper DataGrid's current row. It uses the GetChildren method to make an array of child nodes and then loops through them, adding the Students records' names to the output string. When it has examined all the child rows, the routine displays the string.

The List Parents button finds the Students DataRow corresponding to the lower DataGrid's current row. It uses the GetParentRows method to make an array containing the Students row's parents in the Classes table. It loops through the rows adding values to an output string. When it has examined all the parent rows, the code displays the string.

LISTING 5.9 PROGRAM RELATIONS DEMONSTRATES THE GetChildren AND GetParentRows METHODS

```
Private m_DataSet As DataSet
Private m_dtClasses As DataTable
Private m_dtStudents As DataTable
Private m_DataRelation As DataRelation

Private Sub Form1_Load(ByVal sender As Object, _
    ByVal e As System.EventArgs) Handles MyBase.Load
    ' Build the DataSet.
    m_DataSet = New DataSet()

    ' Build the Classes table.
    m_dtClasses = New DataTable("Classes")
    m_DataSet.Tables.Add(m_dtClasses)
    m_dtClasses.Columns.Add("ClassName", GetType(String))
    m_dtClasses.Columns.Add("ClassNumber", GetType(Integer))
    m_dtClasses.Columns.Add("Department", GetType(String))

    ' Build the Students table.
    m_dtStudents = New DataTable("Students")
    m_DataSet.Tables.Add(m_dtStudents)
    m_dtStudents.Columns.Add("LastName", GetType(String))
    m_dtStudents.Columns.Add("FirstName", GetType(String))
    m_dtStudents.Columns.Add("Major", GetType(String))

    ' Make a DataRelation relating the Department
    ' and Major columns. The constructor's final parameter
    ' says the DataRelation should not create constraints
    ' (which would require a one-to-many relationship).
```

LISTING 5.9   CONTINUED

```
    m_DataRelation = New DataRelation( _
        "ClassStudents", _
        m_dtClasses.Columns("Department"), _
        m_dtStudents.Columns("Major"), _
        False)
    m_DataSet.Relations.Add(m_DataRelation)

    ' Populate the Classes table.
    Dim class_data(2) As Object
    class_data(0) = "Calculus I"
    class_data(1) = 1201
    class_data(2) = "Mathematics"
    m_dtClasses.Rows.Add(class_data)

    ' Code to create more records deleted...

    ' Populate the Students table.
    Dim student_data(2) As Object
    student_data(0) = "Archer"
    student_data(1) = "Audrey"
    student_data(2) = "Mathematics"
    m_dtStudents.Rows.Add(student_data)

    ' Code to create more records deleted...

    ' Accept the data.
    m_DataSet.AcceptChanges()

    ' Attach the DataGrids to the DataTables.
    dgClasses.DataSource = m_dtClasses
    dgStudents.DataSource = m_dtStudents
End Sub

' List the Classes record's child rows.
Private Sub btnListChildren_Click(ByVal sender As System.Object, _
  ByVal e As System.EventArgs) Handles btnListChildren.Click
    Dim class_row As DataRow
    Dim child_rows() As DataRow
    Dim i As Integer
    Dim txt As String

    ' Get the class row.
    class_row = m_dtClasses.Rows(dgClasses.CurrentCell.RowNumber)

    ' Get the children.
    child_rows = class_row.GetChildRows(m_DataRelation)

    ' Loop through the children.
    For i = 0 To child_rows.GetUpperBound(0)
        txt = txt & child_rows(i).Item("FirstName") & " " & _
        child_rows(i).Item("LastName") & vbCrLf
    Next i
    MsgBox(txt, MsgBoxStyle.OKOnly, _
        "Students in the " & class_row.Item("Department") & " department")
End Sub
```

PART

I

CH

5

LISTING 5.9   CONTINUED

```
' List the Student record's parent rows.
Private Sub btnListParents_Click(ByVal sender As System.Object, _
  ByVal e As System.EventArgs) Handles btnListParents.Click
    Dim student_row As DataRow
    Dim parent_rows() As DataRow
    Dim i As Integer
    Dim txt As String

    ' Get the Student row.
    student_row = m_dtStudents.Rows(dgStudents.CurrentCell.RowNumber)

    ' Get the parent.
    parent_rows = student_row.GetParentRows(m_DataRelation)

    ' Display the state's abbreviation.
    For i = 0 To parent_rows.GetUpperBound(0)
        txt = txt & parent_rows(i).Item("ClassName") & vbCrLf
    Next i
    MsgBox(txt, MsgBoxStyle.OKOnly, _
        "Classes in " & student_row.Item("FirstName") & " " & _
            student_row.Item("LastName") & "'s department")
End Sub
```

Program Relations uses two DataGrid controls to display the DataSet's two tables. Because the tables are related by a DataRelation, the DataGrid control can provide some navigation between the tables automatically. If you click on the plus sign to the left of an entry in the upper DataGrid, the control expands the entry to show a list of its child relations. Figure 5.5 shows that the Calculus I entry has a child relation named ClassStudents.

Figure 5.5
The DataGrid lists a record's child relations.

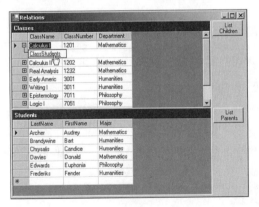

If you click on the relation, the DataGrid displays the row's child rows as shown in Figure 5.6. The rows shown in the top DataGrid are the child rows of the row whose DataRelation you clicked, not all the rows in the Students table. The top of the grid shows the parent row's values. If you click the white left arrow in the grid's upper-right corner, the DataGrid closes the child rows and returns to the parent table shown in Figure 5.5.

Figure 5.6
The DataGrid can follow child relations to display a record's child rows.

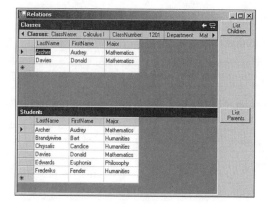

SetUnspecified

The SetUnspecified method takes as a parameter a DataColumn object. It sets the value of the DataRow's field corresponding to that column to Null. The DataColumn object has a ColumnName property giving the name of the column so the following two statements are equivalent:

```
data_row.SetUnspecified(data_column)
data_row.Item(data_column.ColumnName) = DBNull.Value
```

DATACOLUMN

The DataColumn object represents a column in a table. It contains information about the column itself rather than values stored in the column. For example, it holds the column's name but not the column's value for any given row.

The following sections explain some of the DataColumn's most useful properties and methods.

AllowDBNull, MaxLength, ReadOnly, Unique, AND DefaultValue

These properties set simple restrictions on the column's values. These restrictions are not enforced until you finish making changes to the row containing the modified fields. For example, suppose you are using a DataGrid to edit address records. The State field has a MaxLength value of 2 but you enter the value Wash. You can continue to edit that entry and you can even edit other entries in the same row. When you try to move to another row, however, the row finishes editing, checks its constraints, and discovers that you have violated the MaxLength condition. At that point, the program displays an error message and gives you a chance to correct the error.

The definitions of these properties are simple and are listed in Table 5.4.

TABLE 5.4   COLUMN RESTRICTING PROPERTIES

Property	Meaning
AllowDBNull	If AllowDBNull is False, the column cannot take the value Null.
MaxLength	This value gives the maximum number of characters allowed in the field.
ReadOnly	If ReadOnly is True, the column's value cannot be changed after the record is initially created.
Unique	If Unique is True, each row must have a different value for this column.
DefaultValue	This property holds the default value given to the field when a new record is initially created. Once the row is created, the program can assign the field any value it wants (satisfying other restrictions), including Null.

DataType

This property gets or sets the column's data type. The following code shows two ways to create DataColumn objects. The first method adds a new column using the DataTable's Columns collection. It passes the Add method the column's name and data type.

The second method creates the DataColumn first, sets its data type, and then adds it to the DataTable's Columns collection.

```
data_table.Columns.Add("LastName", GetType(String))

data_column = New DataColumn("Salary")
data_column.DataType = GetType(Decimal)
m_dtAddresses.Columns.Add(data_column)
```

The following list gives the Visual Basic .NET data types supported by the DataColumn object:

Boolean	Decimal	Int64
Byte	Double	SByte
Char	Int16	Single
DateTime	Int32	String

AutoIncrement, AutoIncrementSeed, AND AutoIncrementStep

If a DataColumn's AutoIncrement property is True, the column automatically generates values for new rows. It begins with the value specified by the AutoIncrementSeed property and increases the values by AutoIncrementStep each time. Program AutoIncr, shown in Figure 5.7, shows how to use these properties.

Program AutoIncr uses the code shown in Listing 5.10 to create and populate a DataTable. It builds the table and then creates a DataColumn object. It sets that object's AutoIncrement property to True, AutoIncrementSeed to 100, and AutoIncrementStep to 10. When it has finished defining the DataColumn, the program adds it to the table's Columns collection.

Figure 5.7
The DataGrid can follow child relations to display a record's child rows.

The program builds another column and then creates a series of data rows. In each case, it sets the value of the auto-incrementing column to Nothing. That tells the column to generate values itself. Because of the values selected for AutoIncrementSeed and AutoIncrementStep, the records receive the values 100, 110, 120, and so forth.

The Load event handler finishes by attaching the DataTable to the form's DataGrid control.

LISTING 5.10   PROGRAM AUTOINCR DEMONSTRATES AUTO-INCREMENTING FIELDS

```
Private m_DataSet As DataSet
Private m_dtFood As DataTable

Private Sub Form1_Load(ByVal sender As Object, _
    ByVal e As System.EventArgs) Handles MyBase.Load
        ' Build the DataSet.
    m_DataSet = New DataSet()

        ' Build the States table.
    m_dtFood = New DataTable("Food")
    m_DataSet.Tables.Add(m_dtFood)

    Dim number_column As DataColumn
    number_column = New DataColumn("Number", GetType(Integer))
    number_column.AutoIncrement = True
    number_column.AutoIncrementSeed = 100
    number_column.AutoIncrementStep = 10
    m_dtFood.Columns.Add(number_column)

    m_dtFood.Columns.Add("Name", GetType(String))

        ' Populate the Food table.
    Dim food_data(1) As Object
    food_data(0) = Nothing
    food_data(1) = "Apple"
    m_dtFood.Rows.Add(food_data)

    food_data(1) = "Banana"
    m_dtFood.Rows.Add(food_data)

    food_data(1) = "Cherry"
    m_dtFood.Rows.Add(food_data)
```

PART

I

CH

5

LISTING 5.10   CONTINUED

```
    food_data(1) = "Date"
    m_dtFood.Rows.Add(food_data)

    food_data(1) = "Egg"
    m_dtFood.Rows.Add(food_data)

    food_data(1) = "Fig"
    m_dtFood.Rows.Add(food_data)

    ' Accept the data.
    m_DataSet.AcceptChanges()

    ' Attach the DataGrid to the DataTable.
    dgStates.DataSource = m_dtFood
End Sub
```

The column only generates values if you do not specify a value for the column. If you change the previous code so it uses any value other than `Nothing` for `food_data(0)`, the column accepts that value instead of generating one of its own.

ColumnMapping

The `ColumnMapping` property determines how the column is saved in XML representations. This property can take the values `Attribute`, `Element`, `Hidden`, and `SimpleContent`.

Example program ColMapping demonstrates this property. It uses the code shown in Listing 5.11 to build an address table. It gives the table four columns that demonstrate each of the possible `ColumnMapping` property values.

LISTING 5.11   PROGRAM COLMAPPING DEMONSTRATES XML COLUMN MAPPINGS

```
' Build the Addresses table.
m_dtAddresses = New DataTable("Addresses")
m_DataSet.Tables.Add(m_dtAddresses)

data_column = New DataColumn("Street", GetType(String))
data_column.ColumnMapping = MappingType.Attribute
m_dtAddresses.Columns.Add(data_column)

data_column = New DataColumn("City", GetType(String))
data_column.ColumnMapping = MappingType.Element
m_dtAddresses.Columns.Add(data_column)

data_column = New DataColumn("State", GetType(String))
data_column.ColumnMapping = MappingType.Hidden
m_dtAddresses.Columns.Add(data_column)

data_column = New DataColumn("Zip", GetType(String))
data_column.ColumnMapping = MappingType.SimpleContent
m_dtAddresses.Columns.Add(data_column)
```

If you run the program and click the Show XML button, the program displays the DataSet's XML representation. Listing 5.12 shows the program's output. Notice how the different fields are mapped into the XML data. The Street column is saved as an attribute of the Addresses row. The City column is saved as a separate element inside the row. The State column is hidden so it is not saved in the XML data. Finally, the Zip column is saved as a simple text value inside the row.

LISTING 5.12   PROGRAM COLMAPPING GENERATED THIS OUTPUT

```
<NewDataSet>
  <Addresses Street="4537 Main St">
    <City>Boulder</City>80301</Addresses>
  <Addresses Street="#12 Wasserstrasse">
    <City>Deutschberg</City>80764</Addresses>
  <Addresses Street="1 2st St">
    <City>Ash</City>80692</Addresses>
  <Addresses Street="7637 East North St #4">
    <City>Whatever</City>80029</Addresses>
  <Addresses Street="821 Hideaway Ct J-16">
    <City>Hereiam</City>79928</Addresses>
  <Addresses Street="2 First Ave">
    <City>Longwood</City>79873</Addresses>
</NewDataSet>
```

ColumnName

The ColumnName property gives the name of the column. You can use this name to find the DataColumn object in a DataTable's Columns collection as in the following code:

```
data_column = data_table.Columns("Flavor")
```

This is also the name you use to find values in a DataRow's Item collection.

```
last_name = data_row.Item("LastName")
```

Expression

The DataColumn uses the Expression property to filter rows, calculate a value, or create aggregate columns. Example program ColExpression, shown in Figure 5.8, uses an expression to calculate a column value. The Total column's value is equal to the Quantity value times the UnitPrice value.

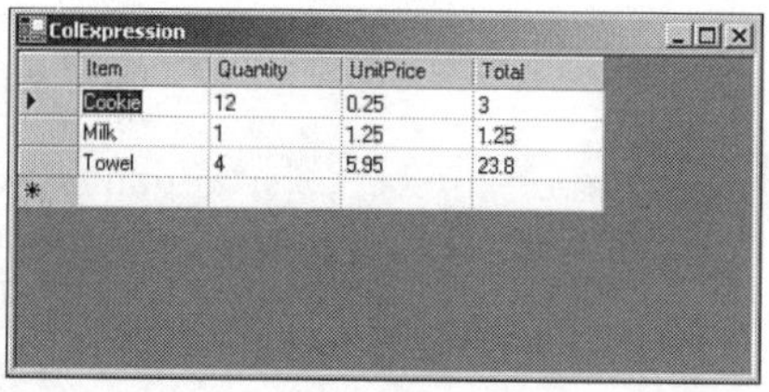

Figure 5.8
Program
ColExpression makes
a column display a
calculated value.

Program ColExpression uses the following code to define its columns. The Item, Quantity, and UnitPrice columns are straightforward. The program sets the Total column's Expression property to Quantity * UnitPrice to make it calculate the value.

```
' Build the Sale table.
m_dtSale = New DataTable("Sale")
m_DataSet.Tables.Add(m_dtSale)

m_dtSale.Columns.Add("Item", GetType(String))
m_dtSale.Columns.Add("Quantity", GetType(Integer))
m_dtSale.Columns.Add("UnitPrice", GetType(Decimal))

data_column = m_dtSale.Columns.Add("Total", GetType(Decimal))
data_column.Expression = "Quantity * UnitPrice"
```

You can also use the Expression property to form aggregates. For example, the Expression value SUM(Child.Price) calculates the total of the Price values in the row's child rows. More general expressions are quite complicated so they are not described further here. See the online help for more details.

Keep in mind that this and many other features of Visual Basic .NET's objects duplicate functions that are also provided by the underlying database. If you attach a DataTable object to a database table, you can use the SQL SELECT statement to include a calculated column in the results. For example, the following SELECT statement creates a calculated Total column similar to the one used by program ColExpression.

```
SELECT Item, Quantity, UnitPrice, Quantity * UnitPrice AS Total
FROM Orders
```

Ordinal

The Ordinal property simply returns the DataColumn's index in the DataTable's Columns collection. This property can be handy if you have a reference to a DataColumn object and want to know which field it represents.

For instance, suppose you use a DataTable's ChildRelations collection to examine the table's child relations. The DataRelation object's ChildColumns and ParentColumns collections give references to the DataColumn objects related through the DataRelation. You can use the DataColumn objects' Ordinal properties to see which fields these objects represent. Then you can use a DataRow's Item method using the Ordinal values to get the related field values for the DataRows.

DATARELATION

The DataRelation object represents a relationship between columns in a child table and columns in a parent table. Often there is a simple one-to-one mapping between the columns. For example, suppose the Customers table contains general customer information and the CustomerAddresses table contains the customers' addresses (mailing address, billing address, shipping address, and so forth). A common CustomerId field links the two tables. In this example, the DataRelation contains references to the CustomerId fields in the two tables. The following code shows how a program might create this relation:

```
customer_addresses_relation = New DataRelation( _
    "Customers_Addresses", _
    addresses_table.Columns("CustomerId"), _
    customers_table.Columns("CustomerId"))
data_set.Relations.Add(customer_addresses_relation)
```

In other cases, fields in one table may be related to fields with different names in another table. For instance, suppose the Employees table contains general employee information. The ProjectStaff table contains information about software project staffing. In this case, the ProjectStaff table's LeaderFirstName and LeaderLastName fields might correspond to the Employees table's FirstName and LastName fields.

Example program MultiColumnRelation uses the code shown in Listing 5.13 to build a relationship similar to this one.

LISTING 5.13   PROGRAM MULTICOLUMNRELATION DEMONSTRATES MULTI-COLUMN RELATIONS

```
' Build the DataSet.
m_DataSet = New DataSet()

' Build the Employees table.
m_dtEmployees = New DataTable("Employees")
m_DataSet.Tables.Add(m_dtEmployees)
m_dtEmployees.Columns.Add("FirstName", GetType(String))
m_dtEmployees.Columns.Add("LastName", GetType(String))
m_dtEmployees.Columns.Add("Phone", GetType(String))

' Build the ProjectStaff table.
m_dtProjectStaff = New DataTable("ProjectStaff")
m_DataSet.Tables.Add(m_dtProjectStaff)
m_dtProjectStaff.Columns.Add("ProjectName", GetType(String))
m_dtProjectStaff.Columns.Add("ProjectNumber", GetType(Integer))
m_dtProjectStaff.Columns.Add("LeaderFirstName", GetType(String))
m_dtProjectStaff.Columns.Add("LeaderLastName", GetType(String))

' Make a DataRelation linking the tables.
Dim parent_columns() As DataColumn = { _
    m_dtEmployees.Columns("FirstName"), _
    m_dtEmployees.Columns("LastName")}
Dim child_columns() As DataColumn = { _
    m_dtProjectStaff.Columns("LeaderFirstName"), _
    m_dtProjectStaff.Columns("LeaderLastName")}
Dim data_relation As DataRelation
data_relation = New DataRelation( _
    "Employees_ProjectStaff", parent_columns, child_columns)
m_DataSet.Relations.Add(data_relation)
```

Compared to some of Visual Basic's other data-related objects, the DataRelation object is relatively simple. The following sections briefly outline some of this object's most useful properties.

PART

I

CH

5

CONSTRUCTOR

The following code shows the syntax for the two most useful variations on the DataRelation object's constructors:

```
DataRelation(relation_name, column1, column2, create_constraints)
DataRelation(relation_name, column_array1(), column_array2(), create_constraints)
```

The first variation takes as parameters the name of the relation and two DataColumn objects that the DataRelation should connect. The second variation is similar except it takes arrays of columns to connect as its second and third parameters.

Both variations take an optional Boolean third parameter that tells the constructor whether it should create constraints for the relation. If this value is True or omitted, the constructor makes child and parent key constraints. See the section "ChildKeyConstraint and ParentKeyConstraint" later in this chapter for information on these constraints.

These constraints require that any child records have only one parent record. For example, suppose the States table has an abbreviation field that is related to the Addresses table's State field. If the constrictor builds these constraints, an Addresses record with a given State value must correspond to a single States record. That makes sense because the States table only needs to contain one record for each state.

In a less common situation, the child and parent tables can both contain multiple related records. For instance, suppose the Classes table contains information about a college's curriculum and the Students table contains information about the college's pupils. The Classes table has a Department field giving the department that teaches each class. The Students table has a Major field that gives the student's department. A particular department can have many classes and many students, so the relationship defined by these fields for these tables is a many-to-many relationship.

To build this relationship in code, the program must tell the DataRelation constructor not to create constraints. Otherwise the ParentKeyConstraint will prohibit duplicate Department field values in the Classes table and prevent you from creating the many-to-many relationship.

Note that this kind of relationship is unusual in database design. A more common design would use a third Departments table linked to the Classes and Students tables with one-to-many relationships.

ChildColumns AND ParentColumns

These properties return arrays containing the relation's child and parent DataColumn objects, respectively. These properties are read-only so you cannot use them to define the relation's columns. Set the relation's columns in its constructor.

ChildTable AND ParentTable

The ChildTable and ParentTable properties return references to the DataRelation's child and parent DataTable objects, respectively. These tables are the tables that own the DataColumn objects returned by the ChildColumns and ParentColumns properties.

ChildKeyConstraint AND ParentKeyConstraint

The ChildKeyConstraint property returns a ForeignKeyConstraint object that determines how changes to a parent row are propagated to child rows. The following code gets a reference to a DataRelation's ChildKeyConstraint. It sets the constraint's UpdateRule value to Rule.Cascade so any changes to the related columns in the parent record are transmitted to the child records.

The code also sets the DeleteRule to Rule.SetNull. If a parent row is deleted, the related fields in the child rows are set to Null. Without this change, the default behavior of the relation is to delete the child rows when the parent row is deleted.

```
Dim foreign_key_constraint As ForeignKeyConstraint
foreign_key_constraint = data_relation.ChildKeyConstraint
foreign_key_constraint.UpdateRule = Rule.Cascade
foreign_key_constraint.DeleteRule = Rule.SetNull
```

The ParentKeyConstraint property returns a reference to the UniqueConstraint object that requires the parent columns to have unique values.

RelationName

As you would probably guess, the RelationName property returns the DataRelation's name. You can use the name as a key to find a particular DataRelation in a DataSet's Relations collection, or in a DataTable's ChildRelations or ParentRelations collection.

DATAVIEW

A DataView object provides a view into a subset of the rows contained in a DataTable. DataView properties let you select rows with a certain state (added, deleted, modified, and so forth) or with certain data values.

A program can use more than one DataView attached to the same DataTable to provide different views of the data. DataViews can act as data sources for bound controls so they make displaying various selections of the data easy.

Example program DataViews, shown in Figure 5.9, uses a DataTable and three DataViews to easily display records in different states. If you add, modify, and delete records in the first DataGrid control, the others show the records that are added, modified, and deleted. This program sets the DataView objects' RowStateFilter properties to select the records they should display. This code is described in more detail in the section "RowFilter and RowStateFilter" that follows.

PART

I

CH

5

Figure 5.9
Program DataViews
uses DataView objects
to provide different
views into a table.

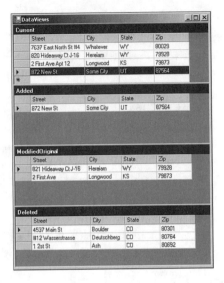

RowFilter AND RowStateFilter

The RowFilter property tells the DataView which data rows to select. This property's value is similar to a SQL SELECT statement's WHERE clause. For instance, the following code selects records from the underlying DataTable where the LastName field begins with S:

```
data_view.RowFilter = "LastName LIKE 'S%'"
```

The RowStateFilter property determines which row states the DataView will consider as it filters the DataTable's rows. The following statement makes the DataView select the original values of rows that have been modified:

```
data_view.RowStateFilter = DataViewRowState.ModifiedOriginal
```

After it loads its data, example program DataViews uses the code shown in Listing 5.14 to display different views of the same data. It attaches the dgCurrent DataGrid control directly to the DataTable holding all of the program's data. It then creates three different DataViews. It sets the RowStateFilter of the first to select added rows and attaches it to the dgAdded DataGrid control. The program makes the second DataView select the original values of rows that have been modified and attaches that view to the dgModified DataGrid. Finally, the program creates a DataView that selects deleted rows and attaches it to the DataGrid control named dgDeleted.

LISTING 5.14 PROGRAM DATAVIEWS DISPLAYS DATA USING THREE DATAVIEWS

```
' Attach dgCurrent to the DataTable.
dgCurrent.DataSource = m_dtAddresses

' Make DataViews to filter the data.
Dim dv As DataView

' Added.
```

LISTING 5.14   CONTINUED

```
dv = New DataView(m_dtAddresses)
dv.RowStateFilter = DataViewRowState.Added
dv.AllowDelete = False
dv.AllowEdit = False
dv.AllowNew = False
dgAdded.DataSource = dv

' Modified.
dv = New DataView(m_dtAddresses)
dv.RowStateFilter = DataViewRowState.ModifiedOriginal
dv.AllowDelete = False
dv.AllowEdit = False
dv.AllowNew = False
dgModified.DataSource = dv

' Deleted.
dv = New DataView(m_dtAddresses)
dv.RowStateFilter = DataViewRowState.Deleted
dv.AllowDelete = False
dv.AllowEdit = False
dv.AllowNew = False
dgDeleted.DataSource = dv
```

The `RowStateFilter` property can take the same `DataViewRowState` values as the DataTable's `Select` method. Those values are summarized in Table 5.1 earlier in this chapter.

AllowNew, AllowEdit, AND AllowDelete

These properties determine what operations are available through the DataView. If the DataView is bound to a control, the control will not let the user perform actions that are prohibited to the DataView. For example, if a DataView's `AllowDelete` property is `False`, a DataGrid control attached to the DataView will not let the user delete rows using the grid.

You can use these properties to prevent changes to the data without disabling bound controls. For instance, setting all three properties to `False` prevents the user from modifying the data using a DataGrid attached to the DataView. Setting the DataGrid's `Enabled` property to `False` would prevent the user from modifying the data, too, but it would also prevent the user from resizing the DataGrid's columns, clicking on its column headers to reorder the data, selecting values to copy to the Clipboard, and taking advantage of the DataGrid's other features.

You may need to use these properties to protect some of the DataTable's data. For example, a program cannot delete a record that is already deleted. If you build a DataView that uses the `RowStateFilter` property to select deleted records and you bind it to a DataGrid, you can make the program crash by deleting a deleted record with the DataGrid. Setting the DataView's `AllowDelete` property to `False` can prevent this problem.

Similarly, some actions might not make much sense. It makes little sense to allow the user to add records through a DataGrid bound to a DataView displaying deleted records. When the

PART
I

CH
5

user creates a new record, it is added to the underlying table but is not visible in the deleted record DataView.

Count AND Item

The Count property returns the number of rows selected by the DataView. The Item method returns a DataRowView item that references one of the rows selected by the DataView. For instance, the following code lists the LastName column in each row selected by a DataView:

```
For i = 0 To data_view.Count - 1
    Debug.WriteLine(data_view.Item(i).Item("LastName"))
Next i
```

AddNew AND Delete

The AddNew method creates a new row in the DataView's underlying table. The following code shows how a program can add a new record:

```
Dim data_row_view As DataRowView

data_row_view = data_view.AddNew()
data_row_view("Street") = "New Street"
data_row_view("City") = "New City"
data_row_view("State") = "New State"
data_row_view("Zip") = "New Zip"
```

The Delete method deletes a record from the DataView's underlying DataTable. The Delete method takes as a parameter the index of the record it should delete. Note that this is the record's index in the DataView not in the underlying table.

Sort AND Find

The Sort property tells the DataView on which columns it should sort its data. This property's value is similar to a SQL SELECT statement's ORDER BY clause. For example, the following code makes a DataView sort records by LastName and FirstName in descending order:

```
data_view.Sort = "LastName DESC, FirstName DESC"
```

The Find method returns the index of a DataView row that contains a specific primary key value. Listing 5.15 shows how a program might search a table for a particular record if the LastName and FirstName fields make up the primary key.

LISTING 5.15   THIS CODE FINDS THE RECORD FOR JEREMY JOHNSON

```
' Build the table.
...

' Build the primary key.
Dim primary_key(1) As DataColumn

primary_key(0) = data_table.Columns("FirstName")
primary_key(1) = data_table.Columns("LastName")
```

LISTING 5.15 CONTINUED

```
data_table.PrimaryKey = primary_key

' Populate the table.
...

' Find the record for Jeremy Johnson.
Dim values() As String = {
    "Jeremy", _
    "Johnson" _
}
Dim row_index As Integer

row_index = data_view.Find(values)
```

The Find method returns -1 if no record has the indicated primary key values.

DATAROWVIEW

The DataRowView object is relatively simple. It is returned by the DataView object's Item method and represents a single row in a DataTable.

The following sections describe the DataRowView's most interesting properties and methods.

Item

The Item method gets or sets the value of the row's indicated field. The following code shows two ways to set the LastName field's value, assuming the LastName field is the row's first field.

```
data_row_view.Item("LastName") = "Stephens"
data_row_view.Item(0) = "Stephens"
```

Row

The Row method returns the underlying DataRow attached to the DataRowView. You can use this property to perform actions on the DataRow that you cannot do with the DataRowView object. For example, you can set and clear errors on the DataRow object but not on the DataRowView object itself.

ROWVERSION

The RowVersion property returns one of the values listed in Table 5.5 to indicate the DataRowView's state.

TABLE 5.5 `DataRowView RowVersion` VALUES

Value	Meaning
`DataRowVersion.Default`	The row contains default values.
`DataRowVersion.Original`	The row has not been modified since it was loaded or the last call to `AcceptChanges` or `RejectChanges`.
`DataRowVersion.Current`	The DataRowView represents the row's current values.
`DataRowVersion.Proposed`	These are proposed modified values that have not yet been saved by a call to `AcceptChanges`.

Delete

The `Delete` method deletes the corresponding DataRow from the underlying DataTable. Like other changes to the DataTable, the deletion is not permanent until the program calls `AcceptChanges`.

SUMMARY

The DataSet object sits at the heart of a large family of objects that correspond closely to objects in a database. The DataSet object itself corresponds to the database. The DataSet contains DataTable objects corresponding to database tables. A DataTable contains DataRow, DataColumn, and constraint objects that correspond to rows, columns, and constraints on the data.

Using the DataSet family of objects, you can model most of the structures you can build using a relational database. This chapter shows how to use those objects and provides some simple examples that used compiled-in data. Chapter 6, "Database Connections," explains how you can move data between these objects and a relational database.

DATABASE CONNECTIONS

Chapter 5, "The DataSet Family of Objects," describes the objects your Visual Basic applications can use to manipulate a database. This chapter explains the objects you can use to move data between those objects and a database.

DATA CONNECTION METHODS

The objects described in Chapter 5 are generic so they work with any kind of database. It doesn't matter to a `DataTable` object whether you loaded its data from an Access database, a SQL Server database, an Oracle database, an XML file, or whether your program generated the data in the DataTable itself. Once the data is loaded, your program can use the DataTable's properties and methods to manipulate the data no matter where it came from.

When you want to move data between these objects and a data source, however, the difference matters. Visual Basic provides several objects and methods for working with different data sources. The most important of these methods work with program-generated data, XML data, SQL Server, and OLE DB.

The following sections describe these data access methods. The last sections in the chapter deal with the `CurrencyManager` class. This class helps coordinate data transfer between bound controls and data loaded using all these methods.

PROGRAM-GENERATED DATA

Chapter 5 explains methods you can use to load program-generated data. Example program ProgramGenerated, shown in Figure 6.1, creates a DataTable object and fills it with data. It then binds the DataTable to a `DataGrid` control to display the results.

The ProgramGenerated example program uses the code shown in Listing 6.1 to display its data. The form's `Load` event handler creates a new DataTable object. It uses the DataTable's `Columns` collection to add new columns to hold the rows' values. It then calls the `AddTableRow` helper subroutine to add the data values to the table.

Subroutine `AddTableRow` uses the DataTable object's `NewRow` method to create a new DataRow object for the table. It sets the values of the DataRow's items and then adds the DataRow to the DataTable's `Rows` collection.

Figure 6.1
Example program
ProgramGenerated
uses compiled-in data
to build a DataTable
and bind it to a
DataGrid control.

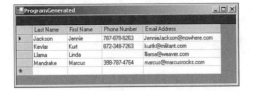

LISTING 6.1 THE PROGRAMGENERATED EXAMPLE LOADS A DATATABLE WITH COMPILED-IN DATA

```
' Create program-generated data.
Private Sub Form1_Load(ByVal sender As Object, _
  ByVal e As System.EventArgs) Handles MyBase.Load
    Dim data_table As New DataTable("Contacts")

    ' Define the columns.
    data_table.Columns.Add("Last Name", GetType(String))
    data_table.Columns.Add("First Name", GetType(String))
    data_table.Columns.Add("Phone Number", GetType(String))
    data_table.Columns.Add("Email Address", GetType(String))

    ' Create some data.
    AddTableRow(data_table, "Jackson", "Jennie", "787-878-8263", _
        "JennieJackson@nowhere.com")
    AddTableRow(data_table, "Kevlar", "Kurt", "872-348-7263",
"kurtk@militant.com")
    AddTableRow(data_table, "Llama", "Linda", "", "lllama@weaver.com")
    AddTableRow(data_table, "Mandrake", "Marcus", "398-787-4764", _
        "marcus@marcusrocks.com")

    ' Bind the DataTable to the DataGrid.
    dgContacts.DataSource = data_table
End Sub

' Add a new row to the DataTable.
Private Sub AddTableRow(ByVal data_table As DataTable, _
 ByVal last_name As String, _
 ByVal first_name As String,_
 ByVal phone_number As String,
  ByVal email_address As String)
    Dim data_row As DataRow

    data_row = data_table.NewRow()
    data_row.Item("Last Name") = last_name
    data_row.Item("First Name") = first_name
    data_row.Item("Phone Number") = phone_number
    data_row.Item("Email Address") = email_address
    data_table.Rows.Add(data_row)
End Sub
```

Using the data objects' properties and methods to build a data application is straightforward but cumbersome. If you only need to display a few values, this method is fine. If you want to display and manipulate a large database, this method can be tedious. It also provides no method for saving changes to the data. The techniques described in the following sections address these problems.

XML Data

XML (Extensible Markup Language) is a relatively new method for storing data. Using a series of tags that you define, you can store data in text files. For example, the XML document shown in Listing 6.2 contains roughly the same values as those created by the ProgramGenerated example program described in the previous section.

LISTING 6.2   A PROGRAM CAN STORE DATA IN AN XML FILE

```
<?xml version="1.0" standalone="yes"?>
<Contacts>
  <Entry>
    <LastName>Jackson</LastName>
    <FirstName>Jennie</FirstName>
    <PhoneNumber>787-878-8263</PhoneNumber>
    <EmailAddress>JennieJackson@nowhere.com</EmailAddress>
  </Entry>
  <Entry>
    <LastName>Kevlar</LastName>
    <FirstName>Kurt</FirstName>
    <PhoneNumber>872-348-7263</PhoneNumber>
    <EmailAddress>kurtk@militant.com</EmailAddress>
  </Entry>
  <Entry>
    <LastName>Llama</LastName>
    <FirstName>Linda</FirstName>
    <EmailAddress>lllama@weaver.com</EmailAddress>
  </Entry>
  <Entry>
    <LastName>Mandrake</LastName>
    <FirstName>Marcus</FirstName>
    <PhoneNumber>398-787-4764</PhoneNumber>
  </Entry>
</Contacts>
```

The XmlLoader example program is similar to the ProgramGenerated example except it uses the code shown in Listing 6.3 to load and save its data in an XML file. The program declares and allocates a `DataSet` object named `m_DataSet`. The form's `Load` event handler uses that object's `ReadXml` method to load the data stored in an XML file. It then binds the DataSet's first and only table to its `DataGrid` control.

When the user closes the program, the form's `Closing` event handler executes. This routine uses the `DataSet` object's `HasChanges` method to see if the user made any changes to the data. If the data is modified, the program calls the DataSet's `WriteXml` method to save the changes back into the XML file.

LISTING 6.3   PROGRAM XMLLOADER LOADS AND SAVES DATA IN AN XML FILE

```
' The DataSet holding the contact data.
Private m_DataSet As New DataSet()
```

LISTING 6.3 CONTINUED

```
' Load the XML data.
Private Sub Form1_Load(ByVal sender As Object, _
  ByVal e As System.EventArgs) Handles MyBase.Load
    ' Read the XML data.
    m_DataSet.ReadXml(DataFileName())

    ' Bind the DataTable to the DataGrid.
    dgContacts.DataSource = m_DataSet.Tables(0)
End Sub

' Save any changes to the data.
Private Sub Form1_Closing(ByVal sender As Object, _
  ByVal e As System.ComponentModel.CancelEventArgs) Handles MyBase.Closing
    ' See if the data was modified.
    If m_DataSet.HasChanges Then
        ' Save the modified XML data.
        m_DataSet.WriteXml(DataFileName())
    End If
End Sub

' Return the name of the XML data file.
' This is in the directory above the initial one.
Private Function DataFileName() As String
    Dim file_name As String

    file_name = Application.StartupPath
    Return file_name.Substring(0, file_name.LastIndexOf("\")) & "\Contacts.xml"
End Function
End Class
```

This method is simple and works extremely well but it has a few disadvantages. First, if the program saves changes to the XML file, it overwrites the file completely. That makes this a poor solution in a multi-user environment. Suppose two users run the program at the same time and both make changes to the data. When the first user exits, the program overwrites the XML file, saving the user's changes. Later, when the second user exits, the program overwrites the XML file again, removing the first user's changes.

XML files also don't have the same power as relational databases. Although the DataSet and DataTable objects provide some features for filtering and sorting data, they cannot match the flexibility of SQL provided by a full database.

Chapter 7, "XML Databases," has a bit more to say about using XML files in Visual Basic but XML is a huge topic that is outside of the scope of this book. For more information on XML, see my book *Visual Basic .NET and XML* (Wiley, 2002, http://www.vb-helper.com/xml.htm).

SQL SERVER

Table 6.1 summarizes the objects a Visual Basic application uses to manipulate SQL Server databases. The following sections describe these objects in detail.

TABLE 6.1   SQL SERVER DATA ACCESS OBJECTS

Class	Purpose
SqlConnection	Connects the application to a SQL Server database
SqlCommand	Represents a stored procedure or SQL statement that the program will execute on a SqlConnection
SqlParameter	Represents a parameter used by a SqlCommand object
SqlDataAdapter	Uses SqlCommand objects to move data between a database and DataSet objects
SqlCommandBuilder	Generates SqlCommand objects
SqlDataReader	Allows the program to read a forward-only set of data
SqlTransaction	Manages SQL transactions in the database

SqlConnection

The SqlConnection object represents a connection to a SQL Server database. All database access must go through a SqlConnection object, although your program doesn't always need to explicitly open the connection by calling its Open method. In some cases, a SqlDataAdapter object opens and closes the connection itself.

The SqlConnection's ConnectionString property contains a semicolon-delimited list of values that tell the object what database to connect to and how to connect to it. Some of these values are duplicated by the SqlConnection's other properties. For instance, the Database property tells which database the SqlConnection is currently using. The SqlConnection object's ConnectionString property can set this value using its Initial Catalog value. The following code shows a ConnectionString setting the SqlConnection's Initial Catalog value to the Contacts database:

```
sql_connection.ConnectionString = _
    "Data Source=Bender\NETSDK;Initial Catalog=Contacts;User Id=sa"
```

Unlike most objects, a database connection is not discarded when a program no longer needs it. Instead, the object is added to a *connection pool*. Later when the same or a different program wants to connect to the same database, the system reuses the connection from the pool. This can improve performance when many applications need access to the same database. Rather than opening a separate connection for each application, the system lets the applications share connections in the pool.

The following sections describe connection pooling in a little more detail. The sections after that explain the most useful properties and methods provided by the SqlConnection object.

CONNECTION POOLING

Microsoft's model for database access in Visual Studio .NET has many applications briefly connecting to a database. A program connects to a database, performs some relatively small operation, such as fetching or updating records, and disconnects from the database.

PART

I

CH

6

To an extent, this mimics the way users work with data. A user pulls up some sort of information, works with it for a while, and then saves any changes. It is only while pulling up and saving information that the user interacts directly with the database.

If each instance of the application has its own permanent connection to the database, a large networked database might need a lot of simultaneous connections. That puts a heavy load on the database server. It can also increase your licensing requirements. For instance, a 100-user system would need a database license allowing 100 users to connect to the database simultaneously even though most of those connections would be idle at any given moment.

To improve this situation, Visual Studio .NET uses connection pooling. When an application opens a SqlConnection, the system compares its ConnectionString to the strings of idle connections in the connection pool. If it finds a match, the system makes the new SqlConnection object use the existing connection. This takes less time than creating a new connection from scratch.

When the program calls the SqlConnection object's Close method, the system puts the underlying database connection back in the pool so this program or another one can later reuse the connection.

The result is a system where a host of applications quickly open and close SqlConnection objects that share the pooled underlying database connections. If the applications typically hold their SqlConnection objects open for only a brief period at a time, they will be able to access the database using a small number of shared connections. The database server will not need to use as many resources holding open a huge number of connections.

To make connection pooling work, you need to satisfy two requirements: The program must open and close SqlConnection objects whenever it needs them and shared connections must use exactly the same ConnectionString value.

CLOSE SQLCONNECTIONS   To use connection pooling, a program must close its SqlConnection objects when it is not actively using them. In a small desktop application, it is common to open a database connection and keep it open while the program is running. Listing 6.4 shows this approach. The form's Load event handler opens a SqlConnection object. As the user interacts with the program, it uses the SqlConnection object to manipulate the database. When the user exits the program, the form's Closing event handler closes the SqlConnection.

LISTING 6.4   SMALL PROGRAMS SOMETIMES KEEP A DATABASE CONNECTION OPEN WHILE THEY ARE RUNNING

```
' The SqlConnection object used by all subroutines.
Private m_SqlConnection As SqlConnection

' Connect to the database.
Private Sub Form1_Load(ByVal sender As Object, _
   ByVal e As System.EventArgs) Handles MyBase.Load
    Dim connect_string As String
```

LISTING 6.4   CONTINUED

```
    ' Build the connect string.
    connect_string = _
        "Data Source=Bender\NETSDK;Initial Catalog=Contacts;User Id=sa"

    ' Connect to the database.
    Try
        m_SqlConnection = New SqlConnection(connect_string)
        m_SqlConnection.Open()
    Catch exc As Exception
        MsgBox(exc.Message)
    End Try
End Sub

' Other subroutines work with the connection while the program runs.
...

' Close the database connection.
Private Sub Form1_Closing(ByVal sender As Object, _
  ByVal e As System.ComponentModel.CancelEventArgs) Handles MyBase.Closing
    m_SqlConnection.Close()
    m_SqlConnection = Nothing
End Sub
```

Because this code keeps the SqlConnection open the whole time the program is running, its resources are not released to a connection pool. If another program needs access to the same database, it must use its own connection.

Instead of opening the connection when it starts and closing the connection when it stops, the program should open and close the connection each time it must interact with the database. Although it may seem more efficient to open and close the connection only once, reconnecting through the connection pool is actually quite fast. Only when the program first connects to the database does the connection take a significant amount of time.

There are still times when it makes sense to use a single connection to perform more than one task. For example, suppose a subroutine needs to fetch records from the database, change their values, and then save the new values back to the database. The routine can use a SqlConnection object's Open method to connect to the database, perform all three database operations, and then call the SqlConnection object's Close method. It would gain little by opening and closing the connection for all three operations separately.

On the other hand, if the program loads data and then waits for the user to modify it before saving the changes, it should open and close the connection separately for each operation. Holding the connection open while the user examines the data will reduce the efficiency of the connection pool. Users are relatively slow so the program should generally close the connection if it must wait for the user to do something.

MATCHING ConnectionStringS   The second requirement for connection pooling is that the SqlConnection objects' ConnectionString properties must match exactly. If two programs use different ConnectionString values, the system will not assign them to the same connec-

PART

I

CH

6

tion pool even if they use the same database. To get the most benefit from connection pools, be sure that your programs use exactly the same ConnectionString values.

Similarly, a single program can use connections from more than one pool. If the program uses one ConnectionString value in one place and another value in another place, the system will not select the connections from the same pool. To avoid using more than one connection, place the ConnectionString in a global string and initialize all SqlConnection objects using that value. Better still, use a shared SqlConnection object that all parts of the program can use, as shown in Listing 6.5.

LISTING 6.5   TO INCREASE POOLING, A PROGRAM CAN USE A GLOBAL SqlConnection OBJECT

```
' The SqlConnection object used by all subroutines.
Private m_SqlConnection As New SqlConnection( _
    "Data Source=Bender\NETSDK;Initial Catalog=Contacts;User Id=sa")

' Fetch Users records.
Private Sub FetchUsers()
    ' Open the connection.
    m_SqlConnection.Open()

    ' Execute the query.
    ...

    ' Close the connection.
    m_SqlConnection.Close()
End Sub
```

ConnectionString

The SqlConnection object's ConnectionString property is a semicolon-delimited list of values used by the object to connect to the database. Table 6.2 lists the most useful values that this string can contain.

Some of the values shown in Table 6.2 have more than one possible name. For instance, the amount of time the system will wait for a new connection before giving up can be called either Connect Timeout or Connection Timeout. The values are case insensitive so you could also call this value connect timeout, connection timeout, or CONNECTION TIMEOUT.

TABLE 6.2   SQLCONNECTION ConnectionString VALUES

Value	Purpose
Connect Timeout Connection	If the system cannot connect to the database after this many seconds, it raises an error. The default is 15 seconds.
Connection Lifetime	When a connection is returned to the connection pool, it is destroyed if it is older than this lifetime in seconds. The default is 0, indicating the connection does not expire.

TABLE 6.2   CONTINUED

Value	Purpose
Data Source Server Address Addr Network Address	The SQL server name or network address.
Initial Catalog Database	The name of the database that the connection should initially open.
Max Pool Size	The maximum number of connections stored in this connection's connection pool.
Pooling	If this is True (the default), the connection is taken from a connection pool if possible.
User ID	The user ID that the system should use to connect to the server.
Password Pwd	The password for the User ID.

For example, the following ConnectionString makes the SqlConnection object connect to the server Bender\NETSDK using the database Contacts. The connection logs on to the server using the user ID sa with no password. By default, the connection may be taken from the connection pool if it is available.

```
Data Source=Bender\NETSDK;Initial Catalog=Contacts;User Id=sa
```

Open

The Open method connects the SqlConnection object to the database. If the system can find an unused connection object in the connection pool that has exactly the right ConnectString value, it attaches that object to the SqlConnection. If the connection pool doesn't contain such an object, the system creates a new database connection for the SqlConnection.

Close

The Close method removes the SqlConnection object's database connection and returns it to the connection pool. A program should close a SqlConnection when it is not actively in use.

Under some circumstances, the SqlDataAdapter object can implicitly open and close a SqlConnection. See the section "SqlDataAdapter" later in this chapter for more information.

State

The State property tells you the SqlConnection object's current state. The value ConnectionState.Open means the SqlConnection is open and connected to the database. The value ConnectionState.Closed means the SqlConnection object has never been opened or it was opened and then the program called its Close method.

ConnectionTimeout

The ConnectionTimeout property is the same as the Connection Timeout value specified in the ConnectionString property. If the system takes more than this many seconds to connect to the database, it gives up and raises an error.

The default value of ConnectionTimeout is 15 seconds. If you set this value to 0, the system never gives up and waits until it can establish a connection. You should generally not use this value because it could make your program hang forever. If your program absolutely must have a database connection to run, use a large value such as 60. If it cannot connect to the database in that much time, chances are it never will. After 60 seconds, it can tell the user there is a problem and either try again or exit.

Database

The Database property is the same as the ConnectionString's Database value. It specifies the database within the server to which the connection is attached. Note that the Database value may change if the connection switches databases using either its ChangeDatabase method or by executing a SQL USE statement. For instance, the following SQL statement makes the connection change to the Contacts database.

```
USE Contacts
```

ChangeDatabase

The ChangeDatabase method makes the SqlConnection switch databases within the server. For example, the following code is equivalent to the SQL statement USE Contacts:

```
sql_connection.ChangeDatabase("Contacts")
```

DataSource

The DataSource property gives the name or network address of the SQL server instance to which the SqlConnection object should connect. It is equivalent to the ConnectionString's DataSource value.

ServerVersion

The ServerVersion property returns the SQL Server version of the server to which the SqlConnection is attached. On the test computer where the examples for this book were written, this property returned 08.00.0194.

BeginTransaction

The BeginTransaction method starts a new SQL transaction and returns a SqlTransaction object representing it. A SQL transaction lets you perform more than one database action as a single unit. See the section "SqlTransation" later in this chapter for more information on transactions.

CreateCommand

The CreateCommand method creates a new SqlCommand object associated with the SqlConnection. The program can then set the SqlCommand's CommandText property and execute the command.

A program can also create a SqlCommand object directly, setting its Connection property either in the call to its constructor or as a separate step. The following code shows three equivalent methods for creating a SqlCommand object associated with the SqlConnection named sql_connection.

```
' Use CreateCommand to set Connection, then set CommandText.
sql_command = sql_connection.CreateCommand()
sql_command.CommandText = query

' Set Connection and CommandText separately.
sql_command = New SqlCommand()
sql_command.Connection = sql_connection
sql_command.CommandText = query

' Set CommandText and Connection in the constructor.
sql_command = New SqlCommand(query, sql_connection)
```

SqlCommand

The SqlCommand object represents a SQL statement or a stored procedure for the program to execute on the SQL Server database. This class provides four methods for executing commands on the server depending on the type of command. These methods are optimized for different kinds of database commands. For example, the ExecuteReader method executes a SQL SELECT statement and returns rows of data. The ExecuteScalar method is optimized for executing queries that return a single value such as the following statement, which returns the number of records in the Customers table.

```
SELECT COUNT(*) FROM Customers
```

These methods and the SqlCommand object's other most useful properties are described in the following sections.

ExecuteReader

The ExecuteReader method executes a SQL SELECT statement and returns a SqlDataReader object that is ready to read the data returned. Example program UseExecuteReader, shown in Figure 6.2, uses this method to display a group of records selected form the Contacts table.

Program UseExecuteReader executes the code shown in Listing 6.6 to display its list of records. The form's Load event handler opens a SqlConnection and builds a SqlCommand object attached to it. It calls the ExecuteReader method to get a SqlDataReader object representing the results of a SQL query.

PART

I

CH

6

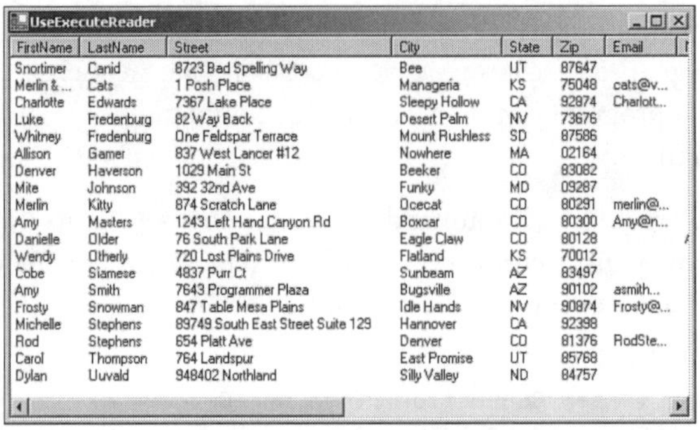

UseExecuteReader

FirstName	LastName	Street	City	State	Zip	Email
Snortimer	Canid	8723 Bad Spelling Way	Bee	UT	87647	
Merlin &...	Cats	1 Posh Place	Manageria	KS	75048	cats@v...
Charlotte	Edwards	7367 Lake Place	Sleepy Hollow	CA	92874	Charlott...
Luke	Fredenburg	82 Way Back	Desert Palm	NV	73676	
Whitney	Fredenburg	One Feldspar Terrace	Mount Rushless	SD	87586	
Allison	Garner	837 West Lancer #12	Nowhere	MA	02164	
Denver	Haverson	1029 Main St	Beeker	CO	83082	
Mite	Johnson	392 32nd Ave	Funky	MD	09287	
Merlin	Kitty	874 Scratch Lane	Ocecat	CO	80291	merlin@...
Amy	Masters	1243 Left Hand Canyon Rd	Boxcar	CO	80300	Amy@n...
Danielle	Older	76 South Park Lane	Eagle Claw	CO	80128	
Wendy	Otherly	720 Lost Plains Drive	Flatland	KS	70012	
Cobe	Siamese	4837 Purr Ct	Sunbeam	AZ	83497	
Amy	Smith	7643 Programmer Plaza	Bugsville	AZ	90102	asmith...
Frosty	Snowman	847 Table Mesa Plains	Idle Hands	NV	90874	Frosty@...
Michelle	Stephens	89749 South East Street Suite 129	Hannover	CA	92398	
Rod	Stephens	654 Platt Ave	Denver	CO	81376	RodSte...
Carol	Thompson	764 Landspur	East Promise	UT	85768	
Dylan	Uuvald	948402 Northland	Silly Valley	ND	84757	

Figure 6.2
Example program UseExecuteReader demonstrates the `SqlCommand` object's ExecuteReader method.

The program uses the SqlDataReader's `GetSchemaTable` method to obtain a DataTable containing information about the selected records' columns. It loops through the rows in this table creating column headers for each.

Then the program uses the SqlDataReader's `Read` method to loop through the data reader's records and uses the `MakeItem` subroutine to add each to the `ListView` control.

Subroutine `MakeItem` creates a new `ListViewItem` holding the SqlDataReader's first item value and adds it to the `ListView` control. It then loops through the record's other items adding them as subitems to the main item.

LISTING 6.6 THE `ExecuteReader` METHOD RETURNS A `SqlDataReader` OBJECT REPRESENTING A QUERY'S RESULTS

```
' Display the Contacts data.
Private Sub Form1_Load(ByVal sender As Object, _
  ByVal e As System.EventArgs) Handles MyBase.Load
    lvwContacts.View = View.Details

    ' Compose the connection string.
    Dim connection_string As String = _
        "Data Source=Bender\NETSDK;Initial Catalog=Contacts;User Id=sa"

    ' Create and open the SqlConnection.
    Dim sql_connection As New SqlConnection(connection_string)
    sql_connection.Open()

    ' Attach a SqlCommand to the SqlConnnection.
    Dim sql_command As New SqlCommand( _
        "SELECT * FROM Contacts ORDER BY LastName, FirstName", _
        sql_connection)

    ' Execute the SqlCommand and get the SqlDataReader.
    Dim data_reader As SqlDataReader = _
        sql_command.ExecuteReader()

    ' Get column information.
    Dim data_table As DataTable
    data_table = data_reader.GetSchemaTable
```

LISTING 6.6 CONTINUED

```
    ' Make the column headers.
    Dim column_header As ColumnHeader
    Dim i As Integer

    For i = 0 To data_table.Rows.Count - 1
        column_header = New ColumnHeader()
        column_header.Text = data_table.Rows(i).Item("ColumnName")
        lvwContacts.Columns.Add(column_header)
    Next i

    ' Make the items.
    Do While data_reader.Read()
        MakeItem(data_reader)
    Loop

    ' Close the data reader and connection.
    data_reader.Close()
    sql_connection.Close()
End Sub

' Add the current row's data to the ListView.
Private Sub MakeItem(ByVal data_reader As SqlDataReader)
    Dim new_item As ListViewItem
    Dim i As Integer

    ' Create the main ListView item.
    new_item = lvwContacts.Items.Add("" & data_reader.Item(0))

    ' Add the subitems.
    For i = 1 To data_reader.FieldCount - 1
        new_item.SubItems.Add("" & data_reader.Item(i))
    Next i
End Sub
```

The section "SqlDataReader" later in this chapter has more to say about the `SqlDataReader` object.

ExecuteNonQuery

The `ExecuteNonQuery` method makes the `SqlCommand` object execute a SQL statement that is not a query. These commands include statements such as INSERT, UPDATE, DELETE, CREATE TABLE, DROP TABLE, and USE.

`ExecuteNonQuery` returns the number of rows affected for SQL statements that directly affect rows. For example, when it executes a DELETE statement, `ExecuteNonQuery` returns the number of rows deleted.

Some statements affect rows indirectly but `ExecuteNonQuery` does not return the number of rows affected. For instance, the DROP TABLE statement effectively removes all the rows from a table as it destroys the table but `ExecuteNonQuery` returns -1 when it executes the DROP TABLE statement.

PART I
CH
6

Example program UseExecuteNonQuery, shown in Figure 6.3, demonstrates the ExecuteNonQuery method. When you click the Create Table button, the program opens the Contacts database and creates a table named TestTable. When you click the Insert Records button, the program inserts three records into the table. When you click Delete Records, the program deletes the records and tells you how many records were affected. Finally, when you click Drop Table, the program removes the TestTable table from the Contacts database.

Figure 6.3
Example program
UseExecuteNonQuery
demonstrates the
SqlCommand object's
ExecuteNonQuery
method.

Program UseExecuteNonQuery uses the code shown in Listing 6.7 to build, populate, empty, and destroy its database table. The program defines a SqlConnection object globally, setting its connection string. The program's button event handlers all use this object to perform their tasks.

The btnCreateTable_Click event handler composes a SQL CREATE TABLE statement and uses it to create a new SqlCommand object attached to the program's SqlConnection. It opens the SqlConnection, calls the SqlCommand object's ExecuteNonQuery method, and closes the SqlConnection.

The btnInsertRecords_Click event handler creates a SqlCommand object attached to the program's SqlConnection, and opens the connection. Then three times it sets the SqlCommand object's CommandText to a SQL INSERT statement and calls the ExecuteNonQuery method. After it has created the new records, the program closes the SqlConnection.

The btnDeleteRows_Click event handler composes a SQL DELETE statement and creates a SqlCommand object using that statement and attached to the program's SqlConnection. It opens the SqlConnection, calls the SqlCommand's ExceuteNonQuery method, and closes the SqlConnection.

Finally, the btnDropTable_Click event handler composes a SQL DROP TABLE statement and creates a SqlCommand object using that statement and attached to the program's SqlConnection. It opens the SqlConnection, calls the SqlCommand's ExceuteNonQuery method, and closes the SqlConnection.

LISTING 6.7   PROGRAM USEEXECUTENONQUERY USES THIS CODE TO CREATE, POPULATE, EMPTY, AND DESTROY A TABLE

```
' The SqlConnection used by all subroutines.
Private m_SqlConnection As SqlConnection = _
    New SqlConnection( _
        "Data Source=Bender\NETSDK;Initial Catalog=Contacts;User Id=sa")
```

LISTING 6.7 CONTINUED

```vb
' Create a test table.
Private Sub btnCreateTable_Click(ByVal sender As System.Object, _
  ByVal e As System.EventArgs) Handles btnCreateTable.Click
    ' Compose the SQL statement.
    Dim cmd As String = _
        "CREATE TABLE TestTable (" & _
        " FirstName VARCHAR(20)    NOT NULL," & _
        " LastName VARCHAR(20)    NOT NULL)"

    ' Make a SqlCommand to execute the statement.
    Dim sql_command As New SqlCommand(cmd, m_SqlConnection)

    Try
        ' Open the database connection.
        m_SqlConnection.Open()

        ' Execute the statement.
        sql_command.ExecuteNonQuery()

        ' If we get here, the statement worked.
        MsgBox("Table created.")
    Catch exc As Exception
        MsgBox(exc.Message, MsgBoxStyle.Exclamation, "Error")
    Finally
        ' Close the database connection.
        m_SqlConnection.Close()
    End Try
End Sub

' Add records to the test table.
Private Sub btnInsertRecords_Click(ByVal sender As System.Object, _
  ByVal e As System.EventArgs) Handles btnInsertRecords.Click
    ' Make a SqlCommand to insert the records.
    Dim sql_command As New SqlCommand("", m_SqlConnection)

    Try
        ' Open the database connection.
        m_SqlConnection.Open()

        ' Create the records.
        sql_command.CommandText _
= "INSERT INTO TestTable VALUES ('Able', 'Andrew')"
        sql_command.ExecuteNonQuery()

        sql_command.CommandText _
= "INSERT INTO TestTable VALUES ('Baker', 'Betty')"
        sql_command.ExecuteNonQuery()

        sql_command.CommandText = _
            "INSERT INTO TestTable VALUES ('Cheever', 'Charles')"
        sql_command.ExecuteNonQuery()

        ' If we get here, the statements worked.
        MsgBox("Records inserted")
    Catch exc As Exception
```

PART

I

CH

6

LISTING 6.7   CONTINUED

```vbnet
            MsgBox(exc.Message, MsgBoxStyle.Exclamation, "Error")
        Finally
            ' Close the database connection.
            m_SqlConnection.Close()
        End Try
    End Sub

    ' Delete the records from the test table.
    Private Sub btnDeleteRows_Click(ByVal sender As System.Object, _
      ByVal e As System.EventArgs) Handles btnDeleteRows.Click
        ' Compose the SQL statement.
        Dim cmd As String = "DELETE FROM TestTable"

        ' Make a SqlCommand to execute the statement.
        Dim sql_command As New SqlCommand(cmd, m_SqlConnection)

        Try
            ' Open the database connection.
            m_SqlConnection.Open()

            ' Delete the records, telling the user
            ' how many records were affected.
            MsgBox(sql_command.ExecuteNonQuery() & " records deleted")
        Catch exc As Exception
            MsgBox(exc.Message, MsgBoxStyle.Exclamation, "Error")
        Finally
            ' Close the database connection.
            m_SqlConnection.Close()
        End Try
    End Sub

    ' Drop the test table.
    Private Sub btnDropTable_Click(ByVal sender As System.Object, _
      ByVal e As System.EventArgs) Handles btnDropTable.Click
        ' Compose the SQL statement.
        Dim cmd As String = "DROP TABLE TestTable"

        ' Make a SqlCommand to execute the statement.
        Dim sql_command As New SqlCommand(cmd, m_SqlConnection)

        Try
            ' Open the database connection.
            m_SqlConnection.Open()

            ' Drop the table.
            sql_command.ExecuteNonQuery()

            ' If we get here, the statement worked.
            MsgBox("Table dropped.")
        Catch exc As Exception
            MsgBox(exc.Message, MsgBoxStyle.Exclamation, "Error")
        Finally
            ' Close the database connection.
            m_SqlConnection.Close()
        End Try
    End Sub
```

Experiment with program UseExecuteNonQuery for a while. The first time you click a button, the program may take a few seconds to connect to the database. The next time you click a button, the program will be able to quickly reuse the previous connection that has been stored in the connection pool.

Try some combinations of commands that do not work to see what happens. For instance, click the Create Table button twice in a row or click the Drop Table button when the database does not contain a table named TestTable.

ExecuteScalar

The ExecuteScalar method executes a SQL statement that returns a single value. Example program UseExecuteScalar, shown in Figure 6.4, demonstrates the ExecuteScalar method.

Figure 6.4
Example program
UseExecuteScalar uses
the SqlCommand
object's
ExecuteScalar
method to fetch a single value from a database.

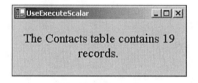

When it starts, program UseExecuteScalar uses the code shown in Listing 6.8 to display the number of records in the database's Contacts table. The program composes a database connect string, uses it to initialize a SqlConnection object, and opens the database connection. It composes a SQL SELECT statement to count the records in the Contacts table and uses that statement to initialize a SqlCommand object.

Next the program invokes the SqlCommand object's ExecuteScalar method. That method returns the single result selected by the SQL statement. The program uses that value to build its result string and displays the result in the lblResult Label control. Finally, the program closes the SqlConnection.

PART

I

CH

6

LISTING 6.8   PROGRAM USEEXECUTESCALAR DEMONSTRATES THE ExecuteScalar METHOD

```
' Display the Contacts data.
Private Sub Form1_Load(ByVal sender As Object, _
  ByVal e As System.EventArgs) Handles MyBase.Load
    ' Compose the connection string.
    Dim connection_string As String = _
        "Data Source=Bender\NETSDK;Initial Catalog=Contacts;User Id=sa"

    ' Create and open the SqlConnection.
    Dim sql_connection As New SqlConnection(connection_string)
    sql_connection.Open()

    ' Attach a SqlCommand to the SqlConnnection.
    Dim sql_command As New SqlCommand( _
        "SELECT COUNT (*) FROM Contacts", _
```

LISTING 6.8 CONTINUED

```
        sql_connection)

    ' Execute the SqlCommand and get the result.
    Dim result As String
    result = sql_command.ExecuteScalar()

    ' Display the result.
    lblResult.Text = "The Contacts table contains " & result & " records."

    ' Close the connection.
    sql_connection.Close()
End Sub
```

You could also use the SqlCommand object's ExecuteReader method to execute this SQL statement. ExecuteReader would return a SqlDataReader object representing the results. You could use the data reader's Read method to fetch the first result record and then look at the record's single field to get the final value.

This method would not only be more complicated than using ExecuteScalar, but it would also be slower. The ExecuteScalar method is optimized for returning a single value and it can do so more quickly than ExecuteReader can. While ExecuteReader needs to package its results into a SqlDataReader object and ship a relatively complex response back to the program, ExecuteScalar returns a single value.

ExecuteXmlReader

The ExecuteXmlReader method works much as the ExecuteReader method does. It executes a query on a SqlConnection and compiles the results. Where ExecuteReader returns the results through a SqlDataReader object, ExecuteXmlReader returns its results via an XmlReader.

One big difference between these two methods is that ExecuteXmlReader must execute a command that returns valid XML data. One way to guarantee this is to include the FOR XML clause in the SQL SELECT statement. That makes the database engine return its results in XML format. For example, the following statement executes a SELECT statement and returns the result in an XML format:

```
SELECT * FROM Contacts
ORDER BY LastName, FirstName
FOR XML AUTO, XMLDATA
```

Example program UseExecuteXmlReader uses the code shown in Listing 6.9 to execute this SELECT statement. When the form loads, the program creates and opens a SqlConnection as usual. It creates a SqlCommand object using the query and calls its ExecuteXmlReader method. A more complicated program could use the returned XmlReader object to process the data itself. This program simply loads the XML data into a DataSet. It attaches the DataSet's first and only table to a DataGrid control to display the results.

LISTING 6.9   PROGRAM UseExecuteXmlReader LOADS DATA IN XML FORMAT

```
' Display the Contacts data.
Private Sub Form1_Load(ByVal sender As Object, _
  ByVal e As System.EventArgs) Handles MyBase.Load
    ' Compose the connection string.
    Dim connection_string As String = _
        "Data Source=Bender\NETSDK;Initial Catalog=Contacts;User Id=sa"

    ' Create and open the SqlConnection.
    Dim sql_connection As New SqlConnection(connection_string)
    sql_connection.Open()

    ' Attach a SqlCommand to the SqlConnnection.
    Dim sql_command As New SqlCommand( _
        "SELECT * FROM Contacts " & _
        "ORDER BY LastName, FirstName " & _
        "FOR XML AUTO, XMLDATA", _
        sql_connection)

    ' Execute the SqlCommand and get the SqlDataReader.
    Dim xml_reader As XmlReader = _
        sql_command.ExecuteXmlReader()

    ' Load the results into a DataSet.
    Dim data_set As New DataSet()
    data_set.ReadXml(xml_reader, XmlReadMode.Fragment)

    ' Bind the first table to the DataGrid.
    dgContacts.DataSource = data_set.Tables(0)

    ' Close the XmlReader and connection.
    xml_reader.Close()
    sql_connection.Close()
End Sub
```

The XmlReader class provides efficient forward-only access to XML data just as the SqlDataReader class provides fast forward-only access to data in a database-oriented format. The XmlReader gives a more XML-oriented view of the data that is outside the scope of this book. For more information, see the online help or my book *Visual Basic .NET and XML* (Wiley, 2002, http://www.vb-helper.com/xml.htm).

PART

I

CH

6

CommandText

The CommandText property gives the SqlCommand object the SQL statement or stored procedure that it should execute.

To tell the SqlCommand object to use parameters, include an @ symbol followed by the name of the parameter. For example, the following statement tells the SqlCommand object that it will fill in the value of the LastNameMatch parameter later:

```
SELECT * FROM Contacts WHERE LastName LIKE @LastNameMatch
```

See the "Parameters" section later in this chapter for more information on parameterized commands.

CommandType

The `CommandType` property tells the `SqlCommand` object what kind of object the text in the `CommandText` property represents. If the command is a SQL statement, set this property to `CommandType.Text`. If the command is the name of a stored procedure, set this property to `CommandType.StoredProcedure`.

CommandTimeout

The `CommandTimeout` property tells the `SqlCommand` object how many seconds to wait for results before giving up and raising an error. If you set this value to `0`, the SqlCommand waits indefinitely. This can be dangerous because the program will hang if the command never returns a result. It is usually better to set this to a relatively large value, such as 60 seconds. Then if the command does not complete within that time, the program can warn the user and either give up or try to execute the command again.

Connection

The `Connection` property indicates the `SqlConnection` object that the SqlCommand will use to communicate with the database. The connection must be open when you call one of the `SqlCommand` object's execute methods.

Parameters

The `Parameters` property is a collection of `SqlParameter` objects that tell the `SqlCommand` object how to fill in values for its parameters. For instance, the following SQL `SELECT` statement selects records where the `LastName` field matches a value specified by the `@LastNameMatch` parameter. A `SqlParameter` object tells the SqlCommand what value to use in place of the string `@LastNameMatch`.

```
SELECT * FROM Contacts WHERE LastName LIKE @LastNameMatch
```

Example program UseParameters, shown in Figure 6.5, uses SqlParameters to select records with certain `LastName` and `FirstName` values. Enter strings to match with `LIKE` statements in the two text boxes and click List. The program lists records where the `FirstName` and `LastName` field match the values you entered. Figure 6.5 displays records where the `LastName` field begins with S and the `FirstName` field has any value.

Figure 6.5
Example program
UseParameters uses
`SqlParameter`
objects to select
records.

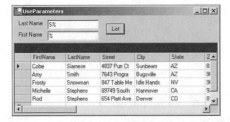

Program UseParameters executes the code shown in Listing 6.10 to display records. It begins by declaring the `SqlConnection` and `SqlCommand` objects it will use later. The form's

Load event handler initializes those objects. It also creates two SqlParameter objects of type VarChar. The first is named @LastNameMatch and the second is named @FirstNameMatch.

When you click the List button, the btnList_Click event handler assigns the values you entered in the text boxes to the two SqlParameter objects. It then opens the connection, calls the SqlCommand object's ExecuteXmlReader method, and uses the resulting XmlReader to fill a DataSet object. The program binds the DataSet's first table to its DataGrid control, and closes the XmlReader and SqlConnection.

LISTING 6.10   PROGRAM USEPARAMETERS DEMONSTRATES PARAMETERIZED QUERIES

```
' The SqlConnection used by all subroutines.
Private m_SqlConnection As SqlConnection

' The SqlCommand object.
Private m_SqlCommand As SqlCommand

' Prepare the SqlConnection and SqlCommand.
Private Sub Form1_Load(ByVal sender As Object, _
  ByVal e As System.EventArgs) Handles MyBase.Load
    ' Prepare the SqlConnection.
    m_SqlConnection = New SqlConnection( _
        "Data Source=Bender\NETSDK;Initial Catalog=Contacts;User Id=sa")

    ' Prepare the SqlCommand.
    Dim query As String = _
        "SELECT * FROM Contacts " & _
        "WHERE LastName  LIKE @LastNameMatch " & _
        "  AND FirstName LIKE @FirstNameMatch " & _
        "FOR XML AUTO, XMLDATA"
    m_SqlCommand = New SqlCommand(query, m_SqlConnection)

    ' Create the SqlCommand object's SqlParameters.
    m_SqlCommand.Parameters.Add("@LastNameMatch", SqlDbType.VarChar)
    m_SqlCommand.Parameters.Add("@FirstNameMatch", SqlDbType.VarChar)
End Sub

' List matching records.
Private Sub btnList_Click(ByVal sender As System.Object, _
  ByVal e As System.EventArgs) Handles btnList.Click
    ' Assign values to the parameters.
    m_SqlCommand.Parameters(0).Value = txtLastName.Text
    m_SqlCommand.Parameters(1).Value = txtFirstName.Text

    ' Open the connection.
    m_SqlConnection.Open()

    ' Execute the command.
    Dim xml_reader As XmlReader
    xml_reader = m_SqlCommand.ExecuteXmlReader()

    ' Copy the results into a DataSet.
    Dim data_set As New DataSet()
    data_set.ReadXml(xml_reader, XmlReadMode.Fragment)
```

PART

I

CH

6

LISTING 6.10   CONTINUED

```
    ' Bind the DataSet to the DataGrid control.
    dgContacts.DataSource = data_set.Tables(0)

    ' Close the XmlReader and connection.
    xml_reader.Close()
    m_SqlConnection.Close()
End Sub
```

An alternative strategy is to compose a new query for the particular values the program should use as parameters. For instance, if the LastName and FirstName parameters are S% and A%, respectively, the program could execute the following query without using parameters.

```
SELECT * FROM Contacts
WHERE LastName  LIKE 'S%'
  AND FirstName LIKE 'A%'
```

Which method you use is largely a matter of preference, although using parameters may be more efficient in combination with the Prepare method described shortly.

CreateParameter

The CreateParameter method creates a new SqlParameter object. Note that this method does not automatically add the SqlParameter to the SqlCommand object's Parameters collection. You still need to add it to the collection if you want the SqlCommand object to use it.

Prepare

The Prepare method makes the database compile the command. Later, when the program executes the command, the database may be able to process the command more efficiently.

Because it is the database that compiles the command, the command's SqlConnection object must be open when the program calls Prepare.

Prepare is often used to execute a single SQL statement many times using different parameters. The program opens the database connection and compiles the SqlCommand. Then it repeatedly sets the command's parameters and executes the command. When it is finished, the program closes the SqlConnection.

Transaction

The Transaction property gets or sets the SqlTransaction object that includes the command's action. The SqlTransaction object's Commit and Rollback methods allow the program to accept or reject this command with the others in the same transaction. See the section "SqlTransaction" later in this chapter for more information about transactions.

Cancel

The Cancel method cancels a command that is currently being processed. Because calls to the SqlCommand object's execution methods run synchronously, only a thread other than the one executing the command can cancel the command.

SqlParameter

A SqlParameter object represents a parameter in a SqlCommand object's command text. The SqlParameter object's most important properties are ParameterName and Value. The ParameterName tells the SqlCommand object which parameter the object represents. The Value property gives the value the SqlCommand object should use in place of the parameter in the SQL statement.

For example, suppose a SqlCommand object has the following command text:

```
SELECT * FROM Customers WHERE AccountBalance > @MinBalance
```

Now if this SqlCommand has a SqlParameter with ParameterName = @MinBalance and Value = 1000, the command translates into the following statement:

```
SELECT * FROM Customers WHERE AccountBalance > 1000
```

The following code fragment shows how a program can set the ParameterName and Value properties:

```
Dim balance_parameter As New SqlParameter()

balance_parameter.PropertyName = "@MinBalance"
balance_parameter.Value = 1000
```

The DataAdapter object, described later in this chapter, uses SqlCommand objects to move data between a database and a DataSet object. Those SqlCommand objects use parameters to get and specify values for their commands. For example, the following code shows an INSERT statement generated by a SqlCommandBuilder object. The 17 parameters @p1 through @p17 correspond to the fields in the Contacts table where the record will be inserted.

```
INSERT INTO Contacts( FirstName , LastName , Street , City , State , Zip ,
 Email , Notes , HomePhone , HomePhoneExtension , HomeFax , HomeFaxExtension ,
 WorkPhone , WorkPhoneExtension , WorkFax , WorkFaxExtension , SnapshotFile )
VALUES ( @p1 , @p2 , @p3 , @p4 , @p5 , @p6 , @p7 , @p8 , @p9 , @p10 , @p11 ,
 @p12 , @p13 , @p14 , @p15 , @p16 , @p17 )
```

When the DataAdapter object updates a DataSet and needs to create a new record, it copies the field values for the record into this SqlCommand object's parameters and then executes the command.

Table 6.3 summarizes the SqlParameter object's most useful properties. Many of them are useful when a DataAdapter is moving data to or from a database. For instance, a program can use the Size property to limit the number of characters in a string that are sent to the database.

PART

I

CH

6

TABLE 6.3   OLE DB DATA ACCESS OBJECTS

Property	Meaning
DbType	The field's generic data type. For example, the String generic data type corresponds to the VarChar SQL Server data type.
Direction	Indicates whether the parameter is used for input, output, both, or whether it is a stored procedure return value.

TABLE 6.3   CONTINUED

Property	Meaning
IsNullable	Indicates whether the corresponding field can accept a Null value.
ParameterName	The name of the parameter in the command text.
Precision	The maximum number of digits for a numeric parameter.
Scale	The maximum number of digits after the decimal place for a numeric parameter.
Size	The maximum size of the field. For binary data and ANSI strings, this value is in bytes. For Unicode strings, the value is in characters. You can set this value to restrict the amount of data sent to the server.
SourceColumn	The database column name for this parameter.
SourceVersion	The version of DataRow data that should be used in an UPDATE statement. This should be DataRowVersion.Current, DataRowVersion.Original, or DataRowVersion.Default.
SqlDbType	The field's SQL Server data type. This type maps to the generic DbType. For example, the SqlDbType NChar maps to the DbType String.
Value	The value the command should use for the parameter.

The SqlParameter object has several different constructors that initialize different combinations of the object's properties when it is created.

SqlDataAdapter

The SqlDataAdapter copies data between a database and a DataSet object. The SqlDataAdapter's Fill method pulls data from the database into the DataSet. Its Update method copies changes back from the DataSet into the database.

The SqlDataAdapter uses SqlConnection and SqlCommand objects to manage its connection to the database and the SQL statements it must execute. You can create these objects yourself or you can let the SqlDataAdapter create its own. For instance, the following code creates a new SqlDataAdapter object. It then sets its SelectCommand property, which the data adapter uses to fetch records from the database, to a new SqlCommand object. It finishes by setting the SqlCommand object's Connection property to a new SqlConnection object.

```
' Make the data adapter.
data_adapter = New SqlDataAdapter()

' Make the SELECT command object.
data_adapter.SelectCommand = New SqlCommand("SELECT * FROM Employees")

' Define the SELECT command object's database connection.
data_adapter.SelectCommand.Connection = New SqlConnection( _
    "Data Source=Bender\NETSDK;Initial Catalog=Employees;User Id=sa")
```

Alternatively, the program can pass the data adapter's constructor the connect and select strings and let the data adapter build its `SelectCommand` object and the corresponding SqlConnection as shown in the following code:

```
' Make the data adapter.
data_adapter = New SqlDataAdapter( _
    "SELECT * FROM Employees", _
    "Data Source=Bender\NETSDK;Initial Catalog=Employees;User Id=sa")
```

A program uses the `Fill` or `Update` methods to move data between the data adapter and a DataSet. If the `SqlConnection` object attached to the corresponding `SqlCommand` object is not already open, the data adapter automatically opens it. When it is finished executing the command, the data adapter returns the `SqlConnection` to its starting state.

This makes it easier for a program to follow the new open/use/close style of using database connections to take advantage of connection pooling. The data adapter automatically opens the connection, uses it, and closes it so it is returned to the connection pool. To allow this convenience, the program should not explicitly open the connection. The only reason it should need to open the connection is if it must perform several actions with the same connection all at once. In that case, the program must remember to close the connection itself when it has finished all of the operations.

The `SqlDataAdapter` class provides several useful properties and methods for controlling data transfer between a database and a `DataSet` object. The following sections describe the more useful of these in detail.

SelectCommand, InsertCommand, DeleteCommand, AND UpdateCommand

The `SqlDataAdapter` object's `SelectCommand`, `InsertCommand`, `DeleteCommand`, and `UpdateCommand` properties are references to `SqlCommand` objects that the DataAdapter uses to move data between the database and a `DataSet` object. The adapter only uses these objects when it needs them so a program may not need to supply them all. For instance, if the program uses the data adapter to load data from the database, it must give the data adapter a `SelectCommand` object. If it never copies changes back to the database, however, it doesn't need to define the `InsertCommand`, `DeleteCommand`, and `UpdateCommand` objects.

Normally a program uses a SQL `SELECT` statement to define the data adapter's `SelectCommand` object. It can then use a `SqlCommandBuilder` object, described later in this chapter, to create the data adapter's other `SqlCommand` objects.

AcceptChangesDuringFill

If this property is `True`, the data adapter calls `AcceptChanges` for each new row it creates during a call to the `Fill` method. If this property is `False`, each row is marked as a new row so the DataSet's `HasChanges` method returns `True`.

Fill

The `Fill` method makes the SqlDataAdapter object copy data from the database into a DataSet or DataTable. The following code shows how a program can create a data adapter and use its `Fill` method to load a DataSet:

```
' Create the SqlDataAdapter.
Dim data_adapter As New SqlDataAdapter(SELECT_STRING, CONNECT_STRING)

' Fill the DataSet.
Dim data_set As New DataSet()
data_adapter.Fill(m_DataSet)
```

By default, the data adapter gives the DataSet a new `DataTable` object with the catchy name `Table`. In other words, after loading the data the value `data_set.Table(0).TableName` returns `Table`. The `TableMappings` collection described next makes the data adapter use more meaningful table names.

TableMappings

The `SqlDataAdapter` object's `TableMappings` property is a collection of `DataTableMapping` objects that define the mappings from database table and column names to DataTable and DataRow names. When a data adapter selects data from a database, it stores the data in the table named `Table`. The table mappings can map this name to a more meaningful one.

The `DataTableMapping` objects contained in the `TableMappings` collection have three important properties. The `SourceTable` property gives the name of the source table in the database. `DataSetTable` gives the name of the DataTable in the DataSet that should receive this table's data. The `ColumnMappings` property, described shortly, determines how database column names are mapped to DataTable column names.

The following code uses the `TableMappings` collection to load data from two different tables. It begins by creating a data adapter to select records from the `Employees` table. It creates a `TableMappings` entry to map the default database table name `Table` to the DataSet name `Employees`. It then calls the data adapter's `Fill` method to load the data.

Next, the code changes the first `DataTableMapping` object's `DataSetTable` value to `Customers`. When the code calls the `Fill` method again, the new data goes into the DataSet's `Customers` DataTable.

When it is finished, the program's DataSet contains two DataTables named `Employees` and `Customers`.

```
' Create the SqlDataAdapter.
Dim data_adapter As New SqlDataAdapter( _
    "SELECT * FROM Employees", _
    "Data Source=Bender\NETSDK;Initial Catalog=Contacts;User Id=sa")

' Create the DataSet.
Dim data_set As New DataSet()

' Load data from the Employees database table into the Employees DataTable.
data_adapter.TableMappings.Add("Table", "Employees")
```

```
data_adapter.Fill(data_set)

' Load data from the Customers database table into the Customers DataTable.
data_adapter.TableMappings(0).DataSetTable = "Customers"
data_adapter.SelectCommand.CommandText = "SELECT * FROM Customers"
data_adapter.Fill(data_set)
```

The DataTableMapping object's third important property is `ColumnMappings`. This is a collection of DataColumnMapping objects that determine how the data adapter maps columns in the database to columns in the DataSet.

The DataColumnMapping object has two important properties, `SourceColumn` and `DataSetColumn`, which give the column's name in the database and in the DataSet. You can use this collection to change the names of specific columns in the database. For instance, the following code makes the data adapter load data from the database's `LastName` field into the DataTable's `Last Name` field.

```
data_adapter.TableMappings.Add("Table", "Contacts")
data_adapter.TableMappings(0).ColumnMappings.Add("LastName", "Last Name")
data_adapter.Fill(data_set)
```

You can get a similar result using an `AS` clause in the SQL `SELECT` statement as in the following code:

```
SELECT LastName AS [Last Name] FROM Contacts
```

MissingMappingAction

The SqlDataAdapter object's `MissingMappingAction` property determines the action the data adapter takes when it does not know how to map an incoming table or column to the DataSet. If this property's value is `MissingMappingAction.Error`, the data adapter raises an error if it encounters a table or column that is not mapped to a corresponding entity in the DataSet.

If this property's value is `MissingMappingAction.Ignore`, the data adapter ignores any data that it cannot map to the DataSet. For example, if the data adapter has no mapping for the `Employees` table, then it simply discards any data selected by its `SelectCommand` object that belongs to the database's `Employees` table. You could use this value to make the data adapter drop certain columns from a query, although it would probably be better to not select those columns in the first place.

If this property's value is `MissingMappingAction.Passthrough`, the data adapter creates a new table or column to hold the data.

FillSchema

The SqlDataAdapter object's `FillSchema` method makes the data adapter load a data structure into a DataSet without loading any data. For example, if the SelectCommand's `CommandText` is `SELECT * FROM Customers`, then the `FillSchema` method makes the data adapter create a new DataTable with the same fields as the `Customer` table's fields in the database.

PART

I

CH

6

The FillSchema's second parameter tells the data adapter whether it should use the adapter's TableMappings. If this parameter is SchemaType.Mapped, the data adapter applies the translations defined by the TableMappings collection. If the parameter is SchemaType.Source, the data adapter ignores the TableMappings collection and creates a structure that duplicates that of the database. Usually this parameter should be SchemaType.Mapped. If you don't want the table structure to include the mappings, you probably won't bother to create the mappings.

Update

The SqlDataAdapter object's Update method makes the data adapter copy changes back from a DataSet to the database. This method makes the data adapter invoke its InsertCommand, UpdateCommand, and DeleteCommand objects for each of the DataSet rows that were inserted, updated, or deleted. You can use the SqlCommandBuilder object described shortly to create these objects.

If you use the TableMappings property to change the name of a table or a table's columns when you load the data, be sure to use the same mappings when you save the data.

RowUpdating

The RowUpdating event fires when a call to the Update method makes the data adapter try to update a row in the database. You can use the event handler's parameters to determine what value is changing.

If the row is new or updated, the program can view and modify its values and the new values will be saved to the database. If the row was deleted, the program cannot view or modify the row's values.

RowUpdated

The SqlDataAdapter object's RowUpdated event fires after a row's changes have been saved to the database. At this point the program can view the row's values but changes to them are too late to affect the database.

SqlCommandBuilder

The SqlDataAdpater uses SqlCommand objects to select, insert, update, and delete records in a database. Typically, you define the select object when you create the SqlDataAdapter as in the following code. The SqlDataAdapter's constructor uses the SQL SELECT statement to create the select SqlCommand object.

```
data_adapter = New SqlDataAdapter( _
    "SELECT * FROM Employees", _
    "Data Source=Bender\NETSDK;Initial Catalog=Employees;User Id=sa")
```

Defining the insert, update, and delete objects is less straightforward. These objects must use SqlParameter objects to define the values that should be used to manipulate the database. Fortunately, you don't have to create these objects yourself. If you attach a SqlCommandBuilder object to the data adapter, the data adapter can use it to make the command objects it needs.

The following code shows how a program can use a SqlCommandBuilder to make the data adapter's insert, update, and delete command objects:

```
Dim data_adapter As SqlDataAdapter
Dim command_builder As SqlCommandBuilder

' Create the DataAdapter.
data_adapter = New SqlDataAdapter(SELECT_STRING, CONNECT_STRING)

' Make the CommandBuilder generate the
' insert, update, and delete commands.
command_builder = New SqlCommandBuilder(data_adapter)

' Save the changes to the data.
data_adapter.Update(m_DataSet)
```

The following code shows the CommandText values of the objects created by a SqlCommandBuilder:

```
*** INSERT ***
INSERT INTO Contacts( FirstName , LastName , Street , City , State , Zip , Email ,
 Notes , HomePhone , HomePhoneExtension , HomeFax , HomeFaxExtension , WorkPhone ,
 WorkPhoneExtension , WorkFax , WorkFaxExtension , SnapshotFile )
VALUES ( @p1 , @p2 , @p3 , @p4 , @p5 , @p6 , @p7 , @p8 , @p9 , @p10 , @p11 , @p12
,
 @p13 , @p14 , @p15 , @p16 , @p17 )

*** UPDATE ***
UPDATE Contacts SET FirstName = @p1 , LastName = @p2 , Street = @p3 , City = @p4 ,
 State = @p5 , Zip = @p6 , Email = @p7 , Notes = @p8 , HomePhone = @p9 ,
 HomePhoneExtension = @p10 , HomeFax = @p11 , HomeFaxExtension = @p12 ,
 WorkPhone = @p13 , WorkPhoneExtension = @p14 , WorkFax = @p15 ,
 WorkFaxExtension = @p16 , SnapshotFile = @p17
WHERE ( FirstName = @p18 AND LastName = @p19 AND Street = @p20 AND City = @p21
  AND State = @p22 AND Zip = @p23 AND Email = @p24 AND Notes = @p25
  AND HomePhone = @p26 AND HomePhoneExtension = @p27 AND HomeFax = @p28
  AND HomeFaxExtension = @p29 AND WorkPhone = @p30 AND WorkPhoneExtension = @p31
  AND WorkFax = @p32 AND WorkFaxExtension = @p33 AND SnapshotFile = @p34 )

*** DELETE ***
DELETE FROM  Contacts
WHERE ( FirstName = @p1 AND LastName = @p2 AND Street = @p3 AND City = @p4
  AND State = @p5 AND Zip = @p6 AND Email = @p7 AND Notes = @p8
  AND HomePhone = @p9 AND HomePhoneExtension = @p10 AND HomeFax = @p11
  AND HomeFaxExtension = @p12 AND WorkPhone = @p13 AND WorkPhoneExtension = @p14
  AND WorkFax = @p15 AND WorkFaxExtension = @p16 AND SnapshotFile = @p17 )
```

Notice that the UPDATE and DELETE statements use WHERE clauses to verify that they are modifying the correct records. Unless every field in the corresponding database record matches the original values stored in the DataSet, the statements do not affect the record.

EXAMPLE PROGRAM USEDATAADAPTER

Example program UseDataAdapter ties together many of the methods described in the previous sections. The program uses the code shown in Listing 6.11 to load data from the Contacts table into a DataGrid. When it exits, the program saves any changes made to the data back into the database.

PART

I

CH

6

When it starts, the program's Load event handler creates a SqlDataAdapter object. It uses the adapter's TableMappings collection to change the default table name Table to the more informative name Contacts. It uses the adapter's Fill method to pull data from the database into a DataSet and binds the program's DataGrid control to the DataSet's table named Contacts.

When the program exits, its Closing event handler checks the DataSet's HasChanges method to see if the data has been modified. If the data has changed, the program makes a new data adapter using the same select and database connection strings as the original data adapter, and it creates the same table mapping. Next the program makes a SqlCommandBuilder object attached to the data adapter and calls the data adapter's Update method to save the changes to the database. You can uncomment the program's Debug.WriteLine statements if you want to see the SQL statements that the SqlCommandBuilder generates.

LISTING 6.11   PROGRAM USEDATAADAPTER USES SQLDATAADAPTERS TO LOAD AND SAVE DATA

```
Private Const SELECT_STRING As String = _
    "SELECT * FROM Contacts ORDER BY LastName, FirstName"
Private Const CONNECT_STRING As String = _
    "Data Source=Bender\NETSDK;Initial Catalog=Contacts;User Id=sa"

' The DataSet that holds the data.
Private m_DataSet As DataSet

' Load the data.
Private Sub Form1_Load(ByVal sender As Object, _
   ByVal e As System.EventArgs) Handles MyBase.Load
    Dim data_adapter As SqlDataAdapter

    ' Create the SqlDataAdapter.
    data_adapter = New SqlDataAdapter(SELECT_STRING, CONNECT_STRING)

    ' Map Table to Contacts.
    data_adapter.TableMappings.Add("Table", "Contacts")

    ' Fill the DataSet.
    m_DataSet = New DataSet()
    data_adapter.Fill(m_DataSet)

    ' Bind the DataGrid control to the Contacts DataTable.
    dgContacts.DataSource = m_DataSet.Tables("Contacts")
End Sub

' Save any changes to the data.
Private Sub Form1_Closing(ByVal sender As Object, _
   ByVal e As System.ComponentModel.CancelEventArgs) Handles MyBase.Closing
    If m_DataSet.HasChanges() Then
        Dim data_adapter As SqlDataAdapter
        Dim command_builder As SqlCommandBuilder

        ' Create the DataAdapter.
        data_adapter = New SqlDataAdapter(SELECT_STRING, CONNECT_STRING)
```

LISTING 6.11   CONTINUED

```
        ' Map Table to Contacts.
        data_adapter.TableMappings.Add("Table", "Contacts")

        ' Make the CommandBuilder generate the
        ' insert, update, and delete commands.
        command_builder = New SqlCommandBuilder(data_adapter)

        ' Uncomment this code to see the INSERT,
        ' UPDATE, and DELETE commands.
        'Debug.WriteLine("*** INSERT ***")
        'Debug.WriteLine(command_builder.GetInsertCommand.CommandText)
        'Debug.WriteLine("*** UPDATE ***")
        'Debug.WriteLine(command_builder.GetUpdateCommand.CommandText)
        'Debug.WriteLine("*** DELETE ***")
        'Debug.WriteLine(command_builder.GetDeleteCommand.CommandText)

        ' Save the changes.
        data_adapter.Update(m_DataSet)
    End If
End Sub
```

SqlDataReader

The SqlDataReader class provides fast, forward-only access to a series of data rows. Its Read method makes the reader advance to the next record. Read returns True if it successfully gets a record and False if there is no more data to read.

The Item property returns the value of one of the row's fields. For example, the following statement saves the value of the LastName field in the last_name variable:

```
last_name = data_reader.Item("LastName")
```

The SqlDataReader also provides a series of methods for getting a field's value in different formats. For example, the statement GetString("FirstName") fetches the value of the FirstName field as a string. These methods perform no data conversions so in this example the field must actually be a string value or the method raises an error. Because these methods perform no conversions, they are slightly faster than the more generic Item method. Table 6.4 lists these methods.

PART I CH 6

TABLE 6.4   SqlDataReader Column Methods

GetBoolean	GetByte	GetBytes	GetChar
GetChars	GetDateTime	GetDecimal	GetDouble
GetFloat	GetGuid	GetInt16	GetInt32
GetInt64	GetString		

Table 6.5 lists methods that get column values as SQL data types.

TABLE 6.5 SQLDATAREADER COLUMN FETCHING METHODS

GetSqlBinary	GetSqlBoolean	GetSqlByte	GetSqlDateTime
GetSqlDecimal	GetSqlDouble	GetSqlGuid	GetSqlInt16
GetSqlInt32	GetSqlInt64	GetSqlMoney	GetSqlSingle
GetSqlString			

Besides these methods for selecting column values, the SqlDataReader provides several properties and methods for manipulating the data. The following sections describe some of the most useful.

See the "ExecuteReader" section earlier in this chapter for an example that uses the SqlDataReader object.

GetFieldType AND GetDataTypeName

The GetFieldType method returns an object representing a column's data type. The GetDataTypeName method returns a string representation of the column's data type. For example, if the first column in the returned data is of type VARCHAR in the database, the following statement displays the value varchar:

```
MsgBox(data_reader.GetDataTypeName(0))
```

GetName AND GetOrdinal

The GetName method returns a column's database field name. The GetOrdinal method returns the index of the column given its name. If data_reader.GetOrdinal("LastName") returns 3, data_reader.GetName(3) should return LastName.

GetSchemaTable

The GetSchemaTable method returns a DataTable object containing information about the SqlDataReader's columns. This is not a DataTable that has columns matching those of the selected data. It is a DataTable with rows that contain values describing the columns. The fields in each row include such values as the column properties ColumnName, ColumnSize, NumericPrecision, IsUnique, IsKey, IsReadOnly, and so forth.

Example program UseExecuteReader (see Listing 6.6 earlier in this chapter) uses GetSchemaTable to build column headers for a ListView control.

GetValue, GetValues, GetSqlValue, AND GetSqlValues

The GetValue method returns an object representing a column's value much as the Item method does. A major difference is that the GetValue method must take the column's index as a parameter, while the Item method can use its name as a key.

The GetValues method returns an array of objects containing the field values for the current row.

The GetSqlValue and GetSqlValues methods are similar to GetValue and GetValues, except they return objects representing the columns' SQL data types.

IsDbNull

The IsDbNull method returns True if the indicated column has a Null value.

NextResult

If the data reader is the result of a batch query containing more than one SQL SELECT statement, the data reader contains the results for each statement separately. The NextResult method makes the data reader move to the next group of results.

SqlTransaction

A *transaction* is a group of database operations that should be treated as a unit. Either they should all take place or none of them should take place.

The classic example of a transaction is an accounting system where each credit must have a corresponding debit. To transfer money from one account to another, you subtract money from one account's record and you add the same amount to another account's record. You need these operations to take place as a single unit to keep the books balanced. If the debit occurs and the corresponding credit does not, the system has lost money. If the credit occurs and the debit does not, the system has magically created money.

A more common scenario involves records in tables with master-detail relationships. For example, suppose the Customers table contains basic customer information. The CustomerAddresses, CustomerPayments, CustomerOperatingAreas, and CustomerOrders tables provide detail. If you delete a Customers record or change the CustomerId field linking these tables, you need to ensure that all the related tables are also updated. If the program crashes or encounters another error before it finishes updating all of the related records, the database will end up with inaccessible detail records that are not linked to any master record.

Note

Under some circumstances you can make the database automatically cascade the changes. If you have cascading disabled, you can protect the database using transactions.

PART

I

CH

6

To prevent these kinds of problems, the related operations should be placed in the same transaction. Databases such as Oracle and SQL Server have transaction capabilities that guarantee that the operations are performed as a single unit. They either all take place or none takes place.

In Visual Basic .NET, the SqlTransaction object ensures that transactions are handled properly. An application uses the SqlConnection object's BeginTransaction method to create a new SqlTransaction object. The program attaches that object to the SqlCommand objects that will perform the tasks that should be part of the same transaction, and the program invokes those command objects to perform the tasks. When it has finished, the program can call the SqlTransaction's Commit method to make the operations permanent or its Rollback method to cancel all the operations.

One particularly useful coding technique is to place the database operations in a Try Catch block. The last statement in the Try block calls the SqlTransaction's Commit method; so if all the database operations succeed, Commit makes them permanent. The Catch block calls the SqlTransaction's Rollback method so if any of the operations fails they are all canceled.

Example program Transaction, shown in Figure 6.6, demonstrates this method. Enter letters in the Letter column and one-digit numbers in the Number column. When you click the Add Records button, the program uses the values you entered to insert two records into the TestTable database table.

Figure 6.6
Example program Transaction uses a SqlTransaction object to ensure that two INSERT commands either both occur or both do not occur.

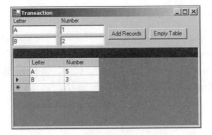

The TestTable table was created with the following SQL statement so the Letter field must be a single character and the Number field must be a one-digit number.

```
CREATE TABLE TestTable (
    Letter    CHAR(1)        NOT NULL,
    Number    NUMERIC(1, 0)  NOT NULL
);
```

If you enter a string with more than one character, the INSERT statement for that record fails. Similarly, if you enter a number with more than one digit, the INSERT statement fails. The program executes both INSERT statements in the same transaction so they either both succeed or they both fail. By entering valid and invalid values, you can experiment with the program's transaction.

For example, enter valid values on the first line and an invalid number on the second. When you click Add Records, the program successfully inserts the first record. It then fails to insert the second record and rolls back both INSERT statements. When the program updates its data display, you will see no change to the table.

If you enter valid values in all four text boxes and click Add Records, both INSERT statements succeed and the program shows the new records in its data display.

Program Transaction executes the code shown in Listing 6.12 when you click the Add Records button. The event handler begins by creating a new SqlConnection to the database and making a `SqlCommand` object attached to the connection. It opens the connection, uses its `BeginTransaction` method to create a new transaction, and attaches the `SqlTransaction` object to the `SqlCommand` object.

Then inside a `Try` block, the program attempts to insert the two new records. If both insertions succeed, the final statement within the `Try` block calls the transaction's `Commit` method to make the insertions permanent.

If either insertion fails, the `Catch` block takes over. It rolls back the `INSERT` statements and displays an error message.

The event handler finishes by closing its database connection and by calling `DisplayData` to redisplay the table's data.

Subroutine `DisplayData` creates a new DataTable, uses a SqlDataAdapter to fill it with the values in the database, and binds the DataTable to the program's DataGrid control.

LISTING 6.12 PROGRAM TRANSACTION USES A TRANSACTION IN A `Try` `Catch` BLOCK.

```
Private Const SELECT_STRING = _
    "SELECT * FROM TestTable ORDER BY Letter, Number"
Private Const CONNECT_STRING = _
    "Data Source=Bender\NETSDK;Initial Catalog=Trans;user id=sa"

Private m_DataAdapter As New SqlDataAdapter(SELECT_STRING, CONNECT_STRING)

' Create both or none of the new records.
Private Sub btnAddRecords_Click(ByVal sender As System.Object, _
  ByVal e As System.EventArgs) Handles btnAddRecords.Click
    ' Prepare the SqlCommand.
    Dim sql_connection As New SqlConnection(CONNECT_STRING)
    Dim insert_command As New SqlCommand( _
        "INSERT INTO TestTable (Letter, Number) " & _
        "VALUES (@Letter, @Number)", _
        sql_connection)

    ' Open the connection.
    sql_connection.Open()

    ' Create the transaction.
    Dim insert_transaction As SqlTransaction = _
        sql_connection.BeginTransaction()

    ' Perform the commands in the transaction.
    insert_command.Transaction = insert_transaction

    ' Perform the actions.
    Try
        ' Insert the first record.
        insert_command.Parameters.Add("@Letter", txtLetter1.Text)
        insert_command.Parameters.Add("@Number", txtNumber1.Text)
        insert_command.ExecuteNonQuery()

        ' Insert the second record.
        insert_command.Parameters(0).Value = txtLetter2.Text
```

PART

I

CH

6

LISTING 6.12   CONTINUED

```
        insert_command.Parameters(1).Value = txtNumber2.Text
        insert_command.ExecuteNonQuery()

        ' Commit the insertions.
        insert_transaction.Commit()
    Catch exc As Exception
        ' Rollback the transaction.
        insert_transaction.Rollback()

        ' Display an error message.
        MsgBox(exc.Message)
    End Try

    ' Close the connection.
    sql_connection.Close()

    ' Display the results.
    DisplayData()
End Sub

' Display the data in the Contacts table.
Private Sub DisplayData()
    Dim data_table As New DataTable()

    ' Fill the DataTable.
    m_DataAdapter.Fill(data_table)

    ' Bind the DataGrid to the DataTable.
    dgContacts.DataSource = data_table
End Sub
```

The SqlTransaction object's Save method creates a *save point*. After creating a save point, the program can later roll the transaction back to that point, keeping any earlier operations it performed. This is a much less commonly used technique than committing or rolling back all changes in a group.

OLE DB

OLE (object linking and embedding) is a specification that defines ways in which different applications can make data available to each other. OLE DB is OLE applied to databases. Using OLE DB providers, an application can work with data from a variety of databases.

Microsoft supplies OLE DB providers for many data sources, including SQL Server, Oracle, Jet (Access databases), AS/400, and VSAM. It also has an ODBC provider that gives access to ODBC-compliant databases, which includes most relational databases.

Visual Basic provides a family of objects that work with OLE DB data providers. Table 6.6 summarizes those objects.

TABLE 6.6   OLE DB DATA ACCESS OBJECTS

Class	Purpose
OleDbConnection	Connects the application to a database using OLE DB
OleDbCommand	Represents a stored procedure or SQL statement that the program will execute on an OleDbConnection
OleDbParameter	Represents a parameter used by an OleDbCommand object
OleDbDataAdapter	Uses OleDbCommand objects to move data between a database and DataSet objects
OleDbCommandBuilder	Generates OleDbCommand objects
OleDbDataReader	Allows the program to read a forward-only set of data
OleDbTransaction	Manages SQL transactions in the database

These classes are exactly analogous to their SQL counterparts. For instance, the OleDbConnection class corresponds to the SqlConnection class.

The SQL versions of these classes are optimized for SQL Server databases. You can use the OleDb classes to access the data in a SQL Server database, but the SQL classes provide better performance. If you know you will be using a SQL Server database, use the SQL versions of these classes. If you know you won't be using a SQL Server database or you don't know what kind of database you will be using, use the OLE DB versions of these classes.

The earlier sections in this chapter describe the SQL Server versions of these classes in some detail so the OLE DB versions are not described further here. In most cases you can use the classes exactly as you would use the SQL Server versions simply by changing the initial "Sql" to "OleDb". The major exception is the database connect string. You need to use the correct connect string for the particular type of database you want to use. For example, the following code shows a connect string for a SQL Server database:

```
Data Source=Bender\NETSDK;Initial Catalog=TestScores;user id=sa
```

The following code shows a similar connect string for an Access database:

```
Provider=Microsoft.Jet.OLEDB.4.0;Data Source=C:\VB DB\Src\Ch04\TestScores.mdb
```

PART

I

CH

6

EXAMPLE PROGRAM RUNSCRIPT

Example Program RunScript, shown in Figure 6.7, ties together several of the objects described in this chapter to execute SQL scripts. Use the File menu's commands to open an Access or SQL Server database. Use the Open Script command to load a text file containing a SQL script or type one in yourself. When you click the Execute button, the program executes the commands in the script and displays the results. The program displays the records returned by queries. For non-query commands, the program displays a success or failure message.

Figure 6.7
Example program
RunScript executes
SQL scripts.

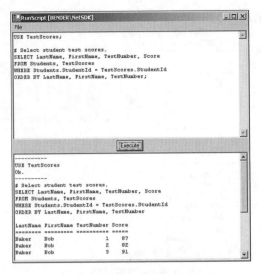

The script should contain one or more SQL statements separated by semicolons. The program uses the # symbol to indicate a comment. When it sees #, the program ignores the rest of the current line.

Program RunScript uses the code in Listing 6.13 to execute scripts. The program uses a SqlConnection object to connect to SQL Server databases or an OleDbConnection object to connect to Access databases. You could easily modify it to connect to other kinds of databases using the OleDbConnection object.

A fair chunk of the program's code deals with processing the script's text rather than executing it using database objects. For example, the RemoveComments function removes comments beginning with # from a string. These routines are important but how they work is not central to this discussion, so they are not described in detail here and their code does not appear in Listing 6.13. Download the program's source code from this book's Web site to see all the details.

When you click the Execute button, the program's btnExecute_Click event handler executes. This routine uses Visual Basic's Split command to break the script into the SQL statements separated by semicolons. It then considers each statement in turn.

For each statement, the program calls the TrimNonPrinting function to remove leading and trailing nonprintable characters. This removes leading and following carriage returns that the script may contain to improve readability.

If the statement is nonblank after trimming, the program processes it. It first adds the statement to the result string. This makes it easier to see which statements produced which results in the output.

The program then determines whether the statement begins with the string SELECT, SP_, or XP_. If the statement begins with SELECT, it is a SELECT statement that returns rows. If it begins with SP_ or XP_, the statement is probably a call to a system stored procedure. Most of those procedures return rows, so the program treats the statement as if it returns rows.

For a particular application, you might want to examine the statement more closely. For example, you may have created stored procedures. In that case, you would need to determine whether the statement invokes one of those procedures and whether it returns rows.

If the statement returns rows, the program calls subroutine ExecuteQuery to execute it. If the statement does not return rows, the program creates either a SqlCommand or an OleDbCommand for the statement and calls its ExecuteNonQuery method to execute it. When the call to ExecuteQuery or the SqlCommand or OleDbCommand object's ExecuteNonQuery method returns, the program adds a success message to its output.

If the program encounters an error while executing the statement, it displays an error message and asks if you want to continue running the rest of the script. The ability to continue is useful because it lets you include statements that may not always work in the script. For instance, a script that creates a new table can first use a DROP TABLE statement to ensure the table does not already exist. If the table doesn't currently exist, the program presents an error message. At that point, you can tell the program to continue running anyway.

After it has processed a statement, the program displays its results so far and you can see that it is making progress.

Subroutine ExecuteQuery executes a query and returns a string containing the results. Depending on the type of database, it creates either a SqlDataAdapter object or an OleDbDataAdapter object using the query and the current database connection. It uses that object to fill a DataSet. Then subroutine ExecuteQuery just needs to format the results in a string.

The subroutine loops over all the returned tables. For each table, the subroutine determines how many columns the table contains and redimensions its col_len array so it has one entry per column. It then loops through the table's columns setting the col_len entry for each to the length of the corresponding column's name.

Next, ExecuteQuery loops through the table's rows. For each row, the subroutine compares the length of each column's data entry with its col_len entry. For Null values, the program uses the length 4 because it will represent the value with the string NULL when it produces the output. For byte arrays, the program uses the length 6 because it represents those values with the string <byte>.

If the length of the data value is longer than the current col_len value, the routine updates col_len. When it has finished checking every row, the col_len entry for a column holds the maximum length of the column's name and all the column's values in every row.

Next, the subroutine loops through the columns creating format strings for each. For a column of 10 characters, the FormatString property returns a string of the form {0,-10} for Boolean, character, DateTime, and string values, and a string of the form {0,10} for numeric values. The program uses these strings later to format the column's results. These values for the format strings make the results blank padded to the column's full length with strings left-justified and numbers right-justified.

ExecuteQuery then loops through the columns adding their names to its result text. It uses the columns' format strings to properly justify the column names. After the column names, the subroutine adds a row of equal signs.

Finally the subroutine begins adding data to the result. For each row, the program loops through the items in the row. For Null values, the subroutine adds the string NULL to the output. For byte arrays, the subroutine adds the value <byte> to the output. For other values, the subroutine adds the value to the output properly justified.

LISTING 6.13 PROGRAM RUNSCRIPT USES THIS CODE TO EXECUTE SQL SCRIPTS

```
' Tells if we are using OleDb versus SQL Server.
Private m_UseOleDb As Boolean

' The database connection.
Private m_OleDbConnection As OleDbConnection
Private m_SqlConnection As SqlConnection

' Execute the user's statements.
Private Sub btnExecute_Click(ByVal sender As Object, _
  ByVal e As System.EventArgs) Handles btnExecute.Click
    Dim oldeb_command As OleDbCommand
    Dim sql_command As SqlCommand
    Dim statements() As String
    Dim statement As String
    Dim sql As String
    Dim i As Integer
    Dim rows_affected As Long
    Dim stop_early As Boolean
    Dim results As String
    Dim data_set As DataSet
    Dim row_returning As Boolean

    Me.Cursor = Cursors.WaitCursor
    txtResults.Text = ""
    Me.Refresh()

    ' Get the user's statements.
    statements = Split(txtStatements.Text, ";")

    ' Process each statement.
    results = ""
    For i = statements.GetLowerBound(0) To statements.GetUpperBound(0)
        ' Get the next statement and see if it is blank.
        statement = TrimNonPrinting(statements(i))
        sql = TrimNonPrinting(RemoveComments(statement))

        If sql.Length > 0 Then
            ' Add the statement to the results.
            results = results & "-----" & vbCrLf & _
                statement & vbCrLf
```

LISTING 6.13 CONTINUED

```
                ' See if this statement returns rows.
                row_returning = _
                    sql.ToUpper.StartsWith("SELECT") Or _
                    sql.ToUpper.StartsWith("SP_") Or _
                    sql.ToUpper.StartsWith("XP_")

                Try
                    If row_returning Then
                        ' Execute the query.
                        results = results & _
                            ExecuteQuery(sql) & _
                            vbCrLf
                    Else
                        ' Execute the non-query statement.
                        ' Create the OleDbCommand object using the
                        ' current script statement.
                        If m_UseOleDb Then
                            ' Use an OleDbCommand.
                            oldeb_command = New OleDbCommand( _
                                sql, m_OleDbConnection)

                            ' Execute the command.
                            rows_affected = oldeb_command.ExecuteNonQuery()
                        Else
                            ' Use a SqlCommand.
                            sql_command = New SqlCommand( _
                                sql, m_SqlConnection)

                            ' Execute the command.
                            rows_affected = sql_command.ExecuteNonQuery()
                        End If

                        ' Display a success message.
                        If rows_affected <= 1 Then
                            results = results & "Ok." & vbCrLf
                        Else
                            results = results & "Ok. " & rows_affected & _
                                " rows affected" & vbCrLf
                        End If
                    End If
                Catch exc As Exception
                    ' Add an error message to the results.
                    results = results & exc.Message & vbCrLf
                    txtResults.Text = results
                    txtResults.Select(0, 0)

                    ' Display the exception's error message and ask
                    ' the user if we should continue with other statements.
                    stop_early = (MsgBox(exc.Message & vbCrLf & _
                        "Continue?", _
                        MsgBoxStyle.Exclamation Or MsgBoxStyle.YesNo, _
                        "SQL Error") = MsgBoxResult.No)
                End Try
            End If ' End If statement.Length > 0
```

PART

I

CH

6

LISTING 6.13 CONTINUED

```
        txtResults.Text = results
        txtResults.Select(results.Length, 0)
        txtResults.ScrollToCaret()
        txtResults.Refresh()

        ' See if we had a problem and the user wants to stop.
        If stop_early Then Exit For
    Next i ' Get the next statement.

    Me.Cursor = Cursors.Default
End Sub

' Execute a query and return the results.
Private Function ExecuteQuery(ByVal query As String) As String
    Dim oldeb_adapter As New OleDbDataAdapter()
    Dim sql_adapter As New SqlDataAdapter()
    Dim results As String
    Dim data_set As New DataSet()
    Dim table_num As Integer
    Dim max_row As Integer
    Dim max_col As Integer
    Dim row As Integer
    Dim col As Integer
    Dim row_string As String
    Dim col_len() As Integer
    Dim col_format() As String
    Dim new_len As Integer

    ' Execute the query and get a DataSet holding the results.
    If m_UseOleDb Then
        ' Use OLE DB.
        oldeb_adapter.SelectCommand = _
            New OleDbCommand(query, m_OleDbConnection)
        oldeb_adapter.Fill(data_set)
    Else
        ' Use SQL Server.
        sql_adapter.SelectCommand = _
            New SqlCommand(query, m_SqlConnection)
        sql_adapter.Fill(data_set)
    End If

    ' Iterate over each table.
    For table_num = 0 To data_set.Tables.Count - 1
        ' Make room for the column sizes.
        max_row = data_set.Tables(table_num).Rows.Count - 1
        max_col = data_set.Tables(table_num).Columns.Count - 1
        ReDim col_len(max_col)

        ' See how big the column names are.
        For col = 0 To max_col
            new_len = data_set.Tables(table_num).Columns(col).ColumnName.Length
            If col_len(col) < new_len Then
                col_len(col) = new_len
            End If
        Next col
```

LISTING 6.13   CONTINUED

```
        ' See how big the column entries are.
        For row = 0 To max_row
            For col = 0 To max_col
                If data_set.Tables(table_num).Rows(row).ItemArray(col).GetType _
                    Is GetType(System.DBNull) Then
                        new_len = 4
                ElseIf data_set.Tables(table_num).Rows(row).ItemArray(col). _
                GetType Is GetType(Byte()) Then
                        new_len = 6
                Else
                        new_len = _
CStr(data_set.Tables(table_num).Rows(row).ItemArray(col)).Length
                End If
                If col_len(col) < new_len Then
                    col_len(col) = new_len
                End If
            Next col
        Next row

        ' Build column formats.
        ReDim col_format(max_col)
        For col = 0 To max_col
            col_format(col) = " " & _
                FormatString( _
                    data_set.Tables(table_num).Columns(col).DataType, _
                    col_len(col))
        Next col

        ' Add the column names to the result.
        row_string = ""
        For col = 0 To max_col
            row_string &= String.Format( _
                col_format(col), _
                data_set.Tables(table_num).Columns(col).ColumnName)
        Next col
        results = row_string.Substring(1) & vbCrLf

        ' Add a row of ====.
        row_string = ""
        For col = 0 To max_col
            ' Add a string of ='s the length
            ' of this column.
            row_string &= " " & _
                New String("="c, col_len(col))
        Next col
        results &= row_string.Substring(1) & vbCrLf

        ' Add the results.
        For row = 0 To max_row
            row_string = ""
            For col = 0 To max_col
                If data_set.Tables(table_num).Rows(row).ItemArray(col).GetType _
                    Is GetType(System.DBNull) Then
                        row_string &= String.Format( _
                            col_format(col), "NULL")
```

LISTING 6.13   CONTINUED

```
                    ElseIf data_set.Tables(table_num).Rows(row).ItemArray(col).GetType
  _
                    Is GetType(Byte()) Then
                        row_string &= String.Format( _
                            col_format(col), "<byte>")
                    Else
                        row_string &= String.Format( _
                            col_format(col),
    data_set.Tables(table_num).Rows(row).Item(col))
                    End If
                Next col
                results &= row_string.Substring(1) & vbCrLf
            Next row
        Next table_num

        Return vbCrLf & results
    End Function
```

The following code shows some sample output. Notice that each SQL statement is repeated in the output followed by its results. Notice also how the numeric TestNumber and Score fields are right-justified in the results of the SELECT statement.

```
— · — — —
USE TestScores
Ok.
— — — —
# Select student test scores.
SELECT LastName, FirstName, TestNumber, Score
FROM Students, TestScores
WHERE Students.StudentId = TestScores.StudentId
ORDER BY LastName, FirstName, TestNumber

LastName FirstName TestNumber Score
======== ========= ========== =====
Baker    Bob                1    87
Baker    Bob                2    82
Baker    Bob                3    91
Baker    Bob                4    86
Carter   Cindy              1    62
Carter   Cindy              2    39
Carter   Cindy              3    71
Carter   Cindy              4    69
Dorph    Donald             1    70
Dorph    Donald             2    65
Dorph    Donald             3    72
Dorph    Donald             4    81
```

This program does some simple checking to determine whether a command is a query or a nonquery statement. You might also want to restrict access to certain statements depending on the user's privileges. For example, you might want to disallow CREATE TABLE, DROP TABLE, and other potentially dangerous statements for most users. You might also want to disallow DELETE statements that do not have WHERE clauses to prevent the user from accidentally deleting every record in a table by omitting the WHERE clause.

You can use the database's privileges to prevent the user from performing some of these actions, but often you need the user to be able to perform these actions using your program but not using an ad hoc script. In that case, you can modify the program to perform these more extensive checks.

This program's database programming code is relatively simple. It only uses a few database objects. Most of its code prepares the script's statements for execution and formats the results. This is still quite a powerful tool. It can perform almost any database operation that you can write using SQL. It can create, populate, and delete tables and even SQL Server databases.

Many of the commercial applications I have written have contained similar tools for use by more advanced users. In some cases, the tools only performed queries. In others, the tools gave database administrators a new method for running their own database maintenance scripts.

SUMMARY

The classes described in this chapter allow a program to connect to a database and move data between it and the classes described in Chapter 5. Between these two groups of classes, an application can insert, update, delete, and select data. It can even create databases and modify their structures. These classes give an application remarkable flexibility when dealing with databases and their data.

CHAPTER 7

XML DATABASES

Relational databases such as Access, SQL Server, and Oracle have many advantages over XML files. These advantages include powerful tools that XML lacks for searching, arranging, grouping, and summarizing data. Relational databases store data in a relatively efficient binary format and use indexes to make searching for particular values fast. They give you access to transactions, privileges, and various record locking schemes to help you protect the data.

On the other hand, XML files do have several advantages over relational databases. They are plain text files with a simple intuitive format so they are easy to read and understand. Visual Basic provides methods for loading, manipulating, and saving XML files. Best of all, Visual Basic provides easy-to-use tools for building and editing XML files. Although these features make XML a poor choice for large, high-performance database needs, they make XML ideal for small, single-user applications, testing, and prototypes.

Chapter 1, "Data Storage Alternatives," describes XML briefly. This chapter explains some of the tools Visual Basic provides for working with XML databases in more detail. It shows how to build and edit an XML file, and how to use XML files in Visual Basic applications.

WHAT IS XML?

XML (Extensible Markup Language) is a text-based data storage language. It uses a series of tags that you define to store data. The file may begin with some XML declaration tags, followed by a single root data node that contains all the other data nodes in a hierarchy.

You do not need to explicitly declare the tags; you just start using them. For instance, Listing 7.1 shows an XML file describing three PhoneNumber records.

LISTING 7.1 A SIMPLE XML FILE

```
<AddressBook>
    <PhoneNumber>
        <LastName>Jenkins</LastName>
        <FirstName>Jeremy</FirstName>
        <HomePhone>987-654-3210</HomePhone>
    </PhoneNumber>
    <PhoneNumber>
        <LastName>Ketterling</LastName>
        <FirstName>Karen</FirstName>
        <WorkPhone>456-769-2340</WorkPhone>
    </PhoneNumber>
```

LISTING 7.1   CONTINUED

```
    <PhoneNumber>
        <LastName>Ludovico</LastName>
        <FirstName>Lawrence</FirstName>
        <HomePhone>983-479-4963</HomePhone>
        <HomeFax>983-479-4963</HomeFax>
    </PhoneNumber>
</AddressBook>
```

Even without an explicit definition of the fields, you can easily understand this file's structure and the data it contains.

The records in an XML file do not need to have an identical format. In this example, the three records have different combinations of HomePhone, WorkPhone, and HomeFax fields.

XML elements can contain other elements to any depth of nesting. For example, Listing 7.2 shows a way you could break the HomePhone element into subfields in the previous code's first record.

LISTING 7.2   AN XML FILE CAN CONTAIN NESTED ELEMENTS

```
<AddressBook>
    <PhoneNumber>
        <LastName>Jenkins</LastName>
        <FirstName>Jeremy</FirstName>
        <HomePhone>
            <CountryCode>1</CountryCode>
            <AreaCode>987</AreaCode>
            <Exchange>654</Exchange>
            <Line>3210</Line>
            <Extension></Extension>
    </PhoneNumber>
    ...
</AddressBook>
```

In this example, breaking the phone number into five subfields is probably overkill.

Although you can nest XML elements to any depth, three relatively simple formats are particularly useful: *single-table*, *multi-table*, and *deep multi-table*. You can build XML files with other formats, although those formats tend to be more confusing and harder to work with, at least when you want to use them to model relational databases.

SINGLE-TABLE

In a single-table XML format, the root data node contains elements of the same type. The nodes each contain a series of elements taken from the same set of element types. This gives the XML hierarchy three levels: root, record, and field.

For instance, in Listing 7.1 the root node AddressBook contains PhoneNumber elements. Those elements contain nodes describing a phone number entry: LastName, FirstName, HomePhone, and so forth. Each PhoneNumber element need not contain all the possible elements, but you know what the possibilities are.

This XML file maps naturally into a simple relational database with one table. The root node corresponds to the database's name. The elements inside the root node correspond to the records in a table. The elements inside those records correspond to the fields in the table's records. In this example, the AddressBook database contains the table PhoneNumber. The PhoneNumber table holds the fields LastName, FirstName, and so forth.

MULTI-TABLE

In a multi-table XML file, the data root element contains records of more than one type. Each record element contains fields as before. Listing 7.3 shows an XML file containing PhoneNumber and ImportantDate elements.

LISTING 7.3   A MULTI-TABLE FORMAT CONTAINS RECORDS FROM MULTIPLE TABLES

```
<AddressBook>
    <PhoneNumber>
        <LastName>Jenkins</LastName>
        <FirstName>Jeremy</FirstName>
        <HomePhone>987-654-3210</HomePhone>
    </PhoneNumber>
    <PhoneNumber>
        <LastName>Ketterling</LastName>
        <FirstName>Karen</FirstName>
        <WorkPhone>456-769-2340</WorkPhone>
    </PhoneNumber>
    <ImportantDate>
        <Date>4/1/1971</Date>
        <Notes>Mary's birthday</Notes>
    </ImportantDate>
    <PhoneNumber>
        <LastName>Ludovico</LastName>
        <FirstName>Lawrence</FirstName>
        <HomePhone>983-479-4963</HomePhone>
        <HomeFax>983-479-4963</HomeFax>
    </PhoneNumber>
    <ImportantDate>
        <Date>12/21/1987</Date>
        <Notes>Nigel's anniversary</Notes>
    </ImportantDate>
    <ImportantDate>
        <Date>2/13/2000</Date>
        <Notes>Olga's birthday</Notes>
    </ImportantDate>
</AddressBook>
```

This file corresponds to an AddressBook database containing two tables: PhoneNumber and ImportantDate. The records in each of those tables contain fields appropriate to the table.

DEEP MULTI-TABLE

Note that the records in a multi-table XML file can be interspersed. In Listing 7.3, PhoneNumber and ImportantDate elements are mixed. It may make the file easier to read, however, if you group similar records. You can make the file even easier to read if you group the records for a table in their own subelement. For example, Listing 7.4 groups the records for each table in its own subelement.

Listing 7.4   Grouping Similar Records Makes an XML File Easier to Read

```
<AddressBook>
    <PhoneNumbers>
        <PhoneNumber>
            <LastName>Jenkins</LastName>
            <FirstName>Jeremy</FirstName>
            <HomePhone>987-654-3210</HomePhone>
        </PhoneNumber>
        <PhoneNumber>
            <LastName>Ketterling</LastName>
            <FirstName>Karen</FirstName>
            <WorkPhone>456-769-2340</WorkPhone>
        </PhoneNumber>
        <PhoneNumber>
            <LastName>Ludovico</LastName>
            <FirstName>Lawrence</FirstName>
            <HomePhone>983-479-4963</HomePhone>
            <HomeFax>983-479-4963</HomeFax>
        </PhoneNumber>
    </PhoneNumbers>
    <ImportantDates>
        <ImportantDate>
            <Date>4/1/1971</Date>
            <Notes>Mary's birthday</Notes>
        </ImportantDate>
        <ImportantDate>
            <Date>12/21/1987</Date>
            <Notes>Nigel's anniversary</Notes>
        </ImportantDate>
        <ImportantDate>
            <Date>2/13/2000</Date>
            <Notes>Olga's birthday</Notes>
        </ImportantDate>
    </ImportantDates>
</AddressBook>
```

Other Formats

You can also make deeply nested XML files that do not represent tables in such a straight-forward manner. The example in Listing 7.2 that breaks PhoneNumber into CountryCode, AreaCode, Exchange, Line, and Extension fields demonstrates this idea. In a similar manner, you can make XML files that contain elements nested to any depth.

For example, you could create an inventory file containing products made up of assemblies, containing parts made up of subparts, and so forth. Deeply nested XML files can also be useful in modeling hierarchical data such as file systems and organizational charts.

These kinds of deeply nested files can be hard to read, particularly if the concept behind the nesting relationship is poorly defined. A parts hierarchy or organizational chart is relatively straightforward. A file containing a one-level employee table, a deeply nested parts table, a one-level customer table, and a random assortment of Web page information could be confusing. It might be better to break this information into separate XML files that each have a tighter focus.

EDITING XML FILES

Editing XML files is fairly easy. Their simple format makes them easy enough to build in any text editor, such as WordPad. Although building XML files using WordPad isn't hard, Visual Basic provides some tools that make editing XML files even easier.

To add an XML file to a Visual Basic project, select the Project menu's Add New Item command. Select the XML File tool and click OK. Figure 7.1 shows Visual Basic's XML editor as it initially appears in XML mode. The XML declaration on the first line is added automatically by Visual Basic and you should not change it. You can type the rest of the XML data directly into the file.

Figure 7.1
Visual Basic's XML editor lets you edit XML code directly.

The XML editor color codes the different parts of the XML file to make it easier to see which parts of the file represent element names, attribute values, and data. When you type in an opening tag, the editor automatically adds a matching closing tag. For instance, if you type `<PhoneNumber>`, the editor adds the tag `</PhoneNumber>` and places the cursor between the tags so you can enter the element's content.

If you click on the Data button on the XML editor's lower-left corner, the editor displays the data in the XML file as shown in Figure 7.2. Click on a table in the column on the left to see that table's data. Click on a field and enter text to change a field's value. Click to the left of the first field to select a record and press Delete to delete that record. Click on the row marked with an asterisk to add a new record.

Figure 7.2
Visual Basic's XML editor lets you edit XML data in a grid display.

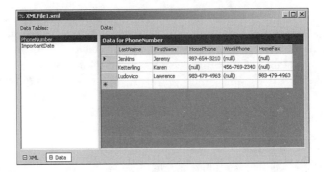

The file used in Figures 7.1 and 7.2 is a multi-table XML file similar to the one shown in Listing 7.3. Its AddressBook root node contains elements of the PhoneNumber and ImportantDate types. The XML editor treats these as two tables.

The editor uses all the fields defined in each record to determine the fields that belong to each table. For example, different PhoneNumber records contain LastName, FirstName, HomePhone, WorkPhone, and HomeFax fields, so those are the fields the editor gives to the PhoneNumber table. If a record is missing one of those values, the editor assigns the record's field the value Null.

Figure 7.3 shows the XML editor viewing a deep multi-table XML file similar to the one shown in Listing 7.4. This file's root node contains two child elements named PhoneNumbers and ImportantDates. Those elements contain PhoneNumber and ImportantDate records, respectively.

Figure 7.3
Visual Basic's XML editor lets you edit XML data in a grid display.

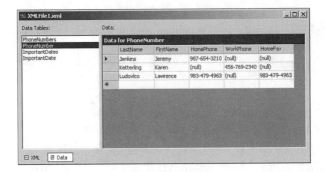

While this structure makes the XML text file easier to understand, it makes editing it in the XML editor a bit more confusing. The PhoneNumber and ImportantDate elements are contained in the PhoneNumbers and ImportantDates elements, but they are all shown in the same way in the XML editor's left hand column.

Other deeply nested XML structures can also be a little confusing. Figure 7.4 shows an XML file where different PhoneNumber records contain HomePhone, WorkPhone, and HomeFax elements. Those elements contain their own subelements so they are shown underlined in

Figure 7.4. If you click on one, the editor displays the fields it contains, as shown in Figure 7.5.

Figure 7.4
The XML editor underlines fields that contain other fields.

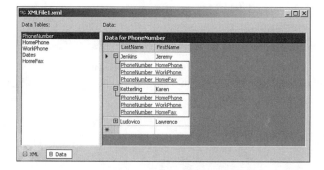

Figure 7.5
Click on an underlined field to see the elements it contains.

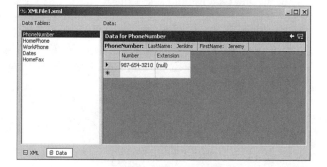

These elements that contain subelements are also listed in the column on the left. If you select one, the XML editor displays those elements as shown in Figure 7.6. It's hard to tell how these values fit into the XML file's overall structure so this display can be quite confusing. Usually it is easier to start with the highest level elements, PhoneNumber and Dates in this example, and move into subelements to see more detail.

Figure 7.6
Select an element with subelements in the left column to see a list of those elements.

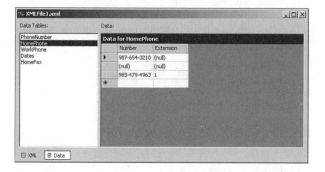

SCHEMAS

A *schema* is a definition of the fields that should appear in an XML document. For example, you can use a schema to tell an XML parser that the file must contain only PhoneNumber elements and that those elements must contain LastName, FirstName, and HomePhone fields. You can even ensure that the HomePhone field's values look like valid phone numbers.

A schema can help ensure that the data your program loads makes sense. Sometimes that lets you reduce the amount of bounds checking and error handling code in your program.

Building and using schemas is a complex subject that is outside the bounds of this book. For more information, see my book *Visual Basic.NET and XML* (Wiley, 2002, http://www.vb-helper.com/xml.htm). Although working with schemas is difficult, the XML editor can build simple schemas for you.

Open the XML file in the XML editor and select the XML menu's Create Schema command. The editor builds a schema for the file and adds it to the Solution Explorer. The schema will have the same name as the XML file except with an xsd extension. For example, with the XML file Customers.xml the editor creates the schema file Customers.xsd. Listing 7.5 shows a schema generated for an XML file containing PhoneNumber and ImportantDate elements.

LISTING 7.5 THE XML EDITOR AUTOMATICALLY GENERATED THIS SCHEMA

```xml
<xsd:schema id="AddressBook" targetNamespace="http://tempuri.org/XMLFile11.xsd"
    xmlns="http://tempuri.org/XMLFile11.xsd"
    xmlns:xsd="http://www.w3.org/2001/XMLSchema"
    xmlns:msdata="urn:schemas-microsoft-com:xml-msdata"
    attributeFormDefault="qualified"
    elementFormDefault="qualified">
  <xsd:element name="AddressBook" msdata:IsDataSet="true"
      msdata:EnforceConstraints="False">
    <xsd:complexType>
      <xsd:choice maxOccurs="unbounded">
        <xsd:element name="PhoneNumber">
          <xsd:complexType>
            <xsd:sequence>
              <xsd:element name="LastName" type="xsd:string" minOccurs="0" />
              <xsd:element name="FirstName" type="xsd:string" minOccurs="0" />
              <xsd:element name="HomePhone" type="xsd:string" minOccurs="0" />
              <xsd:element name="WorkPhone" type="xsd:string" minOccurs="0" />
              <xsd:element name="HomeFax" type="xsd:string" minOccurs="0" />
            </xsd:sequence>
          </xsd:complexType>
        </xsd:element>
        <xsd:element name="ImportantDate">
          <xsd:complexType>
            <xsd:sequence>
              <xsd:element name="Date" type="xsd:string" minOccurs="0" />
              <xsd:element name="Notes" type="xsd:string" minOccurs="0" />
            </xsd:sequence>
          </xsd:complexType>
        </xsd:element>
```

LISTING 7.5   CONTINUED

```
      </xsd:choice>
    </xsd:complexType>
  </xsd:element>
</xsd:schema>
```

This schema doesn't do much. It defines the fields allowed in the PhoneNumber and ImportantDate elements. Because each element's minOccurs value is 0, all the fields are optional. Even without understanding schemas, you could make a field required by changing its minOccurs value to 1. You could also add a maxOccurs value to set an upper limit on the number of times an element can occur. If you learn more about schemas, you can use other attributes to set other properties for the elements.

LOADING XML DATA IN VISUAL BASIC

Visual Basic provides routines that make loading XML data trivial. Example program ReadXml, shown in Figure 7.7, loads XML data into a DataSet object. It then binds the DataSet to a DataGrid control so you can view the data. Use the File menu's Open command to select an XML file.

Figure 7.7
Example program
ReadXml loads XML
files and displays their
data.

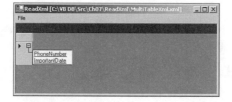

Click on an underlined entry in the DataGrid to expand that object. If you click the PhoneNumber entry in Figure 7.7, the program displays the PhoneNumber records as shown in Figure 7.8. Click the white arrow pointing left in the DataGrid's upper right corner to close the detail view and see the objects shown in Figure 7.7 again.

Figure 7.8
If you click on an
underlined entry, pro-
gram ReadXml shows
the entry's contents.

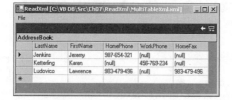

PART

I

CH

7

Example program ReadXml uses the code shown in Listing 7.6 to load and display XML files. After the user selects a file, the program creates a new DataSet object and calls its ReadXml method to load the file. It then binds the DataSet to a DataGrid control and the DataGrid takes care of displaying the data.

If you just want the program to display the data, that's the end of the story. Program ReadXml also prints information about the structure of the DataSet holding the XML file in the Debug window.

Subroutine `DisplayDataSetStructure` begins by printing the number of tables in the DataSet. It then loops through the tables displaying information about each. For each table, the routine displays the table's name and the names of its columns.

The program then loops through the table's `ChildRelations` and `ParentRelations` collections calling subroutine `DisplayDataRelation` to describe each of the relations.

Subroutine `DisplayDataRelation` calls the relation's `ParentRelations` and `ChildRelations` methods to get arrays of DataColumn objects describing the fields that are linked by the relation. It loops through those arrays displaying the table and column names of the related fields.

LISTING 7.6   PROGRAM READXML USES THIS CODE TO LOAD AND DISPLAY XML DATA

```
' Load an XML file.
Private Sub mnuFileOpen_Click(ByVal sender As System.Object, _
  ByVal e As System.EventArgs) Handles mnuFileOpen.Click
    ' Let the user select the file.
    If dlgOpenFile.ShowDialog() = DialogResult.OK Then
        Dim data_set As New DataSet()

        Try
            ' Read the XML data.
            dgAddressBook.DataSource = Nothing
            data_set.ReadXml(dlgOpenFile.FileName)

            ' Bind the DataGrid to the DataSet.
            dgAddressBook.DataSource = data_set

            ' Display the file name in the form's caption.
            Me.Text = "ReadXml [" & dlgOpenFile.FileName & "]"

            ' Display the DataSet's structure.
            DisplayDataSetStructure(data_set)
        Catch exc As Exception
            MsgBox(exc.Message)
            Me.Text = "ReadXml []"
        End Try
    End If
End Sub

' Display the DataSet's structure.
Private Sub DisplayDataSetStructure(ByVal data_set As DataSet)
    Dim data_table As DataTable
    Dim data_column As DataColumn
    Dim data_relation As DataRelation

    ' Tell how many tables.
    Debug.WriteLine(data_set.Tables.Count & " tables")
```

LISTING 7.6   CONTINUED

```vb
    ' Display the tables.
    For Each data_table In data_set.Tables
        ' Display the table's name.
        Debug.WriteLine("******************************")
        Debug.WriteLine("Table " & data_table.TableName)

        ' Display the table's columns.
        For Each data_column In data_table.Columns
            Debug.WriteLine("Column " & data_column.ColumnName & _
                " (" & data_column.DataType.ToString & ")")
        Next data_column

        ' Display the table's child relations.
        For Each data_relation In data_table.ChildRelations
            DisplayDataRelation("Child relation: ", data_relation)
        Next data_relation

        ' Display the table's parent relations.
        For Each data_relation In data_table.ParentRelations
            DisplayDataRelation("Parent relation: ", data_relation)
        Next data_relation
    Next data_table
End Sub

' Display information about this DataRelation.
Private Sub DisplayDataRelation(ByVal relation_name As String, _
  ByVal data_relation As DataRelation)
    Dim parent_columns() As DataColumn
    Dim child_columns() As DataColumn
    Dim i As Integer

    parent_columns = data_relation.ParentColumns
    child_columns = data_relation.ChildColumns
    For i = 0 To parent_columns.GetUpperBound(0)
        Debug.WriteLine(relation_name & _
            parent_columns(i).Table.TableName & "." & _
            parent_columns(i).ColumnName & " = " & _
            child_columns(i).Table.TableName & "." & _
            child_columns(i).ColumnName)
    Next i
End Sub
```

Listing 7.7 shows the output for a deeply nested multi-table XML file. The two "real" tables are PhoneNumber and Dates. The PhoneNumber elements contain HomePhone, WorkPhone, and HomeFax fields. Those fields are broken into subfields so the DataSet makes them separate tables. It automatically creates the PhoneNumber_Id fields to link the tables.

LISTING 7.7   PROGRAM READXML PRODUCED THIS OUTPUT FOR A DEEPLY NESTED
MULTI-TABLE XML FILE

```
5 tables
******************************
Table PhoneNumber
Column LastName (System.String)
```

LISTING 7.7   CONTINUED

```
Column FirstName (System.String)
Column PhoneNumber_Id (System.Int32)
Child relation: PhoneNumber.PhoneNumber_Id = HomePhone.PhoneNumber_Id
Child relation: PhoneNumber.PhoneNumber_Id = WorkPhone.PhoneNumber_Id
Child relation: PhoneNumber.PhoneNumber_Id = HomeFax.PhoneNumber_Id
*******************************
Table HomePhone
Column Number (System.String)
Column PhoneNumber_Id (System.Int32)
Column Extension (System.String)
Parent relation: PhoneNumber.PhoneNumber_Id = HomePhone.PhoneNumber_Id
*******************************
Table WorkPhone
Column Number (System.String)
Column Extension (System.String)
Column PhoneNumber_Id (System.Int32)
Parent relation: PhoneNumber.PhoneNumber_Id = WorkPhone.PhoneNumber_Id
*******************************
Table Dates
Column Date (System.String)
Column Notes (System.String)
*******************************
Table HomeFax
Column Number (System.String)
Column Extension (System.String)
Column PhoneNumber_Id (System.Int32)
Parent relation: PhoneNumber.PhoneNumber_Id = HomeFax.PhoneNumber_Id
```

The ReadXml example program uses a DataGrid to display an XML file's data. After you have loaded the data into a DataSet, however, you can use all of the DataSet properties and methods to modify the data. You can change values, add new rows to tables, and delete records. You can even add new tables programmatically.

SAVING XML DATA FROM VISUAL BASIC

After you make changes to the data loaded from an XML file either manually or programmatically, you may want to save the changes back into the XML file. Example program EditXml is similar to program ReadXml except it allows you to save changes to a modified XML file.

Example program EditXml uses the code in Listing 7.8 to display XML data and save changes. The heart of the program is the DataSet object's WriteXml method, which saves data into an XML file. To ensure that no changes are lost, however, program EditXml must do more than simply calling WriteXml.

When the user selects the File menu's Open command, the program's mnuFileOpen_Click event handler calls the DataSafe function. DataSafe returns True if it safe to discard the currently loaded data. If DataSafe returns False, the event handler exits without discarding the current data and loading a new XML file.

If `DataSafe` returns True, the event handler lets the user select an XML file as before. It creates a new DataSet object and calls its `ReadXml` subroutine to load the file. It then calls the DataSet's `AcceptChanges` method to mark all of the DataSet's data as unmodified. The event handler binds the DataSet to the program's DataGrid control and calls subroutine `DisplayDataSetStructure` much as program ReadXml does.

The `DataSafe` subroutine calls the DataSet's `HasChanges` method to see if the data includes any new changes. If there are no unsaved changes, `DataSafe` returns True.

If there are changes, `DataSafe` asks the user if the program should save them. If the user clicks No, the changes do not need to be saved and the current data is safe to discard. If the user clicks Yes, `DataSafe` calls the `SaveData` subroutine to save the changes. If the user clicks Cancel, `DataSafe` returns False to indicate that it is not safe to discard the changed data.

The rest of the EditXml program is straightforward. When the user selects the File menu's Save command, the event handler calls subroutine `SaveData` to save the data. When the user tries to close the program's form, the `Form1_Closing` event handler uses `DataSafe` to see if it is safe to discard the data. If `DataSafe` returns `False`, the event handler's `e.Cancel` parameter is set to `True` so the form refuses to unload.

Finally, the `SaveData` subroutine simply calls the DataSet's `WriteXml` method to save the data. It then calls the DataSet's `AcceptChanges` method to mark the data as unchanged. Until the data is modified again, this makes the DataSet's `HasChanges` method return `False`.

LISTING 7.8   PROGRAM EDITXML LETS THE USER SAVE CHANGES TO AN XML FILE

```
' The name of the XML file.
Private m_FileName As String

' The DataSet that will hold the data.
Private m_DataSet As New DataSet()

' Load an XML file.
Private Sub mnuFileOpen_Click(ByVal sender As System.Object, _
  ByVal e As System.EventArgs) Handles mnuFileOpen.Click
    ' Make sure the data is safe.
    If Not DataSafe() Then Exit Sub

    ' Let the user select the file.
    If dlgOpenFile.ShowDialog() = DialogResult.OK Then
        Try
            ' Start a new DataSet.
            m_DataSet = New DataSet()

            ' Read the XML data.
            dgAddressBook.DataSource = Nothing
            m_DataSet.ReadXml(dlgOpenFile.FileName)
            m_DataSet.AcceptChanges()

            ' Bind the DataGrid to the DataSet.
            dgAddressBook.DataSource = m_DataSet
```

LISTING 7.8 CONTINUED

```
                ' Display the file name in the form's caption.
                m_FileName = dlgOpenFile.FileName
                Me.Text = "EditXml [" & m_FileName & "]"

                ' Display the DataSet's structure.
                DisplayDataSetStructure(m_DataSet)
            Catch exc As Exception
                MsgBox(exc.Message)
                Me.Text = "EditXml []"
            End Try
        End If
    End Sub

    ' Return True if the data is safe.
    Private Function DataSafe() As Boolean
        ' If there are no pending changes,
        ' the data is safe.
        If Not m_DataSet.HasChanges() Then Return True

        ' Ask the user if we should save the changes.
        Select Case MsgBox("Save changes?", MsgBoxStyle.YesNoCancel, "Save Changes?")
            Case MsgBoxResult.No
                ' The data is safe.
                Return True
            Case MsgBoxResult.Yes
                ' Save the changes.
                SaveData()

                ' Return False if we failed to save
                ' the data for some reason.
                Return (Not m_DataSet.HasChanges())
            Case MsgBoxResult.Cancel
                ' The user wants to cancel this operation.
                ' Do not let the program discard the data.
                Return False
        End Select
    End Function

    ' Save the data.
    Private Sub mnuFileSave_Click(ByVal sender As System.Object, _
      ByVal e As System.EventArgs) Handles mnuFileSave.Click
        SaveData()
    End Sub

    ' Prevent the closing if the data is not safe.
    Private Sub Form1_Closing(ByVal sender As Object, _
      ByVal e As System.ComponentModel.CancelEventArgs) Handles MyBase.Closing
        e.Cancel = (Not DataSafe())
    End Sub

    ' Save the data.
    Private Sub SaveData()
        m_DataSet.WriteXml(m_FileName)
        m_DataSet.AcceptChanges()
    End Sub
```

OVERWRITING FILES

When program EditXml calls the DataSet's `WriteXml` method, that method writes all the DataSet's data into the XML file, overwriting any information that was already there. This is one of the most important differences between XML files and true databases. In a relational database, you can update a single record without modifying the rest of the database's contents. When you modify XML data, you must rewrite the entire XML file.

This makes building a multi-user application with XML difficult. Suppose two users start the application at the same time and they both make changes. The first user saves his changes, overwriting the original XML file, then the second user saves his changes, overwriting the XML file again. The first user's changes are lost.

For this reason, XML files are much less useful than relational databases for multi-user systems. They work well for single-user systems and they are fine for holding read-only data. They are also useful in programs that treat files as documents. For example, a drawing program might store instructions for drawing a picture in an XML file much as a word processor stores a document in a file of its own. If you need to build a large multi-user application, however, you are probably better off using some other form of database.

SUMMARY

XML files do not provide all the features included in a powerful database such as Access, SQL Server, or Oracle. They don't include tools for indexing, grouping, summarizing, and joining records. XML files don't provide transactions, user-based privileges, and the capability to update a single record without rewriting the entire XML file.

For many applications, however, these features are unnecessary. For small single-user applications or applications that load and modify small documents, XML files can be useful database tools. They store data in a text-based format that is easy to read and understand. Loading and saving XML files using a DataSet object's `ReadXml` and `WriteXml` methods is practically trivial. After you have loaded the XML data into a DataSet, you can use all the DataSet's methods to manipulate it.

XML files certainly do not replace databases, but they can be a useful item in your database programming toolkit.

BOUND CONTROLS

Visual Basic lets you bind certain properties of controls to some kinds of data sources. For example, you can use a DataTable object to hold data from records in a database. You can then bind a ComboBox's Text property to the DataTable's State field. When the DataTable visits a record, it automatically updates the ComboBox's Text property to display the value of the record's State field.

The Data Form Wizard described in Chapter 5, "The DataSet Family of Objects," uses binding to display records. Unfortunately, the code generated by the wizard is complicated and hard to understand. It defines classes you can use to manipulate the data with some degree of safety, but the classes are so complex that they add their own measure of danger to any modifications you may later make.

Fortunately data binding is relatively simple, so you can take advantage of it yourself without using the Data Form Wizard. Using data binding, you can delegate relatively simple operations to Visual Basic while you handle more complex tasks yourself.

The following sections describe Visual Basic's data binding features and provide a series of examples putting them to practical use.

BASIC BINDING

The Contacts example program, shown in Figure 8.1, uses bound controls to manage a contacts database. Use the buttons at the bottom to scroll through the entries. Click on the record's fields and type to modify its data. If you move to a different entry and then return to the one you modified, you will see that the program is keeping track of your changes.

Use the Data menu's New command to make a new contact record. Use the Delete command to remove the current record. Finally, use the Save and Cancel Changes commands to save or discard any changes you have made.

If you try to close the program while there are unsaved changes, the program asks you if you want to save them.

Bound controls make building this application relatively easy. Data binding handles the details of moving data to and from the controls. Although you need to add a little code to load and save the data, and to perform other database operations, most of the mundane details are automatic.

Figure 8.1
Program Contacts
uses bound controls
to manage a contacts
database.

CONNECTING TO THE DATABASE

The program stores its data internally in a DataSet object named dsContacts. The DataSet contains a single DataTable holding the records in the database's Contacts table. Almost all the controls shown in Figure 8.1 are bound to this DataTable in one way or another.

To start building the application, create a new Windows Application project. Open its form and select the Toolbox's Data tab. Double-click the DataSet tool to add a new DataSet object to the form. In the dialog shown in Figure 8.2, select an untyped DataSet.

Figure 8.2
Select an untyped
DataSet.

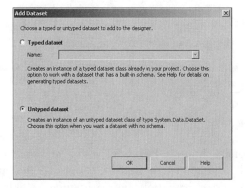

After you add the DataSet object to the form, select it and change its name to dsContacts.

Now on the Toolbox's Data tab, double-click the SqlDataAdapter tool. In the Data Adapter Configuration Wizard, shown in Figure 8.3, select the database connection you want the data adapter to use. If you do not see the connection you want to use, click the New Connection button and make a new one.

This example uses the Contacts database. The scripts ContactsCreate.sql and ContactsPopulate.sql, included in the source code for Chapter 2 available on the book's Web site (http://www.vb-helper.com/vbdb.htm), build and populate a simple Contacts database.

Figure 8.3
Select the data adapter's database connection.

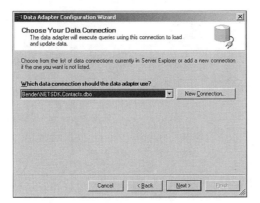

After you select the data adapter's database connection, click Next to see the screen shown in Figure 8.4. Select the Use SQL statement option and click Next.

Figure 8.4
This program's data adapter selects records using a SQL statement.

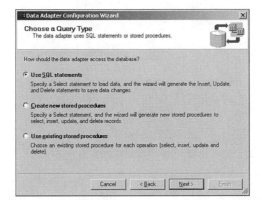

In the screen shown in Figure 8.5, enter the SQL SELECT statement you want to use to select database records. If you prefer, click the Query Builder button to design the query graphically. The statement shown in Figure 8.5 selects all the fields from the Contacts table. The ORDER BY clause makes the adapter order the results by LastName and FirstName.

When you finish building the data adapter, select it and change its name to daContacts. Also select the SqlConnection object that the Data Adapter Configuration Wizard built and rename it conContacts.

DEFINING A DATASET

Now you need to map the data selected by the data adapter to the DataSet. Select the dsContacts object, go to the Properties window, and select the Tables property. Click the ellipsis on the right to display the Tables Collection Editor shown in Figure 8.6.

Figure 8.5
The data adapter uses this statement to select records.

Figure 8.6
Define the Contacts table selected into the DataSet.

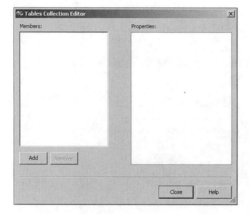

Click the Add button to create a new table entry. Change the table's TableName property to Contacts as shown in Figure 8.7. This sets the name used to identify the table's DataTable object in the DataSet's Tables collection. If you do not change this value, the TableName property has the much less meaningful value Table1.

Figure 8.7
Change the TableName property to Contacts.

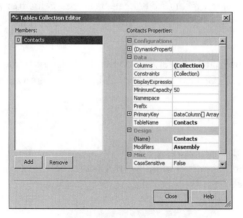

Your program can use the TableName value to locate the table in the DataSet. The following code shows two ways you could find the table. The first method selects entry 0 in the Tables collection. Assuming the DataSet contains information from only one table, that entry is the only entry and therefore it is the desired table.

The second method uses the table's name as a key into the Tables collection. This method is easier to read and correctly selects the Contacts table even if the DataSet contains more than one table:

```
Dim data_table As DataTable

data_table = dsContacts.Tables(0)
data_table = dsContacts.Tables("Contacts")
```

After you have defined the DataSet's new table entry, select its Columns property and click the ellipsis on the right to open the Columns Collection Editor shown in Figure 8.8.

Figure 8.8
The Columns
Collection Editor
defines the columns
selected into the
DataSet.

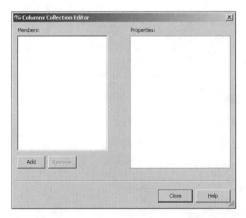

Click Add to create a new column entry. Change the ColumnName property to LastName, the first field selected by the data adapter. Create more column entries for the other fields selected by the adapter. Figure 8.9 shows the results.

Figure 8.9
Define entries for the
fields selected by the
data adapter.

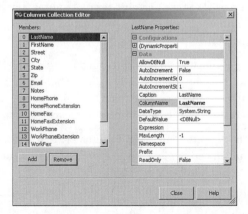

When you have finished defining the DataSet's fields, click Close to close the Columns Collection Editor. Then click Close again to close the Tables Collection Editor.

DISPLAYING DATA

Now add labels and TextBoxes to the form to display the data. Give the TextBoxes reasonable names like txtLastName, txtFirstName, and so forth. For the State address field, create a ComboBox named cboState.

Now select the txtLastName control. In the Properties window, select the (Data Bindings) entry and click on the plus sign to its left to expand it. Within the data bindings, select the Text property and click the drop-down arrow to its right to get a list of possible data sources. Use the TreeView display that appears to select the dsContacts.Contacts.LastName value as shown in Figure 8.10. This binds the txtLastName control's Text property to the LastName field in the Contacts table loaded by the dsContacts DataSet.

Figure 8.10
Bind the
dsContacts.Conta
cts.LastName data
source to the Text
property.

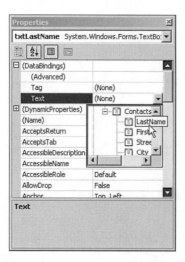

Repeat these steps for each of the other data controls. Bind the cboState ComboBox control's Text property to the DataSet's State field just as you bind the TextBoxes' Text properties. Now when you run the program, the DataSet automatically copies any data it holds into the controls' Text properties.

At this point, you have done as much as you can without writing any code. The program contains a connection to attach to the database, a DataSet to hold data, controls bound to the DataSet, and a data adapter to move data between the database and the DataSet using the connection. Nothing actually tells the data adapter to move any data, however.

To load and save data, you must write some code. Fortunately that code is straightforward. In the form's Load event handler, add the following line of code. This code makes the data adapter daContacts load data into the DataSet dsContacts:

```
daContacts.Fill(dsContacts)
```

Just as you need to add code to load the data, you need to use a little code to save any changes you make to the database. Add the following code to the form's `Closing` event handler. This code makes the data adapter `daContacts` update the database to store any changes made to the DataSet `dsContacts`:

```
daContacts.Update(dsContacts)
```

DISPLAYING PICTURES

Although the DataSet displays most of its records' data automatically, it cannot show the picture indicated by the `SnapshotFile` field. That field contains the name of a file that holds a picture of the person represented by the record. To display the picture, you need to add a little more code.

First, add a PictureBox to the form named `picSnapshot`. If you have not already done so, add a TextBox named `txtSnapshotFile` and bind it to the `SnapshotFile` field.

When the DataSet views a record, it displays the value of the `SnapshotFile` field in the bound TextBox control named `txtSnapshotFile`. That makes Visual Basic raise the control's `TextChanged` event handler. Add the following code to this event handler. Most of the routine is error-handling code. The really important part is the single line that uses the `FromFile` method provided by the `Image` class to load the snapshot file into the PictureBox:

```
' Display the record's snapshot image.
Private Sub txtSnapshotFile_TextChanged(ByVal sender As System.Object, _
  ByVal e As System.EventArgs) Handles txtSnapshotFile.TextChanged
    picSnapshot.Image = Nothing

    ' See if the file name is blank.
    If txtSnapshotFile.Text.Length > 0 Then
        ' The file name is not blank.
        ' Display the image.
        Try
            picSnapshot.Image = Image.FromFile(txtSnapshotFile.Text)
        Catch exc As Exception
            MsgBox("Error displaying file " & _
                txtSnapshotFile.Text & vbCrLf & _
                exc.Message, _
                MsgBoxStyle.Exclamation, _
                "Image Error")
        End Try
    End If
End Sub
```

Normally you don't really want to display the snapshot file's name to the user. The user wants to see the picture, not the name of the file containing the picture. Ideally you would simply set the TextBox's `Visible` property to `False` so the value is hidden. Unfortunately if you do that at design time, the program knows the control is hidden so it doesn't bother to copy data into it. The control's text never changes so the program doesn't receive `TextChanged` events and doesn't display the picture.

To solve this problem, set the control's `Visible` property to `True` at design time. Then in the form's `Load` event handler, set Visible to `False`. That hides the control but still makes the DataSet copy the `SnapshotFile` field value into it.

The user can type new values for most of the DataSet's fields. For example, to change a record's `Street` field, the user can simply click on the `Street` TextBox and type the new value. This won't work for the snapshot picture, however. If you leave the snapshot's TextBox visible, the user could type in a new filename but that would be awkward.

Instead when the user double-clicks on the snapshot picture, the Contacts program uses the following code to display a file selection dialog so the user can select a new picture. If the user selects a file and clicks OK, the program tries to display the file. If it succeeds, the program saves the new file's name in the `txtSnapshotFile` TextBox. That automatically updates the DataSet's `SnapshotFile` field:

```
' Let the user pick a new file.
Private Sub picSnapshot_DoubleClick(ByVal sender As Object, _
  ByVal e As System.EventArgs) Handles picSnapshot.DoubleClick
    If dlgSnapshot.ShowDialog() = DialogResult.OK Then
        Try
            ' Try to load the image.
            picSnapshot.Image = Image.FromFile(dlgSnapshot.FileName)

            ' If we loaded the image, save
            ' the file's name.
            m_CurrencyManager.Current.Row.Item("SnapshotFile") = _
                dlgSnapshot.FileName
        Catch exc As Exception
            MsgBox("Error displaying file " & _
                dlgSnapshot.FileName & vbCrLf & _
                exc.Message, _
                MsgBoxStyle.Exclamation, _
                "Image Error")
        End Try
    End If
End Sub
```

Navigating Through the DataSet

If you run the program at this point, the form's `Load` event handler uses the data adapter to load data into the DataSet. The DataSet automatically displays the data for its first record in the form's bound TextBox and ComboBox controls. If you click on a field and make changes, the DataSet keeps track of the changes. When you close the program, the `Closing` event handler saves those changes to the database.

The program still lacks any means of navigation. The DataSet displays the field values for its first record and nothing else. The program also provides no method for adding or deleting records.

To make the program more useful, add four buttons and a label control at the bottom of the form as shown in Figure 8.1. Name the controls `btnFirst`, `btnPrevious`, `btnNext`, `btnLast`, and `lblPosition`.

To position the DataSet, you need to know a little about a class named CurrencyManager. The CurrencyManager keeps track of the position of the DataSet and coordinates the movement of data from the DataSet to its bound controls. When you want to change the DataSet's position programmatically, you can use its CurrencyManager.

The Contacts program declares the variable m_CurrencyManager to hold a reference to the DataSet's CurrencyManager. It declares the variable using the WithEvents keyword so it can easily catch the object's events.

In the form's Load event handler, the program saves a reference to the CurrencyManager. An object's BindingContext method returns a reference to the CurrencyManager used to handle the data binding for that object and its siblings. Usually a form has only one CurrencyManager and you can use its BindingContext method to get the reference you need. Things become a little more complex if you have controls in different containers bound to multiple data sources. This program uses the following code to save a reference to the CurrencyManager:

```
' The CurrencyManager synchronizes the controls
' with the Contacts DataTable.
Private WithEvents m_CurrencyManager As CurrencyManager

...

Private Sub Form1_Load(ByVal sender As System.Object, _
  ByVal e As System.EventArgs) Handles MyBase.Load
...
    ' Save a reference to the CurrencyManager.
    m_CurrencyManager = Me.BindingContext(dsContacts, "Contacts")
...
End Sub
```

The CurrencyManager's Position property gives the index of the record currently displayed. Its Count property tells how many records there are in all. Using those properties, it is easy to implement the first, previous, next, and last buttons.

The following code shows how the buttons work in program Contacts. Note that the Position property numbers records starting with 0, so the first record is at position 0 and the last is at position m_CurrencyManager.Count - 1:

```
' Move to the first record.
Private Sub btnFirst_Click(ByVal sender As System.Object, _
  ByVal e As System.EventArgs) Handles btnFirst.Click
    m_CurrencyManager.Position = 0
End Sub

' Move to the previous record.
Private Sub btnPrevious_Click(ByVal sender As System.Object, _
  ByVal e As System.EventArgs) Handles btnPrevious.Click
    m_CurrencyManager.Position = m_CurrencyManager.Position - 1
End Sub

' Move to the next record.
Private Sub btnNext_Click(ByVal sender As System.Object, _
```

```
     ByVal e As System.EventArgs) Handles btnNext.Click
        m_CurrencyManager.Position = m_CurrencyManager.Position + 1
End Sub

' Move to the next record.
Private Sub btnLast_Click(ByVal sender As System.Object, _
   ByVal e As System.EventArgs) Handles btnLast.Click
      m_CurrencyManager.Position = m_CurrencyManager.Count - 1
End Sub
```

When the CurrencyManager moves to a different record, it generates a PositionChanged event. Because the program declares its m_CurrencyManager variable using the WithEvents keyword, it can easily catch that event and display the new record's position in the lblPosition label control. The following code shows how you can display the new record's position. The code adds 1 to the position because the records' indexes start at 0:

```
' Display the position.
Private Sub m_CurrencyManager_PositionChanged(ByVal sender As Object, _
   ByVal e As System.EventArgs) Handles m_CurrencyManager.PositionChanged
      lblPosition.Text = m_CurrencyManager.Position + 1 & _
          "/" & m_CurrencyManager.Count
End Sub
```

ADDING AND DELETING RECORDS

The final essential piece to the program is the capability to add and delete records. The CurrencyManager's AddNew method makes the DataSet create a new record. All you need to do to allow the user to create new Contacts records is to add a menu command that invokes this method:

```
Private Sub mnuDataNew_Click(ByVal sender As System.Object, _
   ByVal e As System.EventArgs) Handles mnuDataNew.Click
      m_CurrencyManager.AddNew()
End Sub
```

Deleting a record is just as simple. Simply call the CurrencyManager's RemoveAt method, passing it the index of the record it should delete. Use the CurrencyManager's Position property to delete the currently displayed record:

```
Private Sub mnuDataDelete_Click(ByVal sender As System.Object, _
   ByVal e As System.EventArgs) Handles mnuDataDelete.Click
      m_CurrencyManager.RemoveAt(m_CurrencyManager.Position)
End Sub
```

Note that the Contacts database used for this program defines the LastName and FirstName fields with the NOT NULL attribute. If you try to save the data and you have created a record without a LastName or FirstName value, or if you edit a record and blank one of those fields, the database raises an error.

THE CONTACTS PROGRAM

The previous sections describe the basics of the Contacts program. The actual program, shown in Listing 8.1, provides a few additional features.

The form's Load event handler initializes the cboState ComboBox so it contains a list of valid state abbreviations. It hides the txtSnapshotFile control, uses the data adapter daContacts to fill the DataSet, and saves a reference to the CurrencyManager.

The txtSnapshotFile control's TextChanged event handler displays the record's snapshot file.

The Data menu's New command uses the CurrencyManager's EndCurrentEdit command to accept any changes the user is currently making. It then calls AddNew to create the new record and sets the focus to the Last Name field so the user can start entering data.

The Data menu's Delete command makes the user confirm the deletion before it calls the CurrencyManager's RemoveAt method. It then calls the ShowPosition subroutine to show the CurrencyManager's position in the DataSet because the RemoveAt method does not automatically generate a PositionChanged event.

The Data menu's Save command lets the user save the changes at will. The menu command simply calls the SaveChanges subroutine. SaveChanges verifies that there are changes to save. It then uses the DataSet's GetChanges method to make a new DataSet that contains only the changes. Next the routine uses that DataSet's GetChanges method to extract the changes that represent modified, added, and deleted records. For each type of change, the subroutine calls the corresponding DataSet's Update method to save the changes.

Saving changes grouped by change type like this is more efficient than saving them all at once from the original DataSet. In an application such as this one where it is unlikely that the user will make too many changes all at once, the difference is negligible. In an application that makes many modifications, the savings in time could be substantial.

After it has saved any changes, the SaveChanges subroutine calls the DataSet's AcceptChanges method. This does not actually do anything to the database, it merely makes the changes to the DataSet permanent. After this step, the DataSet's HasChanges method returns False to indicate that the data has not been modified since the call to AcceptChanges. Calling AcceptChanges also makes the changes to the DataSet permanent so you cannot cancel them later.

The Data menu's Cancel Changes command removes any changes the user has made to the data. It first checks the DataSet's HasChanges method to see if there have in fact been any changes. If so, it makes the user confirm before it calls the DataSet's RejectChanges method.

The form's Closing event handler does not save any pending changes automatically. Instead it uses the DataSet's HasChanges method to see if the data has been modified. If the data has been modified since it was loaded or last saved, the event handler asks the user if it should save the changes. If the user answers Yes, the event handler calls subroutine SaveChanges to update the database. If the user answers Cancel, the event handler sets the Cancel field in its CancelEventArgs parameter to True. That makes Visual Basic cancel the form's closing. If the user answers No, the event handler does nothing, so the form closes and the changes are lost.

Finally, the CurrencyManager's ItemChanged event handler fires when the user makes a change and then moves to another record. When this occurs, the program adds an asterisk to the form's title so the user can easily see that the data has been modified. The SaveChanges subroutine and the Cancel Changes menu command remove the asterisk after saving or discarding any pending changes.

LISTING 8.1   PROGRAM CONTACTS USES THIS CODE TO LOAD, DISPLAY, EDIT, AND SAVE RECORDS

```
Public Class Form1
    Inherits System.Windows.Forms.Form

    Private Const APP_TITLE = "Contacts"

    ' The CurrencyManager synchronizes the controls
    ' with the Contacts DataTable.
    Private WithEvents m_CurrencyManager As CurrencyManager

    ' Fill the DataSet.
    Private Sub Form1_Load(ByVal sender As System.Object, _
        ByVal e As System.EventArgs) Handles MyBase.Load
        ' Load the cboState ComboBox.
        Dim states() As String = { _
            "AK", "AL", "AR", "AZ", "CA", "CO", "CT", "DC", "DE", "FL", _
            "GA", "HI", "IA", "ID", "IL", "IN", "KS", "KT", "LA", "MA", _
            "MD", "ME", "MI", "MN", "MO", "MS", "MT", "NC", "ND", "NE", _
            "NH", "NJ", "NM", "NV", "NY", "OH", "OK", "OR", "PA", "RI", _
            "SC", "SD", "TN", "TX", "UT", "VA", "VT", "WA", "WI", "WV", _
            "WY" _
        }
        cboState.Items.Clear()
        cboState.Items.AddRange(states)

        ' Hide the txtSnapshotFile control.
        ' If we do this at design time,
        ' it doesn't get updated by the DataSet.
        txtSnapshotFile.Visible = False

        ' Fill the DataSet.
        daContacts.Fill(dsContacts)

        ' Save a reference to the CurrencyManager.
        m_CurrencyManager = Me.BindingContext(dsContacts, "Contacts")
    End Sub

    ' Display the record's snapshot image.
    Private Sub txtSnapshotFile_TextChanged(ByVal sender As System.Object, _
        ByVal e As System.EventArgs) Handles txtSnapshotFile.TextChanged
        picSnapshot.Image = Nothing

        ' See if the file name is blank.
        If txtSnapshotFile.Text.Length > 0 Then
            ' The file name is not blank.
            ' Display the image.
            Try
```

LISTING 8.1 CONTINUED

```vb
            picSnapshot.Image = Image.FromFile(txtSnapshotFile.Text)
        Catch exc As Exception
            MsgBox("Error displaying file " & _
                txtSnapshotFile.Text & vbCrLf & _
                exc.Message, _
                MsgBoxStyle.Exclamation, _
                "Image Error")
        End Try
    End If
End Sub

Private Sub mnuFileExit_Click(ByVal sender As System.Object, _
  ByVal e As System.EventArgs) Handles mnuFileExit.Click
    Me.Close()
End Sub

' Create a new record.
Private Sub mnuDataNew_Click(ByVal sender As System.Object, _
  ByVal e As System.EventArgs) Handles mnuDataNew.Click
    ' Finish the current edit.
    m_CurrencyManager.EndCurrentEdit()

    ' Add the new record. This automatically
    ' causes the CurrencyManager to reposition
    ' so it displays the new position.
    m_CurrencyManager.AddNew()

    ' Set the focus to the Last Name field.
    txtLastName.Focus()
End Sub

' Delete the current record.
Private Sub mnuDataDelete_Click(ByVal sender As System.Object, _
  ByVal e As System.EventArgs) Handles mnuDataDelete.Click
    ' Finish the current edit.
    m_CurrencyManager.EndCurrentEdit()

    ' Make the user confirm.
    If MsgBox("Delete this record?", MsgBoxStyle.YesNo, _
        "Delete Record?") = MsgBoxResult.No Then Exit Sub

    ' Delete the record.
    m_CurrencyManager.RemoveAt(m_CurrencyManager.Position)

    ' Display the new position.
    ShowPosition()
End Sub

' Save changes to the database and say "Ok".
Private Sub mnuDataSave_Click(ByVal sender As System.Object, _
  ByVal e As System.EventArgs) Handles mnuDataSave.Click
    SaveChanges()

    MsgBox("Ok", MsgBoxStyle.OKOnly Or MsgBoxStyle.Information, _
        "Changes Saved")
End Sub
```

LISTING 8.1   CONTINUED

```
' Save changes to the database.
Private Sub SaveChanges()
    Dim ds_changes As DataSet
    Dim ds_subset As DataSet

    ' Finish the current edit.
    m_CurrencyManager.EndCurrentEdit()

    ' See if there are any changes to save.
    If dsContacts.HasChanges Then
        ' Get a DataSet holding the changes.
        ds_changes = dsContacts.GetChanges()

        ' Save the changes grouped by type.
        ds_subset = ds_changes.GetChanges(DataRowState.Modified)
        If (Not (ds_subset) Is Nothing) Then daContacts.Update(ds_subset)

        ds_subset = ds_changes.GetChanges(DataRowState.Added)
        If (Not (ds_subset) Is Nothing) Then daContacts.Update(ds_subset)

        ds_subset = ds_changes.GetChanges(DataRowState.Deleted)
        If (Not (ds_subset) Is Nothing) Then daContacts.Update(ds_subset)

        ' Mark the modified records as not modified.
        dsContacts.AcceptChanges()
    End If

    ' Update the form's caption to show the data is unmodified.
    Me.Text = APP_TITLE
End Sub

' Cancel the changes.
Private Sub mnuDataCancelChanges_Click(ByVal sender As System.Object, _
  ByVal e As System.EventArgs) Handles mnuDataCancelChanges.Click
    ' Finish the current edit.
    m_CurrencyManager.EndCurrentEdit()

    ' See if there are any changes to cancel.
    If dsContacts.HasChanges Then
        ' Make the user confirm.
        If MsgBox("Discard changes?", MsgBoxStyle.YesNo, _
            "Discard changes?") = MsgBoxResult.No Then Exit Sub

        ' Cancel the changes.
        dsContacts.RejectChanges()
    End If

    ' Update the form's caption to show the data is unmodified.
    Me.Text = APP_TITLE
End Sub

' The application is about to close. Make sure
' any changes to the data are safe.
Private Sub Form1_Closing(ByVal sender As Object, _
  ByVal e As System.ComponentModel.CancelEventArgs) Handles MyBase.Closing
    ' Finish the current edit.
```

LISTING 8.1   CONTINUED

```vb
            m_CurrencyManager.EndCurrentEdit()

            ' See if there are any changes to save.
            If dsContacts.HasChanges Then
                ' Ask the user if we should save the changes.
                Select Case MsgBox("Save changes?", MsgBoxStyle.YesNoCancel, _
                    "Save Changes?")
                    Case MsgBoxResult.Yes
                        ' Save the changes.
                        SaveChanges()
                    Case MsgBoxResult.Cancel
                        ' Cancel the exit.
                        e.Cancel = True
                    Case MsgBoxResult.No
                        ' Do nothing. Just exit.
                End Select
            End If
    End Sub

    ' Move to the first record.
    Private Sub btnFirst_Click(ByVal sender As System.Object, _
        ByVal e As System.EventArgs) Handles btnFirst.Click
        m_CurrencyManager.Position = 0
    End Sub

    ' Move to the previous record.
    Private Sub btnPrevious_Click(ByVal sender As System.Object, _
        ByVal e As System.EventArgs) Handles btnPrevious.Click
        m_CurrencyManager.Position = m_CurrencyManager.Position - 1
    End Sub

    ' Move to the next record.
    Private Sub btnNext_Click(ByVal sender As System.Object, _
        ByVal e As System.EventArgs) Handles btnNext.Click
        m_CurrencyManager.Position = m_CurrencyManager.Position + 1
    End Sub

    ' Move to the next record.
    Private Sub btnLast_Click(ByVal sender As System.Object, _
        ByVal e As System.EventArgs) Handles btnLast.Click
        m_CurrencyManager.Position = m_CurrencyManager.Count - 1
    End Sub

    ' Display the position.
    Private Sub m_CurrencyManager_PositionChanged(ByVal sender As Object, _
        ByVal e As System.EventArgs) Handles m_CurrencyManager.PositionChanged
        ShowPosition()
    End Sub
    Private Sub ShowPosition()
        lblPosition.Text = m_CurrencyManager.Position + 1 & _
        "/" & m_CurrencyManager.Count
    End Sub
End Class

' Change the form's caption to indicate
' that the data has been modified.
```

LISTING 8.1   CONTINUED

```vb
Private Sub m_CurrencyManager_ItemChanged(ByVal sender As Object, _
  ByVal e As System.Windows.Forms.ItemChangedEventArgs) _
  Handles m_CurrencyManager.ItemChanged
    Me.Text = APP_TITLE & "*"
End Sub

' Let the user pick a new file.
Private Sub picSnapshot_DoubleClick(ByVal sender As Object, _
  ByVal e As System.EventArgs) Handles picSnapshot.DoubleClick
    If dlgSnapshot.ShowDialog() = DialogResult.OK Then
        Try
            ' Try to load the image.
            picSnapshot.Image = Image.FromFile(dlgSnapshot.FileName)

            ' If we loaded the image, save
            ' the file's name.
            m_CurrencyManager.Current.Row.Item("SnapshotFile") = _
                dlgSnapshot.FileName
        Catch exc As Exception
            MsgBox("Error displaying file " & _
                dlgSnapshot.FileName & vbCrLf & _
                exc.Message, _
                MsgBoxStyle.Exclamation, _
                "Image Error")
        End Try
    End If
End Sub
```

RECORD SELECTION WITH BOUND CONTROLS

The Contacts program described in the previous sections works but it is rather cumbersome. If the database contains a large number of records, using the <<, <, >, and >> buttons to find a particular record would be tedious. It would be much more convenient if you could list the records' LastName fields and select the one you want.

Figure 8.11 shows the ContactsList program. It is very similar to the initial Contacts program except it uses a ListBox to navigate instead of buttons. Use the list on the left to select a record. Click on fields and type new values to edit the record. The Data menu's Save, Cancel Changes, New, and Delete commands work exactly as they did in program Contacts.

The previous sections show how to bind a control's property to a field provided by a data source. For example, they show how to bind the txtLastName control's Text property to the LastName field provided by the dsContacts DataSet. This is called *simple binding*.

Complex binding allows you to bind more than one data source element to a control in a more complicated way. For example, if you bind a DataGrid control to a DataSet, the control can display all the fields in all the DataSet's records.

Figure 8.11

The ContactsList program allows you to select records from a list instead of using navigation buttons.

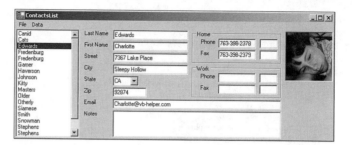

Complex binding also allows a control to interact with the data source in more complicated ways. You can use complex binding with the ComboBox and ListBox controls to allow the user to select the record that a DataSet should display. When the user clicks on the ListBox control, the control makes the DataSet move to the corresponding record and the DataSet automatically displays the new record's fields in the controls bound to it.

Despite its name, complex binding is no more complicated than simple binding. If anything, complex binding is easier.

To add a selection list to the Contacts program, move the existing controls to the right and add a new ListBox. In the Properties window, select the new control's DataSource property, click the drop-down menu to the right, and pick the dsContacts DataSet from the list. Then select the DisplayMember property and click the drop-down arrow to its right. In the resulting TreeView display, open the Contacts entry and select the LastName field.

Remove the navigation buttons and position label, and the code that uses them, and you're done. The ListBox control handles all the navigation for you. If the user adds or deletes a record, the DataSet automatically updates the list. If the user changes a record's LastName value and moves to a new record, the DataSet automatically updates the list to display the new LastName value.

SELECTING A CALCULATED FIELD

The ContactsList program is a big improvement over program Contacts but record selection is still a little awkward. The program lets the user pick a record from a list of LastName field values. It would be better if the list included the FirstName field as well. Then if the database had many records with a LastName value of Stephens, you could decide exactly which of the records to select.

You cannot bind the ListBox's DisplayMember property to more than one data source field, but you can add a calculated field that combines the LastName and FirstName fields to the data source. First, modify the data adapter so it selects the calculated field. Click on the daContacts object and click the Configure Data Adapter link below the property list in the Properties window as shown in Figure 8.12. That starts the Data Adapter Configuration Wizard for the adapter.

Figure 8.12
The Configure Data
Adapter link starts the
Data Adapter
Configuration Wizard.

Use the wizard to change the adapter's SQL SELECT statement to the following:

```
SELECT LastName + ', ' + FirstName AS CombinedName, *
FROM Contacts
ORDER BY LastName, FirstName
```

The first part of this statement selects a calculated field named CombinedName. This field concatenates the LastName and FirstName fields separated by a comma. The asterisk that follows selects all of the fields in the Contacts table.

Next, select the dsContacts DataSet. In the Properties window, select the Tables property and click the ellipsis to the right to open the Tables Collection Editor. Select the Contacts table's Columns property and click its ellipsis to open the Columns Collection Editor.

Click Add to make a new column entry and change the ColumnName property to CombinedName. Click Close twice to close the collection editors.

Now that you have selected the new column and defined it in the DataSet, it is relatively easy to attach it to the record selection list. Select the ListBox, pick its DisplayMember property in the Properties window, and click on the drop-down arrow to the right. Open the Contacts entry and select the CombinedName field at the end of the list.

That is almost all you need to do. At this point, the program automatically displays the CombinedName field in the ListBox. If you click on an entry, the DataSet moves to the record you selected and displays its data.

Unfortunately, the DataSet provides a static snapshot of the database. If you change a LastName or FirstName value, the DataSet does not automatically update the CombinedName field. That means changes you make do not appear in the selection list.

Even worse, when you create a new record, the LastName, FirstName, and CombinedName fields are initially empty so the list displays the new record with a blank value. If you later change the new record's LastName and FirstName values, the list still shows a blank entry.

To fix this, you need to add some code to update the CombinedValue field yourself. The following event handler does just that. When the user modifies a record and moves to a new record, the CurrencyManager's ItemChanged event handler fires. This version of the routine calculates the CombinedName value for the record's current LastName and FirstName values. If the calculated CombinedName is different from the current value, the event handler sets the record's CombinedName value in the DataSet.

Setting the CombinedName value makes the CurrencyManager's ItemChanged event handler fire again. That makes the event handler call itself recursively.

In the second call to the event handler, the CombinedName value has already been updated. When the routine calculates its new value and compares it to the value stored in the DataSet, it finds that the two values are the same, so it does not set the value again. The extra call to the event handler wastes a little time but it doesn't start an infinite series of recursive calls so it does little harm.

This code demonstrates one other trick worth mentioning. When it compares the current and new CombinedName values, the program is comparing the new calculated value to the existing value in the DataSet. If the value in the DataSet was never initialized, if this is a new record for example, that value is NULL. Visual Basic does not allow a program to compare a string to a NULL value so this statement raises an exception. The code exits this event handler so the statement that follows, setting the new CombinedName value, never executes.

To avoid this problem, the code concatenates an empty string to the DataSet's CombinedName value. That converts the value into a string. If the value is NULL, the new string is empty. If the value is not NULL, the new string contains the original value. In either case, the result is a string that the program can safely compare to the new calculated CombinedName value:

```
' If the LastName or FirstName fields have
' changed, update CombinedName.
Private Sub m_CurrencyManager_ItemChanged(ByVal sender As Object, _
  ByVal e As System.Windows.Forms.ItemChangedEventArgs) _
  Handles m_CurrencyManager.ItemChanged
    Dim combined_name As String
    Dim data_row As DataRow

    ' Change the form's caption to indicate
    ' that the data has been modified.
    Me.Text = APP_TITLE & "*"

    ' Update the CombinedName field.
    combined_name = txtLastName.Text & ", " & txtFirstName.Text
    data_row = m_CurrencyManager.Current.Row
    If data_row.Item("CombinedName") & "" <> combined_name Then
        data_row.Item("CombinedName") = combined_name
    End If
End Sub
```

Figure 8.13 shows the new ContactsListCombined program. It behaves exactly as the ContactsList program does except it displays the combined LastName and FirstName in its record selection list.

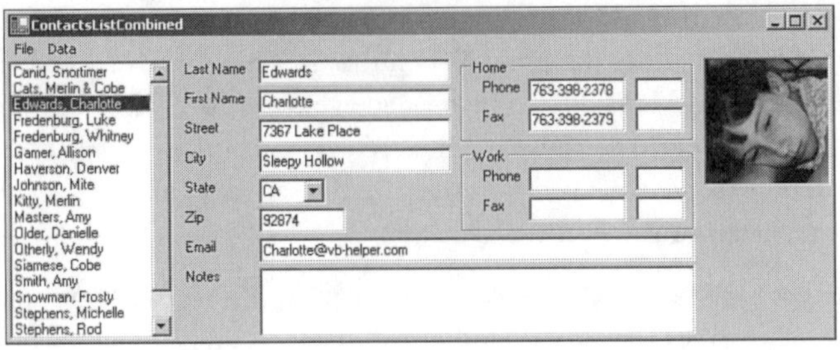

Figure 8.13
Program
ContactsListCombined
lets the user select
LastName/FirstName
pairs.

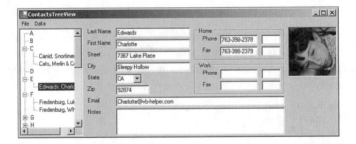

A TREEVIEW DISPLAY

Another possible record selection method uses a TreeView control. The control contains 26 top-level nodes labeled A, B, C, and so forth. Each top-level node contains the nodes representing the DataSet records. A special top-level node at the end, labeled <New>, holds nodes for records that have just been added.

The ContactsTreeView program shown in Figure 8.14 uses this approach. Click on a TreeView node to select a record. Use the Data menu to add and delete records as in the previous versions of the program.

Figure 8.14
Program
ContactsTreeView
uses a TreeView con-
trol for navigation.

Unfortunately, the TreeView control doesn't provide easy properties for you to use in binding it to a data source. You need to use some code to tie the TreeView control to the data.

The code in Listing 8.2 shows the biggest differences between program ContactsTreeView and the previous versions of this program. The form's Load event handler loads the DataSet as before. It then calls subroutine LoadTreeView to prepare the TreeView control for use.

Subroutine LoadTreeView creates TreeView nodes for each of the letters of the alphabet. It then adds a new TreeNode column to the DataSet's Contacts table. The data adapter does not populate this column because the program creates the column after the data adapter loads the data. Besides, the data adapter doesn't know anything about this column. For that reason, the data adapter doesn't try to save the values in this field back to the database when you save changes.

The LoadTreeView subroutine then loops through the records in the DataSet. For each record, the program calculates the record's combined LastName and FirstName value. It creates a new tree node with the combined name as its text and adds it as a child of the appropriate top-level letter node.

The program then sets the TreeView node's Tag property to the DataRow holding the record's data, and it sets the DataRow's TreeNode field to the TreeView node. Later the program can use these values to quickly find the DataRow object from the TreeNode object and vice versa.

After it has added nodes for each of the DataSet's records, the LoadTreeView subroutine creates the special <New> TreeView node to hold nodes for newly created records. Next, it selects the first data record's node. The routine finishes by calling the DataSet's AcceptChanges method. Setting the records' TreeNode fields flags the DataSet as having been modified even though the user has not made changes that need to be saved. Calling AcceptChanges clears the flag so the program can later tell if the user has made any changes.

Program ContactsTreeView creates and deletes records much as the previous programs do, except it must carry out a few extra steps to keep the TreeView control synchronized with the DataSet. The mnuDataNew_Click event handler creates a new record just as the earlier programs do. It then creates a new TreeView node for the new record, making it a child of the special <New> node. It uses the CurrencyManager's Current property to find the DataRow representing the new record and saves a reference to it in the new TreeView node's Tag property. It also saves a reference to the new TreeView node in the DataRow's TreeNode field. The event handler finishes by selecting the new TreeView node so it is highlighted in the TreeView control.

The mnuDataDelete_Click event handler. asks the user to confirm the deletion as in the previous programs. It then locates the TreeView control's current node and the CurrencyManager's current DataRow object. It removes the DataRow object and then removes the TreeView node. The routine finishes by selecting the TreeView node that corresponds to the CurrencyManager's new current record.

Like program ContactsListCombined, this program must take action when the user modifies a record's LastName or FirstName field. In the CurrencyManager's ItemChanged event handler, the program calculates the record's new combined name value. If the record's CombinedName field holds a value different from the new one, the program updates the record and updates the value displayed by the corresponding TreeView node.

The last piece of new code in program ContactsTreeView is used when the user selects a new TreeView node. When that happens, the TreeView control's AfterSelect event handler executes. The routine begins by checking the program's CurrencyManager variable. If the variable has value Nothing, the program is just starting. The event handler doesn't need to display anything yet; it just exits.

Next, the event handler examines the selected TreeView node's Tag property. If the property is Nothing, the TreeView node does not represent a DataSet record. Instead it is a top-level letter node or the <New> node. In that case, the event handler exits without doing anything more.

Finally, if the node represents a DataSet record, the event handler locates the corresponding DataRow object in the CurrencyManager's list of objects. It uses the index of the object in the list to select the DataRow as the CurrencyManager's current record. The CurrencyManager then automatically displays the record's data in the program's bound controls.

LISTING 8.2   PROGRAM CONTACTSTREEVIEW USES THIS CODE

```
' The <New> node.
Private m_NewNode As TreeNode
...
' Fill the DataSet.
Private Sub Form1_Load(ByVal sender As System.Object, _
   ByVal e As System.EventArgs) Handles MyBase.Load
      ' Load the cboState ComboBox.
      Dim states() As String = { _
          "AK", "AL", "AR", "AZ", "CA", "CO", "CT", "DC", "DE", "FL", _
          "GA", "HI", "IA", "ID", "IL", "IN", "KS", "KT", "LA", "MA", _
          "MD", "ME", "MI", "MN", "MO", "MS", "MT", "NC", "ND", "NE", _
          "NH", "NJ", "NM", "NV", "NY", "OH", "OK", "OR", "PA", "RI", _
          "SC", "SD", "TN", "TX", "UT", "VA", "VT", "WA", "WI", "WV", _
          "WY" _
      }
      cboState.Items.Clear()
      cboState.Items.AddRange(states)

      ' Hide the txtSnapshotFile control.
      ' If we do this at design time,
      ' it doesn't get updated by the DataSet.
      txtSnapshotFile.Visible = False

      ' Make the name list as large as possible.
      ArrangeControls()

      ' Fill the DataSet.
      daContacts.Fill(dsContacts)

      ' Load the TreeView.
      LoadTreeView()

      ' Save a reference to the CurrencyManager.
      m_CurrencyManager = Me.BindingContext(dsContacts, "Contacts")
End Sub

' Load the TreeView control with a list of names.
Private Sub LoadTreeView()
    Dim letter_nodes(25) As TreeNode
    Dim letter As Integer
    Dim row_num As Integer
    Dim data_row As DataRow
    Dim record_node As TreeNode
    Dim first_node As TreeNode
    Dim combined_name As String
```

Listing 8.2 Continued

```
        ' Make the letter nodes.
        trvContacts.Nodes.Clear()
        For letter = 0 To 25
            letter_nodes(letter) = trvContacts.Nodes.Add(Chr(letter + Asc("A"c)))
        Next letter

        ' Add a TreeNode column to the table.
        dsContacts.Tables("Contacts").Columns.Add("TreeNode", GetType(TreeNode))

        ' Add each name entry.
        For row_num = 0 To dsContacts.Tables("Contacts").Rows.Count - 1
            data_row = dsContacts.Tables("Contacts").Rows(row_num)
            combined_name = data_row.Item("LastName") & ", " & _
                data_row.Item("FirstName")
            letter = Asc(combined_name.Substring(0, 1).ToUpper) - Asc("A"c)
            record_node = letter_nodes(letter).Nodes.Add(combined_name)
            record_node.Tag = data_row
            data_row.Item("TreeNode") = record_node
            If row_num = 0 Then first_node = record_node
        Next row_num

        ' Make a <New> node.
        m_NewNode = trvContacts.Nodes.Add("<New>")

        ' Select the first node.
        trvContacts.SelectedNode = first_node

        ' Accept the changes (setting the TreeNode field)
        ' so we don't think there are changes yet.
        dsContacts.AcceptChanges()
    End Sub

    ' Create a new record.
    Private Sub mnuDataNew_Click(ByVal sender As System.Object, _
      ByVal e As System.EventArgs) Handles mnuDataNew.Click
        Dim record_node As TreeNode
        Dim data_row As DataRow

        ' Finish any current edits.
        m_CurrencyManager.EndCurrentEdit()

        ' Add the new record. This raises a PositionChanged event.
        m_CurrencyManager.AddNew()

        ' Set the focus to the Last Name field.
        txtLastName.Focus()

        ' Create a new TreeNode for the record.
        record_node = m_NewNode.Nodes.Add(", ")
        data_row = m_CurrencyManager.Current.Row
        record_node.Tag = data_row
        data_row.Item("TreeNode") = record_node

        ' Select the new node.
        trvContacts.SelectedNode = record_node
    End Sub
```

LISTING 8.2 CONTINUED

```
' Delete the current record.
Private Sub mnuDataDelete_Click(ByVal sender As System.Object, _
  ByVal e As System.EventArgs) Handles mnuDataDelete.Click
    ' Finish the current edit.
    m_CurrencyManager.EndCurrentEdit()

    ' Make the user confirm.
    If MsgBox("Delete this record?", MsgBoxStyle.YesNo, _
        "Delete Record?") = MsgBoxResult.No Then Exit Sub

    ' Get the TreeNode.
    Dim data_row As DataRow
    Dim tree_node As TreeNode
    data_row = m_CurrencyManager.Current.Row
    tree_node = data_row.Item("TreeNode")

    ' Delete the record.
    m_CurrencyManager.RemoveAt(m_CurrencyManager.Position)

    ' Remove the TreeNode.
    tree_node.Remove()

    ' Select the current TreeNode.
    data_row = m_CurrencyManager.Current.Row
    tree_node = data_row.Item("TreeNode")
    trvContacts.SelectedNode = tree_node
End Sub

' If the LastName or FirstName fields have
' changed, update CombinedName.
Private Sub m_CurrencyManager_ItemChanged(ByVal sender As Object, _
  ByVal e As System.Windows.Forms.ItemChangedEventArgs) _
 Handles m_CurrencyManager.ItemChanged
    Dim combined_name As String
    Dim data_row As DataRow

    ' Change the form's caption to indicate
    ' that the data has been modified.
    Me.Text = APP_TITLE & "*"

    ' Update the CombinedName field.
    combined_name = txtLastName.Text & ", " & txtFirstName.Text
    data_row = m_CurrencyManager.Current.Row
    If data_row.Item("CombinedName") & "" <> combined_name Then
        data_row.Item("CombinedName") = combined_name

        ' Update the current TreeNode's text.
        Dim tree_node As TreeNode
        tree_node = data_row.Item("TreeNode")
        tree_node.Text = combined_name
    End If
End Sub

' Display the selected record.
Private Sub trvContacts_AfterSelect(ByVal sender As Object, _
```

LISTING 8.2   CONTINUED

```
   ByVal e As System.Windows.Forms.TreeViewEventArgs) _
   Handles trvContacts.AfterSelect
     Dim data_row As DataRow
     Dim data_table As DataTable
     Dim i As Integer

     ' Do nothing if we haven't loaded the data yet.
     If m_CurrencyManager Is Nothing Then Exit Sub

     ' Do nothing if this node has no Tag
     ' value or Tag isn't a DataRow object.
     If e.Node.Tag Is Nothing Then Exit Sub

     ' Display the corresponding record.
     data_table = dsContacts.Tables(0)
     data_row = e.Node.Tag
     For i = 0 To m_CurrencyManager.Count - 1
         If data_row Is m_CurrencyManager.List(i).Row Then
             m_CurrencyManager.Position = i
             Exit For
         End If
     Next i
End Sub
```

DATAVIEWS

A DataView provides a view into a data source. For example, a program can use one or more DataViews to select different records from a DataTable in a DataSet. Program ContactsLetterLists, shown in Figure 8.15, uses a DataView object to make selecting a subset of the records in a DataSet relatively easy. When you select a letter from the ComboBox on the left, the ListBox displays the records that begin with that letter. If you select the ComboBox's special entry <New>, the ListBox displays any new records you have just created. Finally, if you select the <All> item, the ListBox shows all the records in the database.

Figure 8.15
Program
ContactsLetterLists
uses a TreeView control for navigation.

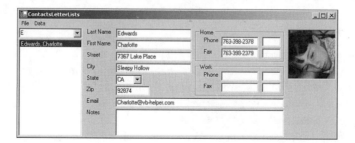

To build this program, open the ContactsListCombined program described earlier in this chapter. Open the form in design mode, go to the Toolbox's Data tab, and double-click the DataView tool. Select the new DataView object and change its name to dvContacts.

In the Properties window, select the DataView's `Table` property and click the drop-down arrow to its right. In the TreeView display that appears, open the `dsContacts` item and select Contacts. That attaches the DataView object to the `Contacts` table in the `dsContacts` DataSet.

Now bind the TextBoxes and other fields on the form to the DataView. For example, select the txtLastName control. In the Properties window, open the (Data Bindings) property, select Text, and click the drop-down arrow to the right. Use the resulting TreeView to select the dvContacts object's LastName field. Repeat these steps for the other controls that should be bound to the data.

Select the existing ListBox named `lstContacts`. In the Properties window, set its `DataSource` property to the DataView dvContacts and set its `DisplayMember` property to `CombinedName`. Now when the user clicks on an item in this list, the ListBox will make the DataView move to the corresponding record.

Next create a new ComboBox named cboLetter and position it above the ListBox. Make its Items collection include the letters A, B, C, and so on, plus the special values <New> and <All>.

That's all you need to do at design time. At runtime, the program needs to use a little code to take advantage of the DataView. Listing 8.3 shows the most interesting code.

The form's `Load` event handler begins as it does in other programs. It initializes the `cboState` ComboBox, hides the `txtSnapshotFile` TextBox, and fills the DataSet. It then saves a reference to the CurrencyManager almost as before. This time, however, it saves a reference to the CurrencyManager that coordinates data transfer for the `dvContacts` DataView instead of for the DataSet. It then sets the `cboLetter` ComboBox's text to the first letter of the `LastName` field in the first record in the DataSet. As you'll see in a moment, that makes the program display the records that have `LastName` values beginning with that letter.

When you invoke the Data menu's New command, the program's `mnuDataNew_Click` event handler executes. This routine sets the cboLetter ComboBox's text to <New>, making the program display the DataSet's new records. It then uses the CurrencyManager's `AddNew` method to create the new record. Because the program is displaying new records, this record appears in the list.

The only other new piece of code is the `cboLetter` ComboBox's `SelectedIndexChanged` event handler. When this routine executes, it checks the ComboBox's value to see what the user selected. If the value is <All>, the event handler sets the DataView's `RowStateFilter` to `DataViewRowState.CurrentRows` so the DataView selects all the DataSet's records. If the ComboBox's value is <New>, the event handler sets the DataView's `RowStateFilter` to `DataViewRowState.Added` so the DataView selects all the DataSet's newly added records.

If the ComboBox's value is not <All> or <New>, then it must be a letter. In that case, the event handler sets the DataView's `RowFilter` property to select records where the `LastName` field begins with that letter. For example, if the user selects the letter S, the program sets the DataView's `RowFilter` property to the statement:

```
LastName LIKE 'S%'
```

The percent character (%) is a wildcard matching zero or more of any character, so this statement matches any record with a LastName starting with S.

The rest is automatic. Setting the RowStateFilter and RowFilter properties makes the DataView update its list of selected records. The CurrencyManager updates the lstContacts ListBox that is bound to the DataView. If the ListBox now displays any records, the first is selected. That makes the DataView automatically display the corresponding record. Finally, that makes the bound TextBoxes and other controls on the form display the newly selected record's field values.

LISTING 8.3   EXAMPLE PROGRAM CONTACTSLETTERLISTS USES THIS CODE TO DISPLAY SUBSETS OF THE DATA

```
' Fill the DataSet.
Private Sub Form1_Load(ByVal sender As System.Object, _
   ByVal e As System.EventArgs) Handles MyBase.Load
      ' Load the cboState ComboBox.
      Dim states() As String = { _
          "AK", "AL", "AR", "AZ", "CA", "CO", "CT", "DC", "DE", "FL", _
          "GA", "HI", "IA", "ID", "IL", "IN", "KS", "KT", "LA", "MA", _
          "MD", "ME", "MI", "MN", "MO", "MS", "MT", "NC", "ND", "NE", _
          "NH", "NJ", "NM", "NV", "NY", "OH", "OK", "OR", "PA", "RI", _
          "SC", "SD", "TN", "TX", "UT", "VA", "VT", "WA", "WI", "WV", _
          "WY" _
      }
      cboState.Items.Clear()
      cboState.Items.AddRange(states)

      ' Hide the txtSnapshotFile control.
      ' If we do this at design time,
      ' it doesn't get updated by the DataSet.
      txtSnapshotFile.Visible = False

      ' Make the name list as large as possible.
      ArrangeControls()

      ' Fill the DataSet.
      daContacts.Fill(dsContacts)

      ' Save a reference to the CurrencyManager.
      m_CurrencyManager = Me.BindingContext(dvContacts)

      ' Select the first record's letter.
      Dim last_name As String = _
          dsContacts.Tables("Contacts").Rows(0).Item("LastName")
      cboLetter.Text = last_name.Substring(0, 1).ToUpper
End Sub

' Create a new record.
Private Sub mnuDataNew_Click(ByVal sender As System.Object, _
   ByVal e As System.EventArgs) Handles mnuDataNew.Click
      ' Finish the current edit.
      m_CurrencyManager.EndCurrentEdit()
```

```
        ' Select the new records.
        cboLetter.Text = "<New>"

        ' Add the new record.
        m_CurrencyManager.AddNew()

        ' Set the focus to the Last Name field.
        txtLastName.Focus()
    End Sub

    ' Display the records for this letter.
    Private Sub cboLetter_SelectedIndexChanged(ByVal sender As System.Object, _
      ByVal e As System.EventArgs) Handles cboLetter.SelectedIndexChanged
        ' Make the DataView select these records.
        If cboLetter.Text = "<All>" Then
            ' Display all records.
            dvContacts.RowFilter = ""
            dvContacts.RowStateFilter = DataViewRowState.CurrentRows
        ElseIf cboLetter.Text = "<New>" Then
            ' Display new records.
            dvContacts.RowFilter = ""
            dvContacts.RowStateFilter = DataViewRowState.Added
        Else
            ' Display records beginning with
            ' this letter.
            dvContacts.RowFilter = "LastName LIKE '" & cboLetter.Text & "%'"
            dvContacts.RowStateFilter = DataViewRowState.CurrentRows
        End If
    End Sub
```

BINDING CONTROLS WITH CODE

The examples presented in this chapter use connections, data adapters, DataSets, and DataViews defined at design time to interact with the database. There's nothing magic about creating these objects at design time, however. All the Visual Basic development environment does is insert code in a region named "Windows Form Designer Generated Code" at the beginning of your program. If you look near the top of your source file, you can find this section. Click on the plus sign to its left to expand the region and look at the code. If you look closely, you will find all these objects defined and initialized in that section.

Instead of creating all these objects at design time, you can write code to create them at runtime. The BindControls subroutine shown in Listing 8.4 does just that. It defines an SqlConnection object and uses it to build a SqlDataAdapter.

Next, the subroutine adds an entry to the data adapter's TableMappings collection telling the adapter to map the default table named Table to the name Contacts. When it loads the table's data, this mapping makes the data adapter give the table the useful name Contacts. That lets the program refer to the table as in m_dsContacts.Tables("Contacts").

The routine then uses a SqlCommandBuilder object to build the INSERT, UPDATE, and DELETE commands that will be needed by the data adapter. It is interesting to look at the command strings created by Visual Basic when you build these objects at design time. Open the automatically generated region of code at the beginning of your program and take a look. You could duplicate this code and build the commands yourself, but they are enormous. Using the SqlCommandBuilder is much easier.

BindControls then creates a DataSet object, uses the data adapter to fill it with data, and creates a DataView object attached to the DataSet.

Next, the subroutine is finally ready to bind the form's controls. It sets the ListBox's DataSource and DisplayMember properties much as you would at design time. The subroutine finishes by adding entries to the other bound controls' DataBindings collections. Each DataBindings entry gives the name of the control's property being bound, the data source, and the name of the data in the data source to use.

LISTING 8.4   SUBROUTINE BindControls BINDS CONTROLS TO DATA SOURCES AT RUNTIME

```
' Bind the controls to the database.
Private Sub BindControls()
    ' Define the connection.
    m_conContacts = New SqlConnection()
    m_conContacts.ConnectionString = _
        "data source=Bender\NETSDK;initial catalog=Contacts;user id=sa"

    ' Define the data adapter.
    m_daContacts = New SqlDataAdapter( _
        "SELECT LastName + ', ' + FirstName AS CombinedName, * " & _
        "FROM Contacts ORDER BY LastName, FirstName", _
        m_conContacts)

    ' Map the default table name "Table"
    '   to "Contacts".
    m_daContacts.TableMappings.Add("Table", "Contacts")

    ' Create the INSERT, UPDATE, and DELETE commands.
    Dim command_builder As New SqlCommandBuilder(m_daContacts)

    ' Create the DataSet.
    m_dsContacts = New DataSet()

    ' Load the DataSet.
    m_daContacts.Fill(m_dsContacts)

    ' Create the DataView.
    m_dvContacts = New DataView(m_dsContacts.Tables(0))

    ' Bind the ListBox to the DataView.
    lstContacts.DataSource = m_dvContacts
    lstContacts.DisplayMember = "CombinedName"

    ' Bind the other fields to the DataView.
    txtLastName.DataBindings.Add("Text", m_dvContacts, "LastName")
    txtFirstName.DataBindings.Add("Text", m_dvContacts, "FirstName")
    txtStreet.DataBindings.Add("Text", m_dvContacts, "Street")
    txtCity.DataBindings.Add("Text", m_dvContacts, "City")
```

LISTING 8.4 CONTINUED

```
    cboState.DataBindings.Add("Text", m_dvContacts, "State")
    txtZip.DataBindings.Add("Text", m_dvContacts, "Zip")
    txtEmail.DataBindings.Add("Text", m_dvContacts, "Email")
    txtNotes.DataBindings.Add("Text", m_dvContacts, "Notes")
    txtHomePhone.DataBindings.Add("Text", m_dvContacts, "HomePhone")
    txtHomePhoneExtension.DataBindings.Add("Text", m_dvContacts, _
        "HomePhoneExtension")
    txtHomeFax.DataBindings.Add("Text", m_dvContacts, "HomeFax")
    txtHomeFaxExtension.DataBindings.Add("Text", m_dvContacts, "HomeFaxExtension")
    txtWorkPhone.DataBindings.Add("Text", m_dvContacts, "WorkPhone")
    txtWorkPhoneExtension.DataBindings.Add("Text", m_dvContacts, _
        "WorkPhoneExtension")
    txtWorkFax.DataBindings.Add("Text", m_dvContacts, "WorkFax")
    txtWorkFaxExtension.DataBindings.Add("Text", m_dvContacts, "WorkFaxExtension")
    txtSnapshotFile.DataBindings.Add("Text", m_dvContacts, "SnapshotFile")
End Sub
```

Example program ContactsLetterLists2 looks exactly like ContactsLetterLists at runtime. The only difference is it creates its database objects explicitly at runtime while program ContactsLetterLists uses objects created at design time.

DATAGRID

The DataGrid control is so powerful that it hardly needs any explanation. It not only displays data, it provides methods for letting the user insert, update, and delete records. To modify a value, simply click on the grid cell and type the new value. To delete a record, click to the left of its grid row to select the row and then press Delete. To create a new record, click on any field in the grid's bottommost row (marked with an asterisk) and start typing.

All these features mean you don't need to add much code to make the DataGrid work. Because the grid displays all rows and columns at once, you don't even need to add any kind of navigation method. The user just points, clicks, and types. Figure 8.16 shows program ContactsGrid displaying Contacts information in a DataGrid control.

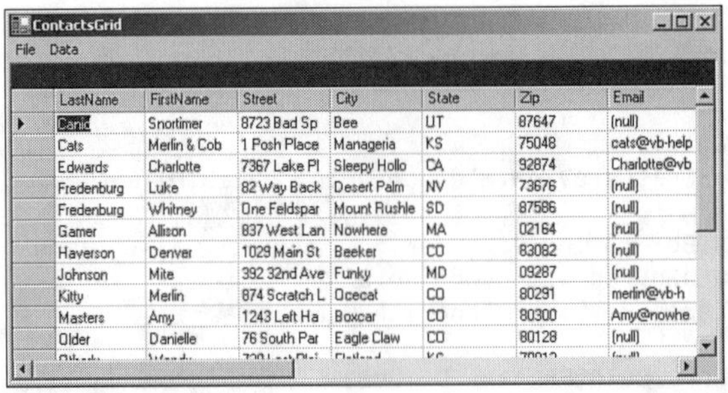

Figure 8.16
Program ContactsGrid uses a DataGrid control to display data.

Making the DataGrid work is relatively simple. Create a data source as described in the previous sections in this chapter. For example, at design time you can make database connection, DataSet, and data adapter objects. Set the DataGrid's `DataSource` property to the DataSet. Then add code to fill the DataSet and to save or cancel changes as appropriate. The rest is automatic.

The remarkable power and simplicity of the DataGrid control makes it very useful for building "quick and dirty" forms that let advanced users manage database tables. For instance, using a DataGrid you can build a simple form to let system administrators view and modify your application's parameters.

If you build the data source objects at runtime instead of using design time objects, you can even use the same form to manage multiple database tables. The code is practically identical no matter what table you want to use. The only change is in the data object's connection string.

SUMMARY

Data binding is a powerful technique. It lets Visual Basic automate the transfer of data between data sources and controls. It also lets controls such as ListBoxes and ComboBoxes manage a data source. For example, when a user selects an item from a ListBox, the ListBox can make its underlying data source select the corresponding record. The data source in turn might then update other bound controls to display the new record's values.

Although data binding cannot solve all your problems, it does make this sort of synchronization easier. With a couple of data objects, a few bound controls, and a little code, you can build applications that give the user flexible and powerful access to a database.

## CHAPTER 9

DATA SAFETY

A database application that does not ensure its data is safe is not very useful. An application that allows a user to work for hours processing customer data and then lets the user accidentally exit without saving the changes will cause more frustration than it is worth.

This chapter explains how an application can ensure that its data is safe before the user exits. It shows how to implement the standard File menu commands New, Open, Save, and Save As. It also shows how to build a most recently used (MRU) file list. Some of these techniques were used in previous chapters. This chapter explains them in more detail.

EASYDRAW

The EasyDraw program, shown in Figure 9.1, demonstrates the ideas described in this chapter. Use the File menu's New command to start a new picture. Select a drawing tool from the toolbar. Then click and drag to draw a new shape. Use the File menu's Save or Save As command to save the drawing. Use the File menu's Open command or MRU list to open a saved drawing.

Figure 9.1
The EasyDraw program lets the user draw simple pictures.

When it knows the name of a drawing's file, the EasyDraw program displays it in the form's caption. When the picture has unsaved changes, the caption includes an asterisk. For example, if you open the file Happy.edr and add a line to the picture, the program's caption is: EasyDraw*[Happy.edr].

When the picture has unsaved changes, the program ensures that you do not discard the changes accidentally. If you try to close the picture, open a new picture, or exit the program, EasyDraw asks if you want to save the changes. If you click Yes, the program saves the changes, possibly asking you to pick a file for the picture if this is a new picture. If you click No, the program discards the changes and lets you continue your action (close the picture, open a new file, or exit). If you click Cancel, the program cancels your action and keeps the picture unchanged.

The following sections explain how EasyDraw protects its data. Although this program is graphical, you can use exactly the same techniques for any other database application. Whether the data is graphical, employee data, inventory records, or purchase orders, each program can use the same methods to protect its data.

STORING DATA

Program EasyDraw uses a document-oriented approach, storing each picture in a separate data file. Because the pictures are stored separately, this application doesn't need to use a relational database.

If you needed to store additional information with the files and search on that information, you could store the pictures in a database. For example, you might give each picture a title and description. In that case, it might be worthwhile to store the title, description, and drawing information in a relational database.

EasyDraw could store drawing information in some sort of customized text or binary format. Visual Basic provides good tools for working with XML, so EasyDraw uses an XML format. XML also gives the files some degree of standardization. Although a program cannot do much with a drawing file without knowing how the drawings work, the XML tags make the format easy for a human to decipher.

The following code shows a small EasyDraw file. Even without instructions, it is easy to understand the data. The file begins with an XML declaration followed by a NewDataSet root element. Each EasyDraw object inside the root element represents a drawing object. The first is an ellipse inside the bounding box with opposite corners at coordinates (87, 69) and (276, 248). The second object is a line from (123, 178) to (145, 208). The last object is a rectangle with opposite corners at coordinates (119, 91) and (245, 59).

```xml
<?xml version="1.0" standalone="yes"?>
<NewDataSet>
  <EasyDraw>
    <Type>Ellipse</Type>
    <X1>87</X1>
    <Y1>69</Y1>
    <X2>276</X2>
    <Y2>248</Y2>
  </EasyDraw>
  <EasyDraw>
    <Type>Line</Type>
    <X1>123</X1>
```

```
    <Y1>178</Y1>
    <X2>145</X2>
    <Y2>208</Y2>
  </EasyDraw>
  <EasyDraw>
    <Type>Rectangle</Type>
    <X1>119</X1>
    <Y1>91</Y1>
    <X2>245</X2>
    <Y2>59</Y2>
  </EasyDraw>
</NewDataSet>
```

The DataSet object has methods for reading and writing XML files so it's easy for the program to use a DataSet to manipulate the drawing internally. The program stores its data in a single table named EasyDraw. That's why the data elements in the previous XML picture file are named EasyDraw.

The rows in this table contain fields named Type, X1, Y1, X2, and Y2. Those parameters describe the picture's drawing objects.

DRAWING EXISTING OBJECTS

Listing 9.1 shows how EasyDraw uses its DataSet and the DataTable it contains to draw graphical objects. The program begins by declaring several variables used for storing and drawing objects. The objects m_DataSet and m_DataTable contain the current picture's data. When the program needs to load or save a picture, it uses the m_DataSet object's ReadXml and WriteXml methods. Rows in the table m_DataTable represent the picture's drawing objects. The program declares m_DataTable using the WithEvents keyword so it can easily receive events for that object.

Subroutine DrawDataSet draws the objects represented by a DataSet. The routine's first parameter is the Graphics object on which it should draw. The program must draw on a couple different Graphics objects so it is important that the subroutine take this as a parameter. This is often the case with drawing programs in Visual Basic .NET.

DrawDataSet begins by clearing the Graphics object. It then loops through the rows in the DataSet's first table, calling DrawDataRow for each.

Subroutine DrawDataRow takes a Graphics object and a DataRow as parameters and draws the DataRow's object on the Graphics object. This routine examines the DataRow's Type field and calls subroutine DrawALine, DrawARectangle, or DrawAnEllipse, accordingly.

Subroutine DrawALine uses the DataRow's X1, Y1, X2, and Y2 fields to draw a line on the Graphics object. Subroutines DrawARectangle and DrawAnEllipse are very similar so they are not shown here. Download the complete project from the book's Web site to see how they work.

LISTING 9.1   THIS CODE DRAWS GRAPHICAL OBJECTS DESCRIBED BY DataRow OBJECTS

```
' The DataSet and DataTable that will hold the data.
Private m_DataSet As DataSet
Private WithEvents m_DataTable As DataTable

' Draw the DataSet's data.
Private Sub DrawDataSet(ByVal gr As Graphics, ByVal data_set As DataSet)
    Dim data_row As DataRow

    ' Clear the canvas.
    gr.Clear(picCanvas.BackColor)

    ' If the DataSet is empty, do nothing more.
    If data_set Is Nothing Then Exit Sub

    ' Loop through the rows drawing their objects.
    For Each data_row In data_set.Tables(0).Rows
        DrawDataRow(gr, data_row)
    Next data_row
End Sub

' Draw this object.
Private Sub DrawDataRow(ByVal gr As Graphics, ByVal data_row As DataRow)
    Select Case data_row("Type")
        Case "Line"
            DrawALine(gr, data_row)
        Case "Rectangle"
            DrawARectangle(gr, data_row)
        Case "Ellipse"
            DrawAnEllipse(gr, data_row)
    End Select
End Sub

' Draw a line.
Private Sub DrawALine(ByVal gr As Graphics, ByVal data_row As DataRow)
    gr.DrawLine(Pens.Black, _
        CInt(data_row("X1")), _
        CInt(data_row("Y1")), _
        CInt(data_row("X2")), _
        CInt(data_row("Y2")))
End Sub
```

You could easily add other drawing objects to program EasyDraw. Define a new object Type and create a new subroutine to draw the object much as subroutine DrawALine draws lines.

You could also define other parameters for the objects. For example, you could add ForeColor, FillColor, LineStyle, LineWidth, and other properties to the objects.

DRAWING NEW OBJECTS

To draw existing objects, program EasyDraw uses the rows in its DataTable object. When the user creates a new object, the program adds a new row to the DataTable. That modifies the data so it is central to the discussion of data safety.

The code in Listing 9.2 shows how program EasyDraw lets the user create a new object. This code uses several global-level variables. The m_DataRow variable represents a drawing object currently being created. The program sets the Boolean value m_Drawing to True while the user is drawing an object. The program uses the Bitmap object stored in m_BackBuffer to erase a new object while the user is drawing it. Finally, the m_SelectedTool object contains a reference to the toolbar button that is currently selected.

When the user clicks on a toolbar button, the tbrDrawingTools_ButtonClick event handler executes. This routine checks whether the clicked button is already selected. If it is, the user is trying to deselect it. The program sets the m_SelectedTool variable to Nothing and resets the drawing area's cursor to the default.

If the user is clicking a new toolbar button, the program deselects the previously selected button and saves a reference to the new button in the m_SelectedTool variable. It then sets the drawing area's cursor to a crosshair to indicate that a tool is selected. In a more elaborate version of the program, you could use different cursors for different tools.

Subroutine SaveBackBuffer saves a snapshot of the current picture in the variable m_BackBuffer. It creates a new Bitmap object sized to fit the drawing area. It then calls subroutine DrawDataSet to make it draw the current picture into the Bitmap.

Subroutine EraseRubberband draws the image saved in m_BackBuffer onto the drawing area. This erases any temporary "rubber band" objects drawn while the user is creating a new object.

When the user moves the cursor over the drawing area and presses the mouse button, the picCanvas_MouseDown event handler fires. If no tool is selected, this subroutine exits. If a tool is selected, the routine indicates that a new object is being drawn by setting m_Drawing to True. It then creates a new DataRow object and sets the new row's Type field value to the name of the new object: Line, Rectangle, or Ellipse. It saves the current mouse position in the row's X1, Y1, X2, and Y2 fields and adds the new row to the DataTable.

Adding the new row to the DataTable modifies the DataTable's data. That raises the DataTable's RowChanged event. The event handler executes and adds an asterisk to the program's caption so the user can easily tell that the data has been modified. The program does not need to take any other action to remember that the data has been changed because adding the row automatically makes the DataSet's HasChanges method return True. The program can use HasChanges later to see if the data has been modified.

This program modifies its data at a single point, so it would be relatively easy to update the form's caption there instead of using the RowChanged event. In other words, the picCanvas_MouseDown event handler could change the caption directly. On the other hand, different applications might change the data in many places. If an application uses bound controls, the user can modify the data directly using the controls without the program's code performing the modification. In those cases, the RowChanged event makes detecting changes easy. As long as the modification is made to the DataSet immediately, the RowChanged event tells the program that a change has occurred.

Some other high-level data objects provide similar change events. For example, the CurrencyManager class provides an Item Changed event. When the user modifies a value displayed in a DataGrid control, its CurrencyManager raises this event so the program can take action.

When the user moves the cursor over the drawing area, the picCanvas_MouseMove event handler fires. If m_Drawing is False, this routine exits without doing anything. If m_Drawing is True, the routine calls EraseRubberband to remove any temporary drawing done while creating the new object. It then saves the current mouse position in the new DataRow's X2 and Y2 fields and calls subroutine DrawDataRow to redraw the new DataRow.

For example, suppose the user is drawing a new line. The MouseMove event handler calls EraseRubberband to erase the previous version of this line. It then calls DrawDataRow to redraw the line in its new position.

When the user releases the mouse button, the picCanvas_MouseUp event handler executes. If m_Drawing is False, the subroutine simply exits. If m_Drawing is True, the event handler indicates that the new object is finished by setting m_Drawing to False. It then sets m_BackBuffer to Nothing because the program doesn't need to erase the object anymore.

You would not need to modify the code in Listing 9.2 to add new drawing objects to the program. That code calls subroutine DrawDataRow in Listing 9.1 to draw the new object. That's where you would need to make the changes.

LISTING 9.2   PROGRAM EASYDRAW USES THIS CODE TO DRAW NEW OBJECTS

```
' The drawing object currently being drawn.
Private m_DataRow As DataRow

' True while we are drawing.
Private m_Drawing As Boolean

' A back buffer used while drawing rubberband objects.
Private m_BackBuffer As Bitmap

' The currently selected drawing tool.
Private m_SelectedTool As ToolBarButton

' Select a new drawing tool.
Private Sub tbrDrawingTools_ButtonClick(ByVal sender As System.Object, _
    ByVal e As System.Windows.Forms.ToolBarButtonClickEventArgs) _
    Handles tbrDrawingTools.ButtonClick
        ' If this is the currently selected tool,
        ' then the user is toggling it off.
        If m_SelectedTool Is e.Button Then
            m_SelectedTool = Nothing
            picCanvas.Cursor = Cursors.Default
            Exit Sub
        End If

        ' Deselect the previously selected tool.
        If Not (m_SelectedTool Is Nothing) Then
```

LISTING 9.2   CONTINUED

```
            m_SelectedTool.Pushed = False
        End If
        m_SelectedTool = e.Button

        ' Set an appropriate mouse cursor.
        picCanvas.Cursor = Cursors.Cross
    End Sub

    ' Display a visible change indication.
    Private Sub m_DataTable_RowChanged(ByVal sender As Object, _
      ByVal e As System.Data.DataRowChangeEventArgs) Handles m_DataTable.RowChanged
        Me.Text = "EasyDraw*[" & FileTitle(m_FileName) & "]"
    End Sub

    ' Make an image of the current drawing to
    ' erase rubberband objects.
    Private Sub SaveBackBuffer()
        ' Make a new bitmap that fits the canvas.
        m_BackBuffer = New Bitmap( _
            picCanvas.Size.Width, _
            picCanvas.Size.Height, _
            picCanvas.CreateGraphics())

        ' Draw the current picture into the back buffer.
        DrawDataSet(Graphics.FromImage(m_BackBuffer), m_DataSet)
    End Sub

    ' Use the back buffer to erase the current
    ' rubberband drawing.
    Private Sub EraseRubberband()
        picCanvas.CreateGraphics().DrawImage(m_BackBuffer, 0, 0)
    End Sub

    ' Start drawing an object.
    Private Sub picCanvas_MouseDown(ByVal sender As Object, _
      ByVal e As System.Windows.Forms.MouseEventArgs) Handles picCanvas.MouseDown
        ' Do nothing if no tool is selected.
        If m_SelectedTool Is Nothing Then Exit Sub

        ' We are now drawing.
        m_Drawing = True

        ' Create a new drawing object.
        m_DataRow = m_DataTable.NewRow()
        m_DataRow("Type") = m_SelectedTool.Tag
        m_DataRow("X1") = e.X
        m_DataRow("Y1") = e.Y
        m_DataRow("X2") = e.X
        m_DataRow("Y2") = e.Y
        m_DataTable.Rows.Add(m_DataRow)

        ' Save a back buffer snapshot.
        SaveBackBuffer()
    End Sub
```

LISTING 9.2   CONTINUED

```
' Continue drawing the object.
Private Sub picCanvas_MouseMove(ByVal sender As Object, _
  ByVal e As System.Windows.Forms.MouseEventArgs) Handles picCanvas.MouseMove
    ' Do nothing if we are not drawing.
    If Not m_Drawing Then Exit Sub

    ' Erase the current rubberband line.
    EraseRubberband()

    ' Save the new point.
    m_DataRow("X2") = e.X
    m_DataRow("Y2") = e.Y

    ' Draw the object.
    DrawDataRow(picCanvas.CreateGraphics(), m_DataRow)
End Sub

' Finish drawing the object.
Private Sub picCanvas_MouseUp(ByVal sender As Object, _
  ByVal e As System.Windows.Forms.MouseEventArgs) Handles picCanvas.MouseUp
    ' Do nothing if we are not drawing.
    If Not m_Drawing Then Exit Sub
    m_Drawing = False

    ' We don't need the back buffer any more.
    m_BackBuffer = Nothing
End Sub
```

DataSafe

The DataSafe subroutine, shown in Listing 9.3, returns True if the current data is safe. If the m_DataSet variable is Nothing, then the program has no drawing loaded so there is no data to protect and DataSafe returns True.

If m_DataSet is not Nothing, the function uses the HasChanges method to see if the data has been modified. If the data has not been modified, the data is safe and DataSafe returns True.

If there are unsaved changes, DataSafe asks the user if the program should save the changes. If the user clicks No, then the program is free to discard the changes and DataSafe returns True to indicate that the changes do not need to be saved.

If the user clicks Yes, the function calls subroutine SaveData to save the data. It then checks the DataSet's HasChanges method to see if the data was saved in case there was an error saving the data. For instance, if this is a new drawing, subroutine SaveData presents a file save dialog so the user can pick the file to hold the data. If the user cancels that dialog, the data is not saved and HasChanges returns True.

Finally, if the user clicks Cancel, DataSafe returns False to indicate that the program cannot discard the modified data.

LISTING 9.3 DataSafe Returns True If It Is Safe to Discard the Data

```
' Return True if the data is safe.
Private Function DataSafe() As Boolean
    ' If there is no DataSet, there is no
    ' data to protect.
    If m_DataSet Is Nothing Then Return True

    ' If there are no pending changes,
    ' the data is safe.
    If Not m_DataSet.HasChanges() Then Return True

    ' Ask the user if we should save the changes.
    Select Case MsgBox("Save changes?", MsgBoxStyle.YesNoCancel, "Save Changes?")
        Case MsgBoxResult.No
            ' The data is safe.
            Return True
        Case MsgBoxResult.Yes
            ' Save the changes.
            SaveData(m_FileName)

            ' Return False if we failed to save
            ' the data for some reason.
            Return (Not m_DataSet.HasChanges())
        Case MsgBoxResult.Cancel
            ' The user wants to cancel this operation.
            ' Do not let the program discard the data.
            Return False
    End Select
End Function
```

Program EasyDraw uses the DataSafe function any time it is about to discard the current data. That happens when the user wants to start a new drawing, open a drawing file, close the current drawing, or exit the program. The following sections describe the code that executes when the user selects these commands from the File menu. You will see calls to DataSafe in that code.

Menu Commands

Program EasyDraw's File menu contains six commands besides the MRU list: New, Open, Save, Save As, Close, and Exit. The code shown in Listing 9.4 manages these functions.

Subroutine FileIsLoaded sets the program's controls to an appropriate state depending on whether a drawing is loaded. If no drawing is loaded, the subroutine disables the File menu's Close, Save, and Save As commands. It also makes the toolbar and drawing area invisible. If a drawing is loaded, the subroutine enables the File menu's commands and makes the toolbar and drawing area visible.

When the user selects the File menu's New command, the mnuFileNew_Click event handler executes. It calls DataSafe to see if it safe to discard the current data and exits if DataSafe returns False. The subroutine then creates a new DataSet. It gives the DataSet a new

DataTable named EasyDraw. It adds the fields Type, X1, Y1, X2, and Y2 to the DataTable. The event handler calls the DataSet's AcceptChanges method to mark the data as unmodified and calls FileIsLoaded to display the toolbar and drawing area. It resets the drawing file's name to blank and calls DrawDataSet to draw the empty picture.

When the user selects the File menu's Open command, the event handler calls DataSafe to see if it safe to discard the current data and exits if DataSafe returns False. It displays a File Open dialog to let the user select a drawing file. If the user selects a file, the program calls the LoadDataFile subroutine to load the file.

Subroutine LoadDataFile creates a new DataSet and uses its ReadXml method to try to load the XML data in the selected file. It calls AcceptChanges to mark the new data as unchanged and calls DrawDataSet to display the new data. If it gets this far, the subroutine makes the module-level variable m_DataSet point at the new DataSet. It is only at this point that the previously loaded data is discarded. If the program could not load the drawing file, for example if it was some other kind of file, then the program still displays the existing picture.

After it has loaded the new data file, LoadDataFile deselects the currently selected drawing tool and calls FileIsLoaded to make sure the toolbar and drawing area are visible. It then calls subroutine MruAdd (described later in this chapter) to add the name of the newly opened file to the MRU list. It finishes by displaying the file's title (name without the path) in the program's caption.

When the user selects the File menu's Close command, the event handler calls DataSafe to see if it is safe to discard the current data and exits if DataSafe returns False. If it is safe to discards the data, the program sets m_DataSet and m_DataTable to Nothing and calls FileIsLoaded to hide the toolbar and drawing area. It finishes by resetting the file's name and the form's caption.

When the user selects the File menu's Save command, the event handler calls the SaveData subroutine, passing it the name of the current drawing's data file.

If its filename is blank, subroutine SaveData displays a File Save dialog so the user can pick the file that should hold the drawing. If the user cancels the file selection, the subroutine exits. Next, SaveData calls the DataSet's WriteXml method to save its contents into the file. It calls AcceptChanges to mark the data as unmodified and calls MruAdd to add the filename to the MRU list. The routine ends after saving the filename in the m_FileName variable and displaying the file's title in the form's caption.

When the user selects the File menu's Save As command, the event handler calls the SaveData subroutine, passing it a blank filename. That makes SaveData display a File Save dialog so the user can pick the drawing's new file.

When the user selects the File menu's Exit command, the event handler calls the form's Close method. The form's Closing event handler does the interesting work. That event handler sets its e.Cancel flag to True if DataSafe returns False. If the data contains unsaved changes, the form refuses to close.

Finally, helper function `FileTitle` returns a file's name without the leading path information. It uses the name's `LastIndexOf` method to find the location of the last backslash in the name and returns whatever comes after that.

LISTING 9.4   PROGRAM EASYDRAW USES THIS CODE TO LOAD, SAVE, CLOSE, AND CREATE NEW DRAWINGS

```
' The name of the drawing file.
Private m_FileName As String

' Set appropriate control properties for when
' a file is loaded or closed.
Private Sub FileIsLoaded(ByVal is_loaded As Boolean)
    ' Enable the Close, Save, and Save As commands.
    mnuFileClose.Enabled = is_loaded
    mnuFileSave.Enabled = is_loaded
    mnuFileSaveAs.Enabled = is_loaded

    ' Show the drawing toolbar and the canvas.
    tbrDrawingTools.Visible = is_loaded
    picCanvas.SetBounds(0, tbrDrawingTools.Size.Height, ClientSize.Width, _
        ClientSize.Height - tbrDrawingTools.Size.Height)
    picCanvas.Visible = is_loaded
End Sub

' Start a new drawing file.
Private Sub mnuFileNew_Click(ByVal sender As System.Object, _
  ByVal e As System.EventArgs) Handles mnuFileNew.Click
    ' Ensure that the data is safe.
    If Not DataSafe() Then Exit Sub

    ' Create a new DataSet and DataTable.
    m_DataSet = New DataSet()
    m_DataTable = m_DataSet.Tables.Add("EasyDraw")
    m_DataTable.Columns.Add("Type", GetType(String))
    m_DataTable.Columns.Add("X1", GetType(Integer))
    m_DataTable.Columns.Add("Y1", GetType(Integer))
    m_DataTable.Columns.Add("X2", GetType(Integer))
    m_DataTable.Columns.Add("Y2", GetType(Integer))

    ' Mark the new data as unmodified.
    m_DataSet.AcceptChanges()

    ' Display controls for a loaded file.
    FileIsLoaded(True)

    ' We have no name for this file yet.
    m_FileName = ""
    Me.Text = "EasyDraw []"
    dlgSaveFile.FileName = ""
    dlgOpenFile.FileName = ""

    ' Redraw the blank file.
    DrawDataSet(picCanvas.CreateGraphics(), m_DataSet)
End Sub
```

LISTING 9.4   CONTINUED

```vb
' Load a drawing file.
Private Sub mnuFileOpen_Click(ByVal sender As System.Object, _
  ByVal e As System.EventArgs) Handles mnuFileOpen.Click
    ' Make sure the data is safe.
    If Not DataSafe() Then Exit Sub

    ' Let the user select the file.
    If dlgOpenFile.ShowDialog() = DialogResult.OK Then
        LoadDataFile(dlgOpenFile.FileName)
    End If
End Sub

' Load a data file by name.
Private Sub LoadDataFile(ByVal file_name As String)
    Try
        ' Start a new DataSet.
        Dim data_set As New DataSet()

        ' Read the drawing data.
        data_set.ReadXml(file_name)
        data_set.AcceptChanges()

        ' Display the new data.
        DrawDataSet(picCanvas.CreateGraphics(), data_set)

        ' If we got this far, replace the
        ' current DataSet with the new one.
        m_DataSet = data_set
        m_DataTable = m_DataSet.Tables(0)

        ' Deselect the selected tool.
        If Not (m_SelectedTool Is Nothing) Then
            m_SelectedTool.Pushed = False
            m_SelectedTool = Nothing
            picCanvas.Cursor = Cursors.Default
        End If

        ' Display appropriate menus.
        FileIsLoaded(True)

        ' Add the file to the MRU list.
        MruAdd(file_name)

        ' Display the file name in the form's caption.
        m_FileName = file_name
        Me.Text = "EasyDraw [" & FileTitle(m_FileName) & "]"
        dlgSaveFile.FileName = file_name
        dlgOpenFile.FileName = ""
    Catch exc As Exception
        MsgBox(exc.Message)
        Me.Text = "EasyDraw []"

        ' Remove the file from the MRU list.
        MruRemove(file_name)
```

LISTING 9.4 CONTINUED

```
            ' Redisplay the data.
            DrawDataSet(picCanvas.CreateGraphics(), m_DataSet)
    End Try
End Sub

Private Sub mnuFileClose_Click(ByVal sender As System.Object, _
  ByVal e As System.EventArgs) Handles mnuFileClose.Click
    ' Make sure the data is safe.
    If Not DataSafe() Then Exit Sub

    ' Destroy the DataSet.
    m_DataTable = Nothing
    m_DataSet = Nothing

    ' Display controls for no loaded file.
    FileIsLoaded(False)

    ' We have no name for this file yet.
    m_FileName = ""
    Me.Text = "EasyDraw []"
End Sub

' Save the data.
Private Sub mnuFileSave_Click(ByVal sender As System.Object, _
  ByVal e As System.EventArgs) Handles mnuFileSave.Click
    SaveData(m_FileName)
End Sub

' Save the data.
Private Sub SaveData(ByVal file_name As String)
    ' See if we know the file name.
    If file_name.Length = 0 Then
        ' Let the user pick the file name.
        If dlgSaveFile.ShowDialog() <> DialogResult.OK Then Exit Sub
        file_name = dlgSaveFile.FileName
    End If

    ' Save the data.
    Try
        m_DataSet.WriteXml(file_name)
        m_DataSet.AcceptChanges()

        ' Add (or readd) the file to the MRU list.
        MruAdd(file_name)

        ' Reset the form's caption.
        m_FileName = file_name
        Me.Text = "EasyDraw [" & FileTitle(m_FileName) & "]"
    Catch exc As Exception
        MsgBox(exc.Message)
    End Try
End Sub

' Save the file with a new name.
```

LISTING 9.4 CONTINUED

```
Private Sub mnuFileSaveAs_Click(ByVal sender As System.Object, _
  ByVal e As System.EventArgs) Handles mnuFileSaveAs.Click
    SaveData("")
End Sub

Private Sub mnuFileExit_Click(ByVal sender As System.Object, _
  ByVal e As System.EventArgs) Handles mnuFileExit.Click
    Me.Close()
End Sub

' Cancel the closing if the data is not safe.
Private Sub Form1_Closing(ByVal sender As Object, _
  ByVal e As System.ComponentModel.CancelEventArgs) Handles MyBase.Closing
    e.Cancel = (Not DataSafe())
End Sub

' Return the file's title (name without path).
Private Function FileTitle(ByVal file_name As String) As String
    Dim pos As Integer

    pos = file_name.LastIndexOf("\")
    If pos < 0 Then Return file_name
    Return file_name.Substring(pos + 1)
End Function
```

MRU List

The last piece to program EasyDraw is the MRU (most recently used file) list. The MRU list shows the four most recently accessed files with the most recent on top. The list appears in the File menu above the Exit command, as shown in Figure 9.2. If you select one of the filenames from the list, the program automatically opens the corresponding file.

Figure 9.2
The MRU list displays the four most recently accessed files.

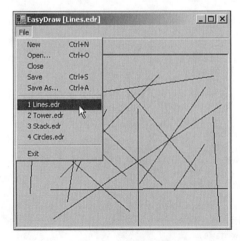

Program EasyDraw uses the code shown in Listing 9.5 to manage its MRU list. The program stores the four MRU filenames in the m_MruFileNames collection. This collection always holds exactly four filenames. If some names are missing, the last names in the list are blank in this collection. For instance, if you try to open a file from the MRU list and that file no longer exists, the program removes it from the list. The other entries are bumped up if necessary so any empty entries appear at the end of the collection and the nonblank entries are displayed in the MRU list.

When the program's form loads, its Load event handler calls subroutine MruLoad to load the initial MRU list. Subroutine MruLoad creates a new m_MruFileNames collection. It then uses Visual Basic's GetSetting function to retrieve the MRU filenames from the System Registry. It looks in the Registry for the application name EasyDraw and the section named MRU. The value names it looks for are File1, File2, File3, and File4. It saves the nonblank values in the new m_MruFileNames collection.

PART
I
CH
9

After it has retrieved all the saved MRU filenames, MruLoad adds blank names until the collection holds exactly four entries. It finishes by calling subroutine MruDisplay display the MRU list in the File menu.

Subroutine MruDisplay places the MRU filenames in the menu items mnuFileMru1, mnuFileMru2, mnuFileMru3, and mnuFileMru4. It hides the menu items that have blank filenames and makes the others visible. It then displays a separator before the first MRU menu item if that item is visible. If that item is hidden, all the MRU items are hidden, and the program hides this separator so two separators don't appear above the Exit command.

When the program changes its MRU list, it calls subroutine MruSave to save the new list into the System Registry. It does this right away instead of waiting until the program ends, so the new MRU list is saved even if the program crashes or the computer loses power. Subroutine MruSave simply calls Visual Basic's SaveSetting routine to save the MRU filenames, overwriting any previous values.

When program EasyDraw opens a file or saves a file with a new name, it calls subroutine MruAdd to add the file's name to the top of the MRU list. Subroutine MruAdd first searches the m_MruFileNames collection to see if the file is already in the list. If the name is in the list, the routine removes it. Note that the code searches the collection from the back to the front. That lets it remove items from the collection without renumbering the remaining items and confusing the For loop.

MruAdd adds the new name to the top of the list and then removes any items that appear after the first four. It calls MruSave to save the new list in the Registry and MruDisplay to display the new list in the File menu.

Subroutine MruRemove removes a specific file from the MRU list. For example, suppose you select a file from the MRU list and the program tries to load that file. If the file has been deleted, the program cannot load it and it removes the file from the MRU list.

MruRemove searches the m_MruFileNames collection to find the file and removes it if it appears. It adds a new blank item to the end of the collection if necessary to give the collection four items. It finishes by calling MruSave to save the new MRU list and by calling MruDisplay to display the new list.

The remaining MRU subroutines let the user select a file from the MRU list. When the user selects a file from the list, the event handler calls subroutine LoadMruFile to load the corresponding file. Subroutine LoadMruFile uses the DataSafe function to see if the current data is safe to discard and it exits if the data is not safe. If the data is safe, LoadMruFile calls LoadDataFile to load the selected file.

LISTING 9.5   THIS CODE MANAGES PROGRAM EASYDRAW'S MRU LIST

```
' The names of the MRU files.
Dim m_MruFileNames As Collection

' Load the MRU list.
Private Sub MruLoad()
    Dim mru_name As String
    Dim i As Integer

    ' Create a new MRU file name collection.
    m_MruFileNames = New Collection()

    For i = 1 To 4
        ' Get the next value from the registry.
        mru_name = GetSetting("EasyDraw", "MRU", "File" & i)

        ' If the value is non-blank, save it.
        If mru_name.Length > 0 Then m_MruFileNames.Add(mru_name)
    Next i

    ' Add blank entries if needed so we have 4.
    Do While m_MruFileNames.Count < 4
        m_MruFileNames.Add("")
    Loop

    ' Display the MRU list.
    MruDisplay()
End Sub

' Display the MRU list.
Private Sub MruDisplay()
    Dim i As Integer
    ' Set the menu captions.
    mnuFileMru1.Text = "&1 " & FileTitle(m_MruFileNames(1))
    mnuFileMru1.Visible = (m_MruFileNames(1).Length > 0)

    mnuFileMru2.Text = "&2 " & FileTitle(m_MruFileNames(2))
    mnuFileMru2.Visible = (m_MruFileNames(2).Length > 0)

    mnuFileMru3.Text = "&3 " & FileTitle(m_MruFileNames(3))
    mnuFileMru3.Visible = (m_MruFileNames(3).Length > 0)
```

LISTING 9.5 CONTINUED

```
        mnuFileMru4.Text = "&4 " & FileTitle(m_MruFileNames(4))
        mnuFileMru4.Visible = (m_MruFileNames(4).Length > 0)

        ' See if the separator should be visible.
        mnuFileMruSep.Visible = mnuFileMru1.Visible
End Sub

' Save the MRU list.
Private Sub MruSave()
        SaveSetting("EasyDraw", "MRU", "File1", m_MruFileNames(1))
        SaveSetting("EasyDraw", "MRU", "File2", m_MruFileNames(2))
        SaveSetting("EasyDraw", "MRU", "File3", m_MruFileNames(3))
        SaveSetting("EasyDraw", "MRU", "File4", m_MruFileNames(4))
End Sub

' Add a name to the MRU list.
Private Sub MruAdd(ByVal file_name As String)
        Dim i As Integer

        ' Remove the file if it is already in the list.
        For i = m_MruFileNames.Count To 1 Step -1
            ' See if this matches the new file name.
            If m_MruFileNames(i) = file_name Then
                ' This name matches. Remove it.
                m_MruFileNames.Remove(i)
            End If
        Next i

        ' Add the new name at the top of the list.
        m_MruFileNames.Add(file_name, , 1)

        ' Make sure we have only 4 entries.
        Do While m_MruFileNames.Count > 4
            m_MruFileNames.Remove(5)
        Loop

        ' Save the updated list.
        MruSave()

        ' Redisplay the list.
        MruDisplay()
End Sub

' Remove this file from the MRU list.
Private Sub MruRemove(ByVal file_name As String)
        Dim i As Integer

        ' Remove the file if it is already in the list.
        For i = m_MruFileNames.Count - 1 To 1 Step -1
            ' See if this matches the target file name.
            If m_MruFileNames(i) = file_name Then
                ' This name matches. Remove it.
                m_MruFileNames.Remove(i)
            End If
        Next i
```

LISTING 9.5   CONTINUED

```
    ' Make sure we have 4 items.
    For i = m_MruFileNames.Count + 1 To 4
        m_MruFileNames.Add("")
    Next i

    ' Save the updated list.
    MruSave()

    ' Redisplay the list.
    MruDisplay()
End Sub

Private Sub mnuFileMru1_Click(ByVal sender As System.Object, _
  ByVal e As System.EventArgs) Handles mnuFileMru1.Click
    LoadMruFile(1)
End Sub
Private Sub mnuFileMru2_Click(ByVal sender As System.Object, _
  ByVal e As System.EventArgs) Handles mnuFileMru2.Click
    LoadMruFile(2)
End Sub
Private Sub mnuFileMru3_Click(ByVal sender As System.Object, _
  ByVal e As System.EventArgs) Handles mnuFileMru3.Click
    LoadMruFile(3)
End Sub
Private Sub mnuFileMru4_Click(ByVal sender As System.Object, _
  ByVal e As System.EventArgs) Handles mnuFileMru4.Click
LoadMruFile(4)
End Sub

' Load a file using the MRU list.
Private Sub LoadMruFile(ByVal index As Integer)
    ' Make sure the data is safe.
    If Not DataSafe() Then Exit Sub

    ' Load the file.
    LoadDataFile(m_MruFileNames(index))
End Sub
```

DATA VALIDATION

Ensuring that changes are saved is only half the data safety problem. A program should also ensure that the saved data values make as much sense as possible. For instance, if the user accidentally types 80201 in a phone number field, the program should not save the data to the database.

At the lowest level, you can use the database itself to validate data. For example, you can use the NOT NULL statement to require a value in a field. You can use CHECK clauses to provide more elaborate validation. For instance, the following SQL statement creates a ZipCodes table. Each record's Zip field must have the format 12345 or 12345-6789.

```
CREATE TABLE Zips (
    Zip VARCHAR(10) UNIQUE NOT NULL
        CHECK ((Zip LIKE '[0-9][0-9][0-9][0-9][0-9]') OR
               (Zip LIKE '[0-9][0-9][0-9][0-9][0-9]-[0-9][0-9][0-9][0-9]'))
)
```

This kind of validation protects the database at its most fundamental level. The database refuses to allow a value that violates its constraints. This provides excellent protection for the data. Unfortunately these validations are applied in the last stages of producing new data. At that point, the user may not remember what the changes were. The database often produces cryptic error messages that don't help the user figure out where the problem lies.

PART
I
CH
9

Sample program DBValidateGrid, shown in Figure 9.3, binds a DataGrid control to the Contacts table. The table's Zip field was defined using a CHECK statement similar to the one shown earlier. You can use the grid to modify records and give them invalid Zip values. The grid shows the new values and provides no clue that there is a problem. When you try to save the data, however, the database raises an error similar to the one shown in Figure 9.3.

Figure 9.3
Program
DBValidateGrid lets
the database validate
the Zip field.

Ideally the program should warn the user about errors as soon as they occur. In program DBValidateGrid, you might think the data you have entered is correct until you try to exit the program. You might then have to fix a lot of errors while the data is no longer fresh in your mind.

Example program ValidateGrid, shown in Figure 9.4, performs its own validation for the state, ZIP code, e-mail, phone number, and extension fields. If you enter an invalid value and move to a new field, the program immediately displays an error message and resets the field to the value it had before you changed it.

Figure 9.4
Program ValidateGrid
validates fields before
the database sees
their values.

Program ValidateGrid uses the code shown in Listing 9.6 to validate its fields. When the user modifies a DataGrid cell, the underlying DataTable object raises a ColumnChanging event. The program's event handler checks the column's name and calls an appropriate validation subroutine.

That subroutine verifies that the new value makes sense. If the value is invalid, the routine displays an error message and restores the original value. For example, the ValidateZip subroutine verifies that a ZIP code value has the format 12345 or 12345-6789.

Notice also how the e-mail, phone number, and extension validation routines allow the user to enter NULL values. The DataGrid itself won't add a NULL value to the database. If the user blanks a cell, the grid normally sends a blank string to the database. The validation subroutines examine the cell's new value. If the value is blank, they convert it into a NULL value. The string (null) immediately appears in the DataGrid.

LISTING 9.6   THIS CODE VALIDATES FIELD VALUES

```
' Validate this change.
Private Sub DataTable1_ColumnChanging(ByVal sender As Object, _
  ByVal e As System.Data.DataColumnChangeEventArgs) _
  Handles DataTable1.ColumnChanging
    Select Case e.Column.ColumnName
        Case "State"
            ValidateState(e)
        Case "Zip"
            ValidateZip(e)
        Case "Email"
            ValidateEmail(e)
        Case "HomePhone", "HomeFax", "WorkPhone", "WorkFax"
            ValidatePhone(e)
        Case "HomePhoneExtension", "HomeFaxExtension", "WorkPhoneExtension", _
                "WorkFaxExtension"
            ValidateExtension(e)
    End Select

    Me.Text = APP_TITLE & "*"
End Sub

' These subroutines validate values with different
' data types. If the value is invalid, they
' present an error message and reset the value.
Private Sub ValidateState(ByVal e As System.Data.DataColumnChangeEventArgs)
    If Not (e.ProposedValue Like "[A-Z][A-Z]") Then
        MsgBox("Invalid state format")
        e.ProposedValue = e.Row.Item(e.Column.Ordinal)
    End If
End Sub
Private Sub ValidateZip(ByVal e As System.Data.DataColumnChangeEventArgs)
    If Not (e.ProposedValue Like "[0-9][0-9][0-9][0-9][0-9]") And _
        Not (e.ProposedValue Like _
_ "[0-9][0-9][0-9][0-9][0-9]-[0-9][0-9][0-9][0-9]")
    Then
        MsgBox("Invalid Zip code format")
        e.ProposedValue = e.Row.Item(e.Column.Ordinal)
    End If
End Sub
Private Sub ValidateEmail(ByVal e As System.Data.DataColumnChangeEventArgs)
    ' Change blank to NULL.
    If e.ProposedValue.length = 0 Then e.ProposedValue = DBNull.Value

    ' Allow a NULL value.
    If e.ProposedValue Is DBNull.Value Then Exit Sub
```

LISTING 9.6   CONTINUED

```
        ' See if the value contains . and @.
        Dim bad_format As Boolean
        Dim test_value As String
        Dim pos As Integer

        test_value = e.ProposedValue
        bad_format = (test_value.IndexOf(".") = -1)
        pos = test_value.IndexOf("@")
        If pos = -1 Then bad_format = True
        pos = test_value.IndexOf("@", pos + 1)
        If pos <> -1 Then bad_format = True

        If bad_format Then
            MsgBox("Invalid email address format")
            e.ProposedValue = e.Row.Item(e.Column.Ordinal)
        End If
    End Sub
    Private Sub ValidatePhone(ByVal e As System.Data.DataColumnChangeEventArgs)
        ' Change blank to NULL.
        If e.ProposedValue.length = 0 Then e.ProposedValue = DBNull.Value

        ' Allow a NULL value.
        If e.ProposedValue Is DBNull.Value Then Exit Sub

        If Not (e.ProposedValue Like "[2-9]-[0-9]") And _
           Not (e.ProposedValue Like "[2-9]-[2-9]-[0-9]") _
        Then
            MsgBox("Invalid phone number format")
            e.ProposedValue = e.Row.Item(e.Column.Ordinal)
        End If
    End Sub
    Private Sub ValidateExtension(ByVal e As System.Data.DataColumnChangeEventArgs)
        ' Change blank to NULL.
        If e.ProposedValue.length = 0 Then e.ProposedValue = DBNull.Value

        ' Allow a NULL value.
        If e.ProposedValue Is DBNull.Value Then Exit Sub

        If Not (e.ProposedValue Like "[0-9]*") Then
            MsgBox("Invalid extension format")
            e.ProposedValue = e.Row.Item(e.Column.Ordinal)
        End If
    End Sub
```

This program's state validation routine is quite elementary. It only verifies that the State field contains two capital letters. A more robust subroutine would check the value against a list of the allowed state abbreviations.

SUMMARY

Visual Basic provides the tools you need to use to ensure that an application's data is safe—but you need to use those tools. A properly implemented DataSafe function can guarantee that the user's changes are not accidentally discarded.

By using the events provided by data objects such as the DataTable, you can learn when a value is changing and validate the new value. When all is said and done, constraints on the underlying tables in the database can ensure that the values makes sense, but you can make the application friendlier and more responsive if you catch errors sooner rather than later.

## CHAPTER 10

A SINGLE-USER EXAMPLE

Many database applications process records having dozens or even hundreds of fields. An application's main record may have links to dozens of detail records, each holding hundreds of its own fields and an unlimited number of records.

Even the simplest possible order fulfillment system must have a Customers table and an Orders table. Information for a customer could include any number of orders, each containing any number of order items. A more complex application might include other tables listing customer addresses, contacts, areas of operation, and more elaborate order tracking information.

When an application needs to display a large number of fields, it cannot simply place each in its own text box because they won't all fit on the screen. This chapter discusses some of the methods you can use to display these large amounts of information in a limited amount of space.

The following sections describe the OrderEntryBig example program. This is a simple order entry application that performs some of the most basic tasks an order entry application must perform. The sections after that explain ways you can improve this application, making its display less cluttered, easier to use, and more efficient.

A more realistic application would need to include other features such as user logins and passwords, screens that search for specific customer and order records, field validations, extensive error checking, order and payment tracking, and probably many other data fields. Most of the customized applications I have seen have included a host of industry-specific fields not found in this simple example.

A ONE-FORM DESIGN

The OrderEntryBig example program shown in Figure 10.1 is a simple order entry application. To make it easier to focus on database-related code, the program performs almost no error checking.

When you select a customer account from the list on the left, the areas on the right display information about that customer. You can use the combo box at the top of the Addresses group box to select one of the customer's address records. You can type directly into the address text boxes to change the values.

Figure 10.1
Example program
OrderEntryBig is a
very simple order
entry application.

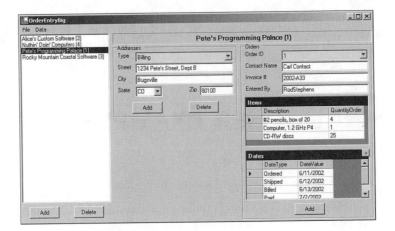

If you click the Add button in the Addresses area, the program displays a dialog that lets you select the type of new address. When you click Ok, the program adds a new address record for the customer. If you click the Addresses area's Delete button, the program removes the current address record from the database.

Similarly, you can use the combo box at the top of the Orders area to select one of the customer's orders. The two grids list the items and dates associated with the order. Click the Add button to add a new order. When you have a new order displayed, a + button appears over the upper-right corner of the item grid. When you click that button, a dialog appears that lets you enter a new item's description and quantity.

This application assumes you never delete an order after it is created. Similarly, the program does not let you add or remove items from an existing order after it has been created. You can add a new date to an order by clicking the + button in the upper-right corner of the date grid.

DATABASE DESIGN

This program's database design is quite simple. The `Customers` table contains basic customer information. In this example, the table only contains the fields `CustomerName` and `CustomerId`.

The `CustomerAddresses` table contains customer address information. It is connected to the `Customers` table by its `CustomerId` field. This table also contains an `AddressId` field used as its primary key. This field is necessary because the program uses a `SqlCommandBuilder` object to generate update and delete commands for this table and `SqlCommandBuilder` can only do its job if it has primary key information for the table.

The `CustomerOrders` table contains basic information about orders, including `ContactName`, `InvoiceNumber`, and `EnteredByUser`. This table's `CustomerId` field links it to the `Customers` table. The table's primary key `OrderId` lets the `SqlCommandBuilder` generate update statements for this table. The application doesn't let you remove order records after they are created, so the `SqlCommandBuilder` doesn't need to generate delete statements for this table.

If the program did not allow you to update the information in the CustomerOrders table, the SqlCommandBuilder would not need the table to include the primary key OrderId, but that field is still necessary to link the CustomerOrders table with the OrderItems and OrderDates tables. Those tables provide details for customer orders. Their OrderId fields link to the CustomerOrders table's OrderId field. The program does not allow you to modify or delete order items or date records after they are created, so these tables do not need primary keys for the SqlCommandBuilder to use.

Figure 10.2 shows the database design graphically.

Figure 10.2
Example program OrderEntryBig uses this simple database design.

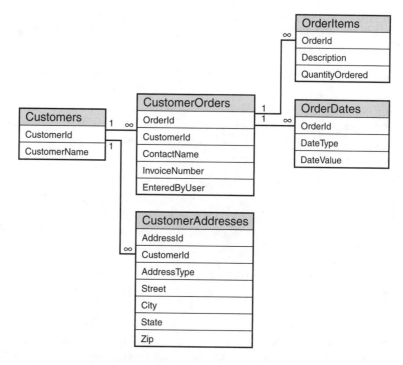

LOADING DATA

Program OrderEntryBig loads all of its database tables into a single DataSet. It keeps references to each DataTable object so it can work with them easily. It uses a separate SqlDataAdapter object to load and save the data in each table.

The program binds its customer list control to the DataTable representing the Customers table. Setting this control's DataSource and DisplayMember properties makes it display the list of customers. When the user picks one, the list automatically selects the corresponding records as the DataTable's current record.

The list control displays entries for all the records in the Customers tables. Most of the program's other controls, however, display only a subset of the data in their tables. For example, the controls in the Addresses area display information from the CustomerAddresses table but only for the currently selected customer.

To make displaying subsets of data easier, the program uses a series of DataViews. Each of the DataViews selects a subset of the records in a DataTable. For example, the m_dvCustomerAddresses DataView selects the CustomerAddresses records for the currently selected customer. The ComboBox in the Addresses area is bound to this DataView so it displays a list of the addresses for the customer. The other controls in the Addresses area are bound to the DataView's currently selected record. When you select an address entry from the ComboBox, the other controls display the information for that address.

Visual Basic uses CurrencyManager objects to coordinate data transfer between a DataTable or DataView and the controls bound to it. A program can use a CurrencyManager to interact with the manager's currently selected record and to add new records to the DataSet. Program OrderEntryBig saves references to each of the CurrencyManagers it will use to manipulate its data.

Listing 10.1 shows the code that program OrderEntryBig uses to load and initialize its data. It begins by declaring the DataSet, DataTable, SqlDataAdapter, DataView, and CurrencyManager objects it will use. The form's Load event handler calls subroutine RestrictControls to place some restrictions on the controls. For instance, RestrictControls sets some TextBox MaxLength properties and initializes the cboState ComboBox's list of state abbreviations.

The event handler then calls subroutine LoadData. The LoadData subroutine repeatedly calls subroutine LoadTable to load data into DataTables in the program's DataSet. Subroutine LoadTable creates a new SqlDataAdapter for the table, attaches a SqlCommandBuilder object to create update and delete commands as needed, and uses the data adapter's Fill method to load the data.

LoadTable optionally also creates a ForeignKeyConstraint object relating the DataTable with a parent table. This object's DeleteRule property determines what Visual Basic does when the program deletes the parent record. If this property has the value Cascade, which it does by default, Visual Basic automatically deletes the related child records. The program uses these constraints to make Visual Basic automatically delete related records. If you delete a record from the Customers DataTable, Visual Basic automatically deletes the related CustomerAddresses and CustomerOrders records. The CustomerOrders records are similarly related to the OrderItems and OrderDates tables, so Visual Basic automatically deletes the corresponding records from those tables, too.

The database uses a similar technique to manage its tables. For example, the following SQL statement shows how the database's CustomerAddresses table is created. The ON DELETE CAS-CADE statement makes the database automatically delete a CustomerAddresses record when the corresponding Customers records is deleted:

```
CREATE TABLE CustomerAddresses (
    AddressId     INT          PRIMARY KEY,
    CustomerId    INT          REFERENCES Customers (CustomerId) ON DELETE CASCADE,
    AddressType   VARCHAR(20)  NOT NULL,
    Street        VARCHAR(40)  NOT NULL,
    City          VARCHAR(40)  NOT NULL,
```

```
    State        CHAR(2)       NOT NULL,
    Zip          VARCHAR(10)   NOT NULL
);
```

In theory the database shouldn't need this statement because the program uses `ForeignKeyConstraints` to ensure that the child records are deleted. In practice, however, making the database cascade deletes is quite useful. In this database, the `OrderItems` and `OrderDates` tables do not have primary keys, so the `SqlCommandBuilder` will not automatically make delete statements for them. While the program's DataTables will automatically delete these records when the corresponding `CustomerOrders` record is deleted, the DataTables cannot update the database without primary keys. Making the database automatically delete these records simplifies things. As you'll see when you read the code that updates the database, however, this doesn't solve every problem.

After subroutine `LoadData` has loaded all the DataTables, the `Load` event handler calls `BindControls` to bind the program's controls to its data objects. Subroutine `BindControls` binds the `lblCustomerName` control to the `m_dtCustomers` DataTable. It creates new DataViews to represent subsets of the `CustomerAddresses`, `CustomerOrders`, `OrderItems`, and `OrderDates` tables. It then binds its controls to the appropriate DataViews.

Subroutine `BindControls` calls subroutine `RemoveGridColumns` to make the program's `DataGrid` controls hide their `OrderId` columns. The subroutine saves references to the data objects' CurrencyManagers and finishes by binding the customer ListBox control to the `m_dtCustomers` DataTable. That makes the list display the customer names and select an initial record.

The `Load` event handler finishes by calling subroutines `DisplayCustomerDetails` and `ArrangeControls`. Subroutine `DisplayCustomerDetails` is described in the next section. Subroutine `ArrangeControls` just arranges the controls and has little to do with database programming so it is not described here. If you want to see the rest of the details, download the example project from this book's Web site (`www.vb-helper.com/vbdb.htm`) and take a look.

LISTING 10.1   PROGRAM ORDERENTRYBIG USES THIS CODE TO LOAD ITS DATA

```
Private Const APP_TITLE = "OrderEntryBig"
Private Const CONNECT_STRING = _
    "data source=Bender\NETSDK;initial catalog=Orders;user id=sa"

' Objects that work with the database.
Private m_DataSet As New DataSet()

' DataTables.
Private m_dtCustomers As DataTable
Private m_dtCustomerOrders As DataTable
Private m_dtCustomerAddresses As DataTable
Private m_dtOrderItems As DataTable
Private m_dtOrderDates As DataTable

' SqlDataAdapters.
```

LISTING 10.1   CONTINUED

```
Private m_daCustomers As SqlDataAdapter
Private m_daCustomerOrders As SqlDataAdapter
Private m_daCustomerAddresses As SqlDataAdapter
Private m_daOrderItems As SqlDataAdapter
Private m_daOrderDates As SqlDataAdapter

' DataViews.
Private m_dvCustomerAddresses As DataView
Private m_dvCustomerOrders As DataView
Private m_dvOrderItems As DataView
Private m_dvOrderDates As DataView

' CurrencyManagers.
Private WithEvents m_cmCustomers As CurrencyManager
Private WithEvents m_cmCustomerOrders As CurrencyManager
Private WithEvents m_cmCustomerAddresses As CurrencyManager
Private WithEvents m_cmOrderItems As CurrencyManager
Private WithEvents m_cmOrderDates As CurrencyManager

Private Sub Form1_Load(ByVal sender As System.Object, _
   ByVal e As System.EventArgs) Handles MyBase.Load
    ' Set restrictions on controls.
    RestrictControls()

    ' Load the data.
    LoadData()

    ' Bind the controls to the data tables.
    BindControls()

    ' Display the details for the initially selected customer.
    DisplayCustomerDetails()

    ' Make the name list as large as possible.
    ArrangeControls()
End Sub

' Set restrictions on the controls.
Private Sub RestrictControls()
    ' Address fields.
    txtStreet.MaxLength = 40
    txtCity.MaxLength = 40
    Dim states() As String = { _
        "AK", "AL", "AR", "AZ", "CA", "CO", "CT", "DC", "DE", "FL", _
        "GA", "HI", "IA", "ID", "IL", "IN", "KS", "KT", "LA", "MA", _
        "MD", "ME", "MI", "MN", "MO", "MS", "MT", "NC", "ND", "NE", _
        "NH", "NJ", "NM", "NV", "NY", "OH", "OK", "OR", "PA", "RI", _
        "SC", "SD", "TN", "TX", "UT", "VA", "VT", "WA", "WI", "WV", _
        "WY" _
    }
    cboState.Items.Clear()
    cboState.Items.AddRange(states)
    txtZip.MaxLength = 10

    ' Order fields.
    txtContactName.MaxLength = 80
```

LISTING 10.1   CONTINUED

```
        txtInvoiceNumber.MaxLength = 10
        txtEnteredBy.MaxLength = 12
End Sub


' Load the data.
Private Sub LoadData()
    ' Load the Customers table.
    LoadTable("Customers", _
        "SELECT CustomerName + ' (' + LTRIM(CustomerId) + ')' " & _
        "AS CombinedName, * FROM Customers ORDER BY CustomerName", _
        "", "", "", _
        m_dtCustomers, m_daCustomers)

    ' Load the CustomerOrders table.
    LoadTable("CustomerOrders", _
        "SELECT * FROM CustomerOrders", _
        "CustomerId", "Customers", "CustomerId", _
        m_dtCustomerOrders, m_daCustomerOrders)

    ' Load the CustomerAddresses table.
    LoadTable("CustomerAddresses", _
        "SELECT * FROM CustomerAddresses ORDER BY AddressType", _
        "CustomerId", "Customers", "CustomerId", _
        m_dtCustomerAddresses, m_daCustomerAddresses)

    ' Load the OrderItems table.
    LoadTable("OrderItems", _
        "SELECT * FROM OrderItems ORDER BY OrderId", _
        "OrderId", "CustomerOrders", "OrderId", _
        m_dtOrderItems, m_daOrderItems)

    ' Load the OrderDates table.
    LoadTable("OrderDates", _
        "SELECT * FROM OrderDates", _
        "OrderId", "CustomerOrders", "OrderId", _
        m_dtOrderDates, m_daOrderDates)
End Sub

' Load a table into the DataSet.
Private Sub LoadTable(ByVal table_name As String, _
  ByVal select_statement As String, ByVal child_column_name As String, _
  ByVal parent_table_name As String, ByVal parent_column_name As String, _
  ByRef data_table As DataTable, ByRef data_adapter As SqlDataAdapter)
    ' Create a data adapter.
    data_adapter = New SqlDataAdapter( _
        select_statement, CONNECT_STRING)

    ' Create INSERT, UPDATE, and DELETE commands.
    Dim command_builder As New SqlCommandBuilder(data_adapter)

    ' Map the default table name "Table" to
    ' the table's real name.
    data_adapter.TableMappings.Add("Table", table_name)

    ' Load the DataSet.
    data_adapter.Fill(m_DataSet)
```

PART

I

CH

10

LISTING 10.1 CONTINUED

```
    ' Save a reference to the new table.
    data_table = m_DataSet.Tables(table_name)

    ' Connect the tables with a foreign key constraint.
    If child_column_name.Length > 0 Then
        Dim parent_table As DataTable = m_DataSet.Tables(parent_table_name)
        Dim foreign_key As New ForeignKeyConstraint( _
            parent_table.Columns(parent_column_name), _
            data_table.Columns(child_column_name))
        data_table.Constraints.Add(foreign_key)
    End If
End Sub

' Bind the controls to the database.
Private Sub BindControls()
    ' ***** Customers *****
    ' Bind data fields.
    lblCustomerName.DataBindings.Add("Text", m_dtCustomers, "CombinedName")

    ' ***** CustomerAddresses *****
    ' Make a DataView for this table.
    m_dvCustomerAddresses = New DataView(m_dtCustomerAddresses)

    ' Bind the cboAddressType record selection
    ' field to the DataView.
    cboAddressType.DataSource = m_dvCustomerAddresses
    cboAddressType.DisplayMember = "AddressType"

    ' Bind data fields.
    txtStreet.DataBindings.Add("Text", m_dvCustomerAddresses, "Street")
    txtCity.DataBindings.Add("Text", m_dvCustomerAddresses, "City")
    cboState.DataBindings.Add("Text", m_dvCustomerAddresses, "State")
    txtZip.DataBindings.Add("Text", m_dvCustomerAddresses, "Zip")

    ' ***** CustomerOrders *****
    ' Make a DataView for this table.
    m_dvCustomerOrders = New DataView(m_dtCustomerOrders)

    ' Bind the cboOrderId record selection
    ' field to the DataView.
    cboOrderId.DataSource = m_dvCustomerOrders
    cboOrderId.DisplayMember = "OrderId"

    ' Bind data fields.
    txtContactName.DataBindings.Add("Text", m_dvCustomerOrders, "ContactName")
    txtInvoiceNumber.DataBindings.Add("Text", m_dvCustomerOrders, "InvoiceNumber")
    txtEnteredBy.DataBindings.Add("Text", m_dvCustomerOrders, "EnteredByUser")

    ' ***** OrderItems *****
    ' Make a DataView for this table.
    m_dvOrderItems = New DataView(m_dtOrderItems)

    ' Bind the dgOrderItems control to the DataView.
    dgOrderItems.DataSource = m_dvOrderItems
    Dim bad_item_columns() As Integer = {0}
    RemoveGridColumns(dgOrderItems, "OrderItems", bad_item_columns)
```

LISTING 10.1   CONTINUED

```
' ***** OrderDates *****
' Make a DataView for this table.
m_dvOrderDates = New DataView(m_dtOrderDates)

' Bind the dgOrderDates control to the DataView.
dgOrderDates.DataSource = m_dvOrderDates
Dim bad_date_columns() As Integer = {0}
RemoveGridColumns(dgOrderDates, "OrderDates", bad_date_columns)

' ***** CurrencyManagers *****
' Save references to important CurrencyManagers.
m_cmCustomers = Me.BindingContext(m_dtCustomers)
m_cmCustomerOrders = Me.BindingContext(m_dvCustomerOrders)
m_cmCustomerAddresses = Me.BindingContext(m_dvCustomerAddresses)
m_cmOrderItems = Me.BindingContext(m_dtOrderItems)
m_cmOrderDates = Me.BindingContext(m_dtOrderDates)

' Bind the ListBox to the DataTable.
lstCustomers.DataSource = m_dtCustomers
lstCustomers.DisplayMember = "CombinedName"
End Sub

' Remove unwanted columns. Note that bad_columns
' should list the column indexes in descending order.
Private Sub RemoveGridColumns(ByVal dg As DataGrid, ByVal table_name As String, _
  ByVal bad_columns() As Integer)
    Dim table_style As New DataGridTableStyle()
    Dim i As Integer

    ' Fill the DataGridTableStyle with information.
    table_style.MappingName = table_name
    dg.TableStyles.Add(table_style)

    ' Remove the unwanted columns.
    For i = 0 To bad_columns.GetUpperBound(0)
        ' Remove this column.
        table_style.GridColumnStyles.RemoveAt(bad_columns(i))
    Next i
End Sub
```

DISPLAYING DATA

When the user selects a customer from the customer list, the list's CurrencyManager raises a CurrentChanged event. The event handler, shown in Listing 10.2, calls subroutine DisplayCustomerDetails.

Subroutine DisplayCustomerDetails gets the selected customer's CustomerId value from the CurrencyManager's currently selected row. It uses that value to compose a row filter statement of the form CustomerId = 10. It sets the RowFilter properties for the m_dvCustomerAddresses and m_dvCustomerOrders DataViews to this expression. That makes the DataViews select records that match the expression. This is roughly equivalent to using a SQL WHERE clause. When the DataViews select new records, the controls bound to them automatically display the new data.

Subroutine `DisplayCustomerDetails` finishes by calling subroutine `DisplayOrderDetails` to display the information for the currently selected order. When the user selects an order from the Order area's ComboBox, the control's event handler also calls `DisplayOrderDetails`.

If the current customer has no orders to display, subroutine `DisplayOrderDetails` sets the DataSource properties of the program's two DataGrid controls to Nothing so the controls display no data. If the customer has orders, the routine makes a row filter much as subroutine `DisplayCustomerDetails` does. It applies the filter to the `m_dvOrderItems` and `m_dvOrderDates` DataViews and ensures that the DataViews are attached to the DataGrid controls. The DataGrids display the data automatically.

LISTING 10.2   PROGRAM ORDERENTRYBIG USES THIS CODE TO DISPLAY DATA WHEN THE USER SELECTS A CUSTOMER OR A CUSTOMER ORDER

```
' Display the data for the selected customer.
Private Sub m_cmCustomers_CurrentChanged(ByVal sender As Object, _
  ByVal e As System.EventArgs) Handles m_cmCustomers.CurrentChanged
    DisplayCustomerDetails()
End Sub

Private Sub DisplayCustomerDetails()
    Dim data_row_view As DataRowView
    Dim customer_id_filter As String

    ' Get the selected record's CustomerId.
    data_row_view = m_cmCustomers.Current()
    customer_id_filter = "CustomerId = " & data_row_view.Item("CustomerId")

    ' CustomerAddresses.
    m_dvCustomerAddresses.RowFilter = customer_id_filter

    ' CustomerOrders.
    m_dvCustomerOrders.RowFilter = customer_id_filter

    ' Display order details for the order.
    DisplayOrderDetails()
End Sub

' Display the data for the selected order.
Private Sub m_cmCustomerOrders_CurrentChanged(ByVal sender As Object, _
  ByVal e As System.EventArgs) Handles m_cmCustomerOrders.CurrentChanged
    DisplayOrderDetails()
End Sub

Private Sub DisplayOrderDetails()
    Dim data_row_view As DataRowView
    Dim order_id_filter As String

    ' See if the CurrencyManager selects any records.
    If m_cmCustomerOrders.Count < 1 Then
        ' There are no order records.
        ' Display no order items or dates.
        dgOrderItems.DataSource = Nothing
```

LISTING 10.2 CONTINUED

```
            dgOrderDates.DataSource = Nothing
            btnOrderItemAdd.Visible = False
            btnOrderDateAdd.Visible = False
        Else
            ' Filter using the selected CustomerOrders
            ' record's CustomerId.
            data_row_view = m_cmCustomerOrders.Current()
            order_id_filter = "OrderId = " & data_row_view.Item("OrderId")

            ' Set the OrderItems filter.
            m_dvOrderItems.RowFilter = order_id_filter

            ' Set the OrderDates filter.
            m_dvOrderDates.RowFilter = order_id_filter

            ' If the DataGrids have no data source,
            ' give them one.
            If dgOrderDates.DataSource Is Nothing Then
                dgOrderItems.DataSource = m_dvOrderItems
                dgOrderDates.DataSource = m_dvOrderDates
            End If

            ' If this order has an original value,
            ' it is not a new order so do not allow
            ' the user to create order items.
            btnOrderItemAdd.Visible = _
                Not data_row_view.Row.HasVersion(DataRowVersion.Original)
            btnOrderDateAdd.Visible = True
        End If
End Sub
```

ADDING RECORDS

When the user clicks one of the program's Add buttons, the program uses the corresponding CurrencyManager to add a new record to the DataSet. For example, the code in Listing 10.3 shows how the program adds a new address record. When you click the Add button, its event handler calls subroutine EndAllEdits. This routine calls the EndCurrentEdit method for each of the program's CurrencyManagers. This makes any changes you have entered in a bound field a permanent part of the DataSet so they are not lost.

The event handler then displays a dialog where you can select the type of the new address the program should create. If you select an address type and click OK, the event handler uses the m_cmCustomerAddresses CurrencyManager's AddNew method to create a new record. It then uses the m_cmCustomers CurrencyManager to get a DataRowView representing the currently selected customer record. It sets the new address record's CustomerId value to the CustomerId value provided by the DataRowView object. It fills in the address type you selected. The program uses the MaxAddressId function to find the largest AddressId value currently in the CustomerAddresses DataTable and adds one to give the new record a unique AddressId. The event handler calls the m_cmCustomerAddresses CurrencyManager's EndCurrentEdit method to save the new record. It finishes by calling the MarkModified subroutine to add an asterisk to the program's title bar.

The MaxAddressId function returns the largest AddressId value in the m_dtCustomerAddresses DataTable. It begins by creating a new DataView object for that DataTable. If the DataView selects no records, the function returns 0. If the DataView does select records, the function sets its Sort property to the string AddressId DESC. This makes the DataView sort its records by AddressId in descending order so the first record contains the largest AddressId. The function returns the AddressId value of that first record.

Subroutine MarkModified uses the DataSet's HasChanges method to see if the data has been modified. If it has, it adds an asterisk to the form's caption so you can see that the data has been changed. Each of the program's CurrencyManagers' ItemChanged event handlers also call MarkModified when you change the value of one of the CurrencyManagers' bound controls.

LISTING 10.3 PROGRAM ORDERENTRYBIG USES THIS CODE TO ADD NEW ADDRESS RECORDS

```
' Add a new address for this customer.
Private Sub btnAddressAdd_Click(ByVal sender As System.Object, _
  ByVal e As System.EventArgs) Handles btnAddressAdd.Click
    ' End any current edits.
    EndAllEdits()

    ' Let the user pick the adress type.
    Dim dlg As New frmNewAddress()
    If dlg.ShowDialog(Me) = DialogResult.OK Then
        ' Create the new record.
        m_cmCustomerAddresses.AddNew()
        Dim cur_address As DataRowView = _
            m_cmCustomerAddresses.Current()
        Dim cur_customer As DataRowView = _
            m_cmCustomers.Current()
        cur_address.Item("CustomerId") = cur_customer.Item("CustomerId")
        cur_address.Item("AddressType") = dlg.cboAddressType.Text
        cur_address.Item("AddressId") = MaxAddressId() + 1
        m_cmCustomerAddresses.EndCurrentEdit()

        ' Mark the data as modified.
        MarkModified()
    End If
End Sub

' Finish any current edits.
Private Sub EndAllEdits()
    m_cmCustomers.EndCurrentEdit()
    m_cmCustomerAddresses.EndCurrentEdit()
    m_cmCustomerOrders.EndCurrentEdit()
    m_cmOrderItems.EndCurrentEdit()
    m_cmOrderDates.EndCurrentEdit()
End Sub

' Return the largest address ID.
Private Function MaxAddressId() As Integer
    Dim data_view As New DataView(m_dtCustomerAddresses)
```

LISTING 10.3   CONTINUED

```
    ' See if there are any records.
    If data_view.Count < 1 Then
        ' There are no records. Return 0.
        Return 0
    Else
        ' There are records. Sort them.
        data_view.Sort = "AddressId DESC"

        ' Get the row with the largest value.
        Dim data_row_view As DataRowView = data_view.Item(0)

        ' Return that value.
        Return data_row_view.Item("AddressId")
    End If
End Function

Private Sub MarkModified()
    If m_DataSet.HasChanges() Then Me.Text = APP_TITLE & " *"
End Sub

Private Sub m_cmCustomerAddresses_ItemChanged(ByVal sender As Object, _
    ByVal e As System.Windows.Forms.ItemChangedEventArgs) _
    Handles m_cmCustomerAddresses.ItemChanged
    MarkModified()
End Sub
```

Program OrderEntryBig uses similar code to add new records to the Customers, CustomerOrders, OrderItems, and OrderDates DataTables. Download the sample code from this book's Web site to see the details.

DELETING RECORDS

Deleting records is easier than adding them. The program uses the appropriate CurrencyManager's Count method to see if the manager has any records to delete. If there are records of the right kind, the program uses the CurrencyManager to get a DataRowView representing the current record. It then calls the DataRowView's Delete method to remove the row from the underlying DataTable.

The following code shows how the program deletes address records:

```
' Delete the current address record.
Private Sub btnAddressDelete_Click(ByVal sender As System.Object, _
    ByVal e As System.EventArgs) Handles btnAddressDelete.Click
    ' Do nothing if there are no records to delete.
    If m_cmCustomerAddresses.Count < 1 Then Exit Sub

    Dim data_row_view As DataRowView
    data_row_view = m_cmCustomerAddresses.Current
    data_row_view.Delete()
End Sub
```

The program deletes records from the Customers and Orders tables in exactly the same manner. Download the example code from this book's Web site and look at it to see the details.

The program does not allow you to delete OrderItems and OrderDates records after they are created.

CANCELING CHANGES

Canceling the changes to the data is easy. When you select the Data menu's Cancel Changes command, the program executes the following code. It uses the DataSet's HasChanges method to see if any changes need to be saved. If there are unsaved changes, the routine asks you to confirm that you really do want to discard them. After they are discarded, the changes are gone forever so the program makes sure you really want to continue.

If you are sure you want to discard the changes, the program calls the DataSet's RejectChanges method. That removes all the changes and restores all the DataTables to the state they were in when they were first loaded.

The event handler finishes by resetting the program's title bar caption so it doesn't contain an asterisk, indicating that there are no unsaved changes:

```
' Cancel the changes.
Private Sub mnuDataCancelChanges_Click(ByVal sender As System.Object, _
   ByVal e As System.EventArgs) Handles mnuDataCancelChanges.Click
      ' Finish the current edit.
    EndAllEdits()

    ' See if there are any changes to cancel.
    If m_DataSet.HasChanges() Then
        ' Make the user confirm.
        If MsgBox("Discard changes?", _
            MsgBoxStyle.YesNo Or MsgBoxStyle.Question, _
            "Discard changes?") = MsgBoxResult.No Then Exit Sub

        ' Cancel the changes.
        m_DataSet.RejectChanges()
    End If

    ' Update the form's caption to show
    ' the data is unmodified.
    Me.Text = APP_TITLE
End Sub
```

SAVING CHANGES

Saving changes is trickier than discarding them. The main complication arises from the fact that the database tables have parent-child relations. When two tables have this kind of relationship, you must create parent records before you can create corresponding child records. On the other hand, you must delete child records before you can delete the corresponding parent record.

For instance, the Customers and CustomerAddresses tables have a parent-child relationship. The CustomerAddresses table's CustomerId field refers to the Customers table's CustomerId field. Before you can make a new CustomerAdddresses record, you need to have already created a Customers record with the proper CustomerId so the new CustomerAdddresses record can refer to it.

For the same reason, you must delete all CustomerAddresses records before you can delete the corresponding Customers record. If you try to delete the Customers record first, the CustomerAddresses records would refer to a CustomerId value that doesn't exist in the Customers table.

All this means the program cannot update all its DataTables in any one order. It must insert parent records before child records but it must delete child records before parent records.

Subroutine SaveData, shown in Listing 10.4, solves this problem. It begins by calling EndAllEdits to ensure that any changes the user is working on are saved. Then it checks the DataSet's HasChanges method and exits if there are no changes to save.

Next SaveData uses subroutine SaveTableChange to insert new records into each of the database's tables. It inserts Customers records first so child records can refer to its CustomerId values. Similarly, it inserts CustomerOrders records before it inserts records into the child tables OrderItems and OrderDates.

After it has inserted all the new records, SaveData uses subroutine SaveTableChange to process any pending records updates. Normally updating records can be tricky, too. For example, suppose the program changes a CustomerId value. If it updates the Customers record first, any related CustsomerAddresses records will refer to a CustomerId value that no longer exists. Conversely, if the program tries to update the CustomerAddresses records first, they will refer to a CustomerId value that does not yet exist. There is no order in which the program can safely change the field linking the two tables.

The solution is to make the database itself propagate changes to the child records. For instance, if the CustomerAddresses table were defined using the following SQL code, then the program would only need to update the Customers record and the database would automatically update the corresponding CustomerId values in the CustomerAddresses table:

```
CREATE TABLE CustomerAddresses (
    AddressId       INT             PRIMARY KEY,
    CustomerId      INT             REFERENCES Customers (CustomerId)
                                    ON DELETE CASCADE
                                    ON UPDATE CASCADE,
    AddressType     VARCHAR(20)     NOT NULL,
    Street          VARCHAR(40)     NOT NULL,
    City            VARCHAR(40)     NOT NULL,
    State           CHAR(2)         NOT NULL,
    Zip             VARCHAR(10)     NOT NULL
);
```

Even this solution doesn't solve all the program's problems, however. The UPDATE statements generated by the SqlCommandBuilder use a WHERE clause to verify every field in the record. For example, the command builder generates the following statement to update the CustomerAddresses table:

```
UPDATE CustomerAddresses
SET AddressId = @p1 , CustomerId = @p2 , AddressType = @p3 , Street = @p4 ,
    City = @p5 , State = @p6 , Zip = @p7
WHERE ( (AddressId = @p8) AND
  ((CustomerId IS NULL AND @p9 IS NULL) OR (CustomerId = @p10)) AND
```

```
((AddressType IS NULL AND @p11 IS NULL) OR (AddressType = @p12)) AND
((Street IS NULL AND @p13 IS NULL) OR (Street = @p14)) AND
((City IS NULL AND @p15 IS NULL) OR (City = @p16)) AND
((State IS NULL AND @p17 IS NULL) OR (State = @p18)) AND
((Zip IS NULL AND @p19 IS NULL) OR (Zip = @p20)) )
```

When it executes this statement, the data adapter plugs in the record's current values for the parameters in the WHERE clause to verify that none of the values have changed since the record was loaded. Unfortunately at this point the database has cascaded the change to the CustomerId field so the WHERE clause does not match the record and the record is not updated. If you made other changes to the record besides changing its CustomerId value, those changes are not moved into the database.

One solution is to compose your own UPDATE statement. The OrderEntryBig program uses the simpler strategy of never changing the CustomerId field values. Fields such as these that are used as primary keys or to link parent and child tables usually have little meaning to the user. They are just arbitrary numbers and there is little need for the user to modify or even look at them.

After it has finished inserting new records and updating existing records (without modifying CustomerId values), the SaveData subroutine calls SaveTableChange to delete records. Because the OrderItems and OrderDates tables are defined in the database with the ON DELETE CASCADE clause, the program does not need to delete records from those tables explicitly. In fact, as the "Loading Data" section earlier in this chapter explains, it cannot successfully delete those records. Because these tables do not have primary keys, the SqlCommandBuilder object cannot automatically create update or delete commands for them so the program cannot easily delete these records.

The program uses SaveTableChange to apply the deletions to the database's other tables, however. It deletes the child records from the CustomerAddresses and CustomerOrders tables first. If it deleted the Customers records first, the database's ON DELETE CASCADE statements would make the database automatically remove any related CustomerAddresses and CustomerOrders records. Then when the program tried to delete those records, it would receive an error because the records wouldn't exist.

After it has deleted the records that it should, subroutine SaveData calls the DataSet's AcceptChanges method to make the changes to the DataSet permanent. This removes any deleted DataRows from the data structures, and marks new and updated DataRows as containing original unmodified values. SaveData finishes by resetting the program's caption so it does not contain an asterisk.

Subroutine SaveTableChange is relatively simple. It uses a DataTable's GetChanges method to create a new DataTable containing only the DataRows in the original table that have the specified change. For example, it might contain all the newly added Customers table rows. The subroutine then uses the table's data adapter to update the database with the changes.

LISTING 10.4   SUBROUTINE SaveData COPIES CHANGES FROM THE PROGRAM'S DATATABLES BACK TO THE DATABASE

```
' Save changes to the database.
Private Sub SaveData()
    ' End any current edits.
    EndAllEdits()

    ' See if there are any changes to save.
    If Not m_DataSet.HasChanges() Then Exit Sub

    ' INSERT.
    SaveTableChange(m_dtCustomers, m_daCustomers, DataRowState.Added)
    SaveTableChange(m_dtCustomerAddresses, m_daCustomerAddresses, _
        DataRowState.Added)
    SaveTableChange(m_dtCustomerOrders, m_daCustomerOrders, DataRowState.Added)
    SaveTableChange(m_dtOrderItems, m_daOrderItems, DataRowState.Added)
    SaveTableChange(m_dtOrderDates, m_daOrderDates, DataRowState.Added)

    ' UPDATE.
    SaveTableChange(m_dtCustomers, m_daCustomers, DataRowState.Modified)
    SaveTableChange(m_dtCustomerAddresses, m_daCustomerAddresses, _
        DataRowState.Modified)
    SaveTableChange(m_dtCustomerOrders, m_daCustomerOrders, DataRowState.Modified)
    SaveTableChange(m_dtOrderItems, m_daOrderItems, DataRowState.Modified)
    SaveTableChange(m_dtOrderDates, m_daOrderDates, DataRowState.Modified)

    ' DELETE.
    ' Note that OrderItems and OrderDates are only
    ' deleted when the Customers record is deleted.
    ' Then a CASCADE statement deletes them so we
    ' don't need to delete them ourselves.
    '    SaveTableChange(g_dtOrderDates, g_daOrderDates, DataRowState.Deleted)
    '    SaveTableChange(g_dtOrderItems, g_daOrderItems, DataRowState.Deleted)
    SaveTableChange(g_dtCustomerOrders, g_daCustomerOrders, DataRowState.Deleted)
    SaveTableChange(g_dtCustomerAddresses, g_daCustomerAddresses, _
        DataRowState.Deleted)
    SaveTableChange(g_dtCustomers, g_daCustomers, DataRowState.Deleted)

    ' Mark the records as unmodified.
    m_DataSet.AcceptChanges()

    ' Update the form's caption to show the data is unmodified.
    Me.Text = APP_TITLE
End Sub

' Save one kind of change to the table.
Private Sub SaveTableChange(ByVal data_table As DataTable, _
  ByVal data_adapter As SqlDataAdapter, ByVal data_row_state As DataRowState)
    Dim changes As DataTable

    changes = data_table.GetChanges(data_row_state)
    If Not (changes Is Nothing) Then
        Try
            data_adapter.Update(changes)
        Catch exc As Exception
            MsgBox(exc.Message)
```

PART

I

CH

10

LISTING 10.4   CONTINUED

```
        End Try
    End If
End Sub
```

A TABBED DESIGN

The form layout shown in Figure 10.1 works but it is very cluttered. It takes up a lot of screen space, filling most of an 800×600 pixel screen. It displays unrelated items on the same screen. For example, the list box on the left displays a list of customers while the rest of the form displays information about a particular customer. Because these displays are only vaguely related, it is unlikely that they really need to be visible at the same time on the same form.

It would be more useful to display more than one customer's data at the same time. You then could compare similar items for the two customers.

The form displays the selected customer's address and order information at the same time. Although it doesn't hurt to display these items simultaneously, it is unlikely that you will need to see an address and an order at the same time. In that case, you can make the form less cluttered by rearranging it to display one or the other but not both at any given moment.

Figure 10.3 shows the redesigned OrderEntryTabs application. This version displays its customer list in a separate window. When you double-click an entry in the list, the program displays a customer detail window. You can then hide the customer list so it doesn't waste screen real estate.

Figure 10.3
Example program OrderEntryTabs lets you display multiple customer records simultaneously.

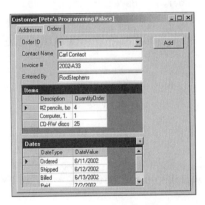

This version lets you display multiple customer records at the same time so you can compare them. Finally, it uses tabs to keep different kinds of customer data separate. Click on the Addresses tab to see the customer's address information. Click on the Orders tab to see order information. While you are looking at one kind of data, the tabs keep unrelated fields from cluttering up the customer display.

A more complex application might have many more tabs than the two used by program OrderEntryTabs. A fuel tax application I once worked on had eight tabs for general information, tax exemptions, fuels used, states where the carrier stored fuel in bulk, operating states, licenses, tax returns, and account information. Many applications could have even more tabs for different kinds of data. With enough tabs, you can display a huge amount of data in a relatively small amount of screen space.

GLOBAL CONTROL

Although example programs OrderEntryBig and OrderEntryTabs look very different, they have many similarities. They use the same database and much of their code is similar. The biggest programming difference is in where the data objects are stored and where the code lies. In program OrderEntryBig, the program's main form contains all the data and practically all the code. Program OrderEntryTabs divides up the data and code a bit more.

Module `DataStuff.vb` contains objects and code that affect the application on a global scale. It declares the main data objects, including the `DataSet`, `DataTable`, and `SqlDataAdapter` objects that the program uses to store and manipulate the data. These objects are similar to those used by program OrderEntryBig. The module also contains the `LoadData` and `SaveData` subroutines that load and save the data to the database, as well as the helper routines that they use.

Module `DataStuff.vb` handles changes to the data in a more centralized way than program OrderEntryBig does. Program OrderEntryBig uses CurrencyManagers to detect changes to the data. Program OrderEntryTabs detects changes using its DataTable's `ColumnChanged` events.

Listing 10.5 shows how the program reacts when the user modifies a value in the `Customers` DataTable. The `ColumnChanged` event handler calls subroutine `CheckModified`. That routine calls subroutine `EndAllEdits` to ensure that any changes the user is currently making are recognized by the program's DataSet object. It then compares the values returned by the DataSet's `HasChanges` method with the Boolean variable `m_DataModified`. If the two values are different, the user has either just modified the data for the first time or the changes have just been saved or canceled. In that case, the subroutine updates the form's caption to show an asterisk if the data has been changed or to show no asterisk if the data is now unmodified.

LISTING 10.5   PROGRAM ORDERENTRYTABS DETECTS CHANGES WITH COLUMNCHANGED EVENTS

```
' True when the data is modified.
Public m_DataModified As Boolean

' Objects that work with the database.
Public g_DataSet As New DataSet()

' DataTables.
Public WithEvents g_dtCustomers As DataTable
```

LISTING 10.5   CONTINUED

```
Public WithEvents g_dtCustomerOrders As DataTable
Public WithEvents g_dtCustomerAddresses As DataTable
Public WithEvents g_dtOrderItems As DataTable
Public WithEvents g_dtOrderDates As DataTable

' SqlDataAdapters.
Public g_daCustomers As SqlDataAdapter
Public g_daCustomerOrders As SqlDataAdapter
Public g_daCustomerAddresses As SqlDataAdapter
Public g_daOrderItems As SqlDataAdapter
Public g_daOrderDates As SqlDataAdapter

' CurrencyManagers.
Public WithEvents g_cmCustomers As CurrencyManager

Public Sub g_dtCustomers_ColumnChanged(ByVal sender As Object, _
  ByVal e As System.Data.DataColumnChangeEventArgs) _
  Handles g_dtCustomers.ColumnChanged
    CheckModified()
End Sub

' Flag the data as modified.
Public Sub CheckModified()
    ' Do not recurse.
    Static running As Boolean
    If running Then Exit Sub
    running = True

    ' Make any pending changes register
    ' with the DataSet.
    EndAllEdits()

    ' See if the current indication is incorrect.
    If g_DataSet.HasChanges <> m_DataModified Then
        ' Update the indication.
        m_DataModified = g_DataSet.HasChanges
        If m_DataModified Then
            g_MdiMain.Text = APP_TITLE & " *"
        Else
            g_MdiMain.Text = APP_TITLE
        End If
        Beep()
    End If

    running = False
End Sub
```

THE CUSTOMER LIST FORM

Program OrderEntryTabs loads and saves its data globally but each form displays and edits data locally. The customer list form displays a list of customers. When the user double-clicks on a customer's entry, the form displays the customer's detail form. When the user clicks the Add or Delete buttons, the customer list form adds or deletes a customer. The form does not load or save data—that's the job of the `DataStuff.vb` module. It also doesn't display customer data—that's the customer detail form's job.

The customer list form uses the code shown in Listing 10.6 to manage customer records. When it loads, the form's `Load` event handler binds its ListBox control to the `g_dtCustomers` DataTable so the control automatically displays the list of customers. It saves a reference to the CurrencyManager that coordinates data transfer between the DataTable and the ListBox.

When the user double-clicks on an entry, the `DoubleClick` event handler calls subroutine `DisplayCustomerForm`. That routine uses the CurrencyManager to find the customer record that the ListBox is currently displaying. It calls the `FindCustomerForm` function to get a reference to the form that is currently displaying the selected customer's information, if such a form exists. If no form is already displaying the customer's data, subroutine `DisplayCustomerForm` creates a new one, sets its `CustomerDataRow` property so it knows which customer to display, and shows it. If a form is already displaying the customer's data, `DisplayCustomerForm` sets focus to it so it moves above any other MDI child forms including the customer list form.

The `FindCustomerForm` function loops through the `MdiChildren` collection of the program's MDI form. It compares each customer form's CustomerId value to a target value. If the values match, the function returns a reference to that form.

When the user clicks the Add button, its Click event handler calls `EndAllEdits` to ensure that any current edits are saved. It then presents a dialog asking the user to enter the new customer's name. If the user enters a value and clicks OK, the program uses the `m_cmCustomers` CurrencyManager to create a new customer record. It calls `CheckModified` to add an asterisk to the form's caption if necessary. It then calls `DisplayCustomerForm` to display the new record. Because it added the record using the CurrencyManager, the new record is already the CurrencyManager's current record; thus, `DisplayCustomerForm` displays it automatically.

When the user clicks the Delete button, its `Click` event handler uses the CurrencyManager to locate the current customer record. It calls the `FindCustomerForm` function to see if a customer detail form is displaying the customer's information. If it finds such a form, the program closes it. It then uses the DataRowView's `Delete` method to remove the record.

LISTING 10.6 THE CUSTOMER LIST FORM USES THIS CODE TO MANAGE CUSTOMERS

```
' Bind the ListBox to the Customers DataTable.
Private Sub frmCustomerList_Load(ByVal sender As Object, _
    ByVal e As System.EventArgs) Handles MyBase.Load
    lstCustomers.DataSource = g_dtCustomers
    lstCustomers.DisplayMember = "CombinedName"

    ' Save a reference to the Customers CurrencyManager.
    g_cmCustomers = Me.BindingContext(g_dtCustomers)
End Sub
```

LISTING 10.6   CONTINUED

```
' Display the selected customer.
Private Sub lstCustomers_DoubleClick(ByVal sender As Object, _
  ByVal e As System.EventArgs) Handles lstCustomers.DoubleClick
    DisplayCustomerForm()
End Sub

' Display the selected customer.
Private Sub DisplayCustomerForm()
    ' Get the customer's ID.
    Dim data_row_view As DataRowView = g_cmCustomers.Current

    ' See if this customer is already displayed.
    Dim frm As frmCustomer = FindCustomerForm(data_row_view.Item("CustomerId"))
    If frm Is Nothing Then
        ' Create and display a new customer form.
        frm = New frmCustomer()
        frm.CustomerDataRow = data_row_view.Row
        frm.MdiParent = Me.MdiParent
        frm.Show()
    Else
        ' Set focus to the existing form.
        If frm.WindowState = FormWindowState.Minimized _
            Then frm.WindowState = FormWindowState.Normal
        frm.Focus()
    End If
End Sub

' Find the customer's display form if it is loaded.
Function FindCustomerForm(ByVal customer_id As Integer) As frmCustomer
    Dim frm As frmCustomer
    Dim child As Form

    For Each child In Me.MdiParent.MdiChildren
        ' Only check frmCustomer forms.
        If child.GetType Is GetType(frmCustomer) Then
            ' See if this form is already displaying
            ' the customer.
            frm = child
            If frm.CustomerId = customer_id Then
                ' This is the form.
                Return frm
            End If
        End If
    Next child

    ' We did not find the form.
    Return Nothing
End Function

' Add a new customer.
Private Sub btnCustomerAdd_Click(ByVal sender As System.Object, _
  ByVal e As System.EventArgs) Handles btnCustomerAdd.Click
    ' End any current edits.
    EndAllEdits()
```

LISTING 10.6   CONTINUED

```vb
        ' Ask the user for the new customer name.
        Dim dlg As New frmNewCustomer()
        If dlg.ShowDialog(Me) = DialogResult.OK Then
            ' Get the customer name and ID.
            Dim customer_name As String = dlg.txtCompanyName.Text
            Dim customer_id As Integer = MaxCustomerId() + 1

            ' Create a new record.
            Dim data_row As DataRow = g_dtCustomers.NewRow()
            data_row.Item("CustomerId") = customer_id
            data_row.Item("CustomerName") = customer_name
            data_row.Item("CombinedName") = customer_name & " (" & customer_id & ")"
            g_dtCustomers.Rows.Add(data_row)

            ' Select the new record.
            g_cmCustomers.Position = g_cmCustomers.Count - 1

            ' Mark the data as modified.
            CheckModified()

            ' Display the new customer.
            DisplayCustomerForm()
        End If
End Sub

' Delete the current customer.
Private Sub btnCustomerDelete_Click(ByVal sender As System.Object, _
  ByVal e As System.EventArgs) Handles btnCustomerDelete.Click
    ' Do nothing if there are no records to delete.
    If g_cmCustomers.Count < 1 Then Exit Sub

    ' Get the DataRowView.
    Dim data_row_view As DataRowView
    data_row_view = g_cmCustomers.Current()

    ' See if this this customer is currently displayed.
    Dim frm As frmCustomer = FindCustomerForm(data_row_view.Item("CustomerId"))
    If Not (frm Is Nothing) Then
        ' Close this form.
        frm.Close()
    End If

    ' Delete the record.
    data_row_view.Delete()

    ' Mark the data as modified.
    CheckModified()
End Sub
```

THE CUSTOMER DETAIL FORM

The customer detail form displays information about a particular customer. In some ways, this form is similar to the main form used by program OrderEntryBig. It contains DataViews and CurrencyManagers for working with the program's DataTables. The main difference is that the form in program OrderEntryBig could display any customer's information while the customer detail form in this program displays the information for a single customer.

Listing 10.7 shows the code that this form uses to display and manipulate its customer's data. The CustomerDataRow property procedures get and set a DataRow object representing the customer that this form represents. When the customer list form sets this property, the Property Set procedure saves a reference to the DataRow object and then calls subroutine LoadData. Subroutine LoadData creates DataViews to display the appropriate data from the Customers, CustomerAddresses, CustomerOrders, OrderItems, and OrderDates tables. It also binds the form's controls to the DataViews and saves references to the CurrencyManagers that manage the bindings. This code is very similar to the BindControls subroutine used by program OrderEntryBig.

The read-only CustomerId property procedure returns the customer's CustomerId value. The customer list form's FindCustomerForm function uses this property to decide whether a form has a particular CustomerId value.

Most of the rest of this form's code is similar to the code used by program OrderEntryBig. For example, when the user selects a new order ID from the ComboBox on the Orders tab, the corresponding CurrencyManager fires its CurrentChanged event. The event handler calls subroutine DisplayOrderDetails to display the order's information.

The form also adds and deletes addresses and records almost exactly as program OrderEntryBig does. The code is so similar that it is not shown here. See the sections about program OrderEntryBig earlier in this chapter for explanation or download the program OrderEntryTabs source code from the book's Web site to see the details.

LISTING 10.7 THE CUSTOMER DETAIL FORM DISPLAYS INFORMATION ABOUT A SINGLE CUSTOMER

```
' DataViews.
Private m_dvCustomerAddresses As DataView
Private m_dvCustomerOrders As DataView
Private m_dvOrderItems As DataView
Private m_dvOrderDates As DataView


' CurrencyManagers.
Private WithEvents m_cmCustomerAddresses As CurrencyManager
Private WithEvents m_cmCustomerOrders As CurrencyManager
Private WithEvents m_cmOrderItems As CurrencyManager
Private WithEvents m_cmOrderDates As CurrencyManager


' This customer's DataRow object.
Private m_DataRow As DataRow
Public Property CustomerDataRow() As DataRow
    Get
        Return m_DataRow
    End Get
    Set(ByVal Value As DataRow)
        m_DataRow = Value
```

LISTING 10.7   CONTINUED

```
        LoadData()
    End Set
End Property

' Load the data for this customer.
Private Sub LoadData()
    Me.Text = "Customer [" & m_DataRow.Item("CustomerName") & "]"

    ' Bind controls to the appropriate objects.
    Dim customer_id As Integer = m_DataRow.Item("CustomerId")

    ' CustomerAddresses.
    m_dvCustomerAddresses = New DataView(g_dtCustomerAddresses)
    m_dvCustomerAddresses.RowFilter = "CustomerId = " & customer_id
    cboAddressType.DataSource = m_dvCustomerAddresses
    cboAddressType.DisplayMember = "AddressType"
    txtStreet.DataBindings.Add("Text", m_dvCustomerAddresses, "Street")
    txtCity.DataBindings.Add("Text", m_dvCustomerAddresses, "City")
    cboState.DataBindings.Add("Text", m_dvCustomerAddresses, "State")
    txtZip.DataBindings.Add("Text", m_dvCustomerAddresses, "Zip")
    m_cmCustomerAddresses = Me.BindingContext(m_dvCustomerAddresses)

    ' CustomerOrders.
    m_dvCustomerOrders = New DataView(g_dtCustomerOrders)
    m_dvCustomerOrders.RowFilter = "CustomerId = " & customer_id
    cboOrderId.DataSource = m_dvCustomerOrders
    cboOrderId.DisplayMember = "OrderId"
    txtContactName.DataBindings.Add("Text", m_dvCustomerOrders, "ContactName")
    txtInvoiceNumber.DataBindings.Add("Text", m_dvCustomerOrders, "InvoiceNumber")
    txtEnteredBy.DataBindings.Add("Text", m_dvCustomerOrders, "EnteredByUser")
    m_cmCustomerOrders = Me.BindingContext(m_dvCustomerOrders)

    ' OrderItems.
    m_dvOrderItems = New DataView(g_dtOrderItems)
    dgOrderItems.DataSource = m_dvOrderItems
    Dim bad_item_columns() As Integer = {0}
    RemoveGridColumns(dgOrderItems, "OrderItems", bad_item_columns)
    m_cmOrderItems = Me.BindingContext(m_dvOrderItems)

    ' OrderDates.
    m_dvOrderDates = New DataView(g_dtOrderDates)
    dgOrderDates.DataSource = m_dvOrderDates
    Dim bad_date_columns() As Integer = {0}
    RemoveGridColumns(dgOrderDates, "OrderDates", bad_date_columns)
    m_cmOrderDates = Me.BindingContext(m_dvOrderDates)

    ' Display the initially selected order's data.
    DisplayOrderDetails()
End Sub

' The form's CustomerId.
Public ReadOnly Property CustomerId() As String
    Get
        CustomerId = m_DataRow.Item("CustomerId")
    End Get
End Property
```

SUMMARY

Example program OrderEntryTabs is a fairly powerful application. It lets the user view and modify data in tables connected by relatively complex parent-child relationships. It shows how a program can display, add, and delete records in both parent and child tables.

Still this program has two serious limitations. First, it can only work reasonably with databases of moderate size. With a few dozen records, this program has no trouble. The user can locate a specific customer's data from the customer list with few problems. If the database contained thousands of records, however, the user might have trouble finding the right customer data. Chapter 12, "Query By Example," shows one solution to this problem. It uses a query-by-example form to let the user search for specific records rather than displaying all the records in a huge list as program OrderEntryTabs does.

Even with this improvement, program OrderEntryTabs could have trouble with large databases. This program loads all the database's data at once when it starts. If the database contains thousands or even millions of records, that may be impractical.

The program's second important limitation is that it is inherently a single-user application. Suppose two users run the program at the same time and they both edit the same customer's data. The first user saves his changes to the database. Now when the second user tries to save his changes, the database update fails. The update command generated by the SqlCommandBuilder object includes a WHERE clause that verifies that the data has not changed since it was originally fetched. Because the first user modified the data, the WHERE clause will eliminate the modified data so the update statement will not save the second user's changes. The SqlDataAdapter object raises an error because it knows that it has changes that it was unable to save. The program can catch this error, but there isn't a lot it can do about it. It would be a huge amount of work to figure out how to merge the first user's changes with the second user's, particularly if the changes conflict. In the end, the second user's changes are lost. The alternative, with the first user's changes overwritten, is just as bad.

Chapter 11, "Multi-User Programming," shows how an application can address these issues.

MULTI-USER PROGRAMMING

The OrderEntryTabs program described in the previous chapter does a fair job of implementing a single-user order entry system. For all but the smallest businesses, however, this example is quite cumbersome. It makes the user select a customer from a single list box. That works if the database contains only a few dozen customers, but it can be difficult if the database contains hundreds or thousands of customers. It also makes the program load and store information about all the customers, although the user will only work with a few of them.

Chapter 12, "Query By Example," shows one way to deal with the problem of selecting a record from a large database. It shows techniques that let the user quickly select a specific record even if the database contains thousands of customer records.

Program OrderEntryTabs has much more serious problems if it is used by multiple, simultaneous users. If more than one user edits the same customer's information at the same time, one of the user's changes are lost. This problem only occurs when users edit the same record at the same time but many systems naturally increase the chances of that happening. For instance, billing clerks often look at the customers with the largest outstanding balances or that are latest with payments. Order fulfillment users look at the orders that have been unfulfilled the longest. In cases such as these, where all the users use the same method for selecting the next record to process, collisions are likely.

This chapter extends the OrderEntryTabs example to show one solution for dealing with the multi-user problem. It shows how the application can allow more than one user to work with the data without allowing two users to make changes to the same customer records at the same time.

PROGRAM ORDERENTRYMULTIUSER

Sample program OrderEntryMultiUser, shown in Figure 11.1, allows multiple users to edit records without overwriting each other's changes. Double-click an entry in the customer list form to see the customer's detail. Click the Edit button to begin editing the customer's information. At that point, the customer is reserved for your use. If another user tries to edit the same customer record, the program displays a message saying another user has already reserved it.

Figure 11.1
Program
OrderEntryMultiUser
allows multiple users
to edit records at the
same time safely.

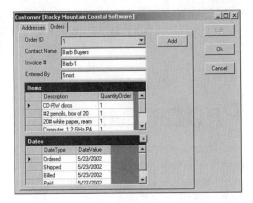

Because more than one user may change the data, the customer list form provides a Refresh button. When you click this button, the program goes back to the database and rebuilds its customer list from scratch so it can take into account any additions or deletions that other users may have made.

DATABASE REDESIGN

Program OrderEntryMultiUser keeps data for each of its customers as independent as possible. Each customer detail form has its own `DataSet`, `DataTable`, `DataView`, and `CurrencyManager` objects to control its own data. That allows each instance of the program to easily separate itself from other instances of the program. It also keeps the customer detail forms separate from each other within a single instance of the program and that simplifies the program's data processing code. When the user clicks the Edit button on a customer detail form, the form's code tries to reserve the customer's data. It does not need to worry about what the program's other forms are doing.

This independence makes the code simpler overall but it does necessitate two small changes to the database design. Figure 11.2 shows the design used by program OrderEntryTabs. The `CustomerOrders` records are linked to `OrderItems` and `OrderDates` records by the tables' `OrderId` fields. This works well in a single-user environment, but causes problems when more than one user may be editing records at the same time.

Suppose User 1 edits a customer and creates a new `CustomerOrders` record. The program examines the `CustomerOrders` records already in the database and discovers that the largest `OrderId` value is 1000 so it gives the new record the `OrderId` value 1001.

While User 1 is still editing that customer, User 2 starts editing a different customer and creates a new `CustomerOrders` record. The program again examines the `CustomerOrders` table. Because User 1 has not committed any changes to the database, the new order for the first customer is not yet present in the `CustomerOrders` table. The program finds that the largest `OrderId` value is still 1000 so it gives the new record for the second customer the `OrderId` value 1001.

Figure 11.2
In this database design, used by program OrderEntryTabs, the `OrderId` fields link the `CustomerOrders`, `OrderItems`, and `OrderDates` records.

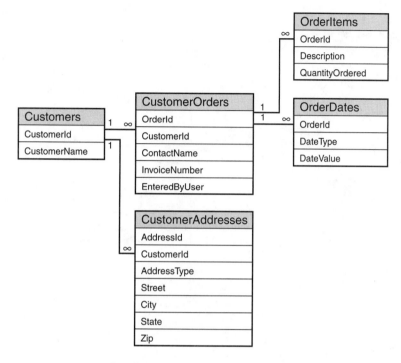

User 1 saves his changes, creating a `CustomerOrders` record with `OrderId` 1001. Now User 2 tries to save his changes and create another `CustomerOrders` record with `OrderId` 1001. Because `OrderId` is that table's primary key, the database does not allow duplicate `OrderId` values, so this fails.

The problem is that an instance of the program cannot create new `CustomerOrders` records completely independently. After the record is created in the database, the program can modify it without affecting other `CustomerOrders` records. To create a new record, however, the program cannot simply take the next `OrderId` value in the sequence without knowing whether another instance of the program is trying to use the same value.

You could build some sort of centralized `OrderId` server to pass out new values to programs as they are needed. The server would ensure that no two records got the same `OrderId`. This would work but would be a relatively complicated solution.

Alternatively, you could have the program create the new record as soon as it needed a new `OrderId`. It would need to delete that record later, however, if the user canceled his changes and did not create the new `CustomerOrders` record after all.

A better solution is to modify the database design slightly. Instead of linking the `CustomerOrders` table to the `OrderItems` and `OrderDates` tables using the single `OrderId` field, you can link the table with the combined `OrderId` and `CustomerId` values as shown in Figure 11.3.

Figure 11.3
This design links the
`CustomerOrders`
table to the
`OrderItems`, and
OrderDates tables
using `OrderId` and
`CustomerId`.

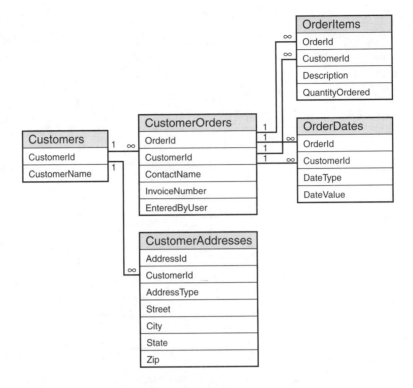

In this database design, two different customers can use the same `OrderId` values because their `CustomerIds` are different. For example, in the original design, Customer 1 might have had `CustomerOrders` records with `OrderId` values 1001, 1010, and 1244. Customer 2 might have had `CustomerOrders` records with `OrderId` values 97 and 1280.

In the new design, Customer 1 would have `CustomerOrders` records with `CustomerId` 1 and `OrderId` values 1, 2, and 3. Customer 2 would have `CustomerOrders` records with `CustomerId` 2 and `OrderId` values 1 and 2. Because the program uses both the `CustomerId` and `OrderId` to link the records in the `CustomerOrders` table to those in the `OrderItems` and `OrderDates` tables, these records can have the same `OrderId`.

Now each customer form can manage its order information completely independently. It can pick new `OrderId` values just by looking at the values already used by the current customer. It doesn't need to know anything about the other `CustomerOrders` records.

RESERVATIONS

One of the most important considerations for any multi-user application is *record locking*. The program must not allow two users to try to edit the same record at the same time. The database features provided by the `SqlDataAdapter` may prevent one user from overwriting the changes made by the other, but it will only do that when the second user tries to save his changes to the database. Allowing the user to make the changes in the first place wastes the user's time and can be very frustrating.

The solution to this problem is to lock the records before allowing the user to edit them. When the user clicks the Edit button, the program can lock the customer's record in the Customers table. When the second user clicks the Edit button, the program tries to lock the record but finds it already locked by another user. The program tells the user that the record is locked and the user can move on to something else.

Unfortunately, different kinds of databases provide different methods for locking records. Some databases also provide little information about who is locking a record and why. One way to solve this problem is to add a ReservedBy field to the database table. When the program wants to edit a record, it puts the user's name in this field. Later when another instance of the program wants to edit the same record, it notices that the ReservedBy field is not empty and it tells its user that another user has the record reserved. When it finishes editing the record, the original instance of the program resets this field to Null to remove its reservation. Figure 11.4 shows the new database design with the ReservedBy field.

Figure 11.4
The ReservedBy
field prevents two
users from editing the
same record at the
same time.

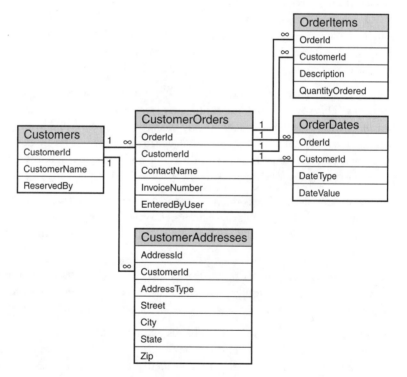

This method does have a few drawbacks. First, it runs on the honor system. The programs that need access to the database must all obey the convention of putting the user's name in the ReservedBy field before editing a record. If one program modifies a record without first reserving it, that program may confuse others that use the same record.

Second, all programs must use the same method for reserving records. The database design shown in Figure 11.4 uses a single ReservedBy field in the Customers table to control access to all customer records, including those in the `Customers`, `CustomerAddresses`, `CustomerOrders`, `OrderItems`, and `OrderDates` tables. All applications must understand that they should reserve the `Customers` record if they want to modify any of the other tables.

Third, because the database engine does not implement this method directly, it cannot reset the `ReservedBy` field if there is a problem. For instance, suppose a program sets the `ReservedBy` field and then crashes. The record's `ReservedBy` field is not `Null`, so no other application can edit it. Restarting the database will reset database locks, but it will not clear the `ReservedBy` field because it is just another piece of data. To handle this situation, you need to write a small application that can reset the `ReservedBy` field to `Null` for specific records that have been left in this state.

SOURCE CODE

Much of the source code used by program OrderEntryMultiUser is similar to the code used by OrderEntryTabs so it is not repeated here. Look at the code shown in Chapter 10, "A Single-User Example," or download the OrderEntryMultiUser sample program from the book's Web site and look at it for yourself. Listing 11.1 shows some pieces of code used by the customer detail form that deserve special mention, however.

When the user clicks the Orders tab's Add button, the `btnOrderAdd_Click` event handler executes. This routine calls subroutine `CustomerFormEndAllEdits` to end any pending edits on the form's CurrencyManagers so any changes are preserved. The event handler then calls function `MaxOrderId` to find the largest `OrderId` value used so far by the current customer's `CustomerOrders` records. It adds 1 to this value and uses the result as the `OrderId` for the new `CustomerOrders` record. It creates the new record and displays it.

Function `MaxOrderId` checks the `m_dtCustomerOrders` table's `Rows.Count` value to see if the current customer has any `CustomerOrders` records. If there are no records, the function returns 0. The `btnOrderAdd_Click` event handler adds 1 to this so the first order has `OrderId` 1.

If the customer does have `CustomerOrders` records, function `MaxOrderId` makes a new DataView listing the customer's `CustomerOrders` records sorted in descending order by `OrderId`. It returns the `OrderId` value of the first record, which has the largest `OrderId` value.

Program OrderEntryTabs begins and ends editing automatically. It starts editing a record when the user changes a value. It finishes editing when the user saves or cancels the changes. Because the user does not start editing explicitly, the program needs to do some work to decide whether its data is safe. Its `DataSafe` function determines whether the data has been modified since the last time it was saved and asks the user if it should save or discard any pending changes.

Protecting data is a bit simpler for program OrderEntryMultiUser. To begin editing, the user must press the Edit button. To end editing, the user must press the OK or Cancel button. This allows the program to always know whether it is editing data. It also makes it clear to the user whether the data has been modified so it is less likely that the user will try to exit the program without saving or canceling changes.

This means the OrderEntryMultiUser program can use a simpler approach to saving data. When the form is closing, its code determines whether the user is currently editing the data. If an edit is in progress, the form tells the user to save or cancel the changes and refuses to close.

When the user clicks the Edit button, its Click event handler calls the ReserveCustomerRecord function to try to reserve the customer's record. Function ReserveCustomerRecord returns the number of records it affected. If the reservation is successful, this should be 1.

If ReserveCustomerRecord makes the reservation, the Click event handler calls subroutine LoadCustomerData to reload the customer's data. It does this for two reasons. First, subroutine LoadCustomerData resets the properties of the form's controls to make them editable so the user can modify their values. Normally, when the user is not editing the customer's data, the controls do not allow the user to make changes.

Second and more importantly, another user may have modified the customer's data between the time the user originally loaded it and the time he clicked the Edit button. The user must reload the data to see any changes and to ensure that the program's data objects can save any changes he may now make. The SqlCommandBuilder object that creates the program's update statement uses a WHERE clause that verifies that the records' data values haven't changed since they were loaded. For example, the command builder generates the following statement to update the CustomerAddresses table:

```
UPDATE CustomerAddresses
SET AddressId = @p1 , CustomerId = @p2 , AddressType = @p3 , Street = @p4 ,
    City = @p5 , State = @p6 , Zip = @p7
WHERE ( (AddressId = @p8) AND
  ((CustomerId IS NULL AND @p9 IS NULL) OR (CustomerId = @p10)) AND
  ((AddressType IS NULL AND @p11 IS NULL) OR (AddressType = @p12)) AND
  ((Street IS NULL AND @p13 IS NULL) OR (Street = @p14)) AND
  ((City IS NULL AND @p15 IS NULL) OR (City = @p16)) AND
  ((State IS NULL AND @p17 IS NULL) OR (State = @p18)) AND
  ((Zip IS NULL AND @p19 IS NULL) OR (Zip = @p20)) )
```

If a second user has modified this record, the values in the WHERE clause will not match those used by the first user's instance of the application. The WHERE clause will not match the record so the UPDATE statement will fail.

Function ReserveCustomerRecord uses an SQL UPDATE statement to set the ReservedBy field to Null or to a customer's name in the Customers table. The statement uses a WHERE clause to ensure that the ReservedBy field is currently Null or holds the user's ID. For instance, the following statement sets the ReservedBy field to Rod for the CustomerId 76. If another user already holds the reservation, the statement fails and leaves the record unchanged:

```
UPDATE Customers SET ReservedBy = 'Rod'
WHERE CustomerId = 76
  AND ReservedBy IS NULL
```

The following code removes the reservation by user Rod from the record with `CustomerId` 76:

```
UPDATE Customers SET ReservedBy = NULL
WHERE CustomerId = 76
  AND ReservedBy = 'Rod'
```

It is important to check and set the `ReservedBy` field in a single SQL statement. If the program fetched the `ReservedBy` value to verify that it was `Null` and then set its value to Rod in a second step, another program could conceivably slip in and make the reservation between the two steps.

After composing its SQL `UPDATE` statement, function `ReserveCustomerRecord` builds a `SqlCommand` object and calls its `ExecuteNonQuery` method to perform the update. `ExecuteNonQuery` returns the number of rows affected (hopefully 1) so `ReserveCustomerRecord` returns that value.

LISTING 11.1   INTERESTING PIECES OF PROGRAM ORDERENTRYMULTIUSER

```
' Create a new order.
Private Sub btnOrderAdd_Click(ByVal sender As System.Object, _
  ByVal e As System.EventArgs) Handles btnOrderAdd.Click
    ' End any current edits.
    CustomerFormEndAllEdits()

    ' Create the new record.
    Dim order_id As Integer = MaxOrderId() + 1
    m_cmCustomerOrders.AddNew()
    Dim cur_order As DataRowView = m_cmCustomerOrders.Current()
    cur_order.Item("CustomerId") = m_CustomerId
    cur_order.Item("OrderId") = order_id
    m_cmCustomerOrders.EndCurrentEdit()

    ' Display the order detail.
    DisplayOrderDetails()

    ' Set focus to the ContactName field.
    txtContactName.Focus()

    ' Mark the data as modified.
    CheckModified()
End Sub

' Return the largest order ID for this customer.
Private Function MaxOrderId() As Integer
    ' See if there are any order records yet.
    If m_dtCustomerOrders.Rows.Count < 1 Then
        ' There are no order records. Return 0.
        Return 0
    Else
        ' Get a DataView listing the IDs
        ' in ascending order.
        Dim data_view As New DataView(m_dtCustomerOrders)
        data_view.Sort = "OrderId DESC"
```

LISTING 11.1   CONTINUED

```
                ' Return the largest value.
                Return data_view.Item(0).Item("OrderId")
        End If
End Function


' Make sure it is safe for this form to close.
Private Sub frmCustomer_Closing(ByVal sender As Object, _
    ByVal e As System.ComponentModel.CancelEventArgs) Handles MyBase.Closing
        If m_Editing Then
            e.Cancel = True
            MsgBox("You must finish editing customer '" & _
                m_DataRow.Item("CustomerName") & _
                "' before you close its form.", _
                MsgBoxStyle.Exclamation, "Edit In Progress")
        End If
End Sub


' Reserve the record so we can edit it.
' Then reload the data in case it has changed.
Private Sub btnEdit_Click(ByVal sender As System.Object, _
    ByVal e As System.EventArgs) Handles btnEdit.Click
        ' Try to reserve the record.
        If ReserveCustomerRecord(True) <> 1 Then
            MsgBox("Unable to reserve this customer." & vbCrLf & _
                "The record may have been deleted or it may be reserved already.", _
                MsgBoxStyle.Information, "Reserve Error")
            Exit Sub
        End If

        ' Reload the data making it not read-only.
        LoadCustomerData(False)
End Sub

' Reserve or unreserve the Customers record.
Private Function ReserveCustomerRecord(ByVal reserve As Boolean) As Integer
        ' Compose the command.
        Dim cmd_text As String
        If reserve Then
            cmd_text = _
                "UPDATE Customers SET ReservedBy = '" & g_UserId & "' " & _
                "WHERE CustomerId = " & m_CustomerId & _
                "  AND ReservedBy IS NULL"
        Else
            cmd_text = _
                "UPDATE Customers SET ReservedBy = NULL " & _
                "WHERE CustomerId = " & m_CustomerId & _
                "  AND ReservedBy = '" & g_UserId & "'"
        End If

        ' Prepare the command.
        Dim conn As New SqlConnection(CONNECT_STRING)
        Dim cmd As New SqlCommand(cmd_text, conn)

        ' Execute the command.
        conn.Open()
```

LISTING 11.1   CONTINUED

```
    Dim records_affected As Integer
    records_affected = cmd.ExecuteNonQuery()
    conn.Close()

    ' If we succeeded, set m_Editing.
    If records_affected = 1 Then m_Editing = reserve

    ' Return the number of records affected.
    Return records_affected
End Function
```

MODIFICATIONS

You could make several modifications to this program depending on your preferences and those of your users. The following sections describe a few of the most useful enhancements you can make.

QUERY-BY-EXAMPLE

The most obvious change to program OrderEntryMultiUser would be to remove the customer list form and add a query-by-example form such as the one described in Chapter 12. That form lets the user search for specific records in a large database without requiring the program to load information about every customer in the database.

The query-by-example form has a List button that rebuilds the list of selected records, providing a convenient equivalent of the customer list's Refresh button. You could also modify the program to automatically refresh the query list each time the user closes a customer detail form so the user can immediately select the next customer.

REAL-TIME CUSTOMER LISTS

In critical applications such as emergency dispatching and network management, the user needs information as quickly as possible. One way to ensure that the user's information is timely is to make the program poll the database. Every few seconds, the application searches the database for new, high-priority items and displays them in its job list.

Blindly rebuilding the user's list of pending items can impose a high load on the database and the network, however. For instance, suppose 10 users are monitoring a list of 100 network faults with different degrees of severity. If the application rebuilds its list of faults every 5 seconds, it makes 2 database queries per second. For each query, the database must fetch the 100 fault records, sort them, and return them to the application. This may very well be possible on a fast computer, but it imposes an unnecessary load. If you add too many users or the fault list gets too big, performance will suffer.

Another strategy is to place a single LastModified record in the database. When an application adds a new record to the faults table, it also updates the LastModified record to show the current time.

The fault tracking application keeps track of the last time it updated its fault list. Every 5 seconds it fetches the LastModified record from the database and compares it to its last update time. Only if the LastModified time is more recent does the program need to download the fault list again. The program still polls the database every 5 seconds, but usually it is asking for much less data and without sorting.

Applications that require even higher performance and true real-time data can use other methods for fetching data. For example, the program can connect to an update server. When an application modifies critical records, it tells the server about the change. The server then tells each of the applications connected to it. If changes are infrequent, each program could then refresh its data from the database. If changes are more frequent, the server could tell each program what records had changed and in what ways so the programs could update their data immediately.

PICKING CUSTOMERS

Even with a record reservation system, there is a chance twousers can waste each other's time with program OrderEntryMultiUser. Suppose two users open the application, list the customers, and they both open the first customer's detail form. User 1 studies the form for a few minutes and then clicks the Edit button. User 2 also studies the form for a few minutes. When he clicks the Edit button, the Customers record is already reserved so User 2 cannot edit it. He can immediately go back to the Customers list and pick another customer, but he has already wasted a few minutes looking at the first one.

PART

I

CH

11

Over the years, businesses have used many approaches to address this problem. One method is to make specific users responsible for groups of customers that have something in common. For example, each user might be responsible for customers in different cities—then two users will not select the same customer at the same time.

Another solution is to have users immediately reserve a record for editing as soon as they look at it, then they cannot waste much time studying a customer's record while another user has already reserved that record. You could make the program automatically reserve records when the user opens them, but that would prevent anyone from looking at the data in a read-only mode.

A final solution is to build an assignment service. Add an AssignedTo field to the Customers table. The assignment service application would periodically look through the Customers table for new records where AssignedTo is Null. It would then assign those records to different users by placing their user IDs in the AssignedTo field. This method works well in conjunction with a query-by-example form because that form lets users select records where the AssignedTo field matches their user IDs.

DISPLAYING RESERVATIONS

Program OrderEntryMultiUser uses a ReservedBy field to prevent a user from beginning to edit a record that another user is already editing but it does not tell the user who is editing the record. Whenever it finds a record is already reserved, you could make the program fetch the ReservedBy value and display it to the user. If the user urgently needed to modify the customer data, he could then go to the user holding the reservation and ask him to finish editing.

This is also useful if someone accidentally leaves for lunch holding a reservation open or if a program crashes while holding a reservation. Knowing who holds the reservation, you can see if the program is editing that record on the person's computer. If you decide that this is a zombie reservation left by a crashed application, you can use an UPDATE statement to reset the ReservedBy field to Null.

SUMMARY

Visual Basic's database objects make working with databases relatively easy. You can load records from any number of tables into a DataSet. You can then add, modify, and delete records, and save your changes to the database.

Although this method is straightforward, it doesn't work well for multi-user applications. If two users try to modify the same record at the same time, one of them gets an error and loses his modifications. Adding a ReservedBy field allows an application to manage record reservations itself in a simple, intuitive way. It allows the application to coordinate its efforts so users don't waste time duplicating their efforts.

Making the application handle individual customer accounts as separately as possible also allows it to reduce the amount of data it must store at any given time. The program only needs to store information about the records it is actually using, not the entire database.

QUERY BY EXAMPLE

Many database applications work with large amounts of data. If a program only needs a few data values, it can easily include them as compiled-in data, or load them from text files or the System Registry. When a program needs a lot of information, a database can be a big advantage.

Many database applications work with thousands or even millions of records. In such large databases, helping the user find particular records can be difficult. You can use different techniques depending on your specific application. For example, a repair dispatch system might present the user with a list of jobs that need attention in their order of priority. A school enrollment system might provide a student search screen that locates student records given a student's name.

One record location technique that is applicable in a variety circumstances is *query by example*. In a query by example, the user enters data values similar to the ones he wants to find. The program uses those values to search for records that match. A well-built query-by-example form allows even inexperienced users who know almost nothing about SQL to perform complex queries and find the records they need.

In specific instances, it is easy to build a query-by-example form. You can put text boxes on the form in which the user can enter values. When the user clicks the Search button, the program uses those values to build a SQL SELECT statement's WHERE clause. It fetches the matching records and displays them in a list.

Building query-by-example forms isn't difficult but it can become tedious. A large application might need several forms to let the user search for different types of records. Building each query form individually can be time consuming.

Fortunately, it isn't too hard to create a generic query-by-example form that can work with different database tables. This chapter explains how you can build a single form that you can use to let the user find records in all of an application's important tables. This tool makes adding a powerful and complex feature to database applications quick and easy.

The following section explains what the query-by-example tool looks like to the user. It explains how the user selects fields and enters values to locate groups of records in the database.

The section after that one shows how you can use the tool in your programs. It explains how to initialize the tool to tell it what tables and columns to manipulate and how to respond when the user double-clicks a row.

The section after that tells how the tool itself works.

The rest of the chapter describes a similar tool that displays its results using a ListView control instead of a DataGrid.

FEATURES

Before you read about the query-by-example tool's internal details, you should understand what the tool looks like to the user. Example program CustomerGrid, shown in Figure 12.1, demonstrates the tool. If you have access to the Internet, take a few moments to download the example code from the book's Web site so you can experiment with the tool as you read about it.

Figure 12.1
Program
CustomerGrid uses a
query-by-example
form to let the user
select customer
records.

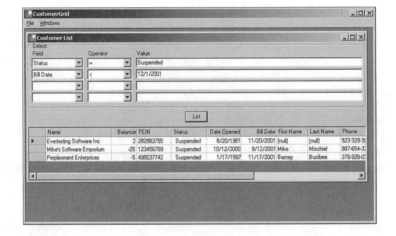

Open the program's Windows menu and select the Customer List command to make a new Customer List window. You can use this command more than once to create more than one Customer List form. Displaying more than one Customer List lets the user create different views of the customer data simultaneously.

On the Customer List form, use the left column of ComboBoxes to select the fields you want to match. In Figure 12.1, the Status field is selected in the first row and the Bill Date field is selected in the second row.

This program lets you select the Id, Name, FEIN, Status, Date Opened, and Bill Date fields. The other fields displayed in the customer list (Balance, First Name, Last Name, Phone, and so forth) are not present in these ComboBoxes so you cannot select them. In general, the programmer determines the fields shown in these controls and the lists could include all the fields in the tables involved in the query.

In the middle ComboBoxes, pick the operations you want to use with the fields you have selected. The operations can be =, !=, >, <, LIKE, IS NULL, or IS NOT NULL.

In the third column, enter the text you want to compare to the field in the first column. If a field's operation is IS NULL or IS NOT NULL, the program ignores the text value.

When you click the List button, the program uses the values you selected to compose a SQL query. The form shown in Figure 12.1 composes a query similar to this one:

```
SELECT *
FROM Customers
WHERE Status = 'Suspended'
  AND BillDate < '12/1/2001'
```

Actually the true query is quite a bit more complicated. For example, the Bill Date field is really called LastBillDate in the database. Several other fields also have aliases like this one. The real query also joins the Customers and Credits tables so the WHERE clause contains a join statement to coordinate the two tables. Finally, the Balance field is the sum of the Amount field values selected from the Credits table. The following code shows the complete query:

```
SELECT Customers.CustomerId AS [Id], CompanyName AS [Name],
    SUM(Amount) AS [Balance], FEIN, AccountStatus AS [Status],
    AccountOpenedDate AS [Date Opened], LastBillDate AS [Bill Date],
    ContactFirstName AS [First Name], ContactLastName AS [Last Name],
    ContactPhone AS [Phone], ContactStreet AS [Street], ContactCity AS [City],
    ContactState AS [State], ContactZip AS [Zip]
FROM Customers, Credits
WHERE Customers.CustomerId = Credits.CustomerId
  AND AccountStatus = 'Suspended'
  AND LastBillDate < '12/1/2001'
GROUP BY Customers.CustomerId, CompanyName, FEIN, AccountStatus,
AccountOpenedDate,
    LastBillDate, ContactFirstName, ContactLastName, ContactPhone, ContactStreet,
    ContactCity, ContactState, ContactZip
ORDER BY CompanyName
```

The program hides all these ugly details from the user form.

After you have built a list of matching customer records, you can click the DataGrid's column headers to reorder the items. For example, click the Balance column's header to sort the records by Balance value. Click that header again to reverse the sort order.

When you double-click the column to the left of a record, the program displays a message box telling you the customer ID of the record you selected. A real application would take some other action, such as displaying a customer detail form that displays the customer's information in greater detail. That form might provide connections to related records (order information, billing information, and so forth), and let you modify the customer information.

PART
I
CH
12

PROGRAMMING THE RECORDLIST FORM

The frmRecordList form implements the query-by-example tool. This section explains how a program can use this form to allow the user to select records. Most of the work is done in initializing the form. After it is initialized, the form does most of its work automatically.

Example program CustomerGrid creates the form when you select the Windows menu's Customer List command. When you invoke this command, the program executes the `mnuWinCustomerList_Click` event handler shown in Listing 12.1.

The first thing the event handler does is create a new instance of the `frmRecordList` form. It defines a database connect string and changes its cursor to the hourglass cursor. It sets the new form's MdiParent property to the program's main MDI form so the customer list appears inside the MDI form.

The program then sets the new form's caption to Customer List. You may wonder why the form itself doesn't have this caption at design time. Remember that the `frmRecordList` form is a generic tool that will work with more tables than this one. To make sense under different circumstances, the program must set the caption when it uses the form.

Next the program registers the main MDI form's `RecordSelected` subroutine as an event handler for the new form's `RecordSelected` event. When the user double-clicks an entry on the Record List form, that form raises its `RecordSelected` event and the main form's `RecordSelected` subroutine fires.

The program then defines the fields the record list form will use to select and display records. For each field, it calls the record selection form's `AddField` method, passing it parameters to indicate how the field should be used and displayed. The following section describes the `AddField` method from the main program's point of view.

After the program defines the fields it needs, it calls the form's `InitializeForm` method. This method gives the form an ID it should use to identify itself when it raises its `RecordSelected` method, and a database connection string. It also includes FROM, JOIN, GROUP BY, and ORDER BY clauses to use in composing the form's SQL SELECT statement.

After all this preparation, the main program displays the record selection form and that form does the rest.

The only remaining piece of interesting code in the main MDI form is its `RecordSelected` method. This method executes when the user double-clicks a record in the record selection form. This routine merely displays a message telling the user which form raised the event and giving the customer's name. A real application would do more. For example, it might display a customer detail form.

The `RecordSelected` event handler receives as a parameter a reference to a DataRowView object representing the record selected. The program can retrieve whatever information it needs from the fields in the corresponding record.

LISTING 12.1 EXAMPLE PROGRAM CUSTOMERGRID USES THIS CODE TO LET THE USER SELECT CUSTOMER RECORDS

```
' Display a new customer list form.
Private Sub mnuWinCustomerList_Click(ByVal sender As System.Object, _
  ByVal e As System.EventArgs) Handles mnuWinCustomerList.Click
    Dim frm As New frmRecordList()
```

LISTING 12.1   CONTINUED

```
Dim connect_string As String = _
    "user id=sa;password=;Data Source=Bender\NETSDK;Database=Customers"

Me.Cursor = Cursors.WaitCursor
Me.Refresh()

' Create the form and set its caption.
frm.MdiParent = Me
frm.Text = "Customer List"

' Make our RecordSelected subroutine handle the form's
' RecordSelected event.
AddHandler frm.RecordSelected, AddressOf Me.RecordSelected

' Define the form's fields.
' CustomerId is a select field but not a display field.
' The Contact fields are display fields but not select fields.
frm.AddField("Customers.CustomerId", "Id", "'", True, False, _
    HorizontalAlignment.Left)
frm.AddField("CompanyName", "Name", "'", True, True, HorizontalAlignment.Left)
frm.AddField("SUM(Amount)", "Balance", "", False, True, _
    HorizontalAlignment.Right)
frm.AddField("FEIN", "FEIN", "'", True, True, HorizontalAlignment.Left)
frm.AddField("AccountStatus", "Status", "'", True, True, _
    HorizontalAlignment.Center)
frm.AddField("AccountOpenedDate", "Date Opened", "'", True, True, _
    HorizontalAlignment.Right)
frm.AddField("LastBillDate", "Bill Date", "'", True, True, _
    HorizontalAlignment.Right)
frm.AddField("ContactFirstName", "First Name", "'", False, True, _
    HorizontalAlignment.Left)
frm.AddField("ContactLastName", "Last Name", "'", False, True, _
    HorizontalAlignment.Left)
frm.AddField("ContactPhone", "Phone", "'", False, True, _
    HorizontalAlignment.Left)
frm.AddField("ContactStreet", "Street", "'", False, True, _
    HorizontalAlignment.Left)
frm.AddField("ContactCity", "City", "'", False, True, _
    HorizontalAlignment.Left)
frm.AddField("ContactState", "State", "'", False, True, _
    HorizontalAlignment.Left)
frm.AddField("ContactZip", "Zip", "'", False, True, HorizontalAlignment.Left)

' Initialize the form's record selection values.
frm.InitializeForm("CustomerList", connect_string, _
    "FROM Customers, Credits", _
    "Customers.CustomerId = Credits.CustomerId", _
    "GROUP BY Customers.CustomerId, CompanyName, FEIN, AccountStatus, " & _
    "AccountOpenedDate, LastBillDate, ContactFirstName, ContactLastName, " & _
    "ContactPhone, ContactStreet, ContactCity, ContactState, ContactZip", _
    "ORDER BY CompanyName")

' Display the form.
frm.Show()
```

```
    Me.Cursor = Cursors.Default
End Sub

' A child list form has selected a record.
' Display its detail.
Private Sub RecordSelected(ByVal form_id As String, _
  ByVal data_row_view As DataRowView)
    MsgBox(form_id & ": " & data_row_view.Item("Name"))
End Sub
```

AddField

The record selection form's `AddField` subroutine gives the form information about one of the fields it needs to manipulate. The following code shows the syntax for the `AddField` method:

```
AddField(db_name, display_name, field_delimiter, is_select_field, _
    is_display_field, field_alignment)
```

The *db_name* parameter tells the form the name of the field as it is stored in the database. If the query will include more than one table that contains the field name so the field would be ambiguous, this name must include the table name as well. For instance, the CustomerGrid program selects records from the `Customers` and `Credits` tables. Both of those tables contain a field named `CustomerId` so the first call to `AddField` specifies this field's database name as `Customers.CustomerId` to be unambiguous.

The *display_name* parameter gives the name of the field as the form should display it to the user. For instance, the CustomerGrid program displays the `CompanyName` field as `Name`. The form uses the display name both in its field `ComboBox` and in the `DataGrid` listing the selected records. The *db_name* and *display_name* parameters are roughly equivalent to using the following column selection in a SQL query:

```
SELECT db_name AS [display_name] FROM ...
```

The *field_delimiter* parameter tells the form what character to use to delimit values for this field. In a SQL statement, string fields must be delimited by single quotes so this value should be a string containing a single quote for those fields. Numeric fields must not be delimited in SQL statements so for numeric fields this parameter should be an empty string. The program uses the delimiter in `WHERE` clauses. For instance, the `CompanyName` field's delimiter is ' so a piece of the `WHERE` clause would look like the following code:

```
... WHERE CompanyName = 'TheName' ...
```

The *is_select_field* parameter should be `True` if you want the query-by-example form to allow the user to select the field in the left column of ComboBoxes. Depending on the application, some fields may not make much sense as selection fields and you can use this parameter to hide those fields. For example, it is unlikely that the user will try to locate a customer's record by entering its contact telephone number so the CustomerGrid example program does not allow the user to select the `ContactPhone` field.

Other fields are not allowed to appear in a WHERE clause. In this example, the Balance field is actually a sum of Value fields taken from the Credits table. Aggregate functions such as SUM cannot normally appear in WHERE clauses so the CustomerGrid program does not allow the user to make it part of the selection criteria.

The *is_display_field* parameter tells the record list form whether it should list the field in the result grid. The CustomerGrid example program sets this parameter to False for the CustomerId field. The user can select records with certain CustomerId values, but the program does not list the CustomerId in its output.

Under some circumstances, a program may want to set a field's *is_select_field* and *is_display_field* parameters both to False. That prevents the user from using the field as a selection criterion and prevents the user from seeing the field in the result grid. The record selection form will select that field, however, and store it with the other field values. When the user double-clicks a record, the RecordSelected event handler includes a DataRowView parameter that represents the selected record and the main program can retrieve the hidden field from the corresponding record.

For instance, suppose the Order record includes an OrderId field that is meaningless to the user but which is the table's primary key. Because the field is meaningless to the user, the user will not want to select records by this field and will not want to see the OrderId in the results. When the user double-clicks a record, however, the main program can use the OrderId to quickly fetch the complete order record.

The final parameter to AddField is *field_alignment*. This value tells the record list form how you want the field's values aligned in the result grid. This value should be one of the following values:

```
HorizontalAlignment.Left
HorizontalAlignment.Center
HorizontalAlignment.Right
```

Generally, numeric values look best right aligned and string values look fine with left alignment.

InitializeForm

The InitializeForm method gives the record selection form more information about how it should compose its SQL SELECT statement. This method has the following syntax:

```
InitializeForm(form_id, connect_string, from_clause, [join_clause,] _
    [group_by_clause,] [order_by_clause])
```

The *form_id* parameter tells the form what ID it should return when it raises its RecordSelected event. If the main program uses the record selection form to display records of more than one type, it can use this ID to determine which kinds of data to display.

For example, the program could use one form to list customers, another to list orders, and a third to list employees. It could give these record selection forms the IDs CustomerList, OrderList, and EmployeeList so it can easily tell whether it should display a customer detail

PART

I

CH

12

form, an order detail form, or an employee detail form.

The second parameter to InitializeForm, *connect_string*, tells the record selection form the database connection string it should use to open the database.

The *from_clause* parameter is the complete FROM clause the form should use in its SELECT statement. This clause should include the keyword FROM as in the value "FROM Customers, Credits".

The optional *join_clause* parameter gives any join conditions needed to combine the records from the tables listed in the *from_clause*. If the form doesn't need any extra join information, this parameter should be blank or omitted. If it is not blank, *join_clause* should not begin with the word WHERE. The record selection form adds the WHERE when it is needed.

The optional *group_by* clause gives the complete GROUP BY statement the record selection form should use. You need to compose the *group_by* parameter to match any aggregate functions you included in the fields described by calls to AddField.

The optional *order_by_clause* parameter provides the complete ORDER BY clause the record selection form uses when it selects records. Be sure to include only fields described by calls to AddField. Also note that the user can click on the DataGrid's column headers to sort the selected records using different columns so the *order_by_clause* parameter really only specifies the records' initial sort order.

RECORDLIST FORM INTERNALS

The record list form performs four main tasks: storing information about the fields it will manipulate, using that information to query the database, displaying the results, and responding when the user double-clicks a record. The next section explains the FieldInfo class that the form uses to store field information. The sections after that explain how the form uses that class to perform its other tasks.

THE FieldInfo CLASS

The form includes a private class named FieldInfo. The following code shows the class definition. FieldInfo is actually quite simple. It contains information analogous to the parameters used by the AddField method described earlier. These data values hold the following information:

- The field's name as it appears in the database
- The field's name as it should be displayed to the user
- A delimiter for the field's values
- A flag telling whether the user should be able to use the field to select records
- A flag telling whether the form should show the field in its results
- The field's alignment in the output

The only method provided by the `FieldInfo` class is a constructor. This routine takes as parameters values for each of the object's data values and it initializes those values:

```
' Stores information about a select field.
Private Class FieldInfo
    Public DbName As String
    Public DisplayName As String
    Public Delimiter As String
    Public IsSelectField As Boolean
    Public IsDisplayField As Boolean
    Public FieldAlignment As HorizontalAlignment

    Public Sub New(ByVal db_name As String, ByVal display_name As String, _
      ByVal field_delimiter As String, ByVal is_select_field As Boolean, _
      ByVal is_display_field As Boolean, _
      ByVal field_alignment As HorizontalAlignment)
        DbName = db_name
        DisplayName = display_name
        Delimiter = field_delimiter
        If Delimiter Is Nothing Then Delimiter = ""
        IsSelectField = is_select_field
        IsDisplayField = is_display_field
        FieldAlignment = field_alignment
    End Sub
End Class
```

This class is little more than a user-defined type with a handy constructor.

INITIALIZING THE FORM

The main program initializes the record selection form in two steps. First, it uses the `AddField` method to give the form information about the fields it will manage. Then it calls the `InitializeForm` method to give the form information about the database and how to compose SQL queries.

The code shown in Listing 12.2 stores the form's information. The form's variables `m_FormId`, `m_ConnectString`, `m_FromClause`, and so on, store information about the database and the SQL query. Subroutine `InitializeForm`, described later in this section, initializes those variables.

The variable `m_FieldInfos` is a collection holding `FieldInfo` objects. The collection uses each field's display name as a key. For instance, if the database field `AccountBalance` will be displayed as `Balance` to the user, then the collection uses the value `Balance` as a key for this field.

The variable `m_DataSet` holds the DataSet returned by the database query. The form will later bind this DataSet to a DataGrid control to display the query results to the user.

When the form loads, its `Load` event handler executes. This routine creates the item lists displayed by the operator ComboBoxes in the form's second column. Notice that the first entry in each ComboBox is blank. That allows the user to select a blank operator if the corresponding condition row is not needed.

The AddField method stores information about a data field. It takes as parameters the values describing the field. It passes those values to the FieldInfo class constructor to make a new FieldInfo object. It adds the new object to the m_FieldInfos collection, using the field's display name as a key.

Because the keys in a collection must be unique, the main program must not try to create more than one field with the same display string. That usually makes sense anyway because you probably don't want to show the user multiple fields with the same name.

The InitializeForm method is almost as simple as the AddField method. This subroutine takes the following parameters:

- An ID string to assign to the form
- A database connection string
- A FROM clause listing the tables taking part in the query
- An optional JOIN clause to add to the query's WHERE statement
- An optional GROUP BY clause to use in the query
- An optional ORDER BY clause to use in the query

The subroutine saves this information for later when the form uses it to compose the SQL query. It then calls the MakeFieldList subroutine to create the lists of fields displayed in the form's left column of ComboBoxes.

Subroutine MakeFieldList clears the ComboBox it is initializing and adds a blank item. That lets the user clear the ComboBox if that selection row is not needed. The routine then loops through the information in the m_FieldInfos collection. For each FieldInfo object in the collection, the routine examines the IsSelectField property. If IsSelectField is True, that field should appear in the ComboBox so the subroutine adds it to the ComboBox's item list.

LISTING 12.2   THIS CODE PREPARES THE RECORD SELECTION FORM FOR USE

```
' We raise this event to tell the main program that
' the user has selected a record.
Public Event RecordSelected(ByVal form_id As String, _
  ByVal data_row_view As DataRowView)

' Used to identify the form.
Private m_FormId As String

' Used to compose and execute the query.
Private m_ConnectString As String
Private m_FromClause As String
Private m_JoinClause As String
Private m_GroupBy As String
Private m_OrderBy As String

' Field information.
Private m_FieldInfos As New Collection()
```

LISTING 12.2   CONTINUED

```
' The DataSet holding the current information.
Private m_DataSet As DataSet

' Initialize the operator ComboBoxes.
Private Sub frmRecordList_Load(ByVal sender As System.Object, _
  ByVal e As System.EventArgs) Handles MyBase.Load
    Dim operators() As String = _
        {"", "=", "!=", ">", "<", "LIKE", "IS NULL", "IS NOT NULL"}

    cboOperator1.Items.Clear()
    cboOperator1.Items.AddRange(operators)
    cboOperator2.Items.Clear()
    cboOperator2.Items.AddRange(operators)
    cboOperator3.Items.Clear()
    cboOperator3.Items.AddRange(operators)
    cboOperator4.Items.Clear()
    cboOperator4.Items.AddRange(operators)

    ' Do not allow the user to edit data from this form.
    grdResults.ReadOnly = True
    grdResults.CaptionVisible = False
End Sub

' Add the field's info to the m_FieldInfos array.
Public Sub AddField(ByVal db_name As String, ByVal display_name As String, _
  ByVal field_delimiter As String, ByVal is_select_field As Boolean, _
  ByVal is_display_field As Boolean, ByVal field_alignment As HorizontalAlignment)
    m_FieldInfos.Add( _
        New FieldInfo(db_name, display_name, field_delimiter, is_select_field, _
            is_display_field, field_alignment), _
        display_name)
End Sub

' Initialize the fields the form will use.
Public Sub InitializeForm(ByVal form_id As String, _
  ByVal connect_string As String, ByVal from_clause As String, _
  Optional ByVal join_clause As String = "", _
  Optional ByVal group_by_clause As String = "", _
  Optional ByVal order_by_clause As String = "")
    ' Save the information for later.
    m_FormId = form_id

    m_ConnectString = connect_string.Trim
    m_FromClause = from_clause

    If join_clause Is Nothing Then join_clause = ""
    m_JoinClause = join_clause.Trim

    If group_by_clause Is Nothing Then group_by_clause = ""
    m_GroupBy = group_by_clause.Trim

    If order_by_clause Is Nothing Then order_by_clause = ""
    m_OrderBy = order_by_clause.Trim
```

LISTING 12.2 CONTINUED

```
    ' Make the field lists.
    MakeFieldList(cboField1)
    MakeFieldList(cboField2)
    MakeFieldList(cboField3)
    MakeFieldList(cboField4)
End Sub

' Make the field list for this ComboBox.
Private Sub MakeFieldList(ByVal cbo As ComboBox)
    Dim field_info As FieldInfo

    cbo.Items.Clear()
    cbo.Items.Add("")
    For Each field_info In m_FieldInfos
        If field_info.IsSelectField Then
            cbo.Items.Add(field_info.DisplayName)
        End If
    Next field_info
End Sub
```

After the main program initializes the form, it should display the form by calling its Show method. That makes the form appear so the user can select fields and operators and enter values to select records.

SELECTING RECORDS

When the user clicks the List button, the btnList_Click event handler shown in Listing 12.3 runs. This routine initializes the variable where_clause to the JOIN clause passed to the form by its InitializeForm method.

It then calls the AddToWhereClause subroutine passing it the values entered by the user. For instance, if the user selects the Customer field and LIKE operator, and enters the value %Software% in the first line of record selection controls, the program passes the AddToWhereClause method the values Customer, LIKE, and %Software%.

When the calls to AddToWhereClause finish, the variable where_clause contains a WHERE clause representing the join conditions and the user's selections. If there is no join condition and the user left all the selection fields blank, then where_clause is blank. If where_clause it not blank, the program adds the text WHERE to the front of it so it can be used to compose the query.

Next, the program builds the SELECT clause. It loops through the field information stored in the m_FieldInfos collection. For each field, the subroutine adds to the SELECT statement a comma and the field's name as it appears in the database. If the field's display name differs from its database name, the subroutine also adds an AS clause giving the field's display name. For example, if the field's database name is CustomerName but its display name is Name, then that field's contribution to the SELECT statement is

```
, CustomerName AS [Name]
```

After it has finished looping through all the fields, the resulting list begins with an extra comma. The program uses the `select_clause` string's `SubString` method to remove the extra comma. It adds the word `SELECT` to the beginning of the string to give valid `SELECT` clause similar to the following:

```
SELECT CustomerName AS [Name], CustomerId, FEIN
```

Now that is has built the pieces of the query, the program combines them. It opens a `SqlConnection` to the database using the connection string given by the `InitializeForm` method. It sets a data adapter's `SelectCommand` property to a new `SqlCommand` object that uses the query to select records. Finally, it calls the data adapter's `Fill` method to copy the selected records into the `DataSet` and calls the `DisplayResults` subroutine described in the next section.

The last piece of code needed to load the data is the `AddToWhereClause` subroutine. This routine begins by checking the operator and name of the field that the user selected. If either of those values is missing, the subroutine returns without modifying the `WHERE` clause. This makes it easy for the user to remove a condition from the form's query. The user only needs to set the field or operator to blank to remove a condition from the query. The form ignores any text the user entered for that condition but the text remains in case the user wants to use it again later.

After the `AddToWhereClause` subroutine knows it has valid values, it begins composing the field's contribution to the `WHERE` clause. It starts by concatenating the field's name and the operator. It then determines whether the operator includes the string `NULL`. If it does, it is either `IS NULL` or `IS NOT NULL`. In either case, the routine does not need to add any text value to the condition.

If the operator does not contain `NULL`, the routine then checks the field's delimiter. If the delimiter is blank, that means the field is numeric and its value should not be surrounded by quotes. It also means the text must be nonblank because a `WHERE` condition cannot have the form `"Field ="` with no following value. If the text is missing, the subroutine ignores the field and exits.

Note that the text can be blank for a string field. For example, the condition can be `"CustomerName = ''"`.

The subroutine now adds the text value, surrounded by a suitable delimiter, to the condition string.

Finally, `AddToWhereClause` adds the new condition to the `WHERE` clause. If the `WHERE` clause already has a nonzero length, the routine adds the word `AND`.

LISTING 12.3 THIS CODE COMPOSES A SQL QUERY BASED ON THE USER'S VALUES AND EXECUTES IT

```
' List the selected records.
Private Sub btnList_Click(ByVal sender As System.Object, _
  ByVal e As System.EventArgs) Handles btnList.Click
```

LISTING 12.3   CONTINUED

```
    Dim where_clause As String
    Dim select_clause As String
    Dim query As String
    Dim sql_connection As SqlConnection
    Dim data_adapter As New SqlDataAdapter()
    Dim field_info As FieldInfo

    Me.MdiParent.Cursor = Cursors.WaitCursor
    Me.Refresh()

    ' Compose the WHERE clause.
    where_clause = m_JoinClause
    AddToWhereClause(where_clause, cboField1.Text, cboOperator1.Text, _
        txtValue1.Text)
    AddToWhereClause(where_clause, cboField2.Text, cboOperator2.Text, _
        txtValue2.Text)
    AddToWhereClause(where_clause, cboField3.Text, cboOperator3.Text, _
        txtValue3.Text)
    AddToWhereClause(where_clause, cboField4.Text, cboOperator4.Text, _
        txtValue4.Text)
    If where_clause.Length > 0 Then where_clause = "WHERE " & where_clause

    ' Compose the SELECT clause.
    For Each field_info In m_FieldInfos
        select_clause = select_clause & ", " & field_info.DbName
        If field_info.DbName <> field_info.DisplayName Then
            select_clause = select_clause & " AS [" & field_info.DisplayName & "]"
        End If
    Next field_info
    select_clause = "SELECT " & select_clause.Substring(2)

    ' Compose the query.
    query = _
        select_clause & " " & _
        m_FromClause & " " & _
        where_clause & " " & _
        m_GroupBy & " " & _
        m_OrderBy

    ' Connect to the database.
    sql_connection = New SqlConnection(m_ConnectString)
    sql_connection.Open()

    ' Execute the command.
    data_adapter.SelectCommand = _
        New SqlCommand(query, sql_connection)
    m_DataSet = New DataSet()
    data_adapter.Fill(m_DataSet)

    ' Display the results.
    DisplayResults()
End Sub

' Add a condition to the WHERE clause.
Private Sub AddToWhereClause(ByRef where_clause As String, _
```

Listing 12.3   CONTINUED

```
ByVal display_name As String, ByVal operator As String, _
ByVal field_value As String)
  Dim condition As String
  Dim field_info As FieldInfo

  ' Do nothing if the field name or operator is blank.
  If operator.Length = 0 Then Exit Sub
  Try
      field_info = m_FieldInfos.Item(display_name)
  Catch
      ' display_name is not a valid index.
      ' Do nothing.
      Exit Sub
  End Try
  If field_info Is Nothing Then Exit Sub

  ' Compose the condition.
  condition = field_info.DbName & " " & operator & " "

  ' See if this is IS NULL or IS NOT NULL.
  If operator.IndexOf("NULL") = -1 Then
      ' This is not IS NULL or IS NOT NULL.
      ' See if this is a numeric field.
      If field_info.Delimiter.Length = 0 Then
          ' This is a numeric type.
          ' See if the value is blank.
          If field_value.Length < 1 Then
              ' A numeric type must have a value.
              ' I.e. we cannot have "Number > ".
              Exit Sub
          End If
      End If

      ' Add the value with appropriate delimiters.
      condition = condition & field_info.Delimiter & _
          field_value & field_info.Delimiter
  End If

  ' Add the condition to the WHERE clause.
  If where_clause.Length > 0 Then where_clause = where_clause & " AND "
  where_clause = where_clause & condition
End Sub
```

Displaying Results

After it has queried the database and filled the program's DataSet with results, the btnList_Click event handler calls subroutine DisplayResults, shown in Listing 12.4, to present the results to the user. The routine begins by clearing the DataGrid and setting its DataSource property. If the program wanted to show the user every field selected by the query, that would be the end of the matter. This form allows some fields to be hidden from the user, however, so the subroutine must do a little more work.

Next, the subroutine creates a new `DataGridTableStyle` object. That object will tell the DataGrid how to format this result table. It sets the object's `MappingName` property to the name of the DataTable containing the data so it knows where to look for values. The program then adds this object to the DataGrid's `TableStyles` collection.

The subroutine then loops through the objects stored in the `m_FieldInfos` collection from back to front. The program checks each field's `IsDisplayField` to see if the field should be displayed to the user. If it should be hidden from the user, the program removes the field's `GridColumnStyles` entry for that field. That makes the DataGrid ignore the field.

If a field should be visible to the user, the program sets the column's alignment to the value that the main program originally specified when it defined the field using the `AddField` method.

At this point, the DataGrid control knows enough about the fields to display those that are appropriate with their correct alignments.

LISTING 12.4 SUBROUTINE `DisplayResults` PRESENTS THE NECESSARY FIELDS TO THE USER

```
' Display the results in the DataGrid.
Private Sub DisplayResults()
    Dim table_style As DataGridTableStyle
    Dim i As Integer

    ' Attach the results to the DataGrid.
    grdResults.TableStyles.Clear()
    grdResults.DataSource = m_DataSet.Tables(0)
    grdResults.PreferredColumnWidth = DataGrid.AutoColumnSize

    ' Create a table style to determine which fields to
    ' display and how to display them.
    table_style = New DataGridTableStyle()
    table_style.MappingName = m_DataSet.Tables(0).TableName

    ' Add the table style to the grid. This creates default
    ' column style objects.
    grdResults.TableStyles.Add(table_style)

    ' Set the column styles.
    For i = m_FieldInfos.Count To 1 Step -1
        ' See if we should display this field.
        If Not m_FieldInfos(i).IsDisplayField Then
            ' Don't show this field. Remove its style entry.
            table_style.GridColumnStyles.RemoveAt(i - 1)
        Else
            ' Show this field. Set its alignment.
            table_style.GridColumnStyles(i - 1).Alignment = _
                m_FieldInfos(i).FieldAlignment
        End If
    Next i

    Me.MdiParent.Cursor = Cursors.Default
End Sub
```

RAISING THE `RecordSelected` EVENT

When the user double-clicks a DataGrid row, the following event handler executes.

This routine simply raises the `RecordSelected` event. It passes the event handler the form's ID and a `DataRowView` object representing the item currently selected in the `DataTable` attached to the DataGrid. The main program can use the hidden and visible field values in that `DataRowView` to take whatever action is necessary:

```
Private Sub grdResults_DoubleClick(ByVal sender As Object, _
    ByVal e As System.EventArgs) Handles grdResults.DoubleClick
    RaiseEvent RecordSelected(m_FormId, _
        grdResults.BindingContext.Item(m_DataSet.Tables(0)).Current)
End Sub
```

LISTVIEW OUTPUT

Example program CustomerListView, shown in Figure 12.2, is similar to program CustomerGrid except it displays its results in a ListView control rather than in a DataGrid.

Figure 12.2
Program CustomerListView displays query–by–example results in a ListView control.

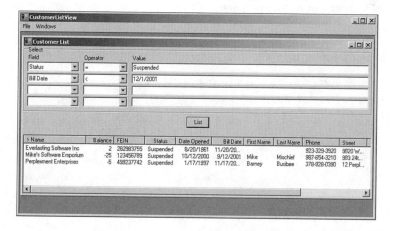

Program CustomerListView works in much the same way as program CustomerGrid so relatively little of its code is shown here. The code the programs use to initialize their forms, build a SQL SELECT statement, and execute the query is the same. The major differences lie in how the programs display their results.

The CustomerListView program uses a ListView control and that makes two large differences in how the program works. First, unlike the DataGrid control, a ListView control does not bind automatically to a data source such as a DataTable. That means the program must copy the data into the ListView itself. Second, the ListView does not automatically provide the same sorting capabilities as the DataGrid so the program needs to do a little more work to let the user sort by the control's columns.

The following sections describe the most interesting code used by program CustomerListView in detail.

SORTING RECORDS

The way in which a ListView's rows are sorted depends on its `ListViewItemSorter` property. This property gets or sets a reference to an object that implements the `IComparer` interface. That interface defines a `Compare` method that the ListView uses when it needs to sort its items.

The `ListViewSorter` class, shown in Listing 12.5, implements this interface. Its `SortColumn` property tells the object which ListView column the user clicked. If the user clicked the first column, the `Compare` method calls the `CompareItems` method, passing it the text displayed by the two ListView items.

Each row in the ListView represents an item followed by subitems. If the user clicked a column other than the first, the program must sort the data using the items' subitems. In that case, the `ListViewSorter` object calls its `CompareItems` method passing it the text displayed by the selected subitems.

The `CompareItems` method uses `StrComp` to compare the text values it is passed. If the control is sorting in ascending order, the method uses `StrComp` to compare the two strings. It returns -1 if the first string is smaller, 1 if it is larger, and 0 of the two strings have the same value. If the control is sorting in descending order, CompareItems reverses the sign of `StrComp`'s result.

When the program loads, it creates an instance of the `ListViewSorter` class and keeps a reference to it. Later, it changes this object's `SortColumn` value to change the list's sort order.

When the user clicks one of the ListView's column headers, the control's `ColumnClick` event handler executes. This routine calls subroutine `SetSortIndicator` to remove the string "> " or "< " from the header of the column that is currently being used for sorting.

The event handler then compares the current sort column to the column the user clicked. If the columns are the same, the program switches the ListView control's `Sorting` property from ascending to descending or vice versa. That automatically makes the control re-sort its data using the `ListViewSorter` object.

If the new sort column is different from the current one, the program examines the ListView's `SortOrder`. If the current `SortOrder` is ascending, the program calls the control's `Sort` method to make it re-sort its data. If the current `SortOrder` is descending, the program changes `SortOrder` to ascending, which automatically makes the control re-sort its data.

Finally, the event handler calls `SetSortIndicator` to add the text "> " to the column's header if the sort is ascending and "< " to the column's header if the sort is descending. This gives the user a visible indication of the column and direction of sort.

Subroutine `SetSortIndicator` removes the initial "> " or "< " from a column's header if such a string is present, and then adds the new string.

LISTING 12.5 THIS CODE ALLOWS THE CustomerListView PROGRAM TO SORT ITS RESULTS

```
' A class to sort ListView items.
Private Class ListViewSorter
    Implements IComparer

    Public SortColumn As Integer

    Public Sub New(ByVal sort_column As Integer)
        SortColumn = sort_column
    End Sub

    Public Overridable Function Compare( _
      ByVal object1 As Object, ByVal object2 As Object) As Integer _
    Implements IComparer.Compare
        Dim item1 As ListViewItem
        Dim item2 As ListViewItem

        ' Convert the objects into ListViewItems.
        item1 = object1
        item2 = object2

        ' See if this is the first column.
        If SortColumn = 0 Then
            ' Compare the items themselves.
            Return CompareItems( _
                item1.Text, _
                item2.Text, _
                item1.ListView.Sorting)
        Else
            ' Compare subitems.
            Return CompareItems( _
                item1.SubItems(SortColumn).Text, _
                item2.SubItems(SortColumn).Text, _
                item1.ListView.Sorting)
        End If
    End Function

    ' Compare the two text values. A fancier version
    ' of the program would compare numeric values
    ' numerically and string values alphabetically.
    Private Function CompareItems(ByVal text1 As String, _
      ByVal text2 As String, ByVal sort_order As SortOrder) As Integer
        If sort_order = SortOrder.Ascending Then
            Return StrComp(text1, text2)
        Else
            Return -StrComp(text1, text2)
        End If
    End Function
End Class

' The ListView column on which we are sorting.
Private m_ListSorter As ListViewSorter

' Initialize the operator ComboBoxes.
Private Sub frmRecordList_Load(ByVal sender As System.Object, _
  ByVal e As System.EventArgs) Handles MyBase.Load
```

PART

I

CH

12

LISTING 12.5   CONTINUED

```
    ' Code omitted...

    ' Select whole rows.
    lvwResults.FullRowSelect = True
    lvwResults.View = View.Details
    lvwResults.MultiSelect = False

    ' Make a new ListView item sorter.
    m_ListSorter = New ListViewSorter(0)
    lvwResults.ListViewItemSorter = m_ListSorter
    lvwResults.Sorting = SortOrder.Ascending
End Sub

' Sort by the clicked column.
Private Sub lvwResults_ColumnClick(ByVal sender As Object, _
  ByVal e As System.Windows.Forms.ColumnClickEventArgs) _
  Handles lvwResults.ColumnClick
    ' Remove the previous sorting indicator.
    SetSortIndicator(m_ListSorter.SortColumn, "")

    ' Set the sort order.
    If m_ListSorter.SortColumn = e.Column Then
        ' It's the same column. Switch the sort order.
        If lvwResults.Sorting = SortOrder.Ascending Then
            lvwResults.Sorting = SortOrder.Descending
        Else
            lvwResults.Sorting = SortOrder.Ascending
        End If
    Else
        ' It's a new column. Start with ascending.
        m_ListSorter.SortColumn = e.Column
        If lvwResults.Sorting = SortOrder.Ascending Then
            ' Make the control resort.
            lvwResults.Sort()
        Else
            ' This makes the control resort.
            lvwResults.Sorting = SortOrder.Ascending
        End If
    End If

    ' Add the new sorting indicator.
    If lvwResults.Sorting = SortOrder.Ascending Then
        SetSortIndicator(m_ListSorter.SortColumn, "> ")
    Else
        SetSortIndicator(m_ListSorter.SortColumn, "< ")
    End If
End Sub

' Set a textual sort indicator for a column.
Private Sub SetSortIndicator(ByVal col As Integer, ByVal indicator As String)
    Dim txt As String

    ' Remove the previous indicator if any.
    txt = lvwResults.Columns(col).Text
    If txt.Substring(0, 2) = "> " Or txt.Substring(0, 2) = "< " _
  Then txt = txt.Substring(2)
```

Listing 12.5   Continued
```
    ' Add the new indicator.
    lvwResults.Columns(col).Text = indicator & txt
End Sub
```

DisplayResults

Subroutine `DisplayResults`, shown in Listing 12.6, is different from the version used by program CustomerGrid. This routine begins by clearing the program's `ListView` control. It loops through its field information looking for fields that it should display. For each visible field, `DisplayResults` adds the field's display name to the `ListView`'s column header collection.

Next the subroutine resets the `ListViewSorter` object's `SortColumn` value to 0. This sorts the new list by the first column. If it did not do this, the program could get confused when it created new output rows. When it initially creates a row, the `ListView` only has the row's primary value and no values for its subitems. At that point, the control will try to position the new item in its list. If the `ListViewSorter` tries to sort using a subitem that does not yet exist, the program crashes. By resetting the `SortColumn` to 0, the program ensures that this initial sort will succeed.

Next, the program loops through the rows returned by its database query. For each row, the program finds the first field that should be displayed and it adds that field's value to the `ListView`. The program saves a reference to the item's DataRow in the new item's `Tag` property for later use.

The program then loops through the remaining fields looking for other fields that it should display. For each visible field, the program adds the field's value to the primary value as a subitem.

Listing 12.6   This Code Displays the Program's Results

```
' Display the DataTable's data in the ListView.
Private Sub DisplayResults()
    Dim data_table As DataTable = m_DataSet.Tables(0)
    Dim row As Integer
    Dim col As Integer
    Dim column_header As ColumnHeader
    Dim data_row As DataRow
    Dim new_item As ListViewItem
    Dim i As Integer

    ' Sort on the first column ascending.
    lvwResults.Clear()

    ' Add the column headers.
    For i = 1 To m_FieldInfos.Count
        ' See if we should display this field.
        If m_FieldInfos(i).IsDisplayField Then
            ' Display this field.
            column_header = New ColumnHeader()
            column_header.Text = m_FieldInfos(i).DisplayName
```

LISTING 12.6   CONTINUED

```
                ' Set the field's alignment.
                column_header.TextAlign = m_FieldInfos(i).FieldAlignment

                lvwResults.Columns.Add(column_header)
            End If
        Next i.

        ' Sort on the first column ascending.
        m_ListSorter.SortColumn = 0
        SetSortIndicator(m_ListSorter.SortColumn, "> ")
        lvwResults.Sorting = SortOrder.Ascending

        ' Add the rows of data.
        For row = 0 To data_table.Rows.Count - 1
            data_row = data_table.Rows(row)

            ' Find the first displayed field.
            For i = 1 To m_FieldInfos.Count
                If m_FieldInfos(i).IsDisplayField Then Exit For
            Next i
            If i > m_FieldInfos.Count Then Exit For

            ' Add the first field.
            new_item = lvwResults.Items.Add("" & data_row.Item(i - 1))
            new_item.Tag = data_row

            ' Add the subitems.
            For i = i + 1 To m_FieldInfos.Count
                If m_FieldInfos(i).IsDisplayField Then
                    new_item.SubItems.Add("" & data_row.Item(i - 1))
                End If
            Next i
        Next row

        Me.MdiParent.Cursor = Cursors.Default
    End Sub.
```

RAISING THE RecordSelected EVENT

When the user double-clicks on the DataGrid in program CustomerGrid, the program uses the DataGrid control's binding context to determine which row was clicked. Because the ListView in program CustomerListView is not data bound, it has no binding context.

To replace this functionality, program CustomerListView stores a reference to a DataRow in each ListView item's Tag property. When the user double-clicks on a row, the program raises the RecordSelected event, passing it the Tag property of the selected row. The main program can then use the selected DataRow for the record that the user selected:

```
' We raise this event to tell the main program that
' the user has selected a record.
Public Event RecordSelected(ByVal form_id As String, ByVal data_row As DataRow)
```

```
' The user has double-clicked a row.
' Display the corresponding record.
Private Sub lvwResults_DoubleClick(ByVal sender As Object, _
   ByVal e As System.EventArgs) Handles lvwResults.DoubleClick
      RaiseEvent RecordSelected(m_FormId, _
         lvwResults.SelectedItems(0).Tag)
End Sub
```

SUMMARY

Programs CustomerGrid and CustomerListView enable you to add a query-by-example feature to your programs quickly and easily. You could streamline these programs by making them gather information from the database directly. For example, they could query the database to learn which fields are contained in a table and how they should be formatted. Although the current implementations require a bit more initialization than necessary, they also give you a lot of flexibility. They let you select data from more than one table, specifying your own join conditions, ORDER BY clauses, and even GROUP BY clauses when necessary.

You may find improvements you can make to these programs, but they give you a solid framework for building useful record selection forms.

CHAPTER 13

DISCOVERING DATABASE STRUCTURE

When you design and build a database, you can keep a record of the database's structure. If you use database design tools, those tools should provide a record of the structure for you. If you use SQL scripts to create the database's tables, you can keep copies of the scripts so you can later see how the tables are built.

In some projects, however, you do not have total control over the database. Someone else may be in charge of the database and that person might change the table structure without telling you. You may have lost the database design or you may be required to work from a legacy database that has little or no documentation. Sometimes it may just be nice to confirm that the database thinks its structure is the same as the structure you think it should have.

SQL Server provides a large collection of stored procedures that describe the structure of servers, databases, tables, and the relationships between tables. You can use those stored procedures to learn about the data environment. You can run them either in your own programs or you can use the RunScript program described in Chapter 6, "Database Connections," to execute them.

You can also use the database objects provided by Visual Studio to learn a lot about a database's structure. For example, the SqlDataReader object's GetSchemaTable method returns a DataTable describing the fields selected by the SqlDataReader.

This chapter explains methods you can use to identify the tables in a database, the fields in those tables, and the relationships between the tables.

LEARNING ABOUT SERVERS

SQL Server provides several stored procedures for learning about a database server. The following sections describe stored procedures that provide this kind of information.

sp_server_info

The SQL Server sp_server_info stored procedure lists information about a server. After connecting to a database server, the program simply executes the SQL statement:

```
sp_server_info
```

The stored procedure returns a series of records with three fields: attribute_id, attribute_name, and attribute_value. The following text shows this procedure's output on the server used to test this book's example programs. Some of the simpler lines give the name of the DBMS (Database Management System) and the DBMS version:

```
 1  DBMS_NAME                    Microsoft SQL Server
 2  DBMS_VER                     Microsoft SQL Server  2000 - 8.00.194 (Intel X86)
    Aug  6 2000 00:57:48
    Copyright (c) 1988-2000 Microsoft Corporation
    Desktop Engine on Windows NT 5.0 (Build 2195: Service Pack 2)

10  OWNER_TERM                   owner
11  TABLE_TERM                   table
12  MAX_OWNER_NAME_LENGTH        128
13  TABLE_LENGTH                 128
14  MAX_QUAL_LENGTH              128
15  COLUMN_LENGTH                128
16  IDENTIFIER_CASE              MIXED
17  TX_ISOLATION                 2
18  COLLATION_SEQ                charset=iso_1 sort_order=nocase_iso charset_num=1
sort_order_num=52
19  SAVEPOINT_SUPPORT            Y
20  MULTI_RESULT_SETS            Y
22  ACCESSIBLE_TABLES            Y
100 USERID_LENGTH                128
101 QUALIFIER_TERM               database
102 NAMED_TRANSACTIONS           Y
103 SPROC_AS_LANGUAGE            Y
104 ACCESSIBLE_SPROC             Y
105 MAX_INDEX_COLS               16
106 RENAME_TABLE                 Y
107 RENAME_COLUMN                Y
108 DROP_COLUMN                  Y
109 INCREASE_COLUMN_LENGTH       Y
110 DDL_IN_TRANSACTION           Y
111 DESCENDING_INDEXES           Y
112 SP_RENAME                    Y
113 REMOTE_SPROC                 Y
500 SYS_SPROC_VERSION            8.00.178
```

sp_helpserver

The `sp_helpserver` stored procedure returns a single record giving additional information about the current server. After connecting to the server, the program executes the SQL statement:

```
sp_helpserver
```

Table 13.1 shows the values returned during one database session.

TABLE 13.1   RESULTS FROM THE sp_helpserver STORED PROCEDURE

Field Name	Value
name	BENDER\NetSDK
network_name	BENDER\NetSDK
status	rpc,rpc out,use remote collation

TABLE 13.1   CONTINUED

Field Name	Value
id	0
collation_name	NULL
connect_timeout	0
query_timeout	0

sp_who

The sp_who stored procedure returns information on the users and processes connected to the server. The following text shows some typical output generated by the RunScript program described in Chapter 6. The RunScript program appears as the second-to-last entry. You can see from the output that the program was connected to the OrderEntry database and was running the SQL SELECT command:

```
spid ecid status             loginame hostname  blk   dbname      cmd
==== ==== ================   ======== ========  ===== ==========  ================
   1    0 background         sa                  0     NULL        LAZY WRITER
   2    0 sleeping           sa                  0     NULL        LOG WRITER
   3    0 background         sa                  0     master      SIGNAL HANDLER
   4    0 background         sa                  0     NULL        LOCK MONITOR
   5    0 background         sa                  0     master      TASK MANAGER
   6    0 background         sa                  0     master      TASK MANAGER
   7    0 sleeping           sa                  0     NULL        CHECKPOINT SLEEP
   8    0 background         sa                  0     master      TASK MANAGER
   9    0 background         sa                  0     master      TASK MANAGER
  10    0 background         sa                  0     master      TASK MANAGER
  11    0 background         sa                  0     master      TASK MANAGER
  51    0 runnable           sa       BENDER     0     OrderEntry  SELECT
  52    0 sleeping           sa       BENDER     0     master      AWAITING COMMAND
```

LEARNING ABOUT DATABASES

In SQL Server, a single server can contain many databases. The following sections explain SQL Server stored procedures that return information about those databases.

sp_databases

The sp_databases stored procedure lists the databases available on a server. After connecting to the server, the program executes this SQL statement:

```
sp_databases
```

The following text shows the results of this statement on the book's test server. The database named master contains information about the server, such as server user login information. Most of the other databases shown here are used by the examples in this book:

```
DATABASE_NAME    DATABASE_SIZE REMARKS
=============== ============= =======
Contacts                 3072 NULL
Customers                3072 NULL
master                  12480 NULL
model                    1152 NULL
msdb                    13312 NULL
MultiUserOrders          3072 NULL
Numbers                  3072 NULL
OrderEntry               3072 NULL
Orders                   3072 NULL
tempdb                   8704 NULL
TestAccounts             3072 NULL
TestRoles                3072 NULL
TestScores               3072 NULL
TestSecurity             3072 NULL
TestViews                3072 NULL
Trans                    3072 NULL
```

sp_helpdb

The sp_helpdb stored procedure returns additional information about the server's databases. The following text shows the results returned for the book's test server. The status field has been truncated because it is very long for some databases:

```
name             db_size        owner dbid created      status
=============== ============= ===== ==== =========== ====================
Contacts          3.00 MB sa       7 Jan  3 2002 NULL
Customers         3.00 MB sa      13 Dec 12 2001 NULL
master           12.19 MB sa       1 Aug  6 2000 Status=ONLINE, ...
model             1.13 MB sa       3 Aug  6 2000 Status=ONLINE, ...
msdb             13.00 MB sa       4 Aug  6 2000 Status=ONLINE, ...
MultiUserOrders   3.00 MB sa      16 Jan 12 2002 NULL
Numbers           3.00 MB sa       9 Dec  5 2001 NULL
OrderEntry        3.00 MB sa       5 Nov  5 2001 Status=ONLINE, ...
Orders            3.00 MB sa      15 Jan  9 2002 NULL
tempdb            8.50 MB sa       2 Jan 16 2002 Status=ONLINE, ...
TestAccounts      3.00 MB sa       8 Dec  3 2001 NULL
TestRoles         3.00 MB sa      10 Dec  7 2001 Status=ONLINE, ...
TestScores        3.00 MB sa       6 Nov  7 2001 Status=ONLINE, ...
TestSecurity      3.00 MB sa      11 Dec  7 2001 Status=ONLINE, ...
TestViews         3.00 MB sa      12 Dec  7 2001 Status=ONLINE, ...
Trans             3.00 MB sa      14 Dec 28 2001 Status=ONLINE, ...
```

The following text shows a typical status value for one record. In the results returned by sp_helpdb, this is one long string. It is shown here with each value on a separate line so it is easier to read:

```
Updateability=READ_WRITE,
UserAccess=MULTI_USER,
Recovery=SIMPLE,
Version=539,
Collation=SQL_Latin1_General_CP1_CI_AS,
SQLSortOrder=52,
IsAutoClose,
IsAutoShrink,
IsTornPageDetectionEnabled,
```

```
IsAutoCreateStatistics,
IsAutoUpdateStatistics
```

sp_helpfile

The `sp_helpfile` stored procedure returns file information about the database that the program is currently using. The following text shows the results returned when a program was connected to a database named OrderEntry. The results show the database's data and log files, their current and maximum sizes, the amounts by which they are enlarged when they are too small, and whether they are used to store data or log entries. These values correspond to the parameters used by the SQL CREATE DATABASE statement:

```
name      fileid  filename                 filegroup  size     maxsize   growth   usage
========  ======  =======================  =========  =======  ========  =======  =========
oe_data        1  C:\Temp\OrderEntry.mdf   PRIMARY    2048 KB  10240 KB  2048 KB  data only
oe_log         2  C:\Temp\OrderEntry.ldf   NULL       1024 KB  5120 KB   1024 KB  log only
```

For more information on CREATE DATABASE, see Appendix A, "SQL."

sp_spaceused

The `sp_spaceused` stored procedure gives information about the space used by the database the program is using. The following output shows that this database reserved 1136KB, used 424KB for its data and 608KB for its indexes, and had 104KB unused:

```
reserved  data    index_size  unused
========  ======  ==========  ======
1136 KB   424 KB  608 KB      104 KB
```

sp_help

The `sp_help` stored procedure gives information about a database object. For example, the following SQL statement retrieves information about the `CustomerOrders` table in the current database:

```
sp_help CustomerOrders
```

The following text shows the output produced by this statement:

```
Table is referenced by foreign key
===========================================================
OrderEntry.dbo.OrderDates: FK__OrderDate__Order__092A4EB5
OrderEntry.dbo.OrderItems: FK__OrderItem__Order__064DE20A
```

The output states that the `CustomerOrders` table is referenced by two foreign key constraints in the `OrderDates` and `OrderItems` tables. Those constraints were created without explicit names so the database created the somewhat ugly names shown here.

LEARNING ABOUT TABLES

SQL Server provides several stored procedures that list the tables available in a database and that describe how those tables are related. The following sections describe these procedures.

sp_tables

The sp_tables stored procedure lists the tables in a database. The following text shows the output generated by this procedure for the database OrderEntry:

```
TABLE_QUALIFIER  TABLE_OWNER  TABLE_NAME           TABLE_TYPE     REMARKS
===============  ===========  ==================   ============   =======
OrderEntry       dbo          syscolumns           SYSTEM TABLE   NULL
OrderEntry       dbo          syscomments          SYSTEM TABLE   NULL
OrderEntry       dbo          sysdepends           SYSTEM TABLE   NULL
OrderEntry       dbo          sysfilegroups        SYSTEM TABLE   NULL
OrderEntry       dbo          sysfiles             SYSTEM TABLE   NULL
OrderEntry       dbo          sysfiles1            SYSTEM TABLE   NULL
OrderEntry       dbo          sysforeignkeys       SYSTEM TABLE   NULL
OrderEntry       dbo          sysfulltextcatalogs  SYSTEM TABLE   NULL
OrderEntry       dbo          sysfulltextnotify    SYSTEM TABLE   NULL
OrderEntry       dbo          sysindexes           SYSTEM TABLE   NULL
OrderEntry       dbo          sysindexkeys         SYSTEM TABLE   NULL
OrderEntry       dbo          sysmembers           SYSTEM TABLE   NULL
OrderEntry       dbo          sysobjects           SYSTEM TABLE   NULL
OrderEntry       dbo          syspermissions       SYSTEM TABLE   NULL
OrderEntry       dbo          sysproperties        SYSTEM TABLE   NULL
OrderEntry       dbo          sysprotects          SYSTEM TABLE   NULL
OrderEntry       dbo          sysreferences        SYSTEM TABLE   NULL
OrderEntry       dbo          systypes             SYSTEM TABLE   NULL
OrderEntry       dbo          sysusers             SYSTEM TABLE   NULL
OrderEntry       dbo          AddressTypes         TABLE          NULL
OrderEntry       dbo          Cities               TABLE          NULL
OrderEntry       dbo          CustomerAddresses    TABLE          NULL
OrderEntry       dbo          CustomerOrders       TABLE          NULL
OrderEntry       dbo          Customers            TABLE          NULL
OrderEntry       dbo          DateTypes            TABLE          NULL
OrderEntry       dbo          dtproperties         TABLE          NULL
OrderEntry       dbo          Inventory            TABLE          NULL
OrderEntry       dbo          OrderDates           TABLE          NULL
OrderEntry       dbo          OrderItems           TABLE          NULL
OrderEntry       dbo          Pupils               TABLE          NULL
OrderEntry       dbo          States               TABLE          NULL
OrderEntry       dbo          TestScores           TABLE          NULL
OrderEntry       dbo          Users                TABLE          NULL
OrderEntry       dbo          Zips                 TABLE          NULL
OrderEntry       dbo          sysconstraints       VIEW           NULL
OrderEntry       dbo          syssegments          VIEW           NULL
```

Notice that this output contains several system tables with names beginning with "sys." These tables describe various objects in the database. For example, the sysusers table gives information about users and roles defined in the database. You can query these tables directly to get information about the database's objects. For instance, the following SQL statement gets a list of the users and roles defined in the database:

```
SELECT name FROM sysusers
```

Sometimes querying the system tables directly is more convenient than using the system stored procedures.

sp_depends

The sp_depends stored procedure lists the objects that depend on a database object. For example, it lists the views and procedures that depend on a table. The following SQL script creates a view named CustomerList that selects data from the Customers and CustomerAddresses tables. It then uses sp_depends to see what objects depend on the CustomerAddresses table:

```
USE OrderEntry;

CREATE VIEW CustomerList
AS SELECT CustomerName, CustomerAddresses.* FROM Customers, CustomerAddresses
WHERE Customers.CustomerId = CustomerAddresses.CustomerId;

sp_depends CustomerAddresses;
```

The following output shows that the CustomerList view depends on the CustomerAddresses table:

```
name              type
================= ====
dbo.CustomerList  view
```

LEARNING ABOUT RELATIONSHIPS

The following sections describe SQL Server stored procedures that describe relationships between tables.

sp_pkeys

The sp_pkeys stored procedure gives information about a table's primary key. The following text shows the output of the SQL statement sp_pkeys CustomerOrders. The PK_NAME column is truncated to fit on the page.

```
TABLE_QUALIFIER TABLE_OWNER TABLE_NAME      COLUMN_NAME KEY_SEQ PK_NAME
=============== =========== =============== =========== ======= ===================
OrderEntry      dbo         CustomerOrders  OrderId           1 PK__CustomerOrd...
```

This output indicates that the CustomerOrders table's primary key is the single field OrderId. The key's full name is PK__CustomerOrders__027D5126.

sp_fkeys

The sp_fkeys stored procedure gives information about a table's foreign keys. This procedure returns quite a few columns describing the table's foreign keys. Two of the most useful columns are PKTABLE_NAME and PKCOLUMN_NAME, which give the name of the key's table and fields in the table used in the sp_fkeys statement. The FKTABLE_NAME and FKCOLUMN_NAME columns give the name of the table and fields in the foreign key table.

For example, in the OrderEntry database the OrderDates and OrderItems tables both have OrderId fields that refer to the CustomerOrders table's OrderId field. The PKTABLE_NAME,

PKCOLUMN_NAME, FKTABLE_NAME, and FKCOLUMN_NAME values returned by the SQL statement sp_fkeys CustomerOrders are:

```
PKTABLE_NAME      PKCOLUMN_NAME  FKTABLE_NAME  FKCOLUMN_NAME
===============   =============  ============  =============
CustomerOrders    OrderId        OrderDates    OrderId
CustomerOrders    OrderId        OrderItems    OrderId
```

The sp_fkeys stored procedure returns several other values, including the tables' owners, the keys' update and delete rules, and the keys' names, but the table and column names are the easiest values to understand.

sp_helpconstraint

The sp_helpconstraint stored procedure returns information about a table's constraints. The following output shows the results of the SQL statement sp_helpconstraint CustomerOrders. The output indicates that two foreign keys reference the CustomerOrders table:

```
Table is referenced by foreign key
========================================================
OrderEntry.dbo.OrderDates: FK__OrderDate__Order__092A4EB5
OrderEntry.dbo.OrderItems: FK__OrderItem__Order__064DE20A
```

The SQL statement sp_helpconstraint OrderDates generates a very different result. The OrderDates table's DateType and OrderId fields refer to the fields DatesTypes.DateType and CustomerOrders.OrderId. In this case, sp_helpconstraint returns the constraint type, constraint name, delete action, update action, enabled status, replication status, and keys describing the constraints.

sp_helpindex

The sp_helpindex stored procedure gives information about a table's indexes. For example, the following output shows the results from the SQL statement sp_helpindex CustomerOrders. This result describes the index that the database automatically created for the table's primary key:

```
index_name                          index_description
index_keys
===========================  ==================================================
==========
PK__CustomerOrders__027D5126 clustered, unique, primary key located on PRIMARY
OrderId
```

LEARNING ABOUT FIELDS

If you know that a table exists in a database, learning about the fields it contains is relatively easy. The following sections describe several ways a program can obtain information about the table's fields.

FILLING A DATATABLE

One method to get information about a table's fields is to use a data adapter to fill a DataTable with the results of the query SELECT * FROM *table_name*. The DataTable object's Columns collection contains information about the table even if the query returns no records.

Example program TableColumns, shown in Figure 13.1, demonstrates this technique. The program uses the code in Listing 13.1 to display information about a table's columns.

Figure 13.1
Program TableColumns uses a data adapter to get information about a table's fields.

The code uses a data adapter to fill a DataTable with the results of a query of the form SELECT TOP 0 FROM CustomerAddresses. The TOP 0 clause makes the command return the first zero rows from the database, minimizing the amount of data the database must send back to the program.

The code loops through the DataTable's Columns collection, examining its DataColumn objects to learn about the columns. Although the DataTable object contains no rows, its Columns collection describes the data it would have returned if the SELECT statement had selected any rows.

As you can see from the code, the DataColumn object gives quite a bit of information about the database field it represents, including its name, data type, caption, default, and maximum length. It also tells whether the field allows Null values, is an auto-incrementing field (an IDENTITY field), is read-only, and whether the field's values must be unique.

Program TableColumns connects to a specific server hard coded into the program. You could modify the code to connect the program to your server. Alternatively you could make the user enter the name of the server and use it to build the database connect string at run-time.

PART

I

CH

13

LISTING 13.1   PROGRAM TABLECOLUMNS USES THIS CODE TO DESCRIBE A TABLE'S FIELDS

```
Private Sub btnGo_Click(ByVal sender As System.Object, _
  ByVal e As System.EventArgs) Handles btnGo.Click
    txtStructure.Text = Nothing
    Cursor = Cursors.WaitCursor
    Refresh()

    ' Make a SqlDataAdapter to execute the query.
    Dim select_string As String = _
        "SELECT TOP 0 * FROM " & cboTableName.Text
    Dim data_adapter As New SqlDataAdapter(select_string, CONNECT_STRING)

    ' Execute the query.
    Dim data_table As New DataTable()
    data_adapter.Fill(data_table)

    ' Display the result.
    Dim txt As String
    Dim data_column As DataColumn
    Dim default_value As String
    For Each data_column In data_table.Columns
        If data_column.DefaultValue Is DBNull.Value Then
            default_value = "<null>"
        Else
            default_value = data_column.DefaultValue.ToString
        End If
        txt = txt & _
            "Name:         " & data_column.ColumnName & vbCrLf & _
            "  Type:         " & data_column.DataType.FullName & vbCrLf & _
            "  AllowDBNull:  " & data_column.AllowDBNull & vbCrLf & _
            "  AutoIncrement:" & data_column.AutoIncrement & vbCrLf & _
            "  Caption:      " & data_column.Caption & vbCrLf & _
            "  Default:      " & default_value & vbCrLf & _
            "  MaxLength:    " & data_column.MaxLength & vbCrLf & _
            "  ReadOnly:     " & data_column.ReadOnly & vbCrLf & _
            "  Unique:       " & data_column.Unique & vbCrLf & _
            vbCrLf
    Next data_column
    txtStructure.Text = txt

    Cursor = Cursors.Default
End Sub
```

Program TableColumns fills a DataTable with zero rows of data to learn about a table's fields. Perhaps a more typical use of this technique is to learn about the columns returned by a query that selects rows. After the program fills a DataTable with data, it can examine its Columns collection to learn about the query's fields. This works whether the query selects all the fields from a database table, only some of the fields, or fields from multiple tables.

Note also that the DataTable's Columns collection is indexed by the column names. If you want to learn about a particular column, you can use its name to find its DataColumn element as shown in the following code:

```
' Fill the DataTable.
    :
' Get information about the Salary field.
Dim salary_data_column As DataColumn = data_table.Columns("Salary")
```

FILLING A SqlDataReader

A program can use a data adapter to load data from a database into a DataTable. The previous section shows how to use the DataTable's Columns collection to learn about the loaded fields.

A program can also load data using a SqlDataReader object. The program creates a SqlCommand object and uses its ExecuteReader method to create a SqlDataReader object that represents the results. It can then use the reader to move through the returned rows processing the data.

A SqlDataReader object can also provide information about the returned fields much as a DataTable object can. Example program TableColumns2, shown in Figure 13.2, demonstrates this technique. The program uses the code in Listing 13.2 to list information about a table's columns.

Figure 13.2
Program TableColumns2 uses a SqlDataReader object to get information about a table's fields.

The code creates and opens a connection to the database. It then creates a SqlCommand object and uses it to execute a SELECT statement that selects all the fields from the selected database table. The TOP 0 clause makes the command return only the first zero records selected by the statement, minimizing the amount of data the database must send back to the program.

The code uses the SqlCommand object's ExecuteReader method to retrieve a SqlReader object representing the results. Although this object contains no rows, its GetName and GetDataTypeName functions return the names and data types of the columns the query would have returned if it had selected any rows. The code loops through these values, adding them to its output.

Like program TableColumns, program TableColumns2 connects to a specific server hard coded into the program. You could modify the code to connect the program to your server or build a connect string at runtime connecting the program to your server.

LISTING 13.2 PROGRAM TABLECOLUMNS2 USES A SqlDataReader TO LEARN ABOUT A TABLE'S FIELDS

```
Private Sub btnGo_Click(ByVal sender As System.Object, _
  ByVal e As System.EventArgs) Handles btnGo.Click
    txtStructure.Text = ""
    Cursor = Cursors.WaitCursor
    Refresh()

    ' Create and open the SqlConnection.
    Dim sql_connection As New SqlConnection(CONNECT_STRING)
    sql_connection.Open()

    ' Attach a SqlCommand to the SqlConnnection.
    Dim sql_command As New SqlCommand( _
        "SELECT TOP 0 * FROM " & cboTableName.Text, _
        sql_connection)

    ' Execute the SqlCommand and get the result.
    Dim sql_reader As SqlDataReader
    sql_reader = sql_command.ExecuteReader()

    ' Display the result.
    Dim txt As String
    Dim i As Integer
    For i = 0 To sql_reader.FieldCount - 1
        txt = txt & Format(sql_reader.GetName(i), "{0,-20}") & _
            sql_reader.GetDataTypeName(i) & vbCrLf
    Next i

    txtStructure.Text = txt

    ' Close the connection.
    sql_connection.Close()

    Cursor = Cursors.Default
End Sub
```

USING GetSchemaTable

The SqlDataReader object provides only two methods for learning about a returned field: GetName and GetDataTypeName. This is much less information than is available using the DataColumn objects provided by a DataTable. However, the SqlDataReader's GetSchemaTable method returns a DataTable filled with information about the SqlDataReader's selected fields. Example program TableColumns3, shown in Figure 13.3, uses this DataTable to display information about a table.

Listing 13.3 shows program TableColumns3's most interesting code. The program creates a SqlDataReader object exactly as program TableColumns2 does. It then calls that object's GetSchemaTable method to get a DataTable containing information about the fields selected. The program binds the DataTable to a DataGrid control to display the results automatically.

Figure 13.3
Program
TableColumns3 uses a
`SqlDataReader`'s
`GetSchemaTable`
method to obtain
information about a
table's columns.

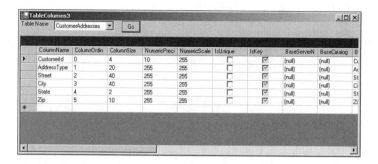

Like programs TableColumns and TableColumns2, program TableColumns3 connects to a specific server hard coded into the program. You could modify the code to connect the program to your server or build a connect string at runtime connecting the program to your server.

LISTING 13.3   PROGRAM TABLECOLUMNS3 USES THIS CODE TO DISPLAY INFORMATION ABOUT A TABLE'S FIELDS

```
Private Sub btnGo_Click(ByVal sender As System.Object, _
  ByVal e As System.EventArgs) Handles btnGo.Click
    grdStructure.DataSource = Nothing
    Cursor = Cursors.WaitCursor
    Refresh()

    ' Create and open the SqlConnection.
    Dim sql_connection As New SqlConnection(CONNECT_STRING)
    sql_connection.Open()

    ' Attach a SqlCommand to the SqlConnnection.
    Dim sql_command As New SqlCommand( _
        "SELECT TOP 0 * FROM " & cboTableName.Text, _
        sql_connection)

    ' Execute the SqlCommand and get the result.
    Dim sql_reader As SqlDataReader
    sql_reader = sql_command.ExecuteReader()

    ' Get a DataTable describing the columns.
    Dim data_table As DataTable = sql_reader.GetSchemaTable()

    ' Attach this table to a DataGrid.
    grdStructure.DataSource = data_table

    ' Close the connection.
    sql_connection.Close()

    Cursor = Cursors.Default
End Sub
```

Whether you should get field information using a DataTable's `Columns` collection or using a SqlDataReader's `GetSchemaTable` method depends largely on how you want to use the

PART

I

CH

13

information. A DataTable's `Columns` collection is indexed by the field names so you can easily locate information about a particular field. `GetSchemaTable` returns a DataTable that you can bind to a DataGrid, making reporting easy.

sp_columns

The `sp_columns` stored procedure lists information about a table's columns. The following SQL script invokes the `sp_columns` procedure for the `OrderEntry` database's `CustomerAddresses` table:

```
USE OrderEntry;
sp_columns CustomerAddresses;
```

The result contains too many columns to easily display here. Some of the more interesting fields returned by `sp_columns` include column name, data type code, data type name, precision, length, and a flag indicating whether the field can accept `Null` values.

sp_column_privileges

The `sp_column_privileges` stored procedure gives information about a table's column privileges. The following statement lists the column privileges for the `CustomerAddresses` table:

```
sp_column_privileges CustomerAddresses;
```

The results include the table's database, owner, and name. For each of the table's columns, the results also include the column's name, the privilege granted (INSERT, SELECT, UPDATE, and so forth), the grantor and grantee, and a flag indicating whether the grantee can also grant the privilege.

META-LEARNING

SQL Server provides a couple of stored procedures that can be helpful in discovering what you can learn about. Using these methods, you can explore some of the hidden corners of the database and the server.

sp_stored_procedures

The `sp_stored_procedures` stored procedure lists the stored procedures in the current database. Unless you create stored procedures in your databases, `sp_stored_procedures` will usually return no results for them. The master database, however, is full of system-defined stored procedures. On this book's test server, `sp_stored_procedures` returned a list of 1,030 stored procedures in the master database, including all the stored procedures described in this chapter. In fact, `sp_stored_procedures` even lists itself.

The most useful value returned for each procedure is PROCEDURE_NAME. The REMARKS field would also be useful except it is `Null` for the system stored procedures.

sp_helptext

Using `sp_stored_procedures` you can get a list of the stored procedures in a database. Unless you have some idea of what a procedure is supposed to do, however, knowing its name isn't very useful. The `sp_helptext` stored procedure can help. This procedure returns the text definition of a stored procedure or function, trigger, view, or rule. Although the text won't directly tell you what the procedure is supposed to do, you can at least look at the code and try to figure it out for yourself.

For example, the following SQL script creates a view named `CustomerList` that joins information from the `Customers` and `CustomerAddresses` tables:

```
CREATE VIEW CustomerList AS
  SELECT CustomerName, CustomerAddresses.*
  FROM Customers, CustomerAddresses
  WHERE Customers.CustomerId = CustomerAddresses.CustomerId
```

After you create the `CustomerList` view, the following statement returns the exact text of this `CREATE` statement (with some extra blank lines inserted by the stored procedure):

```
sp_helptext CustomerList
```

The `sp_helptext` stored procedure is useful if you lose the definition of a view or stored procedure. It is even more useful for learning about stored procedures that you did not create. You can even use `sp_helptext` to learn about the SQL Server system stored procedures described in this chapter. For example, the following SQL script retrieves the definition of the `sp_server_info` system stored procedure described at the beginning of this chapter:

```
USE master;
sp_helptext sp_server_info;
```

The following text shows the result with some extraneous blank lines removed:

```
create proc sp_server_info (
                  @attribute_id  int = null)
as
    if @attribute_id is not null
          select *
          from master.dbo.spt_server_info
          where attribute_id = @attribute_id
    else
          select *
          from master.dbo.spt_server_info
          order by attribute_id
```

If you look at this result, you can see that the `sp_server_info` stored procedure is nothing more than a SELECT statement that pulls records from the `spt_server_info` table in the master database. If you pass the procedure a parameter, the procedure selects the record with that `attribute_id` value. If you omit the parameter, the procedure selects all the `spt_server_info` records and orders them by `attribute_id`.

Most of the other system stored procedures are much longer than `sp_server_info`. For instance, the `sp_columns` stored procedure selects information from several tables, including

PART

I

CH

13

syscolumns, so you might assume the procedure is simple. The sp_columns stored procedure actually is 195 lines long, not counting blank lines. The sp_fkeys stored procedure is 304 lines long.

Besides helping you figure out what a stored procedure does, sp_helptext can help you learn how to build stored procedures. All of the system stored procedures are complicated but they show useful techniques for examining parameters, branching, and selecting data.

sp_datatype_info

The sp_datatype_info stored procedure returns information about the database's supported data types. This procedure is usually used to convert a data type code into a data type name. The procedure also returns other information, such as the data types' precisions and the prefixes and suffixes used to delimit the data types' values.

The following text shows some of the more interesting fields returned by sp_datatype_info. From this information you can see, for example, that a text variable can have a length of up to 2,147,483,647 characters and should begin and end with a single quote. Similarly a money value should have a $ symbol prefix and no suffix:

```
TYPE_NAME            DATA_TYPE  PRECISION LITERAL_PREFIX LITERAL_SUFFIX
==================== ========= ========== ============== ==============
sql_variant             -150       8000 NULL            NULL
uniqueidentifier        -11          36 '               '
ntext                   -10   1073741823 N'              '
nvarchar                 -9        4000 N'              '
sysname                  -9         128 N'              '
nchar                    -8        4000 N'              '
bit                      -7           1 NULL            NULL
tinyint                  -6           3 NULL            NULL
tinyint identity         -6           3 NULL            NULL
bigint                   -5          19 NULL            NULL
bigint identity          -5          19 NULL            NULL
image                    -4   2147483647 0x              NULL
varbinary                -3        8000 0x              NULL
binary                   -2        8000 0x              NULL
timestamp                -2           8 0x              NULL
text                     -1   2147483647 '               '
char                      1        8000 '               '
numeric                   2          38 NULL            NULL
numeric() identity        2          38 NULL            NULL
decimal                   3          38 NULL            NULL
money                     3          19 $               NULL
smallmoney                3          10 $               NULL
decimal() identity        3          38 NULL            NULL
int                       4          10 NULL            NULL
int identity              4          10 NULL            NULL
smallint                  5           5 NULL            NULL
smallint identity         5           5 NULL            NULL
float                     6          15 NULL            NULL
real                      7           7 NULL            NULL
datetime                 11          23 '               '
smalldatetime            11          16 '               '
varchar                  12        8000 '               '
```

PROGRAM EXPLORESERVER

Example program ExploreServer, shown in Figure 13.4, uses SQL Server's stored procedures to study a server. It uses the `sp_databases` stored procedure to list the server's databases. For each database in the server, it uses `sp_tables` to list the database's tables. For each table in the databases, it uses `sp_columns` to list the table's columns.

Figure 13.4
Program
ExploreServer uses
SQL Server's system
stored procedures to
list a server's data-
bases, tables, and
columns.

Program ExploreServer uses the code shown in Listing 13.4 to display the server's structure. When the user selects the File menu's Server command, the `mnuFileServer_Click` event handler executes. This code displays a small `dlgSqlServerLogin` form to let the user enter a server name, user name, and password. If the user clicks the form's Ok button, the program calls subroutine `ExploreServer` to display information about the indicated server.

Subroutine `ExploreServer` adds a node giving the server's name to the program's TreeView control. It makes a `SqlConnection` object connected to the server and opens the connection. It uses the connection to create a `SqlCommand` object that executes the `sp_databases` stored procedure. The routine calls the `SqlCommand`'s `ExecuteReader` method to run the procedure and return the results through a `SqlDataReader` object. It loops through the records returned by the `SqlDataReader`, saving the `DATABASE_NAME` field values in a collection.

When it has finished building a list of the server's databases, `ExploreServer` closes the `SqlDataReader`. It then loops through the database names calling subroutine `ExploreDatabase` for each. When it has finished, the subroutine closes the connection to the server.

Subroutine `ExploreDatabase` adds a node to the TreeView control giving the database's name, making the new node a child of the server's node. It then makes a `SqlCommand` object that executes the SQL USE statement to select the database on the server. For example, if the

PART

I

CH

13

database's name is OrderEntry, then the `SqlCommand` object executes the statement USE
OrderEntry.

`ExploreDatabase` then resets the `SqlCommand` object so it calls the `sp_tables` stored procedure. It calls the `SqlCommand` object's `ExecuteReader` method to fetch the results via a
`SqlDataReader` object. It loops through the `SqlDataReader`'s returned records, saving the
`TABLE_NAME` values in a collection. After it finishes making a list of the tables in the database,
`ExploreDatabase` loops through them, calling subroutine `ExploreTable` to display information about each table.

Subroutine `ExploreTable` creates a new TreeView node giving the table's name. It makes the
new node a child of the database's node.

The subroutine then creates a `SqlCommand` object that invokes the `sp_columns` stored procedure. Note that this routine does not need to execute a SQL USE statement first because the
calling instance of subroutine `ExploreDatabase` already did that so the `SqlConnection` object
is still attached to the desired database.

Subroutine `ExploreTable` calls the `SqlCommand` object's `ExecuteReader` method to fetch the
results with a `SqlDataReader` object. It loops through the returned records, pulling out the
`COLUMN_NAME` and `TYPE_NAME` values. For columns of the char or varchar data type, the routine adds the column's `PRECISION` value to indicate the number of characters allowed in the
column. If the column's `IS_NULLABLE` value is not YES, the routine adds the text NOT NULL to
the column's description. Finally, the routine adds the column's description to the TreeView
control as a child node of the table's node.

You could make the program perform other tests at this point. For example, it could do
some more work to figure out which columns in the table are part of keys, indexes, and references to other tables. The ExploreServer program is fairly slow already, so you might
want to do this only for selected tables that you want to study in greater depth rather than
examining every table at this level of detail.

One more feature of program ExploreServer is worth mentioning at this point. The
`ExploreServer` and `ExploreDatabase` subroutines use a `SqlDataReader` to make lists of database and table names. They then loop through those lists processing their entries. You
might like to skip building the lists and make the code process each item as the
`SqlDataReader` encounters it. For example, as subroutine `ExploreServer` loops through the
records returned by its `SqlDataReader`, it would call subroutine `ExploreDatabase`.

Unfortunately, this is not completely straightforward. Subroutine `ExploreDatabase` uses its
own `SqlDataReader` to loop through the names of the database's tables. Meanwhile, the
`SqlDataReader` created by subroutine `ExploreServer` is still open. A `SqlConnection` object
can be associated with only one open `SqlDataReader` at a time so subroutine
`ExploreDatabase` cannot use the same `SqlConnection` to open its `SqlDataReader`. It would
need to create another connection to the database.

Similarly, subroutine `ExploreTable` uses a `SqlDataReader` to list the columns in a database
table. If subroutine `ExploreDatabase` calls `ExploreTable` as it loops through the records it

has found, subroutine ExploreTable would need to create a new database connection to manage its SqlDataReader object.

You could certainly modify program ExploreServer to use three SqlConnection objects to manage three SqlDataReaders simultaneously. This version of ExploreServer avoids that by reading all the data provided by each SqlDataReader and then closing the reader before processing its values.

LISTING 13.4   EXAMPLE PROGRAM EXPLORESERVER USES THIS CODE TO DISPLAY A SERVER'S STRUCTURE

```
' Let the user select the server.
Private Sub mnuFileServer_Click(ByVal sender As System.Object, _
  ByVal e As System.EventArgs) Handles mnuFileServer.Click
    ' Let the user select the database.
    Dim dlg As New dlgSqlServerLogin()
    If dlg.ShowDialog() = DialogResult.Cancel Then Exit Sub

    trvResults.Nodes.Clear()
    Me.Cursor = Cursors.WaitCursor
    Me.Refresh()

    ' Explore the server.
    ExploreServer(dlg.txtServer.Text, dlg.txtUserId.Text, dlg.txtPassword.Text)

    Me.Cursor = Cursors.Default
End Sub

' Display information about the server.
Private Sub ExploreServer(ByVal server_name As String, _
ByVal user_name As String, _
  ByVal user_password As String)
    ' Make a node for the server.
    Dim server_node As TreeNode = trvResults.Nodes.Add(server_name)

    Me.Text = "ExploreServer - connecting..."
    Me.Refresh()

    ' Connect to the server.
    Dim connect_string As String = _
        "User Id=" & user_name & ";" & _
        "Password=" & user_password & ";" & _
        "Data Source=" & server_name
    Dim sql_connection As New SqlConnection(connect_string)
    sql_connection.Open()

    ' Make a list of the databases.
    Dim cmd As New SqlCommand("sp_databases", sql_connection)
    Dim data_reader As SqlDataReader = cmd.ExecuteReader()
    Dim database_names As New Collection()
    Do While data_reader.Read()
        database_names.Add(data_reader.Item("DATABASE_NAME"))
    Loop
    data_reader.Close()
```

PART

I

CH

13

LISTING 13.4   CONTINUED

```
        ' Explore the databases.
        Dim database_name As String
        For Each database_name In database_names
            Me.Text = "ExploreServer - " & database_name
            Me.Refresh()
            ExploreDatabase(sql_connection, server_node, database_name)
        Next database_name

        sql_connection.Close()
        Me.Text = "ExploreServer"
End Sub

' Explore a database.
Private Sub ExploreDatabase(ByVal sql_connection As SqlConnection, _
  ByVal server_node As TreeNode, ByVal database_name As String)
        ' Add a node for the database.
        Dim database_node As TreeNode = server_node.Nodes.Add(database_name)

        ' Select the database.
        Dim cmd As New SqlCommand("USE " & database_name, sql_connection)
        cmd.ExecuteNonQuery()

        ' Make a list of the database's tables.
        cmd.CommandText = "sp_tables"
        Dim data_reader As SqlDataReader = cmd.ExecuteReader()
        Dim table_names As New Collection()
        Do While data_reader.Read()
            table_names.Add(data_reader.Item("TABLE_NAME"))
        Loop
        data_reader.Close()

        ' Explore the tables.
        Dim table_name As String
        For Each table_name In table_names
            ExploreTable(sql_connection, database_node, table_name)
        Next table_name
End Sub

' Explore a table.
Private Sub ExploreTable(ByVal sql_connection As SqlConnection, _
  ByVal database_node As TreeNode, ByVal table_name As String)
        ' Add a node for the table.
        Dim table_node As TreeNode = database_node.Nodes.Add(table_name)

        ' Make a list of the table's columns.
        Dim cmd As New SqlCommand("sp_columns " & table_name, sql_connection)
        Dim data_reader As SqlDataReader = cmd.ExecuteReader()
        Dim txt As String
        Dim type_name As String
        Do While data_reader.Read()
            ' Make a TreeView node for the column.
            type_name = data_reader.Item("TYPE_NAME")
            txt = data_reader.Item("COLUMN_NAME") & "    " & type_name
            If (type_name = "char") Or (type_name = "varchar") Then
                txt = txt & "(" & data_reader.Item("PRECISION") & ")"
            End If
```

LISTING 13.4   CONTINUED

```
        If data_reader.Item("IS_NULLABLE").ToLower <> "yes" Then
            txt = txt & " NOT NULL"
        End If

        table_node.Nodes.Add(txt)
    Loop
    data_reader.Close()
End Sub
```

PROGRAM EXPLORERELATIONS

Example program ExploreRelations uses SQL Server's stored procedures to study the relations between tables in a database. Select the File menu's Server command to pick a server and database to examine. The program loads information about the database's tables and displays it in a DataGrid control. Initially the grid is collapsed. Click on the plus sign to see a list of tables similar to the one shown in Figure 13.5.

Figure 13.5
Program ExploreRelations lists the tables in a database.

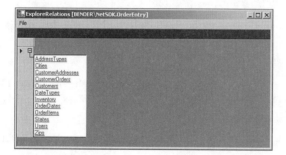

When you click on one of the tables, the DataGrid displays information about the table's columns. Figure 13.6 shows the results for the CustomerOrders table in the OrderEntry database.

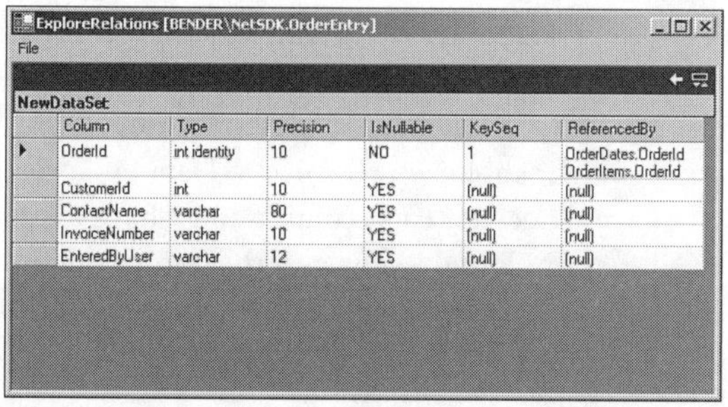

Figure 13.6
Program ExploreRelations shows information about a table's columns.

PART

I

CH

13

The display gives some basic information, such as the columns' data types and precision. It also indicates whether a column is part of a key and whether another column refers to the column. Figure 13.6 shows that the OrderId field is the only column in the table's key. If the table had a composite key, such as LastName combined with FirstName, the numbers in the KeySeq column would show their order of inclusion in the key.

Figure 13.6 also indicates that the OrderId column is referenced as a foreign key by the OrderDates table's OrderId column, and by the OrderItems table's OrderId column.

Program ExploreRelations uses the code shown in Listing 13.5 to study the relationships among a database's tables. The program begins by declaring a DataSet object. It later fills the DataSet with information about the database tables' relationships and then binds it to a DataGrid control for display.

When the user selects the File menu's Server command, the mnuFileServer_Click event handler displays a dialog box where the user can enter a server name, user name, password, and database. If the user then clicks OK, the event handler calls subroutine ExploreRelations to display information about the database.

Subroutine ExploreRelations connects to the server and executes a SQL USE statement to use the database you selected. It then executes the sp_tables stored procedure to make a list of the tables in the database much as program ExploreServer does.

ExploreRelations creates a new DataSet object to remove any data it might contain from a previous run. The routine then loops through its list of tables calling subroutine ExploreTable for each.

Subroutine ExploreTable adds a new DataTable object to the program's DataSet. It creates new columns in the DataTable to hold the Column, Type, Precision, IsNullable, KeySeq, and ReferencedBy values for each column.

Next ExploreTable uses the sp_columns stored procedure to get a list of the table's columns. For each column, the routine adds a new row to the DataTable and copies the column's COL-UMN_NAME, TYPE_NAME, PRECISION, and IS_NULLABLE values into the new row.

After it has finished loading the columns' basic information, subroutine ExploreTable uses the stored procedure sp_pkeys to get information about the table's primary key columns. For each returned row, the routine uses the DataTable's Select method to find the corresponding DataRow object in the DataTable. For example, suppose sp_pkeys returns a row with COLUMN_NAME equal to OrderId. Then the routine calls the DataTable's Select method with parameter Column = 'OrderId'. The Select method returns an array of DataRow objects matching this criterion. Because each row in the DataTable represents a different column in the database table and because each column must have a different name, the rows in the DataTable all have different Column values so this array contains only one DataRow object. The subroutine sets that object's KeySeq value to indicate the column's primary key sequence.

After it processes the primary key information, subroutine ExploreTable uses similar code to fetch information about the table's columns that are referenced as foreign keys by other tables. The routine executes the sp_fkeys stored procedure. It loops through the results, using the DataTable's `Select` method to find the corresponding row's `DataRow` object. It then sets the DataRow's `ReferencedBy` value to show the row's foreign key table and foreign key column names.

When subroutine `ExploreRelations` finishes, the program has built a `DataSet` object containing a DataTable for each of the database's tables. The DataTables hold information about each table's columns, primary keys, and foreign key references. Binding the DataSet to the DataGrid control does the rest.

LISTING 13.5   THIS CODE USES SQL SERVER STORED PROCEDURES TO DISPLAY INFORMATION ABOUT TABLE RELATIONSHIPS

```
Private m_DataSet As DataSet

' Let the user select the server.
Private Sub mnuFileServer_Click(ByVal sender As System.Object, _
  ByVal e As System.EventArgs) Handles mnuFileServer.Click
    ' Let the user select the database.
    Dim dlg As New dlgSqlServerLogin()
    If dlg.ShowDialog() = DialogResult.Cancel Then Exit Sub

    grdResults.DataSource = Nothing
    Me.Cursor = Cursors.WaitCursor
    Me.Refresh()

    ' Explore the database's relations.
    ExploreRelations(dlg.txtServer.Text, dlg.txtUserId.Text, _
        dlg.txtPassword.Text, dlg.txtDatabase.Text)

    Me.Cursor = Cursors.Default
End Sub

' Display information about the database's relations.
Private Sub ExploreRelations(ByVal server_name As String, _
  ByVal user_name As String, ByVal user_password As String, _
  ByVal database_name As String)
    Me.Text = "ExploreServer - connecting..."
    Me.Refresh()

    ' Connect to the server.
    Dim connect_string As String = _
        "User Id=" & user_name & ";" & _
        "Password=" & user_password & ";" & _
        "Data Source=" & server_name
    Dim sql_connection As New SqlConnection(connect_string)
    sql_connection.Open()

    ' Use the database.
    Dim cmd As New SqlCommand("USE " & database_name, sql_connection)
    cmd.ExecuteNonQuery()

    ' Make a list of the tables.
    cmd.CommandText = "sp_tables"
    Dim data_reader As SqlDataReader = cmd.ExecuteReader()
    Dim table_names As New Collection()
```

PART

I

CH

13

LISTING 13.5   CONTINUED

```
    Do While data_reader.Read()
        ' Save only normal TABLEs.
        If data_reader.Item("TABLE_TYPE") = "TABLE" Then
            table_names.Add(data_reader.Item("TABLE_NAME"))
        End If
    Loop
    data_reader.Close()

    ' Remove the previous data.
    m_DataSet = New DataSet()

    ' Explore the tables.
    Dim table_name As String
    For Each table_name In table_names
        Me.Text = "ExploreServer - " & table_name
        Me.Refresh()
        ExploreTable(sql_connection, table_name)
    Next table_name

    sql_connection.Close()
    grdResults.DataSource = m_DataSet
    Me.Text = "ExploreServer [" & server_name & "." & database_name & "]"
End Sub

' Explore a table.
Private Sub ExploreTable(ByVal sql_connection As SqlConnection, _
  ByVal table_name As String)
    ' Make a DataTable to hold the column data.
    Dim data_table As New DataTable(table_name)
    m_DataSet.Tables.Add(data_table)

    ' Make the DataTable columns.
    data_table.Columns.Add("Column", GetType(String))
    data_table.Columns.Add("Type", GetType(String))
    data_table.Columns.Add("Precision", GetType(String))
    data_table.Columns.Add("IsNullable", GetType(String))
    data_table.Columns.Add("KeySeq", GetType(String))
    data_table.Columns.Add("ReferencedBy", GetType(String))

    ' Make a list of the table's columns.
    Dim cmd As New SqlCommand("sp_columns " & table_name, sql_connection)
    Dim data_reader As SqlDataReader = cmd.ExecuteReader()
    Dim data_row As DataRow
    Do While data_reader.Read()
        ' Add a DataRow for the column.
        data_row = data_table.NewRow()
        data_row.Item("Column") = data_reader.Item("COLUMN_NAME")
        data_row.Item("Type") = data_reader.Item("TYPE_NAME")
        data_row.Item("Precision") = data_reader.Item("PRECISION")
        data_row.Item("IsNullable") = data_reader.Item("IS_NULLABLE")
        data_table.Rows.Add(data_row)
    Loop
    data_reader.Close()

    ' Get information about the table's primary keys.
    cmd.CommandText = "sp_pkeys " & table_name
```

LISTING 13.5   CONTINUED

```
    data_reader = cmd.ExecuteReader()
    Do While data_reader.Read()
        ' Find the column's DataRow.
        Dim data_rows() As DataRow = _
            data_table.Select("Column = '" & _
                data_reader.Item("COLUMN_NAME") & "'")

        ' Set the column's KeySeq value.
        data_rows(0).Item("KeySeq") = data_reader.Item("KEY_SEQ")
    Loop
    data_reader.Close()

    ' Get information about foreign keys
    ' referencing this table's columns.
    cmd.CommandText = "sp_fkeys " & table_name
    data_reader = cmd.ExecuteReader()
    Do While data_reader.Read()
        ' Find the column's DataRow.
        Dim data_rows() As DataRow = _
            data_table.Select("Column = '" & _
                data_reader.Item("PKCOLUMN_NAME") & "'")

        ' Set the column's ReferencedBy value.
        Dim txt As String = "" & data_rows(0).Item("ReferencedBy")
        If txt.Length > 0 Then txt = txt & vbCrLf
        txt = txt & _
            data_reader.Item("FKTABLE_NAME") & "." & _
            data_reader.Item("FKCOLUMN_NAME")
        data_rows(0).Item("ReferencedBy") = txt
    Loop
    data_reader.Close()
End Sub
```

SUMMARY

Visual Basic's DataTable and SqlDataReader objects, and the SqlDataReader's GetSchemaTable method can give you information about a table or the fields selected by a database query. SQL Server stored procedures give you even more information about database objects. They can list a server's databases, a database's tables, and a table's columns. They can tell you about the properties of a database, column, or table, and they can describe the relationships among a database's tables.

When you build a database, you can keep track of its structure by recording the steps you take to build it. If you build it using SQL scripts, just be sure to keep copies of the scripts. For databases you did not create, Visual Basic's database objects and the stored procedures described here can help you discover the database's structure.

PART

I

CH

13

SQL

SQL (Structured Query Language) is an industry standard language for building and manipulating relational databases and their content. SQL includes statements for adding, selecting, ordering, and deleting records. It also contains statements for defining the database structure.

Unfortunately not every database implements all SQL statements in exactly the same way. Some provide extra features that are not available in other database engines. This book focuses on Transact-SQL, the version of SQL implemented by SQL Server. You can find detailed information on Transact-SQL at Microsoft's Web site. Currently this information is available at:

```
http://msdn.microsoft.com/library/en-us/tsqlref/ts_tsqlcon_6lyk.asp
```

Sometimes Microsoft moves its links. If you cannot find this page, search the MSDN site for "Transact-SQL Overview."

Several good books have also been written about SQL programming, including *SQL Server 2000 Programming by Example* (2001, Guerrero and Rojas, Que).

If you decide to switch database engines for some reason, you may find some statements work slightly differently in the new database. For the most part, however, you should be able to use the scripts you write to build and populate your SQL Server database to quickly move to the new database engine.

Probably the biggest difference between the databases Visual Basic programmers are most likely to use is the fact that Visual Basic applications each connect directly to an Access database, as shown in Figure A.1. On the other hand, an application connects to a SQL Server or Oracle database through a server, as shown in Figure A.2.

This difference has some implications when the applications connect to the database. It has larger implications when a program wants to create or delete a database. When the program is connected to a server, it can send the server the CREATE DATABASE and DROP DATABASE commands to create and destroy a database.

When the program is connected directly to an Access database, there is no server to execute those commands. In that case, the application can manipulate an Access database created by another program (such as Access), but it cannot create the database itself. It can remove the database by simply deleting the .mdb file that contains it. See the CREATE DATABASE and DROP DATABASE statements described later in this appendix for more information.

Figure A.1
Visual Basic programs connect directly to Access databases.

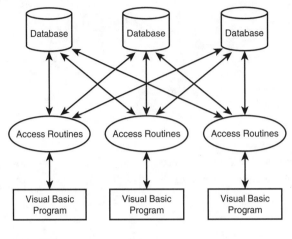

Figure A.2
SQL Server, MSDE, and Oracle control access to many databases with a single database server.

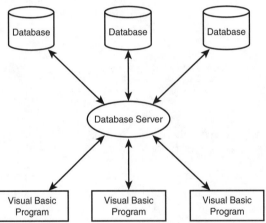

CREATE DATABASE

Databases such as SQL Server, MSDE, and Oracle use database servers to control access to any number of databases as shown in Figure A.2. A Visual Basic application connects to the server and can use SQL to make the server create databases, add and update records, and so forth.

The CREATE DATABASE command makes the server create a new database. The basic syntax of the CREATE DATABASE command is

```
CREATE DATABASE database_name
```

The *database_name* parameter names the new database.

Different database engines allow you to use additional arguments to specify the location of the database's storage and log files. SQL Server and MSDE databases give you much more detailed control over how the database grows. With these databases, you can use this syntax:

```
CREATE DATABASE database_name
[ON
  (NAME = logical_file_name,
   FILENAME = 'physical_file_name',
   SIZE = initial_size,
   MAXSIZE = maximum_size,
   FILEGROWTH = increment)
]
[LOG ON
  (NAME = logical_file_name,
   FILENAME = 'physical_file_name',
   SIZE = initial_size,
   MAXSIZE = maximum_size,
   FILEGROWTH = increment)
]
```

The optional ON clause defines the files that will contain the database's content. You can repeat the file definition section inside the parentheses several times if separated by commas to make the database use more than one file.

The optional LOG ON clause defines the files used to record database logging information.

The following list describes the parameters in the ON and LOG ON clauses:

- logical_file_name—Gives the logical name of the file in the database.
- physical_file_name—Gives the name of the file on the physical disk. By convention, database storage files should have an .mdf extension and log files should have an .ldf extension.
- initial_size—Gives the initial size of the database file. You can add the suffixes KB, MB, GB, or TB to indicate kilobytes, megabytes, gigabytes, or terabytes.
- maximum_size—Gives the maximum size to which the file is allowed to grow.
- increment—Gives the amount by which the file is enlarged when it is too small.

```
The following code shows an example CREATE DATABASE statement:CREATE DATABASE
OrderEntry
ON (
  NAME = oe_data,
  FILENAME = 'C:\Data\OrderEntry\order_entry_data.mdf',
  SIZE = 10MB,
  MAXSIZE = 1GB,
  FILEGROWTH = 10MB
)
LOG ON (
  NAME = oe_log,
  FILENAME = 'C:\Data\OrderEntry\order_entry_log.ldf',
  SIZE = 5MB,
  MAXSIZE = 100MB,
  FILEGROWTH = 5MB
)
```

Access does not manage databases through a server. Instead, each database is contained in its own file. A Visual Basic program uses Access routines to connect to the individual database directly.

PART
I
APP
A

Because a Visual Basic program using an Access database doesn't use a server, it cannot send a CREATE DATABASE statement to the server to create a database.

The Visual Data Manager included in Visual Basic 6 could create an Access database, but Visual Basic .NET does not provide a similar tool and cannot create an Access database by itself. The best strategy for dealing with this issue is to use MSDE instead. Using MSDE, a Visual Basic program can connect to the database server and issue a CREATE DATABASE command.

If you really must use an Access database and you don't have Microsoft Access itself, make a copy of any Access database you can find. Write a small application to open the database, use DROP TABLE statements to remove the database's existing content, and add new tables and relations of its own. You can also use the RunScript program described in Chapter 6, "Database Connections," to open the database and remove its tables.

DROP DATABASE

As you can probably guess, the DROP DATABASE statement deletes a database.

A program connects to an Access database by opening it directly. Because it doesn't connect to the database using a server, there is no server to process the DROP DATABASE command. If you want to destroy an Access database, simply delete the .mdb file that contains it.

A program connects to Oracle, SQL Server, and MSDE databases through a server as shown in Figure A.2. A program connecting to a server like this can destroy a database using the DROP DATABASE statement.

The server will not drop the database while any program is connected to it, however. Even the program attempting to drop the database must be disconnected from it. If the program has been working with the database, it can use the command SET MASTER to connect to the server's master database. That disconnects the program from the target database so the server can drop the database.

The following script shows how an application can connect to the TempCalculations database, work with it for a while, disconnect from the database, and drop it:

```
# Connect to the TempCalculations database.
USE TempCalculations;

# Work with the database.
...

# Disconnect from the database.
USE Master;

# Drop the TempCalculations database.
DROP DATABASE TempCalculations;
```

ALTER DATABASE

The ALTER DATABASE command lets you change the properties of the files in which the database is stored. For example, you could use this command to change the database file's logical names or to change their sizes. These are unusual operations so they are not described here. See Microsoft's online documentation for more information.

CREATE TABLE

After you create a database, you need to add tables to it. Tables hold a lot of information about the database structure. They hold the table's field definitions, index definitions, and relational information.

Because tables hold so much information, the CREATE TABLE statement is quite complicated. The basic syntax looks like this:

```
CREATE TABLE table_name (
    field_name data_type [(size)] [DEFAULT default] [NOT NULL]
[column_constraint],
    field_name data_type [(size)] [DEFAULT default] [NOT NULL]
[column_constraint],
    ...
    field_name data_type [(size)] [DEFAULT default] [NOT NULL] [column_constraint]
[, CONSTRAINT table_constraint, ...]
)
```

The meanings of the parameters are

- field_name—Gives the name of the table's field.

- data_type—Gives the field's data type. The section that follows lists the most common data types.

- size—For string data types, this parameter gives the string's maximum length.

- default—If you include the DEFAULT clause, default gives the value the database should use when an INSERT statement omits the value.

- NOT NULL—If you include the NOT NULL clause, the database will not accept a record that has no value for this field.

- column_constraint—Adds restrictions to the field. For example, it can make a single field the table's primary key, or it can mark the field as unique so all records must have different values for the field. See the section "Column Constraints" later in this appendix for more details.

- table_constraint—Defines constraints similar to those defined by a column_constraint. It can also define constraints that include multiple fields. See the section "Table Constraints" later in this appendix for more details.

PART

I

APP

A

The following simple example creates a Customers table with two fields. CustomerId is an integer field. CustomerName is a variable length string with a maximum length of 50 characters. Both fields are declared NOT NULL so records must have a value for both fields:

```
CREATE TABLE Customers (
    CustomerId INTEGER NOT NULL,
    CustomerName VARCHAR (50) NOT NULL
)
```

DATA TYPES

Different database engines may support slightly different data type implementations. Table A.1 lists some of the most useful data types supported by SQL Server databases.

TABLE A.1   USEFUL SQL SERVER DATA TYPES

Data Type	Description
BIGINT	8-byte integer between -2^{63} and $2^{63} - 1$ (roughly $-9E18$ to $9E18$).
INT	4-byte integer between $-2,147,483,648$ and $2,147,483,647$. This is the preferred integer data type.
SMALLINT	2-byte integer between $-32,768$ and $32,767$.
TINYINT	1-byte unsigned integer between 0 and 255.
BIT	A single bit value (0 or 1).
DECIMAL	Fixed-precision decimal value between $-10^{38} + 1$ and $10^{38} - 1$.
NUMERIC	Same as DECIMAL.
MONEY	8-byte monetary value between -2^{63} and $2^{63} - 1$ with accuracy of 0.0001.
SMALLMONEY	4-byte monetary value between $-214,748.3648$ and $214,748.3647$ with accuracy of 0.0001.
FLOAT	Floating point value between $-1.79E + 308$ and $1.79E + 308$.
REAL	Floating point value between $-3.40E + 38$ and $3.40E + 38$.
DATETIME	8-byte date and time value between January 1, 1753, and December 31, 9999, with accuracy of 0.00333 seconds.
SMALLDATETIME	4-byte date and time value between January 1, 1900, and June 6, 2079, with accuracy of 1 minute.
CHAR	Fixed-length string with maximum length of 8,000 characters.
VARCHAR	Variable-length string with maximum length of 8,000 characters.
TEXT	Variable-length string with maximum length of 2,147,483,647 characters.
CCHAR	Fixed-length Unicode string with maximum length of 4,000 characters
NVARCHAR	Variable-length Unicode string with maximum length of 4,000 characters

TABLE A.1   CONTINUED

Data Type	Description
NTEXT	Variable-length Unicode string with maximum length of 1,073,741,823 characters
BINARY	Fixed-length binary data up to 8,000 bytes.
VARBINARY	Variable-length binary data up to 8,000 bytes.
IMAGE	Variable-length binary data up to 2,147,483,647 bytes.

Many data type declarations can take parameters indicating their size or precision. The following sections describe these declaration parameters and some other special features of certain data types.

DECIMAL AND NUMERIC

The DECIMAL and NUMERIC types can take parameters indicating their precision and scale. *Precision* indicates the total number of decimal digits the value can have before and after the decimal point. *Scale* gives the number of digits allowed after the decimal point. You can calculate the number of digits allowed before the decimal point using the equation (digits before) = (precision) – (scale).

For example, the following declaration indicates a value with six digits, two of which can come after the decimal point:

```
Salary NUMERIC(6, 2)
```

In this case, the database would allow the value 1234.56 and 123.4 because they have no more than six digits and no more than four come before the decimal point. The database would not allow the value 12345.6 because it has five digits before the decimal point.

The database would accept the value 1234.567 but it would round the value up to 1234.57 so it would fit the field's definition.

FLOAT AND REAL

The FLOAT data type can take a parameter indicating the number of bits the database should use to store the mantissa of the value in scientific notation. For instance, in the value 1.234E12 the mantissa is 234.

The database adjusts the number of bits so the value fits in either 4 or 8 bytes. If the number of bits is between 1 and 24, the database stores the value in 4 bytes and gives you 7 digits of precision. If the number of bits is between 25 and 53, the database stores the value in 8 bytes and gives you 15 digits of precision.

The REAL data type is a FLOAT value with 24 bits of precision, so the following declarations are equivalent:

```
Temperature FLOAT(24)
Temperature REAL
```

CHAR, VARCHAR, NCHAR, **AND** NVARCHAR

The parameter to the CHAR data type indicates the length of the character data. The parameter's default value is 1; therefore, omitting the parameter is equivalent to the following declaration:

```
Preference CHAR(1)
```

If a value is not long enough to fill a CHAR field, the database pads it with spaces on the right.

The parameter for the VARCHAR data type indicates the value's maximum allowed length. The following declaration allows strings of any length up to 50 characters:

```
Lastname VARCHAR(50)
```

Usually applications use the CHAR data type when the values in a field will always have exactly the same length. For instance, state abbreviations are always exactly two characters long, so you could declare a State field like this:

```
State CHAR(2)
```

Use the VARCHAR data type for fields with values that will vary greatly in length. The storage used by VARCHAR fields depends on the length of the actual data, not on the maximum length allowed. If you are uncertain about the maximum length, err on the long side. If you think your customers' names will be at most 20 characters long, you might want to set the limit at 40 or 50 characters just to be safe.

On the other hand, keep the limit reasonable so the database can catch obvious errors. If you declare the LastName field to be of type VARCHAR(5000), a program could accidentally store the contents of a text file in the field.

The NCHAR and NVARCHAR data types are similar to CHAR and VARCHAR respectively except they hold Unicode text instead of ASCII text.

All four of these data types are limited to 8,000 bytes of character storage. ASCII text uses one byte per character so the CHAR and VARCHAR types can hold up to 8,000 characters. Unicode strings use two bytes per character; as such, the NCHAR and NVARCHAR types are limited to 4,000 characters.

TEXT, NTEXT, **AND** IMAGE

Although these data types can hold huge chunks of data, they have some restrictions. The database cannot use them in ORDER BY clauses, so you cannot sort a query's results using these fields. You also cannot use them in WHERE clauses except with the IS NULL or LIKE keywords. To keep the ability to search and order text fields, use the CHAR and VARCHAR data types unless you really need to store enormous values.

BINARY **AND** VARBINARY

The parameters for these data types are analogous to those for the CHAR and VARCHAR data types. For the BINARY data type, the parameter indicates the exact number of bytes in the field. For the VARBINARY data type, the parameter indicates the maximum number of bytes allowed in the field.

Both of these data types can hold a maximum of 8,000 bytes of data so they are only big enough to hold small pictures. The IMAGE data type can hold up to 2,147,483,647 bytes so it is more appropriate for large amounts of data such as those in a big photograph.

IDENTITY

If you add the IDENTITY keyword to a column's definition, the database automatically generates values for that column. That makes it easy to generate records with unique ID numbers. Often IDENTITY fields are used as primary keys.

An IDENTITY field must have data type BIGINT, INT, SMALLINT, TINYINT, DECIMAL, or NUMERIC. A table can have only one IDENTITY field.

The IDENTITY statement takes two optional parameters, seed and increment. The seed parameter gives the value the database should assign to the first row it adds to the table. The increment parameter tells the database how much it should add to the column's values between rows.

The following statement creates an Employees table where the database automatically generates EmployeeId field values. The first Employees record will receive the EmployeeId value 1001. Subsequent records will receive the values 1002, 1003, and so forth:

```
CREATE TABLE Employees (
    EmployeeId    INT           IDENTITY (1001, 1) PRIMARY KEY,
    FirstName     VARCHAR(40)   NOT NULL,
    LastName      VARCHAR(40)   NOT NULL,
)
```

Because the database generates the IDENTITY field's values automatically, you cannot specify the value when you create a new record. The following statement would fail because it specifies the value for the EmployeeId field:

```
INSERT INTO Employees VALUES (1010, 'Rod', 'Stephens')
```

The following statement works because it does not give a value for the EmployeeId field. The database automatically generates the value:

```
INSERT INTO Employees (FirstName, LastName) VALUES ('Rod', 'Stephens')
```

The seed and increment parameters must either both be included or both be omitted. If they are omitted, the database uses a default value of 1 for both the seed and increment.

COLUMN CONSTRAINTS

If you want to refer to a constraint by name later, you can begin it with the keyword CONSTRAINT followed by the constraint's name. Constraint names must be unique within the database. If you give a constraint a meaningful name, you won't need to worry about name collisions. For example, you might start constraint names with "con" followed by the table name and the column name separated by underscores. The name for a constraint on the

CompanyId field in the Order table would be con_Order_CompanyId. If you don't give a constraint name, the database creates a default name that it uses in any error messages it generates.

In many cases, an application will never need to refer explicitly to a constraint. In that case, you can leave out the CONSTRAINT keyword and the constraint name. For example, the following statement creates a table where both fields are marked with NOT NULL constraints but only the first constraint has a name:

```
CREATE TABLE People (
    LastName   VARCHAR(50)  CONSTRAINT con_People_LastName NOT NULL,
    FirstName  VARCHAR(50)  NOT NULL
)
```

The types of column constraint are PRIMARY KEY, NOT NULL, UNIQUE, FOREIGN KEY, and CHECK. The following sections describe these kinds of constraints.

PRIMARY KEY

Primary key fields must contain unique values. In other words, you cannot add two records to the table that have the same primary key value.

A primary key field also cannot take a NULL value, so all records must have some value for the field.

NOT NULL

If a field is marked NOT NULL, the database will not allow you to create a record that has a NULL value for the field.

Note that a NULL value is not the same as a blank value. For instance, suppose a VARCHAR field is marked NOT NULL. Then in the following script, the first INSERT statement works because it is inserting a blank value. The second INSERT statement fails because it is inserting a NULL value:

```
CREATE TABLE Names (
    Name VARCHAR(50) NOT NULL
);

INSERT INTO Names VALUES ('');    # This is ok. Blank is not NULL.
INSERT INTO Names VALUES (NULL);  # This fails.
```

For consistency, you can also specify NULL as a constraint. What this really means is "not NOT NULL" and few designers bother with this statement.

UNIQUE

If a field is marked UNIQUE, the database will not allow you to add two records with the same value for that field. Note that this includes NULL values. You can insert one record with a NULL value in the field but you cannot insert a second.

Many fields marked UNIQUE should also not allow NULL values anyway. They should also be marked NOT NULL.

FOREIGN KEY

A foreign key provides referential integrity to a field in another table. That field must be declared PRIMARY KEY or UNIQUE to be used as a foreign key.

The clause begins with the optional words FOREIGN KEY. The keyword REFERENCES must follow. After that, the statement should include the name of the foreign table followed by the field in that table in parentheses.

The following script creates a Students table. The StudentId field is marked as the table's primary key. The script then creates the TestScores table. Its StudentId field references the Students table's StudentId field. In this table definition, you could leave out the words FOREIGN KEY:

```
CREATE TABLE Students (
    StudentId    NUMERIC        PRIMARY KEY,
    LastName     VARCHAR(50),
    FirstName    VARCHAR(50)
);
CREATE TABLE TestScores (
    StudentId    NUMERIC        FOREIGN KEY REFERENCES Students(StudentId),
    TestNumber   NUMERIC,
    Score        NUMERIC
);
```

In this example, when you try to create a new TestScores record, the database verifies that the value for the StudentId field matches the value in some record in the Students table. If the Students table does not contain a record with that value, the database won't let you add the new TestScores record.

After you have added records to both tables, the database will not normally let you delete a Students record if any TestScores record refers to its StudentId value because that would violate the constraint.

The database will also not let you drop the Students table while the TestScores table still exists because its constraint refers to the Students table.

Finally, the database will not let you change the value of the foreign key field while a constrained record refers to it. In this example, you cannot change the value of a Students record's StudentId value if any TestScores record uses it.

If the database is set to cascade deletes or updates, it will automatically delete or update the corresponding TestScores records when you delete or modify a Students record. See Chapter 2, "Database Design," for more information on cascading deletes and updates.

You can also specify cascading deletes and updates on the field constraint itself. If you add ON DELETE CASCADE to the constraint, the database automatically deletes the corresponding records whenever it deletes the master record. In this case, if you delete a Students record the database would automatically delete any corresponding TestScores records.

The following script creates the `Students` and `TestScores` tables with the `ON DELETE CAS-CADE` statement:

```
CREATE TABLE Students (
    StudentId    NUMERIC       PRIMARY KEY,
    LastName     VARCHAR(50),
    FirstName    VARCHAR(50)
);
CREATE TABLE TestScores (
    StudentId    NUMERIC       REFERENCES Students(StudentId) ON DELETE CASCADE,
    TestNumber   NUMERIC,
    Score        NUMERIC
);
```

You can explicitly turn off cascading deletes with the statement `ON DELETE NO ACTION`.

Similarly you can enable or disable cascading updates using the `ON UPDATE CASCADE` and `ON UPDATE NO ACTION` clauses.

CHECK

A `CHECK` constraint provides additional range checking on values entered in the field. For example, the following `CREATE` statement ensures that test scores lie between 0 and 100:

```
CREATE TABLE TestScores (
    StudentId    NUMERIC       REFERENCES Students(StudentId) ON DELETE CASCADE,
    TestNumber   NUMERIC,
    Score        NUMERIC       CHECK (Score >= 0 AND Score <= 100)
);
```

The condition in a column's `CHECK` statement can refer only to the current column. A table-level `CHECK` constraint can refer to more than one column in the table.

TABLE CONSTRAINTS

When you define a column, you can define a column constraint to restrict the column's values and determine its behavior. You can also define constraints after you have defined all the table's columns.

After the final column definition, add the constraint much as you would define it for a column. Enter the field name or names in parentheses after the type of constraint.

The following example makes the `StudentId` field the table's primary key after it has defined all the table's fields. It then uses a `UNIQUE` constraint to prevent duplicates of the combination of `FirstName` and `LastName`. Different records can have the same `FirstName` value, or the same `LastName` value, but they cannot have both. You cannot create multicolumn constraints like this one when you define the columns; you can only create them after you have defined all the columns:

```
CREATE TABLE Students (
    StudentId    NUMERIC,
    LastName     VARCHAR(50),
    FirstName    VARCHAR(50),
    CONSTRAINT pk_Students PRIMARY KEY (StudentId),
```

```
        CONSTRAINT uni_Students_Names UNIQUE (FirstName, LastName)
);
```

If you don't need to create a name for the constraints, leave them out as you would when you create a constraint in a column definition. The following statement defines the same constraints as the previous example without the CONSTRAINT keyword and constraint names:

```
CREATE TABLE Students (
    StudentId    NUMERIC,
    LastName     VARCHAR(50),
    FirstName    VARCHAR(50),
    PRIMARY KEY (StudentId),
    UNIQUE (FirstName, LastName)
);
```

Similarly you can define multicolumn foreign keys as in this example:

```
CREATE TABLE Students (
    LastName     VARCHAR(50),
    FirstName    VARCHAR(50),
    PRIMARY KEY (FirstName, LastName)
);
CREATE TABLE TestScores (
    TestNumber   NUMERIC,
    Score        NUMERIC,
    LastName     VARCHAR(50),
    FirstName    VARCHAR(50),
    FOREIGN KEY (FirstName, LastName) REFERENCES Students(FirstName, LastName)
);
```

Remember that the fields referenced in the foreign table must be a PRIMARY KEY or be declared UNIQUE.

A table-level CHECK constraint can compare more than one field in the table, though it cannot refer to fields in other tables. The following example defines a Salary table containing Salary and Bonus fields. CHECK constraints on the fields ensure that Salary is greater than zero and that Bonus is at least zero. A table-level CHECK constraint verifies that Bonus is no more than 10 percent of Salary:

```
CREATE TABLE Salary (
    FirstName    VARCHAR(50),
    LastName     VARCHAR(50),
    Salary       NUMERIC(9, 2) CHECK (Salary > 0),
    Bonus        NUMERIC(9, 2) CHECK (Bonus >= 0),
    CHECK (Bonus <= Salary * 0.1)
);
```

ALTER TABLE

The ALTER TABLE statement lets you redefine a table's structure. It lets you add or delete columns and constraints. The syntax is similar to the syntax used to define parts of a table except this statement begins with ALTER TABLE. For example, the following script creates a Salary table. Successive ALTER TABLE statements then add additional fields and constraints and drop the original EmployeeName field:

PART

I

APP

A

```
# Create the Salary table.
CREATE TABLE Salary (
    EmployeeName    VARCHAR(100) NOT NULL
);

# Add the FirstName field with a NOT NULL constraint.
ALTER TABLE Salary
    ADD FirstName VARCHAR(50) NOT NULL DEFAULT '';

# Add the LastName field with a NOT NULL constraint.
ALTER TABLE Salary
    ADD LastName VARCHAR(50) NOT NULL DEFAULT '';

# Drop the EmployeeName field.
ALTER TABLE Salary
    DROP COLUMN EmployeeName;

# Add the Salary and Bonus fields with CHECK constraints.
ALTER TABLE Salary
    ADD Salary      NUMERIC(9, 2) CHECK (Salary > 0),
        Bonus       NUMERIC(9, 2) CHECK (Bonus >= 0);

# Add a multi-column CHECK constraint.
ALTER TABLE Salary
    ADD CHECK (Bonus <= Salary * 0.1);
```

Naturally this would be an incredibly inefficient way to create a table. It would be much better to get the definition right during the initial CREATE TABLE statement. You should only need to modify the table to make small changes, not rebuild the entire table. If you build your database using scripts, it will often be easier to modify the script and recreate the table from scratch.

Table modifications such as these are subject to many restrictions. You cannot delete the only column from a table. That's why the previous example adds new columns first. You cannot drop a column used in an index or if it is used in a CHECK, FOREIGN KEY, UNIQUE, or PRIMARY KEY constraint. You can get around these restrictions by first removing the constraint, but such major changes to a table might indicate a fundamental problem with your database design. You also cannot add a column unless it can take NULL values or you provide a default value with the DEFAULT clause.

Dropping columns can also alter the data. If you drop a column, all its data is lost.

You can use ALTER TABLE statements to drop and create constraints. The following example removes the named constraint con_Salary_Salary and creates a new table-level constraint with the same name:

```
# Make the con_Salary_Salary constraint more restrictive.
ALTER TABLE Salary
    DROP CONSTRAINT con_Salary_Salary;
ALTER TABLE Salary
    ADD CONSTRAINT con_Salary_Salary CHECK (Salary > 1000 AND Salary < 10000000);
```

ALTER TABLE can modify a column's definition. The following example changes the LastName field's length to 20 characters:

```
ALTER TABLE Salary
    ALTER COLUMN LastName VARCHAR(20);
```

If any of the table's records have a `LastName` value longer than 20 characters, the database will balk at this change.

Like the `CREATE TABLE` statement, `ALTER TABLE` has a lot of clauses and options that give it great flexibility and that make it quite confusing. If you need to do something more elaborate than the examples described here, consult Microsoft's online documentation.

DROP TABLE

The `DROP TABLE` statement removes a table and all its contents from the database. After you remove a table, the data it contains is gone forever; therefore, you should be careful with this command.

The database will not let you drop a table that is the master table in a relational constraint. For instance, consider the following SQL script. In this example, the `EmployeeId` field in the `Departments` table refers to the `EmployeeId` field in the `Employees` table. The database will not let you drop the `Employees` table even if there are no records in either table:

```
CREATE TABLE Employees (
  EmployeeId NUMERIC UNIQUE NOT NULL
);

CREATE TABLE Departments (
  DepartmentId NUMERIC NOT NULL,
  EmployeeId NUMERIC REFERENCES Employees(EmployeeId)
);

DROP TABLE Employees;
DROP TABLE Departments;
```

To drop the `Employees` table in this example, you would need to either drop the `Departments` table first or delete the referential constraint.

Some databases, such as Oracle, allow you to add the keywords `CASCADE CONSTRAINTS` to override this behavior. The following statement tells the database to drop the `Employees` table and any tables that depend on it:

```
DROP TABLE Employees CASCADE CONSTRAINTS
```

Because `CASCADE CONSTRAINTS` is vendor-specific, you should probably not use it in your programs unless you are absolutely certain you will be using a database that supports it for quite a while.

PART

I

APP

A

CREATE INDEX

The `CREATE INDEX` statement adds an index to a table or view. When you create an index, the database builds data structures to make searching and sorting on the fields in the index faster. The data structures take a little more space in the database and they make adding and updating records a little slower, so you shouldn't go overboard with indexes. Use indexes to speed queries that you execute often but don't index every field.

The optional UNIQUE keyword makes the index require unique values. If a set of fields forms a unique index, you cannot add two records to the table with the same values for those fields. The basic syntax for the statement is

```
CREATE [UNIQUE] INDEX index_name ON table_name (column, column2, ...)
```

For example, the following statement creates an unique index for the FirstName and LastName fields in the Employees table.

```
CREATE UNIQUE INDEX idx_EmpNames ON Employees (FirstName, LastName)
```

The CREATE INDEX statement can take several optional parameters that help the database build the indexing data structure. The following sections describe some parameters that can have a big impact on your database's performance.

FILLFACTOR

The FILLFACTOR parameter is a percentage that tells the database how full to make the leaf nodes in the index tree. The details of how the database builds the index are unimportant. It is important to know that it takes longer to add a new item to the index if the index tree is completely full. If you add a new record when there is no room in the index data structure, the database may need to do a lot of rearranging to make room. You can make this faster by initially creating the index with a FILLFACTOR less than 100 percent.

For example, suppose you have a database that already contains 100,000 customer records. You could create an index for the records and specify a FILLFACTOR of 50 percent. Then you could add a lot of records to the table before the index would need major reorganization. If the new records are evenly distributed through the index values, you could add roughly another 100,000 records before the database would need to start rearranging the index structure. This statement might look like this:

```
CREATE UNIQUE INDEX idx_Customers ON Customers (CustomerId)
    WITH FILLFACTOR=50
```

After you create the index, you have no control over the amount of empty space in the index data structures. As you add new records, the index will start to fill up.

Using a large FILLFACTOR when you create an index makes later insertions faster. The downside is it makes the index data structures larger. The size of the structure depends on the size of the fields in the index, not on the size of the entire record. For example, suppose you have employee records that are 10KB in size. If you index on the SocialSecurityNumber field, the size of the index depends on the size of the SocialSecurityNumber field not the 10KB records. Increasing the size of the index structures by setting FILLFACTOR to 50 will not double the size of the database.

You need to use your knowledge of the data to pick the best FILLFACTOR. If you don't plan to add a lot of new records later, you may want to use a large FILLFACTOR. If you know you have only loaded about half of the records you will eventually have, you may want to set FILLFACTOR smaller.

PAD_INDEX

The PAD_INDEX property indicates whether the database should allocate empty space in the middle of the index data structure. FILLFACTOR indicates the percentage of the index tree's leaf nodes that should be filled. If you include the PAD_INDEX keyword, the database also uses the FILLFACTOR value to decide how much space to leave in the middle of the tree.

Adding space in the middle of the tree reduces the amount of rearranging the database will need to do when it needs to reorganize the index structure. Typically the index tree contains much less space in its interior than it does in its leaf nodes, so including PAD_INDEX doesn't increase the size of the tree all that much and it can make inserting new records faster.

The following statement creates an index with empty space in its leaves and internally:

```
CREATE UNIQUE INDEX idx_Customers ON Customers (CustomerId)
    WITH PAD_INDEX, FILLFACTOR=80
```

DROP_EXISTING

Sometimes you may want to rebuild an index. For example, if the index data structures are too full, you might want to rebuild the index so you can use the FILLFACTOR parameter to add space to the index. Conversely, if you have loaded all the data you will ever load into the table, you could rebuild the index with a FILLFACTOR of 100 to remove any empty space in the index data structure.

You could use the DROP INDEX statement to remove the index and then use CREATE INDEX to build it again. You also can use CREATE INDEX with the DROP_EXISTING keyword to make the database rebuild the index in one step. This can be much faster if you are not changing the fields in the index because it allows the database to use the existing index to sort the records as it builds the new index. The following example shows how a script can build an index and rebuild it later to remove extra space:

```
# Add a bunch of records.
...
# Create the index.
CREATE UNIQUE INDEX idx_EmployeesSSN ON Employees (SSN)
    WITH PAD_INDEX FILLFACTOR=50;

# Work with the database, add more records, etc.
...

# We are done adding records.
# Compact the index to remove empty space.
CREATE UNIQUE INDEX idx_EmployeesSSN ON Employees (SSN)
    WITH FILLFACTOR=100, DROP EXISTING;
```

DROP INDEX

The DROP INDEX statement removes an index from a table or view. The following script creates an index and then later drops it:

```
# Create the Social Security number index.
CREATE UNIQUE INDEX idx_SSN ON Employees (SSN);

# Work with the database for a while.
...

# Drop the Social Security number index.
DROP INDEX Employees.idx_SSN;
```

The DROP INDEX statement cannot remove the indexes built by PRIMARY KEY or UNIQUE constraints used when building a table. For example, it cannot remove the index named con_EmpId in the following script:

```
# Create the Employees table.
CREATE TABLE Employees (
    EmployeeId NUMERIC CONSTRAINT con_EmpId UNIQUE NOT NULL,
    FirstName  VARCHAR(50),
    LastName   VARCHAR(50),
    etc.
);

# Work with the database for a while.
...

# This fails.
DROP INDEX Employees.con_EmpId;
```

To remove an index associated with a PRIMARY KEY or UNIQUE constraint, use the ALTER TABLE statement.

CREATE VIEW

A view is a virtual table that represents the data in one or more tables. You can use a view to prepackage a query to make it easy to use. You can also give different permissions to tables and views (in a database that provides that level of permission) to restrict access to the data. For example, supervisors might need to see some employee data but not salary information. You could create a view that selects the employee data except for the Salary field and give the supervisors access to that view instead of the entire Employees table.

The basic syntax for a CREATE VIEW statement is

```
CREATE VIEW view_name [(column_name, column_name, ...)]
AS select_statement
```

The column_name values give the names the view will use for the values it selects. If you omit these names, the view uses the same names as the tables from which it is selecting data. These names are required if the column names in the select statement are ambiguous.

The *select_statement* can be any SELECT statement using one or more tables or other views. The select statement cannot include an ORDER BY clause. The view defines a set of records much as a table does, so it does not define an ordering of the records. You can include an ORDER BY clause when you use the view.

After you have created a view, you can use it much as you would a table. You can select records from it, use a WHERE clause to place restrictions on the records, use an ORDER BY clause to order the results, and join the results with other views and tables. You can even join a view with the tables that define the view, though that would be rather strange and might indicate a problem in your database design.

The following example creates a view that selects fields from the Employees and Departments tables. It then uses the view to display a list of employees and their departments:

```
# Create the Departments lookup table.
CREATE TABLE Departments (
    DepartmentId   NUMERIC       UNIQUE NOT NULL,
    DepartmentName VARCHAR(40)   NOT NULL
);

# Create the Employees table.
CREATE TABLE Employees (
    DepartmentId NUMERIC       REFERENCES Departments (DepartmentId),
    FirstName    VARCHAR(40) NOT NULL,
    LastName     VARCHAR(40) NOT NULL,
    etc.
);

# Create a view listing employees and their departments.
CREATE VIEW EmployeeDepartments AS
    SELECT FirstName, LastName, DepartmentName
    FROM Employees, Departments
    WHERE Employees.DepartmentId = Departments.DepartmentId

# List employees in the Network Lab department.
SELECT * FROM EmployeeDepartments
WHERE DepartmentName = 'Network Lab'
ORDER BY FirstName, LastName
```

A view is really more like a stored query than a separate table. You cannot create a view if the tables that define it do not exist, but in some versions of SQL Server you can delete the tables that define the view without deleting the view. If you try to execute the view after deleting one of its defining tables, the database raises an error.

DROP VIEW

The DROP VIEW statement removes a view from the database. The following statement demonstrates this statement's simple syntax:

```
DROP VIEW EmployeeDepartments
```

This statement is so straightforward that there's really nothing more to say about it.

SELECT

The SELECT statement is one of the most complicated SQL statements. It's so complicated that only its most useful variations are described here.

The SELECT statement lets you select data and return it to your application, insert it in another table, use it to create a temporary table, or use it in another query.

The basic syntax for a SELECT statement is

```
SELECT [DISTINCT] [TOP number [PERCENT]] fields
[INTO table]
FROM tables
[WHERE where_conditions]
[GROUP BY group_by_expression]
[HAVING search_conditions[
[ORDER BY order_fields [ASC | DESC]]
```

The following sections describe the different SELECT statement clauses.

SELECT

The fields parameter indicates the fields that should be selected by the statement. If the fields are all taken from a single table, you only need to list the field names. If the query involves more than one table, you need to prefix a field's name with its table if fields of the same name appear in more than one table.

For instance, suppose a query selects values from the Accounts and Customers tables and both tables have an AccountNumber field. Then you would indicate the AccountNumber field from the Accounts table as Accounts.AccountNumber.

The asterisk (*) indicates the query should select all fields. For example, the following statement selects all the fields from the Employees table:

```
SELECT *
FROM Employees
```

You can prefix the asterisk with a table name if the query involves more than one table. The following statement selects all the fields in the Students table but only the Score field from the TestScores table:

```
SELECT Students.*, Score
FROM Students, TestScores
WHERE Students.StudentId = TestScores.StudentId
```

The DISTINCT keyword tells the database to return its data without duplicates. If the results contain two records with exactly the same values for every selected field, the database returns only one of them.

The TOP number clause tells the database to return only the first several records selected. For instance, the following statement selects 10 records from the Customers table. The records are arranged in descending order of AccountBalance so the accounts with the largest

AccountBalance values come first. The result is a query that selects the 10 records with the largest AccountBalances:

```
SELECT TOP 10 *
FROM Customers
ORDER BY AccountBalance DESC
```

Adding the keyword PERCENT after TOP makes the database return a percentage of the total records selected. The following statement selects the 20 percent of the Customers records that have the largest AccountBalance values:

```
SELECT TOP 20 PERCENT *
FROM Customers
ORDER BY AccountBalance DESC
```

You can follow a field's name with an AS clause to give the field a new name in the returned data. For example, the following statement returns the FirstName and LastName fields from the Students table, renaming the fields First and Last:

```
SELECT FirstName AS First, LastName AS Last
FROM Students
```

The AS clause is useful when you want to rename a field with a confusing or very long name. It is also useful when you select a calculated field. For instance, the following statement concatenates the FirstName and LastName fields separated with a space and renames the result Name:

```
SELECT FirstName + ' ' + LastName AS Name
FROM Students
```

If your Visual Basic program will process the returned data, the names of the fields don't matter much. If you want to feed the result into a new table, report, or some other object for further processing, changing the name can be useful.

INTO

The INTO clause tells the database to insert the selected records into a new table with the given name. For example, the following query selects records from the TestScores tables and inserts them in a new HighScores table:

```
SELECT *
INTO HighScores
FROM TestScores
WHERE Score >= 90
```

If the new table already exists, this statement generates an error.

The database uses the fields selected to decide what fields to make in the new table.

FROM

The FROM clause tells the database from which tables it should select data. The fields in the SELECT clause must come from the tables listed in the FROM clause.

PART

I

APP

A

Usually when you select fields from more than one table, the WHERE clause includes statements linking the tables. For example, the following statement selects student names from the Students table and test scores from the TestScores table. The WHERE clause tells the database which Students records go with which TestScores records:

```
SELECT LastName, FirstName, TestNumber, Score
FROM Students, TestScores
WHERE Students.StudentId = TestScores.StudentId
ORDER BY LastName, FirstName, TestNumber
```

WHERE

The WHERE clause tells the database which records it should select. The WHERE clause allows standard operators such as =, >, <, >=, <=, and !=. For example, the following statement selects all Students records where LastName is not equal to Stephens:

```
SELECT *
FROM Students
WHERE LastName != 'Stephens'
```

The WHERE clause can also contain some more database-oriented operators such as IS NULL, IS NOT NULL, and LIKE.

Usually a Visual Basic variable has a value. If txt is a string, then txt has some value even if your code has not yet assigned txt a value. Before your code gives it a value, txt has a default text value: a zero-length string "".

A text field in a database can also have the special value NULL, meaning the field has never been assigned a value. The difference between NULL and a "nothing" value like "" can sometimes be confusing, particularly for text fields. The NULL value is quite different from a zero-length string.

When you select records from the database, the NULL value does not match anything. For example, the following statement selects records where the LastName field is a zero-length string. If a record has a LastName value that has never been initialized, that value is NULL and it does not match this WHERE clause:

```
SELECT *
FROM Students
WHERE LastName = ''
```

This is exceptionally confusing when you try to match records where a field does not have a certain value. For example, the following statement selects Students records where the LastName field is not Smith. If a record's LastName value is NULL, this statement will not match it because NULL values never match anything:

```
SELECT *
FROM Students
WHERE LastName != 'Smith'
```

In fact, the following statement seems to select every record. Actually it doesn't find any record that has a NULL LastName value:

```
SELECT *
FROM Students
WHERE LastName  = 'Smith'
   OR LastName != 'Smith'
```

To select fields with NULL values, you can use the IS NULL operator as in this statement:

```
SELECT *
FROM Students
WHERE LastName IS NULL
```

To select all records where a field's value is not null, use IS NOT NULL as in this example:

```
SELECT *
FROM Students
WHERE LastName IS NOT NULL
```

The LIKE operator is a little easier to understand although it provides more options than IS NULL and IS NOT NULL. The LIKE operator performs limited pattern matching on a field. For each record, the database compares the field with the LIKE operator's pattern string. The pattern can include the wildcards listed in Table A.2.

TABLE A.2 PATTERN MATCHING COMMANDS FOR THE LIKE OPERATOR

Character(s)	Purpose
_	Matches any single character.
%	Matches a string of zero or more characters.
[aeiou]	Matches any one of the characters in the brackets.
[a–z]	Matches any one character in the range a–z.
[^aeiou]	Matches any one character other than a, e, i, o, or u.

For example, the following statement selects Students records where the LastName value begins with A–S or a–s:

```
SELECT *
FROM Students
WHERE LastName LIKE '[A-Sa-s]%'
```

GROUP BY

The GROUP BY clause tells the database how to group results contained in aggregate functions. For instance, the following statement selects the FirstName and LastName fields from the Students table. It also selects the average of the students' Score values and renames the result Ave. If it did not rename this calculated value, the database would return it with the name Column1.

The aggregate function AVG calculates the average of the values in the TestScores table's Score field. The GROUP BY clause tells the database to calculate averages using records grouped by FirstName and LastName. In other words, for each distinct FirstName/LastName combination, the database averages the Score values.

The ORDER BY clause arranges the results by Score in descending order:

```
SELECT FirstName, LastName, AVG(Score) AS Ave
FROM Students, TestScores
WHERE Students.StudentId = TestScores.StudentId
GROUP BY FirstName, LastName
ORDER BY Ave DESC
```

The following code shows some sample output produced by this query:

```
LastName FirstName Ave
======== ========= ===
Anderson Amy          93
Baker    Bob          86
Dorph    Donald       72
Carter   Cindy        60
```

HAVING

The HAVING clause is similar to a WHERE clause. It specifies additional conditions for an aggregate function or GROUP BY statement.

Sometimes you can replace a HAVING clause with additional WHERE clauses. For example, the following two statements select the same records:

```
SELECT FirstName, LastName, AVG(Score) AS Ave
FROM Students, TestScores
WHERE Students.StudentId = TestScores.StudentId
  AND LastName = 'Anderson'
GROUP BY FirstName, LastName
ORDER BY Ave DESC

SELECT FirstName, LastName, AVG(Score) AS Ave
FROM Students, TestScores
WHERE Students.StudentId = TestScores.StudentId
GROUP BY FirstName, LastName
HAVING LastName = 'Anderson'
ORDER BY Ave DESC
```

An aggregate function cannot normally appear in a WHERE clause, however, so you need to use a HAVING clause if you want to select aggregated values that satisfy a certain condition. The following statement selects students' names and test score averages. The HAVING clause makes it select only results where the average is less than 70:

```
SELECT FirstName, LastName, AVG(Score) AS Ave
FROM Students, TestScores
WHERE Students.StudentId = TestScores.StudentId
GROUP BY FirstName, LastName
HAVING AVG(Score) < 70
ORDER BY Ave DESC
```

ORDER BY

The ORDER BY clause makes the database sort its results. The clause can include more than one field to use in breaking ties. For example, the following statement selects test score information. It orders the results by Score. If more than one entry has the same Score, they are also ordered by LastName. If multiple entries have the same Score and LastName values, they are also ordered by FirstName. Any entries that have the same Score, FirstName, and LastName are returned in arbitrary order:

```
SELECT Score, FirstName, LastName, TestNumber
FROM Students, TestScores
WHERE Students.StudentId = TestScores.StudentId
ORDER BY Score, LastName, FirstName
```

Each field listed in the ORDER BY clause can have its own ASC or DESC parameters to indicate the database should sort that field ascending or descending. The following statement is the same as the previous one except it lists the highest Score values first. The LastName and FirstName values keep their default sort order ascending:

```
SELECT Score, FirstName, LastName, TestNumber
FROM Students, TestScores
WHERE Students.StudentId = TestScores.StudentId
ORDER BY Score DESC, LastName, FirstName
```

The following listing shows some sample output. Amy Anderson's score of 87 comes before Bob Baker's, and Bob's 82 comes before Cindy Carter's because of the LastName field in the ORDER BY clause:

```
Score FirstName LastName TestNumber
===== ========= ======== ==========
   98 Amy       Anderson          1
   96 Amy       Anderson          2
   94 Bob       Baker             4
   93 Amy       Anderson          4
   92 Cindy     Carter            3
   91 Bob       Baker             3
   87 Amy       Anderson          3
   87 Bob       Baker             1
   85 Donald    Dorph             4
   82 Bob       Baker             2
   82 Cindy     Carter            1
   72 Donald    Dorph             3
   70 Donald    Dorph             1
   69 Cindy     Carter            4
   65 Donald    Dorph             2
   39 Cindy     Carter            2
```

UNION

The UNION operator combines the results of multiple SELECT statements into one result. The following example makes a list of company and individual customers with an outstanding balance greater than $50. The first SELECT statement takes data from the CompanyAccounts table and the second pulls data from the IndividualAccounts table:

```
# Select accounts with balances greater than $50.00.
SELECT CompanyName, FEIN, AccountBalance
FROM CompanyAccounts
WHERE AccountBalance > 0
  UNION
SELECT FirstName + ' ' + LastName, SSN, AccountBalance
```

```
FROM IndividualAccounts
WHERE AccountBalance > 0
```

The one important rule for combining queries with the UNION operator is that the queries' fields must match. Each query must return the same number of fields and corresponding fields must have compatible data types. In the previous example, the first two columns are text and the third is monetary so the queries return compatible values.

INSERT

The INSERT statement adds a new record to a database table. There are two main variations on the INSERT statement. The first explicitly lists the names of the fields for which the statement is specifying values:

```
INSERT INTO table_name
(field1, field2, ...)
VALUES (value1, value2, ...)
```

To insert a NULL value in a field, simply omit the field. For example, suppose the People table has the fields LastName, FirstName, and PhoneNumber. The following statement creates a new record with a NULL PhoneNumber value:

```
INSERT INTO People
(LastName, FirstName)
VALUES ('Crissy', 'Canon')
```

Alternatively, you can list the field and explicitly give it a NULL value as in this example:

```
INSERT INTO People
(LastName, FirstName, PhoneNumber)
VALUES ('Crissy', 'Canon', NULL)
```

In the second variation on the INSERT statement, you do not list any fields, so you must include a value for every field in the order in which they are defined by the table. For example, if the People table defines the FirstName, LastName, and PhoneNumber fields in that order, the following statement is equivalent to the previous one:

```
INSERT INTO People
VALUES ('Crissy', 'Canon', NULL)
```

When you use this variation, you must include values for every field and the values must appear in their proper order. If you want to leave a field's value undefined, use the NULL value.

Fields defined with the IDENTITY attribute are the exception to this rule. When you define an IDENTITY field, the database automatically generates values for the field so you should not specify its value. Include values for the other fields in their proper order and just pretend the IDENTITY field doesn't exist.

For example, suppose you define the Employees table using this command:

```
CREATE TABLE Employees (
    EmployeeId   INT            IDENTITY (1001, 1) PRIMARY KEY,
```

```
    FirstName    VARCHAR(40)    NOT NULL,
    LastName     VARCHAR(40)    NOT NULL
)
```

When you create new Employees records, the database automatically generates the EmployeeId value starting with the value 1001 and incrementing the value by 1 every time you add a new record. The following statement adds a new record to the Employees table, ignoring the EmployeeId value:

```
INSERT INTO Employees
VALUES ('Daniel', 'Disappear')
```

The following statement uses the earlier INSERT syntax to add the same record:

```
INSERT INTO Employees
(FirstName, LastName)
VALUES ('Daniel', 'Disasper')
```

For more information on IDENTITY fields, see the "IDENTITY" section earlier in this appendix.

UPDATE

The UPDATE statement modifies a record in a table. The basic syntax is

```
UPDATE table_name
SET field1 = value1, field2 = value2, ...
[WHERE condition]
```

The following statement fixes a typographical error, changing the Employees table's LastName field value to Jones in every record that currently has a LastName value of Jone:

```
UPDATE Employees
SET LastName = 'Jones'
WHERE LastName = 'Jone'
```

It is important to remember that the database modifies every record in the database that meets the statement's WHERE conditions. If there happened to be a second record that was really supposed to have the LastName value Jone, this statement would modify that record, too.

To prevent possible accidents like this one, many tables have a primary key that acts as a unique unchanging identifier. For example, the Employees table might use an EmployeeId field. When you edit an Employees record, the application uses the EmployeeId to save any changes. The following statement shows how a program might fix the Jone error without damaging any records that really should have that value:

```
UPDATE Employees
SET LastName = 'Jones'
WHERE EmployeeId = 18278
```

A common mistake when using UPDATE statements is forgetting to include the WHERE clause entirely. The following statement changes the LastName value of every record in the table to Jones:

PART

I

APP

A

```
UPDATE Employees
SET LastName = 'Jones'
```

You should be suspicious of any UPDATE statement that has no WHERE clause. Mistakes like this one can cause a huge amount of damage in an instant.

Whenever you try to modify a record, the database verifies that any constraints involving the record are still satisfied. For example, suppose the CustomerOrders table contains a SoldBy field that references the Employees table's EmployeeId field. Now suppose you try to change an Employees record's EmployeeId value. If there are no CustomerOrders records referring to that EmployeeId, the modification succeeds. If any CustomerOrders record refers to that EmployeeId value, the UPDATE statement causes an error.

If the reference from the CustomerOrders table to the Employees table was defined with the ON UPDATE CASCADE clause, the database will perform the update and automatically modify any CustomerOrders records to match. See the section "FOREIGN KEY" earlier in this appendix for more information on cascading updates.

DELETE

The DELETE statement removes a record from a table. The basic syntax is

```
DELETE FROM table_name
[WHERE condition]
```

Like the UPDATE statement, the DELETE statement applies to all the records selected by the statement, so you need to be careful when you write this statement's WHERE clause. If you specify a unique and never changing value in the clause, such as a primary key value, the statement will delete only the record you want. If you use a set of fields that may not be unique, you may delete more than you bargain for.

As is the case with the UPDATE statement, forgetting the WHERE clause completely is a common mistake when using the DELETE statement. If you omit the WHERE clause, the database removes every record from the table.

Note that you do not need to remove the records from a table before you drop the table. If you want to destroy the table itself, just issue a DROP TABLE command. See the section "DROP TABLE" earlier in this appendix for more information.

Whenever you try to delete a record, the database verifies that any constraints involving the record are still satisfied. For example, suppose the CustomerOrder table contains a SoldBy field that references the Employees table's EmployeeId field. Now suppose you try to delete an Employees record. If there are no CustomerOrder records referring to that EmployeeId, the deletion succeeds. If any CustomerOrder record refers to that EmployeeId value, the DELETE statement causes an error.

If the reference from the CustomerOrders table to the Employees table was defined with the ON DELETE CASCADE clause, the database will perform the deletion and automatically delete any matching CustomerOrders records. See the section "FOREIGN KEY" earlier in this appendix for more information on cascading deletions.

AGGREGATE FUNCTIONS

Aggregate functions perform an operation on a group of values taken from a series of records. For example, the AVG function computes the average of a field's value over the selected records. The following statement calculates the average Score value for records with StudentId value 1001:

```
SELECT AVG(Score)
FROM Scores
WHERE StudentId = 1001
```

Table A.3 describes aggregate functions available in SQL Server.

TABLE A.3   USEFUL AGGREGATE FUNCTIONS

Function	Purpose
AVG	Calculates the average of the selected values.
COUNT	Returns the number of selected records.
MAX	Returns the largest value selected.
MIN	Returns the smallest value selected.
SUM	Returns the sum of the selected values.
STDEV	Calculates the statistical standard deviation of the selected values.
STDEVP	Calculates the statistical standard deviation of the population of selected values.
VAR	Calculates the statistical variance of the selected values.
VARP	Calculates the statistical variance of the population of selected values.

The COUNT, AVG, and SUM functions can take the optional parameter DISTINCT to indicate they should consider only distinct rows. For example, the following statement selects the StudentId field from the TestScores table where the corresponding Score value is less than 70. The COUNT function counts the distinct StudentId values so this query returns the number of students who had a test score below 70:

```
SELECT COUNT (DISTINCT StudentId)
FROM TestScores
WHERE Score < 70
```

Older versions of SQL allow the MAX and MIN functions to take the DISTINCT parameter, although it doesn't change the value returned by those functions. The maximum of a set of values is the same as the maximum of the distinct values. To remain compatible with more recent SQL implementations, do not use DISTINCT with the MAX and MIN functions.

JOINS

A *join* is query that selects more than one table. Normally the tables are linked by fields that have the same meaning. The linking fields do not need to have the same names, although joins are less confusing if the do.

Suppose the Students table has a StudentId field. The TestScores table also has a StudentId field indicating the student who got a particular score. The two StudentId fields link the tables. The following query joins the two tables to select student information from the Students table plus test scores from the TestScores table:

```
SELECT TestNumber, LastName, FirstName, Score
FROM Students, TestScores
WHERE Students.StudentId = TestScores.StudentId
ORDER BY TestNumber, LastName, FirstName, Score
```

In many cases, that's as much as you need to know about joins. If every record in the Students table has corresponding records in the TestScores table and vice versa, joining the tables in this kind of query is straightforward. Things only get strange when records in one table do not have corresponding records in the other.

For example, suppose a new student enters the class. That student hasn't taken any tests yet so the TestScores table contains no records for the new student. When you join the two tables, what should the database return? Should it return the new Students record and give it NULL values for the Score field? Or should it ignore the new record and return nothing for this student?

The previous query ignores the new StudentId record because it does not match any TestScores record but SQL defines a join syntax that tells the database exactly what it should do in this situation.

The basic join syntax is

```
SELECT fields
FROM table1 join_clause table2
[ON on_clause1 [ON on_clause2]...]
[WHERE conditions]
[ORDER BY fields]
```

The join_clause tells the database how to resolve unmatched records in both tables. The following sections describe the four different kinds of join clauses. For the examples in those sections, assume the Numbers database has two tables named Ordinals and SpelledValues that map numeric values (1, 2, 3) to ordinal values (First, Second, Third) and spelled values (One, Two, Three). The tables have the following records:

```
Ordinals
1    First
2    Second
3    Third
4    Fourth

SpelledValues
1    One
```

```
2    Two
5    Five
6    Six
```

INNER JOIN

An inner join selects records from both tables that have matching records in the other table. This is the default if you use the JOIN keyword without any other modifiers, if you use the keywords CROSS JOIN, and when you don't use a join clause. The following queries all produce the same result:

```
# INNER JOIN
SELECT Ordinals.NumericValue, OrdinalValue, SpelledValue
FROM Ordinals INNER JOIN SpelledValues
  ON Ordinals.NumericValue = SpelledValues.NumericValue
ORDER BY Ordinals.NumericValue

# JOIN
SELECT Ordinals.NumericValue, OrdinalValue, SpelledValue
FROM Ordinals JOIN SpelledValues
  ON Ordinals.NumericValue = SpelledValues.NumericValue
ORDER BY Ordinals.NumericValue

# CROSS JOIN
SELECT Ordinals.NumericValue, OrdinalValue, SpelledValue
FROM Ordinals CROSS JOIN SpelledValues
WHERE Ordinals.NumericValue = SpelledValues.NumericValue
ORDER BY Ordinals.NumericValue

# WHERE
SELECT Ordinals.NumericValue, OrdinalValue, SpelledValue
FROM Ordinals, SpelledValues
WHERE Ordinals.NumericValue = SpelledValues.NumericValue
ORDER BY Ordinals.NumericValue
```

The following shows the result of these queries:

```
NumericValue OrdinalValue SpelledValue
============ ============ ============
           1 First        One
           2 Second       Two
           3 Third        NULL
           4 Fourth       NULL
```

LEFT JOIN

A left join selects all records from the left table even if there are no matching records in the right table. The following query selects all Ordinals records even if there are no corresponding SpelledValues records:

```
# LEFT JOIN
SELECT Ordinals.NumericValue, OrdinalValue, SpelledValue
FROM Ordinals LEFT JOIN SpelledValues
  ON Ordinals.NumericValue = SpelledValues.NumericValue
ORDER BY Ordinals.NumericValue
```

This query produces the following result:

```
NumericValue OrdinalValue SpelledValue
============ ============ ============
           1 First        One
           2 Second       Two
           3 Third        NULL
           4 Fourth       NULL
```

This clause can include the optional word OUTER to emphasize the fact that it is not an inner join, as in:

```
SELECT Ordinals.NumericValue, OrdinalValue, SpelledValue
FROM Ordinals LEFT OUTER JOIN SpelledValues
  ON Ordinals.NumericValue = SpelledValues.NumericValue
ORDER BY Ordinals.NumericValue
```

RIGHT JOIN

A right join selects all records from the right table even if there are no matching records in the left table. The following query selects all SpelledValues records even if there are no corresponding Ordinals records:

```
# RIGHT JOIN
SELECT Ordinals.NumericValue, OrdinalValue, SpelledValue
FROM Ordinals RIGHT JOIN SpelledValues
  ON Ordinals.NumericValue = SpelledValues.NumericValue
ORDER BY Ordinals.NumericValue
```

This query produces the following result:

```
NumericValue OrdinalValue SpelledValue
============ ============ ============
        NULL NULL         Five
        NULL NULL         Six
           1 First        One
           2 Second       Two
```

This clause can include the optional word OUTER to emphasize the fact that it is not an inner join as in:

```
SELECT Ordinals.NumericValue, OrdinalValue, SpelledValue
FROM Ordinals RIGHT OUTER JOIN SpelledValues
  ON Ordinals.NumericValue = SpelledValues.NumericValue
ORDER BY Ordinals.NumericValue
```

FULL JOIN

A full join selects all records from both tables even if there are no matching records in the other table. The following query selects all Ordinals and SpelledValues records:

```
# FULL JOIN
SELECT Ordinals.NumericValue, OrdinalValue, SpelledValue
FROM Ordinals FULL JOIN SpelledValues
  ON Ordinals.NumericValue = SpelledValues.NumericValue
ORDER BY Ordinals.NumericValue
```

This query produces the following result:

```
NumericValue OrdinalValue SpelledValue
============ ============ ============
        NULL NULL         Five
        NULL NULL         Six
           1 First        One
           2 Second       Two
           3 Third        NULL
           4 Fourth       NULL
```

This clause can include the optional word OUTER to emphasize the fact that it is not an inner join as in:

```
SELECT Ordinals.NumericValue, OrdinalValue, SpelledValue
FROM Ordinals FULL OUTER JOIN SpelledValues
  ON Ordinals.NumericValue = SpelledValues.NumericValue
ORDER BY Ordinals.NumericValue
```

SUMMARY

SQL is a relatively intuitive language. Usually you can look at an SQL statement and figure out what it means in a few seconds. After you have some experience with SQL, you will probably be able to read scripts and understand what they do with few problems.

The details can be a little tricky, particularly for complex SELECT statements and joins. When you are writing scripts, you may still need to occasionally refer to this appendix or to the online documentation.

PART

I

APP

A

THE VISUAL BASIC .NET DEVELOPMENT ENVIRONMENT

The Visual Basic .NET development environment comes with a bewildering assortment of tools, wizards, and windows for building, examining, and modifying Visual Basic projects. The environment is extremely configurable, letting you dock, undock, resize, hide, and reconfigure its windows and toolbars. This lets you build an environment that suits your particular development style. Unfortunately, it also allows you to confuse yourself by removing important tools and making your environment look nothing like the pictures shown in this book or other Visual Basic .NET books.

This appendix explains some of the basics of using the Visual Basic .NET development environment. It shows how you can build customized toolbars, shows where you can find some of the environment's more useful features, and tells how you can find windows that may have disappeared.

If you have not worked with Visual Basic before, you will probably find this information helpful. Even if you have used previous versions of Visual Basic, you may want to skim this material. A lot has changed since Visual Basic 6 and a few minutes now may save you a lot of trouble later.

GETTING STARTED

When you first start Visual Basic, the development environment looks like Figure B.1. Although no project is loaded, the environment already contains some tools. The Server Explorer tab on the left lists database connections and servers. Figure B.1 shows information about the server BENDER, the test server used to write this book.

To open an existing solution, select the File menu's Open Solution command. Use the file selection dialog to find the solution's `.sln` file and select it. Figure B.2 shows the development environment with the ExploreServer program described in Chapter 13 loaded.

Figure B.1
The Visual Basic development environment starts empty.

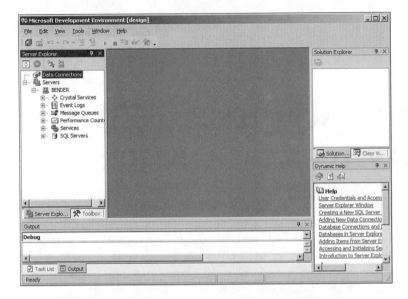

Figure B.2
The environment's toolbars depend on the type of file displayed.

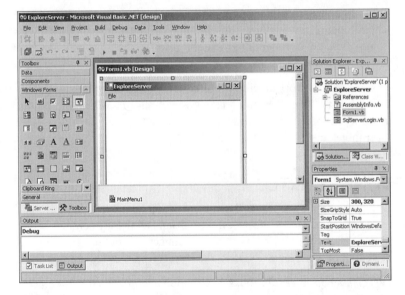

Because the program's main form is displayed in design mode, the development environment shows toolbars that are appropriate for editing a form. Similarly, the Toolbox window on the left shows tabs appropriate for editing a form. The following sections say a bit more about the toolbars and the Toolbox tabs.

CREATING A NEW SOLUTION

To create a new solution, select File, New, Project. In the New Project dialog shown in Figure B.3, select the project template for the type of project you want to create. Normally if you are building straightforward desktop applications, you will select the Windows Application template.

Figure B.3
The environment's toolbars depend on the type of file displayed.

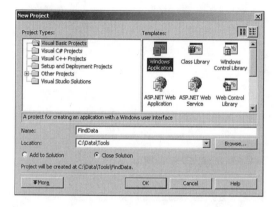

Be careful if you select some other kind of application. The next time you create a new project, the New Project dialog selects the template you last used by default. For example, suppose you normally build Windows applications but one day you need to make a class library. The next time you start a new project, the Class Library template is selected by default. If you don't notice, you may create the wrong kind of application.

Enter the directory where you want the new project created in the Location text box. Enter the name of the new project in the Name text box. When you click OK, the environment creates a new directory for the project inside the directory you specified in the Location text box. For example, if you set the Name to `FindData` and the Location to `C:\Data\Tools` as shown in Figure B.3, Visual Basic puts the project in the directory `C:\Data\Tools\FindData` and it names the main solution file `C:\Data\Tools\FindData\FindData.sln`.

TOOLBARS

The development environment contains 28 different toolbars to help you perform different tasks. It includes toolbars for editing images, building reports with Crystal Reports, debugging code, formatting controls on forms, and working with XML data.

The environment automatically hides and displays some of these toolbars depending on the file you are examining. For example, when you open a form in design mode, the environment displays tools for aligning controls on the form. When you display the form's code, the environment hides those tools.

You can easily configure these toolbars to suit your preferences. When you select the Tools menu's Customize command, the dialog shown in Figure B.4 appears. Use the check boxes to determine which toolbars are visible.

Figure B.4
You can customize the developer environment's toolbars.

Rather than modifying predefined toolbars, hide any you don't want and click the New button to create a new one. The new toolbar appears floating somewhere on the screen. Drag it to the bottom of the development environment's toolbars.

Next click the Commands tab to see the commands available as shown in Figure B.5. Select the category of command in the list on the left. Then click and drag commands from the list on the right into the new toolbar. In Figure B.5, you can see five debugging commands in the new toolbar just above the Toolbox on the left. When you finish building your new toolbar, close the Customize dialog.

Figure B.5
Use the Commands
tab to add commands
to your toolbar.

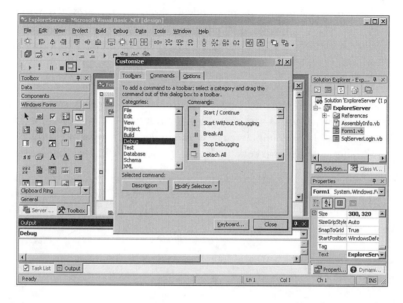

TOOLBOX TABS

Like the environment's toolbars, the Toolbox tabs adjust so they are appropriate for the type of file you are editing. When you open a textual file like the form code shown in Figure B.6, the Toolbox's only interesting tab is the Clipboard Ring. In Figure B.6, the mouse is hovering over the first Clipboard item so the environment is displaying that item's text in a tooltip. Click and drag one of the items into the text window to paste the text into the code.

Figure B.6
The Toolbox shows a
Clipboard Ring tab
when you open a
form's code view.

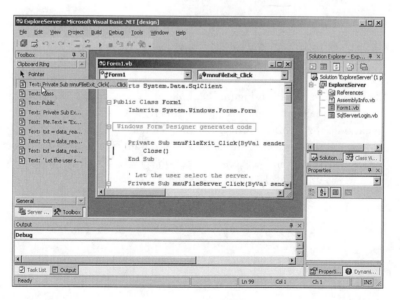

When you open a form in design mode as shown in Figure B.2, the Toolbox window displays the Data, Components, Windows Forms, and Clipboard Ring tabs. The Windows Forms tab is similar to the toolbox used by previous versions of Visual Basic and contains Windows controls that you can place on the form.

Many of these controls will be familiar to you if you have used a previous version of Visual Basic, with some minor variations. One difference between Visual Basic .NET and previous versions is that controls with no visible components appear below the form rather than on the form itself. For example, the MainMenu control shown in Figure B.2 appears below the form. This area may also contain database objects such as SqlConnections and DataSets.

Right-click on the tab and check the List View option to make the tab display its items in a one-column list including the tools' names. Figure B.7 shows the Toolbox window undocked and showing the Components tab in a List View. The Components tab contains non-graphical tools other than database tools.

Figure B.7
The Components tab holds non-graphical, non-data tools.

The Data tab, shown in Figure B.8, holds database-related tools such as DataSet, DataView, and database connection objects. You can create these objects at design time by dragging them onto the form. You can also create them at runtime using code. That method more closely matches the way a Visual Basic 6 program creates database objects, such as the ADODB.Connection and ADODB.Recordset objects. Other chapters in this book, particularly Chapters 5 and 6, explain how to use these objects.

Figure B.8
The Data tab holds
database object tools.

PROPERTIES

The Properties window is reminiscent of those used by previous versions of Visual Basic, although it has several new features. When you click on a control or other object in a form's design view, the Properties window displays that object's properties. Click on a property's value and enter a new value to change the property.

When you select some properties, the Properties window displays an ellipsis or drop-down arrow on the right. If you click this, a dialog box or drop-down list appears to let you select the property's new value.

Many properties are objects in their own right and they have their own properties. Click the plus sign to the left of the property to expand it and see its properties. Figure B.9 shows a form's Font property expanded to show its properties. You can set these subproperties individually or you can click the ellipsis to the right of the Font entry to define the font in a font selection dialog.

Some objects provide configuration functions as well as properties. Links to these functions appear immediately below the properties in the Properties window. For example, Figure B.10 shows the Properties window for an OleDbDataAdapter object named OleDbDataAdapter1. Below the Modifiers property are three links: Configure Data Adapter, Generate Dataset, and Preview Data. Click those links to invoke the object's configuration functions.

When you select an object that has configuration functions, the functions also often appear in the development environment's menus. When you select an OleDbDataAdapter object, for example, the Configure Data Adapter, Generate Dataset, and Preview Data commands appear in the Data menu.

Figure B.9
The Font property is an object with properties of its own.

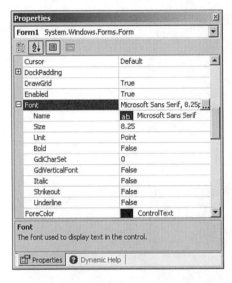

Figure B.10
The OleDbDataAdapter object provides Configure Data Adapter, Generate Dataset, and Preview Data commands.

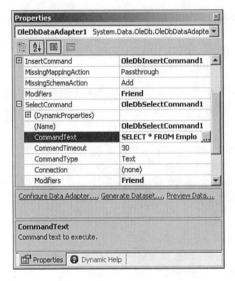

FINDING LOST WINDOWS

Sometimes you can lose a window. For instance, when you run a and step through the code in debug mode, the environment hides the Server Explorer window by default. To restore the window, select the View menu's Server Explorer command.

You can use the View menu's other commands to find other lost windows. Use the Other Windows submenu to restore the Command window or Output window if you close them and want them back.

Note that some windows don't display meaningful data under all circumstances. For example, the Properties window is empty unless you have a form open in design mode. While the program is executing and when you have a text module open, the Properties window is empty.

SUMMARY

This appendix explains only a few of the many new features in the Visual Basic .NET development environment. It is not intended as a comprehensive description of the environment's new tools but as an introduction to some of the areas that may slow you down while you try to read this book. Having learned how to customize the environment's toolbars and how to find lost windows, you should be able to understand why your development environment doesn't look exactly like the pictures in this book.

PART

I

APP

B

INDEX

SYMBOLS

1NF (first normal form), 41-42

2NF (second normal form), 42-46

3NF (second normal form), 46-47

A

AcceptChanges method, 106-107, 121, 128
    in LoadTreeView subroutine, 229
    in SaveChanges subroutine, 219

AcceptChangesDuringFill property, 171

AcceptRejectRule property, 119

Access, 27-29, 55-60, 68

access
    controlling with views, 76-77
    revoking, 80
    stored procedures, 79-80

Access Database Wizard, 55-57

account_id parameter, 73

Added row state, 128

AddField method, 304-307

AddNew method, 144, 218, 273

AddRange method, 9

Address value, 155

AddressId field, 264

AddTableRow subroutine, 147

AddToWhereClause method, 312-315

ADO.NET
    Datacolumn object, 133
    DataRelation object, 138-139
    DataRow object, 126
    DataRowView object, 145
    DataSet object, 105-106
    DataTable object, 113
    DataView object, 141

ADODB.Connection object, 390

ADODB.Recordset object, 390

AfterSelect event handler, 229

aggregate functions, 379

AllowDBNull property, 133-134

AllowDelete property, 143-144

AllowEdit property, 143-144

AllowNew property, 143-144

ALTER DATABASE command, 355

ALTER TABLE statement, 363-365

application designs, 35
    entities, 36-38
    refining, 38-40
    requirements, 36

AppName parameter, 11

ArrangeControls subroutine, 267

AS clause, 371

AssignedTo field, 299

attribute_id field, 326

attribute_name field, 326

attribute_value field, 326

AutoIncr program, 134-136

AutoIncrement property, 134-136

AutoIncrementSeed property, 134-136

AutoIncrementStep property, 134-136

AVG function, 379

B

BACKUP DATABASE privilege, 73

BACKUP LOG privilege, 73

BeginEdit method, 128

BeginTransaction method, 156, 180

BENDER server, 385

BIGINT data type, 356

BINARY data type, 357, 359

BindControls subroutine, 236-238

binding, 209

BindingContext method, 217

BIT data type, 356

bitmap, 245

bound controls, 209
    codes in, 236-238
    selecting records with, 224-225

btnCreateTable_Click event handler, 160

btnDeleteRows_Click event handler, 160

btnDropTable_Click event handler, 160

btnExecute_Click event handler, 184

btnInsertRecords_Click event handler, 160

btnList_Click event handler, 167

btnOrderAdd_Click event handler, 294

btn_Click event handler, 312, 315

C

calculated fields, 225-227

Cancel method, 168

CancelChanges command, 219

CancelEdit method, 128

Cascade value, 119

CaseSensitive property, 114-115

Catch block, 180-181

ChangeDatabase method, 156

CHAR data type, 356, 358

CHECK clauses, 258

CHECK constraint, 362

CheckModified subroutine, 281

ChildColumns property, 140

ChildKeyConstraint property, 141

ChildRelations method, 117, 202

ChildTable property, 141

Class Library template, 387

Clear Errors button, 122-123

Clear method, 105-106, 121

ClearErrors method, 123

Clerks role, 81-83

Clipboard Ring, 389

Clone method, 110, 124

Close method, 155

Closing event handler, 149
closing SqlConnection with, 152

saving changes to databases with, 216, 219

ColMapping program, 136-137

column constraints, 355, 359-360

Column Error button, 122

ColumnChanged event handler, 281-282

ColumnClick event handler, 318

ColumnMapping property, 136-137

ColumnName property, 137

ColumnnChanged event handler, 124

ColumnnChanging event handler, 124

Columns collection, 114

Columns Collection Editor, 213, 226

Columns property, 226

CombinedName field, 226-227

ComboBox, 9-10, 214, 234

comma-separated value (CSV) files, 14-15

Commands tab, 388

CommandText property, 98, 157, 165

CommandTimeout property, 166

CommandType property, 166

Commit method, 180

Compare method, 318

CompareItems method, 318

compiling, 9-10

complex binding, 224

Components tab, 390

composite indexes, 50-51

Configure Data Adapter link, 226

Connect Timeout value, 154

Connection Lifetime value, 154

connection pooling, 152-154

Connection property, 157, 166

Connection Timeout value, 154

ConnectionString property, 87-90, 151-155

ConnectionTimeout property, 156

connect_string parameter, 308

CONSTRAINT keyword, 359-360

constraints, 51-52
column, 359-360
keyword, 359-360
stored procedures for, 332
table, 362-363

Constraints class, 117

constructors, 140

Contacts program, 209-211, 218-224

ContactsCreate.sql, 210

ContactsLetterLists program, 233-236

ContactsList program, 224-225

ContactsListCombined program, 225-227

ContactsPopulate.sql, 210

ContactsTreeView program, 228-233

Copy method, 110, 124

COUNT function, 379

Count method, 275

Count property, 144, 217

CREATE DATABASE command, 352-354

CREATE DATABASE privilege, 73-74

CREATE DEFAULT privilege, 73

CREATE FUNCTION privilege, 73

CREATE INDEX statement, 366

CREATE PROCEDURE privilege, 73

CREATE TABLE privilege, 73-74

CREATE TABLE statement, 355-356

CREATE VIEW privilege, 73

CREATE VIEW statement, 368-369

CreateCommand method, 157

CreateParameter method, 168

Crystal Reports, 387

CSV (comma-separated value) files, 14-15

CurrencyManager class, 217-218

Customer Addresses table, 265-266

customer detail forms, 285-287

Customer List command, 302

customer list forms, 282-285

CustomerAddresses table, 264-266, 276-278

CustomerFormEndAllEdits subroutine, 294

CustomerGrid program, 302-303
    RecordList form in, 303-306

CustomerID field, 139, 277-278

CustomerListView program, 317
    displaying records in, 321-322
    RecordSelected event in, 322-323
    sorting records in, 318-321

CustomerOrders table, 264-265, 290-292

Customers table, 263-265, 276-277

D

data
    binding, 209
    compiling, 9-10
    displaying, 214-215, 271-273

    merging related sets of, 116
    ordering, 26
    program-generated, 147-148
    safety of, 241
    storing, 9
        in EasyDraw program, 242-243
    validating, 258-261
    XML, 149-150

Data Adapter Configuration Wizard, 99-100

data adapters, 99-103

Data Form Wizard, 90-94

data forms, 95

Data Link Properties dialog, 87-90

Data Source value, 155

Data tab, 390

data types, 134, 356-357
    stored procedures for, 340

data-centric application design, 35

Database property, 156

Database value, 155-156

databases
    access to, 79-80
    adding tables to, 355-356
    altering, 355
    application designs, 35-40
    connecting to, 210-211
    creating, 352-354
        with Microsoft Access, 55-60
        with SQL, 61-65
    data types, 340
    default, 79-80
    deleting, 354
    design tools, 54-55
    entities, 36-38
    grouping in, 373-374
    hacking, 70-71
    indexes, 26, 49-50
    keys, 48-49
    normalization, 41-47
    passwords, 68-71
    physical security, 72
    privileges, 72-73
    products, 27-29
    reformatted diagrams, 47-48
    relational, 23
    roles, 80-81
    security, 27, 67-68

    selecting records from, 372-373
    servers, 325-327
    sorting in, 374-375
    stored procedures for, 37, 327-329
    structures, 325
    updating, 53-54
    validating data in, 258-261
    XML, 193

database_object parameter, 74

DataColumn, 133-138

DataErrors program, 122-124

DataEvents program, 125-126

DataGrid, 132, 143

DataGrid control, 238-239

DataGridTableStyle object, 316

DataRelation, 129, 138-139
    constructors, 140
    properties, 140-141

DataRow, 126
    methods, 126-133
    properties, 127-128

DataRowVersion.Current value, 146

DataRowVersion.Default value, 146

DataRowVersion.Original value, 146

DataRowVersion.Proposed value, 146

DataRowView, 145, 317

DataSafe function, 204-205, 294

DataSafe subroutine, 248-249

DataSet, 101-106, 210-211
    adding and deleting records in, 218
    collections, 105-106
    defining, 211, 213-214
    displaying data in, 214-215
    displaying pictures in, 215-216
    methods, 106-113
    navigating through, 216-218

DataSource property, 156, 237, 239

DataStuff.vb module, 281

DataTable, 113
  Constraints collection, 117-121
  events, 124-126
  filling, 333-334
  methods, 115-117, 122-124
  properties, 114-115

DataType property, 134

DataView, 141, 233-236
  method, 144-145
  properties, 142-145

DataViewRowState.Added value, 115

DataViewRowState.Current Rows value, 115

DataViewRowState.Deleted value, 115

DataViewRowState.Modified value, 115

DataViewRowState.Modified Original value, 115

DataViewRowState.None value, 115

DataViewRowState.Original Rows value, 115

DataViewRowState. Unchanged value, 115

DATETIME data type, 356

DBAs role, 81

DbType property, 169

DBValidateGrid program, 258-259

db_name parameter, 306

debugging, 387-388

DECIMAL data type, 356-357

deep multi-table XML files, 195-196

DEFAULT clause, 355

default database, 79-80

default language, 80

DefaultValue property, 133-134

Delete command, 209

Delete method, 129, 144, 275

DELETE privilege, 74

DELETE statement, 378-379

DeleteCommand property, 171

Deleted row state, 128

DeleteRule property, 119, 266

DeleteSetting routine, 11

denormalization, 47

DENY statement, 75

Detached row state, 128

Direction property, 169

DisplayCustomerDetails subroutine, 267, 271-273

DisplayCustomerForm subroutine, 283

DisplayData subroutine, 181

DisplayDataRelation subroutine, 202

DisplayDataStructure subroutine, 202

DisplayMember property, 225, 234, 237

DisplayOrderDetails subroutine, 286

DisplayResults subroutine, 315-316, 321-322

display_name parameter, 306

DISTINCT keyword, 370

Dock property, 96-97

DoubleClick event handler, 283

DrawALine subroutine, 243-244

DrawAnEllipse subroutine, 243

DrawARectangle subroutine, 243

DrawDataRow subroutine, 243, 246

DrawDataSet subroutine, 243, 250

DROP DATABASE command, 354

DROP EXISTING keyword, 367

DROP INDEX statement, 368

DROP TABLE statement, 159, 185, 365

DROP VIEW statement, 369

E

EasyDraw program, 241-242
  DataSafe subroutine, 248-249
  drawing
    existing objects in, 243
    new objects in, 244-248
  menu commands, 249-254
  MRU (most recently used) list, 254-258
  storing data in, 242-243

EditXml program, 204-206

Enabled property, 143

encryption, 79

End Try statement, 96

EndAllEdits subroutine, 273, 281

EndCurrentEdit command, 219

EndCurrentEdit method, 273

EndEdit method, 128

entities, 36-38

ER (entity-relationship) diagrams, 38

EraseRubberband subroutine, 245

EXECUTE privilege, 75

ExecuteNonQuery method, 159-163, 296

ExecuteQuery subroutine, 185-186

ExecuteReader method, 157-159

ExecuteScalar method, 157, 163-164

ExecuteXmlReader method, 164-165

ExploreDataBase subroutine, 342-343

ExploreRelations program, 345-349

ExploreRelations subroutine, 346-347

ExploreServer program, 341-345

ExploreServer subroutine, 342-343

ExploreTable subroutine, 342-347

Expression property, 137-138

Extensible Markup Language. *See* XML

F

FieldInfo class, 308-309

fields, 23
indexes, 49
keys, 48-49

field_alignment parameter, 307

field_delimeter parameter, 306

file names, 353

file sizes, 353

FileIsLoaded subroutine, 249-250

FileTitle helper function, 251

Fill method, 170-172, 176

FILLFACTOR parameter, 366-367

FillSchema method, 173-174

Find method, 144

Find property, 145

first normal form (1NF), 41-42

FirstName field, 225-227

fixed-length records, 15-17

FLOAT data type, 356-357

Font property, 391

FOREIGN KEY constraint, 361-362

foreign keys, 48-49, 118, 331-332

ForeignKeyConstraint, 118-121, 266-267

FormatString property, 186

forms
creating, 90-94
customizing, 95-97
grid, 95-96
single-record, 97

form_id parameter, 307-308

frmRecordList form, 303-306

FROM clause, 371

FromFile method, 215

from_clause parameter, 308

full joins, 382-383

G

Generate Dataset command, 101, 391

GerOrdinal method, 178

GetAllSettings function, 11

GetBoolean method, 177

GetByte method, 177

GetBytes method, 177

GetChanges method, 107-110, 121, 219

GetChar method, 177

GetChars method, 177

GetChildrenMethod, 130-132

GetChildRows method, 129

GetColumnError method, 127

GetColumnsinError method, 123, 127

GetDataTypeName method, 178

GetDateTime method, 177

GetDecimal method, 177

GetDouble method, 177

GetErrors method, 122-124

GetFieldType method, 178

GetFileContents function, 14-15

GetFloat method, 177

GetGuid method, 177

GetInt16 method, 177

GetInt32 method, 177

GetInt64 method, 177

GetName method, 178

GetParentRow method, 129

GetParentRows method, 129-132

GetSchemaTable method, 158, 178, 336-338

GetSetting routine, 11-13

GetSqlBinary method, 178

GetSqlBoolean method, 178

GetSqlByte method, 178

GetSqlDateTime method, 178

GetSqlDecimal method, 178

GetSqlDouble method, 178

GetSqlGuid method, 178

GetSqlInt16 method, 178

GetSqlInt32 method, 178

GetSqlInt64 method, 178

GetSqlMoney method, 178

GetSqlSingle method, 178

GetSqlString method, 178

GetSqlValue method, 178-179

GetSqlValues method, 178-179

GetString method, 177

GetValue method, 178-179

GetValues method, 178-179

GetXml method, 111, 113

GetXmlSchema method, 113

global control, 281

GRANT statement, 73-75

grid forms, 95-96

GROUP BY clause, 373-374

H

hacking, 70-71

HasChanges method, 106,
checking changes in data with, 149, 219,
in DataSafe subroutine, 248
in OrderEntryBig program, 276

HasErrors method, 107, 121, 127

HAVING clause, 374

I

IComparer interface, 318
IDENTITY field, 359,
    376-377
Image class, 215
IMAGE data type, 357-358
ImportRow method, 115
increment parameter, 359
indexes, 26, 49-50
    composite, 50-51
    creating, 366
    duplicates in, 51
    empty spaces in, 367
    rebuilding, 367
    removing, 368
    stored procedures for, 332
INI files, 17-21
Initial catalog value, 151, 155
InitializeForm method, 304,
    307-312
IniToXml subroutine, 18-21
inner joins, 381
INSERT privilege, 74, 83
INSERT statement, 180-181,
    376-377
InsertCommand property, 171
INT data type, 356
Internet, 68
INTO clause, 371
IS NOT NULL operation,
    303
IS NULL operation, 303
IsDbNull method, 179
IsNullable property, 170
IsSelectField property, 310
is_display_field parameter, 307
is_select field parameter,
    306-307
Item method, 126-127,
    144-145
ItemArray method, 127
ItemChanged event handler,
    220, 229

J

JOIN clause, 312
joins, 380-383
join_clause parameter, 308

K

Key parameter, 11
keys, 48-49
    primary, 116
    stored procedures for,
        331-332

L

LastIndexOf method, 251
LastModified record, 298
LastName field, 225-227
lblCustomerName control,
    267
lblPosition label control, 218
left joins, 381-382
LIKE operator, 373
List Errors button, 122-123
ListBox, 234
ListView
    displaying results in, 321-322
    output, 317
    sorting records in, 318-321
ListViewItemSorter class, 318
ListViewSorter class, 318
Load event handler, 217, 219,
    267
LoadData subroutine, 266
LoadDataFile subroutine, 250,
    256
LoadDataRow method, 115
LoadMruFile subroutine, 256
LoadMruList subroutine, 12
LoadTable subroutine, 266
LoadTreeView subroutine,
    228-229
LOG ON clause, 353

logical file name, 353
login information, 80
Login program, 69-71
lookup tables, 52

M

MakeFieldList subroutine, 310
many-to-many relationships,
    38-40
many-to-one relationships, 40
MappingName property, 316
MarkModified subroutine,
    273-274
master-detail relationships, 40
MAX function, 379
Max Pool Size value, 155
MaxAddressId function, 274
MaxLength property, 133-134,
    266
MaxOrderId function, 294
MdiChildren collection, 283
Merge method, 110
Microsoft Access, 27-29
MIN function, 379
MissingMappingAction prop-
    erty, 173
MissingSchemaAction.Add
    value, 110
MissingSchemaAction.AddWit
    h Key value, 110
MissingSchemaAction.Error
    value, 110
mnuDataNew_Click event
    handler, 229
mnuDataNew_Delete event
    handler, 229
mnuFileNew_Click subrou-
    tine, 250
mnuFileOpen_Click event
    handler, 204
mnuFileServer_Click event
    handler, 341, 346
mnuWinCustomerList_Click
    event handler, 304

Modified row state, 128

Modifiers property, 391

MONEY data type, 356

MRU (most recently used) files, 12-13

MRU (most recently used) list, 254-258

MruAdd subroutine, 255

MruLoad subroutine, 255

MruRemove subroutine, 255

MruSave subroutine, 255

MskeItem subroutine, 158

multi-table XML files, 195

multi-user order-entry system, 289-290

   database design, 290-292

   picking customers in, 299

   query-by-example form, 298

   real-time customer lists, 298-299

   reservations in, 292-294, 299

   source codes, 294-298

MultiColumnRelation program, 139

m_Backbuffer variable, 245

m_ConnectString variable, 309

m_DataRow variable, 245

m_DataSet object, 243

m_DataSet variable, 309

m_DataTabl object, 243

m_Drawing variable, 245

m_FieldInfos collection, 316

m_FieldInfos variable, 309

m_FormdId variable, 309

m_FromClause variable, 309

m_MruFileNames collection, 255-256

m_SelectedTool variable, 245

N

NCHAR data type, 358

nested XML files, 196-197

Network Address value, 155

network packet analyzer, 72

network security, 68

New command, 209

New Project dialog box, 387

NewRow method, 116

NextResult method, 179

no-security databases, 67

None value, 119

normalization, 41-47

NOT NULL clause, 355

NOT NULL constraint, 360

NTEXT data type, 357-358

NUMERIC data type, 357

NVARCHAR data type, 356, 358

O

object linking and embedding. *See* OLE DB

OCHAR data type, 356

OLE DB, 182-183

OleDataAdapter class, 183

OleDbCommand class, 183

OleDbCommandBuilder class, 183

OleDbConnection class, 183

OleDbDataAdapter object, 391

OleDbDataReader class, 183

OleDbParameter class, 183

OleDbTransactions class, 183

ON clause, 353

one-to-many relationships, 39-40

Open method, 151, 155

Open Solution command, 385

ORDER BY clause, 374-375

order-entry applications, 263

   adding records in, 273-275

   canceling data changes in, 276

   customer detail form, 285-287

   customer list form, 282-285

   database design, 264-265

   deleting records in, 275-276

   displaying data in, 271-273

   global control in, 281-282

   loading data in, 265-271

   multi-user, 289-299

   one-form design, 263-264

   saving changes in, 276-280

   tabbed design, 280-281

OrderEntryBig program, 263

   adding records in, 273-275

   canceling data changes in, 276

   database design, 264-265

   deleting records in, 275-276

   displaying data in, 271-273

   loading data in, 265-271

   one-form design, 263-264

   saving changes in, 276-280

OrderEntryMultiUser program, 289-290

   database design, 290-292

   displaying reservations in, 299

   picking customers in, 299

   query-by-example form, 298

   real-time customer lists, 298-299

   reservations in, 292-294

   source codes, 294-298

OrderEntryTabs program, 280-281, 290

   customer detail form, 285-287

   customer list form, 282-285

   global control in, 281-282

OrderId field, 265, 290-292, 307

Orders table, 263

order_by_clause parameter, 308

Ordinal property, 138

orphaned records, 53

P

PAD INDEX property, 367

ParameterName property, 170

Parameters property, 166-168

ParentColumns property, 140

ParentKeyConstraint property, 141

ParentRelations method, 117, 202

ParentTable property, 141

Password value, 155

passwords, 68-72

PERCENT keyword, 371

physical file name, 353

picCanvas_MouseDown event handler, 245

picCanvas_MouseMove event handler, 246

picCanvas_MouseUp event handler, 246

picSnapshot field, 215

PictureBox, 215

Pooling value, 155

Position property, 217

PositionChanged event, 218-219

Precision property, 170

Prepare method, 168

Preview Data command, 391

PRIMARY KEY constraint, 360

primary keys, 48-49, 116, 331

PrimaryKey property, 116

privileges, 72-76

ProgramGenerated program, 147-148

Properties window, 391

Q

Query Builder, 97-99, 211

query-by-example form, 298, 301-303

R

range tables, 52-53

Read method, 158

ReadOnly property, 133-134

ReadXml method, 111, 113, 250

ReadXml program, 201-204

ReadXmlSchema method, 113

REAL data type, 356-357

real-time customer lists, 298-299

record locking, 292

record selection forms
AddField method, 306
InitializeForm method, 307-308
initializing, 309-312

RecordList form, 308

records, 23

RecordSelected event, 317, 322

RecordSelected method, 304

Recordset, 105

REFERENCES privilege, 74-75

referential constraints, 51-52

Registry, 11-13

RejectChanges method, 106-107, 121, 128, 276

relational databases, 23-24
indexes, 26
ordering data in, 26
products, 27-29
relationships, 24-26
security, 27
stored procedures, 27

RelationName property, 141

Relations collection, 105

relationships, 24-26
many-to-many, 38-40
master-detail, 40
one-to-many, 39-40
stored procedures for, 331-332

RemoveAt method, 218-219

RemoveComments function, 184

RemoveGridColumns subroutine, 267

ReserveCustomerRecord function, 295-296

ReservedBy field, 293-296

RestrictControls event handler, 266

REVOKE statement, 76

right joins, 382

roles, 80-82

Rollback method, 180

root elements, 242

Row method, 145

RowChanged event handler, 125, 245

RowChanging event handler, 125

RowDeleted event handler, 125

RowDeleting event handler, 125

RowError property, 122, 127

RowFilter property, 142-143, 235

Rows collection, 114

RowState property, 128

RowStateFilter property, 142-143, 235

RowUpdated event handler, 174

RowUpdating event handler, 174

RowVersion property, 145

Rule enumeration, 119

RunScript program, 183-191, 327

S

Save command, 219

SaveBackBuffer subroutine, 245

SaveChanges subroutine, 219-220

SaveData subroutine, 205, 248-250, 277-280

SaveSetting routine, 11-13

SaveTableChange subroutine, 277-280

Scale property, 170

schemas, 200-201

second normal form (2NF), 42-46

Section parameter, 11

security, 27, 67-68, 72

seed parameter, 359

Select nethod, 114-115

SELECT privilege, 74-75, 83

SELECT statement, 370-371
   building, 97-99, 312-313
   changing, 226
   clauses, 371-375
   executing, 164

SelectCommand property, 171, 313

SelectedIndexChanted event handler, 234

SelectSingleNode method, 22

Server Explorer, 385

Server value, 155

servers, 325-327

ServerVersion property, 156

Set Database Password command, 68

SET MASTER command, 354

SetColumnError method, 122, 127

SetDefault value, 119

SetNull value, 119

SetParentRow method, 129

SetSortIndicator subroutine, 318

Setting parameter, 11

SetUnspecified method, 133

Show method, 312

ShowPosition subroutine, 219

simple binding, 224

single-record forms, 97

single-table XML files, 194-195

Size property, 170

SLN file, 385

SMALLDATETIME data type, 356

SMALLINT data type, 356

SMALLMONEY data type, 356

SnapshotFile field, 215-216

Sort property, 144-145

SortColumn property, 318, 321

Sorting property, 318

SortOrder, 318

source codes, 9-10, 294-298

SourceColumn property, 170

SourceVision property, 170

sp_addlogin procedure, 78, 80

sp_addrole procedure, 81-82

sp_columns stored procedure, 338

sp_columns_privileges stored procedure, 338

sp_column_privileges procedure, 84

sp_databases stored procedure, 327-328

sp_datatype stored procedure, 340

sp_default language procedure, 80

sp_defaultdb procedure, 80

sp_denylogin procedure, 78-79

sp_depends stored procedure, 331

sp_droplogin procedure, 79

sp_fkeys stored procedure, 331-332

sp_grantdbaccessprocedure, 79

sp_grantlogin procedure, 78

sp_help stored procedure, 329

sp_helpconstraint stored procedure, 332

sp_helpdb stored procedure, 328-329

sp_helpfile stored procedure, 329

sp_helpindex stored procedure, 332

sp_helplanguage procedure, 83

sp_helplogins procedure, 82

sp_helprole procedure, 82

sp_helprolemember procedure, 83

sp_helpserver stored procedure, 326

sp_helptext stored procedure, 339-340

sp_helpuser procedure, 82

sp_password procedure, 80

sp_pkeys stored procedure, 331

sp_revokedbaccess procedure, 80

sp_revokelogin procedure, 78

sp_server_info stored procedure, 325-326, 339

sp_spaceused stored procedure, 329

sp_stored_procedures stored procedure, 338

sp_tables stored procedure, 330

sp_table_privileges procedure, 83

sp_who stored procedure, 327

SQL (Structured Query Language), 351
   building databases with, 61-65
   SELECT statement, 97-99

SQL Server, 151
   access to, 78
   authentication, 78-79
   data access objects, 150
   DENY statement, 75
   GRANT statement, 73-75
   REVOKE statement, 76
   SELECT statement, 226
   stored procedures, 77-85, 325-332, 338-340

SqlCommand class, 313
   methods, 157-165, 168
   properties, 165-168
   purpose of, 151

SqlCommandBuilder class, 174-175
   in BindControls subroutine, 237
   in database design, 264-265
   purpose of, 151
   WHERE clause, 295

SqlConnection class, 313
   closing, 152-153
   connection pooling, 151-152
   ConnectionString values, 154
   methods, 155-157
   Open method, 69
   properties, 154-156
   purpose of, 151

SqlDataAdapter class, 170-171
   events, 174
   example program, 175-177
   loading data with, 265
   methods, 171-174
   properties, 171-174
   preventing overwriting by, 292
   purpose of, 151

SqlDataReader class, 177-178
   filling, 335-336
   methods, 178-179
   purpose of, 151

SqlDbType property, 170

SqlParameter class, 151, 166-170

SqlTransaction class, 151, 168, 179-182

State property, 155

STDEV function, 379

STEDVP function, 379

stored procedures, 27, 77-79, 84-85
   column privileges, 338
   columns, 338
   database access, 79-80
   database information, 82-84
   databases, 327-328
   datatype info, 340
   depends, 331
   foreign keys, 331-332
   help, 329
   help server, 326
   helpconstraint, 332
   helpdb, 328-329
   helpfile, 329
   helpindex, 332
   helptext, 339-340
   login information, 80, 82-84
   primary keys, 331
   server info, 325-326
   server information, 82-84
   spaceused, 329
   stored procedure, 338
   tables, 330
   user info, 327

Structured Query Language. See SQL

SubString method, 313

SUM function, 379

Supervisors role, 81-82

sysusers table, 330

T

table constraints, 355, 362-363

TableColumns program, 333-334

TableColumns2 program, 335-336

TableColumns3 program, 337-338

TableMappings collection, 236

TableMappings property, 172-173

TableName property, 114, 211-213

tables, 23
   adding indexes to, 366
   adding records to, 376-377
   altering, 363-365
   constraints, 362-363
   creating, 355-356
   creating new entries, 212-213
   deleting records from, 378-379
   fields, 332-334
   inserting records into, 371
   keys, 48-49
   names, 114
   privileges for, 74, 83
   range, 52-53
   removing, 365
   selecting data from, 371
   stored procedures for, 329-330
   updating, 53-54, 377-378
   using names as keys, 213

Tables collection, 105

Tables Collection Editor, 211, 226

Tables property, 211, 213

Tag property, 322

tbrDrawingTools_ButtonClick event handler, 245

TEXT data type, 356, 358

Text property, 214

TextBox, 214-215, 234

TextChanged event handler, 219

third normal form (3NF), 46-47

TINYINT data type, 356

toolbars, 387-388

Toolbox tabs, 389-390

TOP number clause, 371

Transaction program, 181-182

Transaction property, 168

transactions, 179-182

TreeNode field, 228-229

TreeView control, 228-233

TrimNonPrinting function, 184

Try block, 180-181

Try Catch block, 180-182

Try statement, 96

txtSnapshotFile control, 219

U

Unchanged row state, 128

UNION operator, 375-376

UNIQUE constraint, 361

Unique property, 133-134

UniqueConstraint, 117-118

Update method, 171, 174

UPDATE privilege, 74-75

UPDATE statement, 377-378

UpdateCommand property, 171

UpdateRule property, 119

UseDataAdapter program, 175-177

UseExecuteNonQuery program, 160-163

UseExecuteReader program, 157, 159

UseExecuteScalar program, 163-164

UseExecuteXmlReader program, 164-165

UseParameters program, 167-168

user id, 79

User ID value, 155

user passwords, 68-71

user-centric application design, 35

V

ValidateGrid program, 259-261

ValidateZip subroutine, 259

Value property, 170

VAR function, 379

VARBINARY data type, 357, 359

VARCHAR data type, 356, 358

VarChar type, 167

VARP function, 379

views
    adding indexes to, 366
    controlling access with, 76-77
    creating, 368-369
    privileges for, 74
    removing, 369

Visible property, 215

Visual Basic
    editing XML files in, 197-199
    loading XML data in, 201-204
    saving XML data from, 204-206

Visual Basic .NET, 385
    creating new solutions in, 387
    data types, 134
    finding lost windows in, 392-393
    Properties window, 391
    starting, 385-386
    toolbars, 387-388
    Toolbox tabs, 389-390

Visual Data Manager Add-In, 29

Visual Studio .NET, 152

W

WHERE clause, 25-26, 372-373
    adding new conditions to, 313-315
    in SqlCommandBuilder, 295

where_clause variable, 312

Windows Application template, 387

Windows Forms, 390

Windows NT authentication, 78

WithEvents keyword, 217, 243

wizards, 87
    Access Database Wizard, 55-57
    Data Adapter Configuration Wizard, 99-100
    Data Form Wizard, 90-94
    Data Link Properties, 87-90
    Query Builder, 97-98

WordPad, 197

WriteXml method, 111-113, 204-205, 250

WriteXmlSchema method, 113

X

XML (Extensible Markup Language), 21-23
    storing data in, 149-150
    files, 193-194

XML editor, 197-199

XML files, 149-150, 193-194
    deep multi-table, 195-196
    editing, 197-199
    loading in Visual Basic, 201-204
    multi-table, 195
    nested, 196-197
    overwriting, 207
    saving from Visual Basic, 204-206
    schemas, 200-201
    single-table, 194-195

XmlDocument class, 21

XmlLoader program, 149-150

XmlNodeValue function, 22

XmlWriteMode.DiffGram value, 111

XmlWriteMode.IgnoreSchema value, 111

Hey, you've got enough worries.

Don't let IT training be one of them.

Get on the fast track to IT training at InformIT,
your total Information Technology training network.

 www.informit.com

■ Hundreds of timely articles on dozens of topics ■ Discounts on IT books from all our publishing partners, including Que Publishing ■ Free, unabridged books from the InformIT Free Library ■ "Expert Q&A"—our live, online chat with IT experts ■ Faster, easier certification and training from our Web- or classroom-based training programs ■ Current IT news ■ Software downloads ■ Career-enhancing resources